REGRESSION AND APOCALYPSE

REGRESSION AND APOCALYPSE:

Studies in North American Literary Expressionism

Sherrill E. Grace

UNIVERSITY OF TORONTO PRESS

Toronto Buffalo London

© University of Toronto Press 1989
Toronto Buffalo London
Printed in Canada

ISBN 0-8020-5816-7

Printed on acid-free paper

Canadian Cataloguing in Publication Data

Grace, Sherrill E., 1944–
Regression and apocalypse

Bibliography: p.
Includes index.
ISBN 0-8020-5816-7

1. Canadian fiction (English) – 20th century –
History and criticism.* 2. American fiction –
20th century – History and criticism. 3. Canadian
drama (English) – 20th century – History and
criticism.* 4. American drama – 20th century –
History and criticism. 5. Expressionism. I. Title.

PS8101.E9G72 1989   C813'.5'09   C89-094284-6
PR9185.5.E9G72 1989

This book has been published with the help of a grant from the Canadian
Federation for the Humanities, using funds provided by the Social Sciences
and Humanities Research Council of Canada.

IN MEMORY OF MY FATHER

ALFRED A. PERLEY

1913–1965

and

for John, Elizabeth, and Malcolm

Contents

Part Four: The Expressionist Legacy

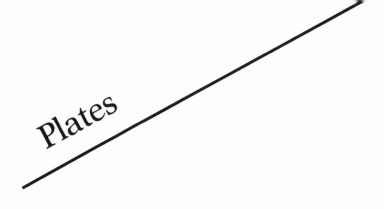

Plates

Preface

This study has required many years of research in three countries to bring to fruition. When I began my work on Expressionism in 1976, only a few English literature specialists in North America were familiar with the term or aware of the movement's strategic importance to modernism, and Neo-expressionism had scarcely been heard of in North American circles.

Over the past decade, however, I have been fortunate to receive constant encouragement from scholars, and it is a great pleasure to be able to thank them publicly now. The most important of these is Armin Arnold, Professor of German, specialist in literary Expressionism and a Joyce scholar; to him I owe a special debt of thanks for his suggestions regarding chapters 1 and 2 and, perhaps most importantly, for his belief in the task at moments when it seemed next to impossible to complete. For their numerous useful suggestions and interest I also want to thank Dr Maria Tippett and my colleagues Professors K Edgington, Joel Kaplan, Patricia Merivale, and Roger Seamon, who read proof or chapters of the work in progress. Errors and shortcomings that remain are my own.

In some instances my work would have been more difficult if I had not had the generous co-operation of some of the authors under discussion. For submitting to interviews, answering letters and many questions, and for the privilege of their friendship, it is a pleasure to thank Sheila Watson and Herman Voaden. So many other individuals, curators, and archivists in Canada, the United States, and West Germany have given me invaluable help that I can only hope to mention a few of them here: Gerald Hallowell of University of Toronto Press for his friendly and expeditious help; Susan Kent Davidson, for her interest and her meticulous copy-editing;

the late Dr Max Stern, owner of Montreal's Dominion Gallery; Dr Anton Wagner, who first brought Herman Voaden's work to my attention; Professor Dr Helmut Bonheim, Head of the Englisches Seminar at the Universität zu Köln; and my research assistants Helen Knutti, Sheryl Salloum, and Stefan Haag. To my husband, Professor John Grace, who shares my love for modern art, go my warmest thanks as always. Together we have watched with great interest as Neo-expressionism has taken North America by storm over the past few years.

For permission to reprint passages from my previously published material, to quote from the works of others, and to reproduce paintings, graphics, photographs, or manuscript materials I wish to thank the following individuals, editors, publishers, copyright holders, and private collectors: Anne Smith, formerly of Vision Press; Richard Plant, editor of *Theatre History in Canada*; Eugene Benson, editor of *Canadian Drama*; Peter Matson and the Malcolm Lowry Estate; Random House and Faber and Faber Ltd; Herbert Mitgang for the Authors League Fund, New York, and the Historic Churches Preservation Trust, London, the literary executors of the Djuna Barnes Estate; Harcourt Brace Jovanovich Inc.; Herman Voaden, Sheila Watson, Ruth Müller-Stein, Olda Kokoschka, John Willett, Dr Wolfgang and Ingeborg Henze, the Essen theatre, the Lawren Harris Estate, the Schaubühne theatre, the Deutsches Theatermuseum München, John H.G. Korner, Renate Shapiro and the Mary Boone Gallery / Michael Werner Gallery, Max Pechstein, the Saint Louis Art Museum, the Städtische Galerie im Lenbachhaus, Munich, the Basel Kunstmuseum, the Solomon R. Guggenheim Museum, the Düsseldorf Kunstmuseum and VIS-ART Copyright Inc., the Art Institute of Chicago, the Städtische Kunsthalle in Mannheim, the Staatsgalerie moderner Kunst in Munich, the Museum of Modern Art in New York, the East German Staatliches Filmarchiv, Transit-Film-Gesellschaft MBH, the New York Public Library, the National Gallery of Canada, and the Nasjonalgalleriet in Oslo. Every reasonable effort has been made to contact copyright holders; if the author is notified of errors or omissions, corrections can be made to the next edition of the book.

Finally, for the research funds that make projects like this possible, I am pleased to thank the Social Sciences and Humanities Research Council of Canada, the West German government for a DAAD Fellowship, the University of British Columbia for a series of small but essential grants that kept the research going in its early stages, McGill University for the initial grant that started the whole process, and the Canadian Federation for the Humanities, whose grant in aid of publication has brought it to this close.

S.E.G.
Vancouver 1989

1 Oskar Kokoschka, detail from *Self-Portrait of a Degenerate Artist* (1937), which was painted in London after the artist fled Hitler's Germany. Kokoschka, along with many other modern artists, had been branded 'degenerate' by the Nazis. Private collection

2 Ernst Ludwig Kirchner, *Girl Circus Rider* (1912). This treatment of the popular
circus theme, with its lurid orange and sickly green, its distortion of figure
and perspective, is typical of Kirchner. Also typical is his structural focus on the
nude female that, unlike the dizzying blur of spectators, is sharply controlled
and centred through the woman in the foreground with her raised lorgnette.
Copyright Dr Wolfgang and Ingeborg Henze, Campione d'Italia

3 Karl Schmidt-Rottluff, *Rising Moon* (1912). Both in its colour (green sky, red
   moon, blue houses) and in its abstracted forms (leaning, angular houses
   that merge with mountain peaks), this painting is a fine example of early
   Expressionism by a *Brücke* artist.
   Collection of the Saint Louis Art Museum

4 Erich Heckel, *The Glassy Day* (1913). Although the blue sky and water and the green and brown tones of earth are more naturalistic than the colours in many expressionist works, the figure of the nude bather is made to merge with the natural setting through the abstract handling of figure and ground. Collection of the Städtische Galerie im Lenbachhaus, Munich

5 Franz Marc, *The Fate of the Animals* (1913). The diagonal shafts and eruptions of brilliant colour that surround or intersect with the highly stylized
animals (green horses, pink cows, and the central shape of a blue deer) in Marc's
painting suggest the apocalyptic energy of imminent war. Marc's abstract
handling of pigment, line, and figure find unmistakable echoes in the work of
Kathleen Munn and Bertram Brooker.
Collection of the Öffentliche Kunstsammlung Basel, Kunstmuseum

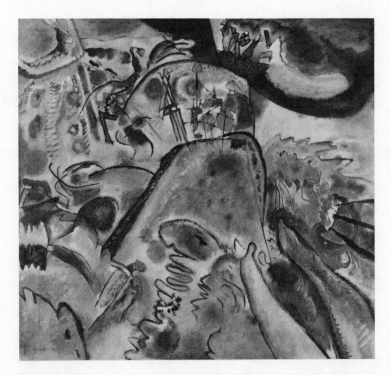

6 Vasily Kandinsky, *Small Pleasures* (1913). This non-objective oil with its joyful orchestration of colour is typical of Kandinsky's early abstract work. Collection of the Solomon R. Guggenheim Museum, New York
Photo: David Heald

OPPOSITE

7 Max Beckmann, *The Night* (1918–19). This large (133 × 154 cm) canvas is a powerful denunciation of a world seething in violence, lust, and madness. Beckmann's claustrophobic crowding of figures and collapse of perspective, together with his sickly whites and greyish yellows, are the hallmark of his work. A drawing of *The Night* formed part of the series in Beckmann's *Die Hölle* (1919). Collection of the Kunstsammlung Nordrhein-Westfalen, Düsseldorf. Copyright Max Beckmann 1989 VIS*ART Copyright Inc.

8 Max Pechstein, *An Alle Künstler!* (1918). Pechstein's drawing for the cover of the revolutionary pamphlet *An Alle Künstler!* depicts the central role and the apocalyptic energy of the artist in expressionist political thought.
Copyright Pechstein/Hamburg-Tökendorf

9 Pablo Picasso, *Portrait of Daniel-Henry Kahnweiler* (1910), oil on canvas,
100 × 72.8 cm. This analytical cubist handling of a portrait reduces the human
figure and its context to a maze of facets crowding the picture surface. By
contrast, an expressionist portrait attempts to capture the inner being of
its subject by distorting or stressing recognizable features; see Plates 1, 10, and
22 for comparison.
Collection of the Art Institute of Chicago. Gift of Mrs Gilbert W. Chapman in
Memory of Charles B. Goodspeed, 1948. 561. Copyright 1988 the Art Institute
of Chicago

10 Oskar Kokoschka, *Portrait of Auguste Forel* (1910). Kokoschka's expressionist portraits were described by a contemporary critic as 'massacres in paint.' The eminent scientist Forel rejected this portrait, but the artist believed he had captured the inner emotion and reality of his sitter.
Collection of the Städtische Kunsthalle, Mannheim

11 Emil Nolde, *Dance around the Golden Calf* (1910). This image of erotic,
abandoned female dancers in vivid yellows and oranges depicts a common
expressionist response to sexuality: essentially female, animalistic, pagan, and
uncontrolled, its dionysiac energy is viewed as both seductive and dangerous.
Collection of the Staatsgalerie moderner Kunst, Munich

12 Ernst Ludwig Kirchner's 1916 woodcut illustration for A. von Chamisso's
    Peter Schlemihl is an archetypal expressionist image of violence, sexuality,
    and psychological distress.
    Copyright Dr Wolfgang and Ingeborg Henze, Campione d'Italia

13 Mary Wigman. This photograph of Wigman's expressive dance style is
reprinted from John Willett's *The Weimar Years*.

14 Kurt Jooss's ballet *The Green Table* (1932). This photo of the original Essen
production shows Jooss as Death and Rudi Pescht as the dying soldier.
Photo: Lipnitzki, Paris

15 The frame scene, showing the masked politicians sitting around the green
table, from the Essen Theatre's 1985 production of *The Green Table*.
Photo: Armin Wenzel

16 The dramatic expressionist set by Hans-Dieter Schaal for the 1985 Paris
   Opera production of *Woyzeck*.
   Courtesy of the Théâtre National de l'Opéra de Paris
   Photo: Jacques Moatti

17 Robert Wiene's classic expressionist film *The Cabinet of Dr Caligari* (1919).
The distorted, angular sets with sharp diagonals and dramatic chiaroscuro
evoke the demonic and violent forces gathering in the story and within
the characters; note the reward notice about 'Murder' at the extreme left
of the image.
Collection of the Stills Archive of the Staatliches Filmarchiv der DDR, Berlin

18 The final scene – the Cashier in front of the cross – of Karl Heinz Martin's
1920 film version of Kaiser's play *From Morn to Midnight*. Ernst Deutsch
starred as the Cashier. John Willett describes this silent film as 'even eerier'
than the original play.
Reprinted from J.L. Styan's *Modern Drama in Theory and Practice 3*.

19 A still from Robert Wiene's film *The Hands of Orlac* (1924), showing Conrad
Veidt in the title role. Veidt's acting captures the perfect expressionist image of
madness and murderous obsession.
Collection of the Staatliches Filmarchiv der DDR

20 A scene from the 1919 production of Ernst Toller's *Transfiguration,* with
production by Karl Heinz Martin and sets by Robert Neppach. The transfiguration envisaged here leads humanity to the utopian state of a revolutionary
new world.
Courtesy the Deutsches Theatermuseum München

21 Robert Edmond Jones's drawing of the famous 1921 Volksbühne production of
Toller's *Masses and Man* by Jürgen Fehling, with sets by Hans Strobach.
This drawing depicts the machine-gun attack on the workers and illustrates the
expressive handling of light and massed figures.
Illustration from *Continental Stagecraft* by Kenneth Macgowan and Robert
Edmond Jones.
Copyright Harcourt Brace Jovanovich, Inc. Reprinted by permission

22 Ludwig Meidner, *The City and I* (1913). In this expressionist self-portrait,
Meidner presents an apocalyptic vision of the artist's private *Angst* and his
prophecy of social catastrophe. (See also colour plate.)
Private collection

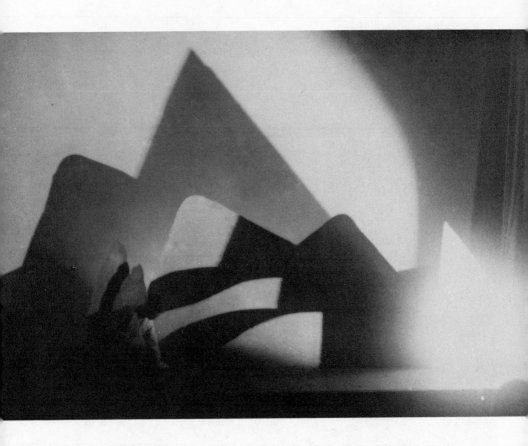

23 Herman Voaden's production of Jesse Edgar Middleton's *Lake Doré*, with sets
    by Lowrie Warrener and E.H. Thomas. The inspiration of the Group of Seven,
    notably of Lawren Harris, can be seen in the abstraction of mountain forms
    and in the colours, which range from silver grey to cold blue and green.
    Reprinted from Herman Voaden's *Six Canadian Plays*
    Photo: Allan Sangster

24 Eugene O'Neill's *The Hairy Ape*, scene six, showing Louis Wollheim as Yank
in his Rodin 'Thinker' pose in prison. The sets for the 1922 première of the
play at the Provincetown Theater, New York, were designed by Cleon
Throckmorton and Robert Edmond Jones.
Collection of the New York Public Library at Lincoln Center

25 *The Hairy Ape*, scene five, as Yank confronts the toffs on Fifth Avenue.
Collection of the New York Public Library at Lincoln Center

26 Roland Schäfer as Yank in Peter Stein's 1987 Schaubühne production of
   The Hairy Ape at the National Theatre, London.
   Courtesy the Schaubühne am Lehnimer Platz, Berlin
   Photo: Ruth Walz

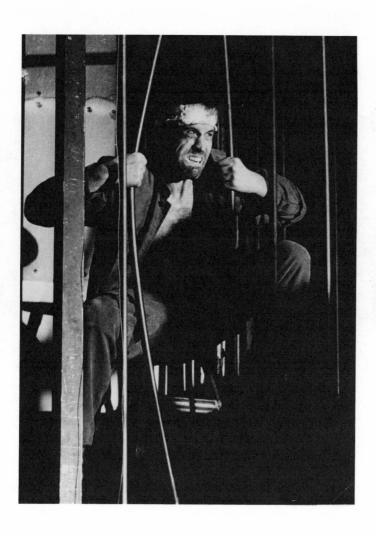

27 The final scene of transfiguration from Herman Voaden's *Rocks*.
The sets were designed for Voaden's 1932 Workshop production;
they illustrate his 'symphonic expressionist' use of a highly abstract stage
and his symbolic handling of light.
Collection of Herman Voaden

28 Lawren Harris, *North Shore, Lake Superior* (1926). Harris's famous painting
illustrates the expressionist abstraction of his work, its stress on transfiguration, and his influence on Voaden's theatre production.
Collection of the National Gallery of Canada

29 Edvard Munch, *The Scream* (1893). Munch's lithograph and painting *Geschrei* have come to be seen as the expressionist sign of anxiety-ridden twentieth-century humanity. The image has not, however, lost its power to disturb, as is clear from Georg Baselitz's recent parodies of it.
Collection of the Nasjonalgalleriet, Oslo

30 Georg Baselitz, *The Resurrection* (1984). Many works by this contemporary German artist are painted upside-down. The thick paint, muddy yellows, blues and blacks, and the Munch-like shape of this image create a disturbing, ambiguous sense of *déjà vu* that hovers on the edge of parody.
Collection of Renate Shapiro
Courtesy the Mary Boone Gallery/Michael Werner Gallery, New York

REGRESSION AND APOCALYPSE

To talk about the first half of the twentieth century

without mentioning Expressionism

would not only be unjust;

it would mean leaving a gaping hole.

MAX KRELL

Introduction

'The problems of Expressionism will continue to be worth pondering until they have been superseded by better solutions than those put forward by its exponents.' So announced Ernst Bloch, philosopher, utopian idealist, and apologist for Expressionism, before reminding his readers that the 'heritage of Expressionism has not ceased to exist, because we have not yet even started to consider it.'[1] Bloch made these remarks in a 1938 defence of expressionist art against attacks by the Marxist critics Georg Lukács and Alfred Kurella, who had argued during the thirties that German Expressionism led directly to fascism. In 1938 the 'heritage' of political and social rebirth, once so dear to the expressionists and ardently believed in by Bloch, had certainly 'not yet even started' to be considered.

At the time when he spoke out, the early ideals of Expressionism seemed dead; the extreme right had seized power in Germany, and most traces of the movement known as German Expressionism had been wiped out by the National Socialists. Expressionism, however, involved more than vague utopian ideals, and this study addresses other aspects of the expressionist heritage that still need to be considered. Bloch's statement, coming as it did in 1938 as a response to criticism from the left, is an immediate reminder of the four preceding years, 1933 to 1937, when the Nazis waged a fanatical campaign to wipe expressionist art (and its artists) from the face of Germany. Today Bloch's remarks force us to question the past and the sources, nature, and significance of this art that could arouse such hostility in the fascist heart. But Bloch also invites us to contemplate the present, both in Germany and elsewhere, in other countries, languages, and cultural experiences where Expressionism, in one form or another, had and still has a significant impact.

The fundamental assumption of a study such as this one is that Expressionism was more than an exclusively German development. Although it is accurate to speak of a German expressionist movement in the arts that began in 1905 and continued until sometime in the mid-twenties, and although any appreciation of Expressionism must begin with the Germans, it is also true that the expressionists were highly inter-nationalist in their sources and subsequent contacts and influences as well as in their socio-political thinking, and that Expressionism – as a style, subject-matter, vision, and aesthetic – has been an international phenom-enon and a major impulse of modernism.

The aims of this study arise, then, from my desire to look back in order to discover what Expressionism was, why it has been so neglected in the English-speaking world's understanding of what constitutes modernism, and where and how a small number of very interesting American and Canadian writers came to be influenced by Expressionism. In Part One I examine the art that Hitler labelled 'degenerate' in 1937 and provide a discussion of expressionist poetics. Part Two explores the expressionist features of the drama of Eugene O'Neill and Herman Voaden in the context of theatrical developments in New York and Toronto during the twenties and thirties, while Part Three is devoted to the fiction of Djuna Barnes, Malcolm Lowry, Sheila Watson, and Ralph Ellison. In Part Four I consider a variety of contemporary experiments in painting, theatre, and fiction that illustrate a vital renewal of interest in Expressionism. In today's context it is important to ask why we are experiencing a flood of so-called neo-expressionist painting, from the work of German 'neuen Wilden' or the apocalyptic vision of the New Zealander Patrick Hanly to the ecclesiastic expressionism of a Quebec group of painters and the socio-mythopoeic violence of New York's Julian Schnabel, or why today there are frequent revivals of expressionist classics, such as the stunning performance of *Woyzeck* at the Paris Opera in the spring of 1985 (see Plate 16) and a highly self-conscious, parodic use of Expressionism in many postmodern plays, novels, and other works.

Among the specific topics considered in chapters 3 through 9 are the central thematics of expressionist literature – questions of language and style, particularly in the expressionist monologues that are crucial to the discourse of plays and novels and find their parallel in the expressionist painters' obsession with portraiture; generic adaptations of structure; character conception and portrayal; and the interdependent codes of regression and apocalypse, which are set forth in chapter 1. In the final chapter these topics are re-examined in the context of a postmodernist vision and against the background of neo-expressionist painting.

It seems to me that an investigation of this sort cannot take place by considering one art in isolation from the others or one national literature apart from another. Modernism was essentially interartistic and international: the artists often lived and worked together, exchanged views, experimented in various media, shared influences, and discussed their common goals. This is especially true of Expressionism, and it is also true, to varying degrees, of the North American writers who are the main subject of this study. Nevertheless, there are many problems raised by interdisciplinary and comparative studies, and I do not pretend to have addressed them all. What I do claim is that by examining these plays and novels together with painting and film against a historical background that includes all the arts and a major non-English source of influence, it is possible to shed new, interesting light on a specific author or text, on the issues raised by interdisciplinary, comparative thinking, and on the nature of the expressionist poetics shaping the texts under discussion.

Equally challenging for this study are the many questions raised in any discussion of modern art by the problem of artistic representation. With Expressionism these questions are inescapable: What is meant by the term 'representation,' which is mistakenly conflated with mimesis? How can representation in a painting or a novel be distinguished from what is usually spoken of as its opposite, abstraction? Because these stylistic tendencies, or more properly artistic modes, are of particular importance to Expressionism, they must be carefully weighed. Finally, what vocabulary, precise but not esoteric, exists to articulate interartistic parallels and comparisons? What does it mean to speak, for example, of abstraction in a painting or representation in a novel, especially when the artists were deliberately defying tradition and overturning the conventional operations of their media? All these questions lie behind the following chapters, and I have drawn attention to them wherever possible and used a semiotic vocabulary when interartistic comparisons make it necessary.

There are, of course, essential and inevitable limitations to a study such as this one. First of all, I do not analyse German expressionist art and literature at length – this has been done by many able Germanists – but simply provide an overview of what constitutes Expressionism so that the art (painting, sculpture, film, drama, fiction, and poetry) can be more readily appreciated by North American readers and seen as what seems to me an essential and important aspect of what we usually speak of as modernism. This overview, which may be unnecessary for experts in modern German literature and art history, is useful here because critics approaching modernism from an English-speaking perspective tend to be unfamiliar with this material, and the North American understanding of modernism continues, even today, to be dominated by literary and art-historical interest in France.[2] Because I have a primarily English-speaking audience in mind, I have provided translations of all quotations and of titles and key terms; unless otherwise indicated, translations are my own. In a few special instances, however, I have retained the German word or phrase, either because a translation is imprecise and cumbersome or because the term is already familiar.

Chapters 1 and 2 are devoted to background, comparisons, description, and theory without, on the one hand, resorting to lists of indigestible dates or bald facts that oversimplify a complex phenomenon or, on the other, indulging in unnecessary discussion of fascinating issues and favorite works of art that would take me further and further from my specific topic. Most important for my purposes is that only such a preliminary wide-ranging exploration of the roots and works of German Expressionism illuminates what I consider to be a distinctive expressionist poetics. Second, although I make many references to the fine arts and film, which are veritable touchstones in any study of Expressionism, this study is primarily a work of literary criticism. Third, my selection of the North American modernists with whom I deal has been governed by two principles: in each case the writer in question was arguably influenced by and demonstrably acquainted with some form(s) of German expressionist art, and each writer chosen for detailed examination is either influential in his or her own national literature (such as Eugene O'Neill and Sheila Watson) or, if less well known, is of special importance for certain innovative and unique qualities (such as Djuna Barnes and Herman Voaden).

My selection of these particular authors makes it possible to demonstrate the variety of expressionistic writing in the United States and Canada and to suggest a coherent way of thinking about a group of interesting writers who stand somewhat outside the generally accepted central traditions in both countries. While this selection allows me to focus closely on a few authors and texts, it also means that I must pass quickly over some writers and ignore others.[3] It is my hope that readers of *Regression and Apocalypse* will be stimulated into finding other artists who might be included, because there is much recuperative and critical work to be done on Expressionism, especially in Canada, which has tried very hard to ignore this presumably 'un-Canadian' style and subject-matter. Readers of this book may also object to the authors I have chosen.

So much the better. The issues raised by placing them in this perspective deserve continuing argument and attention.

In addition to my selection of specific authors, I have had to place other kinds of restrictions on this study. For example, Expressionism can and has been discussed in the early work of Australian novelist Patrick White, in T.S. Eliot and in D.H. Lawrence, James Joyce, Wyndham Lewis, and other British modernists, but the style and subject-matter are at most tangential to the main concerns of all of them except Lewis.[4] Thus, to expand an already broad study to include these writers seems doubly unnecessary. I have also deliberately avoided discussion of Expressionism in modern American and Canadian poetry, not because it is not present but because poetry, especially in its structural and linguistic features, requires a separate study.[5]

If I can claim only to make a beginning in the process of looking back at the heritage of Expressionism in modern North American writing, it is even more true to say that my speculations about postmodern neo-expressionism are tentative. The two novelists about whom I comment, Hubert Aquin and Thomas Pynchon, are major contemporary authors (Aquin committed suicide on 15 March 1977 at the age of forty-seven) who have attracted much critical attention, but neither has been placed squarely in an expressionist context before now and both reveal some interesting qualities when perceived in this way or when compared with a leading German painter like Georg Baselitz (see Plate 30) and viewed as part of contemporary neo-expressionist trends in the arts.

The contemporary revival of Expressionism is the living proof of Ernst Bloch's prediction: the legacy of Expressionism is still alive, and we who are its most recent inheritors have much to learn from an art that could not be destroyed and a vision that continues to haunt the Western imagination in distorted images of violence and transfiguration, atavism and utopian dream, ecstasy and despair, and in convulsions of the mind and soul that prefigure either an apocalyptic purging of the world or a slide into regression and oblivion.

PART ONE

'Entartete Kunst' –
Modernism in Germany

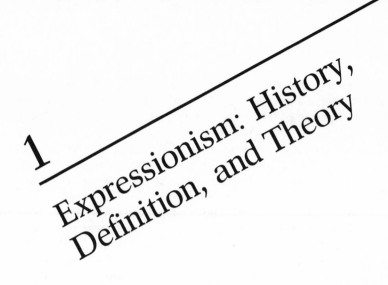

1 Expressionism: History, Definition, and Theory

May God help us, we are headed towards difficult times.
EDVARD MUNCH, ca 1909*
We shall see a whole series of suicides.
KURT TUCHOLSKY, 1933†

Arguments abound as to when and why German Expressionism died. Some contemporaries claimed that, as a movement, it died with the young artists killed in the First World War. Others were certain that it had been stamped out with the repression of the Spartacist uprisings in 1919 or with the return to a new objectivity (*neue Sachlichkeit*) in painting after the war, while still others believed that the peak of expressionist theatre during the early twenties was Expressionism's last gasp. But as late as 1933 Adolf Hitler knew that the spirit of Expressionism had not died, and hindsight shows that John Willett is closer to the mark when he suggests that Expressionism (by which Hitler and Goebbels understood modern art in general) was not finally driven from Germany until 1937. And even then its destruction was incomplete.

---

* When first shown woodcuts by Karl Schmidt-Rottluff, Munch was silent for a while before exclaiming: 'Gott soll uns schützen, wir gehen schweren Zeiten entgegen.' Quoted by Peter Selz, *German Expressionist Painting* (Berkeley: University of California Press 1957), 107
† From a letter written to Walter Hasenclever on 14 September 1933, quoted in Harold L. Poor, *Kurt Tucholsky and the Ordeal of Germany, 1914–1935* (New York: Charles Scribner's Sons 1968), 204

The Third Reich's concerted attack on 'entartete Kunst,' the so-called 'degenerate art,' began officially in 1933, shortly after Hitler's assumption of power on 31 January of that year. It began with the infamous 'Black List' of books by Jews and Marxists, of books criticizing war and demanding peace and social reforms, books by Erich Maria Remarque, Arnold Zweig, Heinrich Mann, Ernst Toller, Ludwig Rubiner, Jack London, Brecht, Tucholsky, and Freud. It began with the slogan 'Aktion "Wider den undeutschen Geist"' (action against the un-German spirit) and reached its first destructive peak on the night of 10 May 1933 in the Berlin Opernplatz. On that spring night Nazi students and professors staged a massive *auto-da-fé* of some twenty thousand books that had been confiscated from various libraries and collections. Goebbels himself appeared on the scene to praise the act as a purgative fire from which the phoenix of the true German spirit would rise, freed from Jewish intellectualism and Bolshevik corruption.[1] Other book-burnings followed in other German cities; the Black List was extended, and publishers and booksellers were controlled. In these vicious acts lies the reality behind the nightmarish visions of Peter Kien in Elias Canetti's remarkable expressionistic novel of 1935, *Die Blendung* (*The Blinding*), which was translated into English as *Auto da Fé* in 1946.

Of course, from the perspective of today, 1933 is an ominous, prophetic year – the year when Max Reinhardt, perhaps the most influential and famous individual in German theatre of the period, an extraordinary director, and a Jew, was stripped of his Berlin theatres. He left for the United States in 1934. Nineteen thirty-three: the year when the Nazis finally succeeded in closing the Bauhaus in its Berlin factory home (it had already been driven from Weimar in 1924 and Dessau in 1932); the year that saw Heinrich Campendonk, Max Beckmann, and Otto Dix removed from their professorships and Alfred Döblin, Georg Kaiser, Leonhard Frank, René Schickele, and Franz Werfel expelled from the Prussian Academy (Käthe Kollwitz and Heinrich Mann had already resigned); the year that Fritz Lang, one of the greatest of German silent film directors, fled the country, only hours after Goebbels offered him a key post in the National Socialist film industry. In 1933 Kaiser's plays were burned and proscribed. In August, Ernst Toller, whose works had also been burned, the staging of his plays forbidden, was stripped of German citizenship after writing a strong letter of protest to Goebbels.[2]

Kaiser, who was stripped of his citizenship in June 1935, went into exile in Switzerland in 1938, where he died a lonely, embittered man in 1945, still protesting against fascism and war. Toller fled first to England and then to the United States, where he committed suicide in 1939 in a final gesture of protest. In his moving introduction (dated 17 October 1934) to the English publication of his *Seven Plays*, Toller reminds his English readers of the power of art to expose dictators and social injustice:

> The increasing persecution of the products of the mind indicates that the dictators of this world have realized the power of the word and the moral nature of art – and are afraid ... Four of these plays were written in prison, others were banned. And, finally, when a dictator came to power in Germany, a man who tolerated no writers unless they were prepared to become his slaves and obey him like dogs and glorify his inhuman teachings, they were one and all publicly burnt ... But even the power of dictators is limited. They can kill the mind for a time and they can kill it in any one land. But across the border they are impotent; across the border the power of the word can save itself and harbour itself; the word, which in the long run is stronger and greater than any dictator, and which will outlast them all.[3]

Kandinsky, Döblin, Walter Hasenclever, Arnold Schönberg, and Kurt Wolff left for other countries, and thus began the calculated removal of all Jewish, socialist, intellectual, pacifist, determined critics of the regime from all the universities, academies, museums, galleries, theatres, publishing houses, and film studios of the Third Reich.[4]

Between 1933 and 1937 the Nazis systematically destroyed all the prompt-books for major expressionist plays,[5] but it is 19 July 1937 that marks the climax of their assault on the movement and on modern art in general. Not content to have burned books, banned plays, censored publishing and filming, and to have driven hundreds of artists, publishers, art dealers, and intellectuals into exile, despair, suicide – or into concentration camps (for example, Paul Kornfeld died in Lodz in 1942) – Hitler attacked the actual paintings, drawings, sculpture, and graphics of the so-called 'degenerate' artists.

Propaganda against modern art had begun at least as early as 1929, when figural works by Nolde, Picasso, and others were compared with photographs of diseased and deformed people.[6] The implication was clear: these paintings were by diseased individuals and depicted deformed, degenerate subjects. By contrast, National Socialism called for an art depicting healthy, muscled bodies, noble deeds, and family solidarity in a kitschy neo-classical monumental style. Adolf Behne, who was among the first to speak up for expressionist art after the war, described Munich art during the Third Reich: 'Bulging muscles, steaming with sweat and all completely accurate and recognizable, in service to rattling flags, fanfaring festival music, pretty parades, girls dressed only in the German fashion, such was the art of the Third Reich: loud and gaudy, banal and servile – and for many very beautiful.'[7]

On 30 June 1937 Hitler signed a decree authorizing Adolf Zeigler, a mediocre Munich painter and president of the fine arts division in the Kulturkammer, to confiscate 'decadent' art in German state, provincial, and municipal collections. Zeigler seized 730 works for a hastily erected exhibit that opened at the Archaeological Institute of Munich on 19 July 1937 under the title 'Entartete Kunst.' Before the exhibit closed at the end of August, over a million visitors had surveyed these paintings, sculptures, and graphics displayed against slogans, derogative graffiti, and reminders of the public funds spent on museum acquisition of such work. The criteria for selecting this 'degenerate' art included work by Jews, Jewish themes, pacifist or socialist subjects, unsightly forms ('unschöne Gestalten' – as in the work of Barlach and Otto Mueller), abstract art, and 'all Expressionism, even if it is by the "northern" Nolde' ('aller Expressionismus, auch wenn er vom "nordischen" Nolde stammt').[8] In the months that followed, thousands of paintings, sculptures, and graphics, totalling approximately 17,000 pieces, were confiscated from museums and galleries across Germany – 1,273 from the Folkwang Museum in Essen alone. Some were sold at public auctions, like the ones in Lucerne and Zurich in 1939; some disappeared into the private collections of men like Hermann Goering. Others were sold abroad, as was the case with Nolde's *Reife Sonnenblumen*, which was removed from the Berlin National Gallery, displayed as 'degenerate art,' then sold for four hundred dollars by the Reich. It is now in the Detroit Institute of Art, which received it as a gift in 1954. Ernst Ludwig Kirchner's *Strassenszene* suffered a similar fate before finding a home in the Museum of Modern Art in New York. From his exile in England Oskar Kokoschka painted his sad and eloquent comment on the events of this year: *Self-Portrait of a Degenerate Artist* (1937; see Plate 1).

Not all of the confiscated works survived. In his list of the paintings Franz Roh indicates that many were destroyed and the whereabouts (as of 1962) of others was unknown.[9] Almost five thousand works were burnt in Berlin alone in 1939 and bronze sculptures were melted down for scrap metal. Perhaps the most infamous example of this destruction is the case of Barlach's *Angel*, the war memorial for the Gustrow cathedral that was dismantled by the Nazis in 1937. A second casting from the original mould was made in 1952, and this is now installed in Cologne's Antoniterkirche.[10]

And so the thread was lost until 30 June 1945, seven weeks after the fall of Hitler's Reich, when the true story of these purges began to be told. The scene again was Munich, but this time it was a photography exhibit called 'Entartete Kunst – eine Hitlerlüge,' or 'Degenerate Art – A Hitler-Lie,' and its organizer, Adolf Behne, showed photographs of paintings that had been attacked, confiscated, and defamed. In his pamphlet *Entartete Kunst*, published two years later, he includes an excerpt from the lecture that accompanied his exhibit.[11] To all appearances it was a passionate condemnation of the fascist mentality and a moving plea for the understanding of modern, specifically expressionist, art. In words reminiscent of Bloch, Behne concludes that despite the confiscations, burnings, and wholesale looting, the Nazis failed to kill the expressionist spirit.

But what was Expressionism? Who were the expressionists? And what was it about Expressionism that could arouse criticism (like Lukács's) from the political left as well as vicious persecution from the extreme right? Even today, when an enormous amount of research and recovery has already taken place, these questions remain complex and much debated; therefore, I can only hope to trace some of the most important features of this controversial movement and discuss a very few of its most influential practitioners.

More than other artistic movements, German Expressionism was deeply embroiled in the socio-political struggles of the day, and as is clear from the Nazi persecution, it cannot be separated, either in its origins or in its demise, from this context. When Germany became a unified state in 1871, it was not a full parliamentary democracy (that had to wait until the Weimar Republic was announced – almost by accident – in 1918) but a constitutional monarchy designed by Bismarck, the first chancellor, and ruled by the Prussian king Wilhelm I, who was declared the German emperor at Versailles. This system was conservative, militaristic, and extremely authoritarian. Neither Wilhelm I nor his grandson Wilhelm II was an effective or enlightened monarch, and Kaiser Wilhelm II was in part to blame for the revolution that overthrew him and brought an end to the war.

The years between unification and the outbreak of the First World War were marked by tremendous social upheaval caused by rapid urbanization and industrialization, which transformed the country from a fragmented, largely agrarian society into a modern state within the space of two generations.[12] Tension, social conflict, alienation, and disaffection, especially among the young, mounted steadily as individuals struggled to find stability and a younger generation rebelled against the repressive forces, outdated mores, and oppressive materialism of a flourishing bourgeoisie. Wilhelmine Germany (1888–1918), symbolized by Kaiser Wilhelm II but represented in practice by the Kaiser's personal interference in daily affairs and by strict, authoritarian fathers, seemed increasingly insupportable to young men and women around the turn of the century. For example, outraged by the 1892 exhibit of Edvard Munch's work at the prestigious Rotunda Room in Berlin – an exhibit, moreover, invited by the Berlin Artist's Association – Wilhelm ordered it closed.[13] And closed it was, within the week, though not without repercussions from the dissenting members of the association, who formed the famous Berlin *Sezession* and began separate exhibits, of their own and foreign works, in 1899.

Although the closing of an exhibit is but a footnote to the history of a nation, it is a detail that illustrates the repressive mentality of the time, and in this instance (in many ways a parallel to more momentous issues) the heavy hand of authority elicited a response that would lead to the shake-up of the entire art world in Germany. The mentality of Wilhelmine Germany and its effect upon the young are graphically set forth in Frank Wedekind's play *Spring Awakening* (*Frühlings Erwachen*, 1891) and Heinrich Mann's novel *Man of Straw* (*Der Untertan*, 1914). The best critical overview of these troubled and turbulent years that I have discovered, not least for the light it throws on the reasons for artistic revolt, the degree of left-wing sympathy among expressionists, and the close relationships among artists of different nationalities is Theda Shapiro's *Painters and Politics: The European Avant-Garde and Society, 1900–1920* (1976).

The most widely accepted date to mark the beginning of Expressionism is 1905 because the Dresden group of expressionist painters known as *Die Brücke* came together at this time. But the precise date is almost irrelevant because the term 'expressionism' did not come into use until 1911, when it was applied generally to modern painting, including the Fauves, Braque, and Picasso, in the catalogue for the Berlin *Sezession* summer exhibit, and to literature by Kurt Hiller.[14] When we explore the years immediately preceding 1905, we may not find the word expressionism, but we do find a crucial network of international and German influences that lead directly to this modernist phenomenon: influences such as Matisse, Munch (himself a proto-expressionist and major inspiration for the Germans), and Vincent Van Gogh, the latter two given major exhibits in Germany during these years, Whitman and Dostoevsky, who both enjoyed enormous popularity in Germany at the time, with the former becoming something of a cult figure, August Strindberg and Frank Wedekind, Matthias Grünewald, whose stunning Isenheim altarpiece (1505–16) inspired painters as different as Kokoschka and Beckmann, the entire Art Nouveau craze (called Jugendstil in its German context), and, of course, Friedrich Nietzsche.[15]

The philosophical roots of Expressionism have been variously traced to the Romantics, Hegel, Kant, Nietzsche, Schopenhauer, and Husserl, and there is some basis to each claim. Certainly the expressionists' location of creativity in the individual imagination harks back to Romanticism, as does their idealization of nature in the face of an increasingly dehumanized, mechanized world. As far as Walter Sokel is concerned, the expressionists' rejection of mimesis and their sense of estrangement from the world derives from Kant, for whom art became an end in itself rather than a means of revelation or representation.[16] Others, however, argue that the expressionist belief in brotherhood stems from Schopenhauer and that their general aesthetic position either derives from Hegel, who, in *Phenomenology of Mind* (1807), announced the end of representation as the mind turns to direct knowledge of itself, or is best explained by Husserl, who came closest to formulating the basic premises of Expressionism in his *Logical Investigations* (1901) and *Transcendental Phenomenology* (1913), where he argued for the importance of insight, as opposed to empirical observation, in understanding what he spoke of as a transcendental subject – a consciousness beyond the personal, pragmatic self.[17]

The problem with each of these 'explanations' of the philosophical underpinnings of Expressionism is that the young artists and writers of Wilhelmine Germany were not likely to be well read in Kant, Hegel, or Husserl (indeed, Husserl could be seen as part of the expressionist phenomenon rather than as an influence upon it), although they may well have known something of their theories. Nietzsche was by far the most popular philosophical figure of the period, and it is Nietzsche's views that are most closely reformulated by the expressionists. In an ecstatic rhetoric that frequently foreshadows Expressionism (for example, in *Thus Spoke Zarathustra*) Nietzsche celebrates animal and human instinct, the power of will, feeling and the superiority of the sensuous body over reason, and the radical subjectivity of the individual at last freed from metaphysical constraints by the death of God. It could be argued as well that the expressionist withdrawal into a subjectivity bordering on solipsism was a response to scientific explanations of the self as a set of functions and relations. Nietzsche's concept of the *Übermensch*, his vitriolic attacks on a philistine bourgeoisie, and his apocalyptic vision of rebirth (a *Götterdämmerung* followed by a *Morgenröte*, or new day) all elicited a deep response from the young expressionists. Both extremes of Expressionism, what Wilhelm Worringer, speaking of the psychology of style, called 'empathy' and 'abstraction,' are fundamental to Nietzsche, who thought of the individual subject as a volatile 'field of conflicting forces and drives' susceptible to either extreme.[18] Although Hegel and Kant (and the ethics of neo-Kantians) may constitute the philosophical background for Expressionism and Husserl may explain the expressionist desire to connect the individual inner life with a wider, cosmic, and transcendent subject (especially for the *blaue Reiter* expressionists, who are discussed below), the rebellious heart and soul of Expressionism is Nietzschean.

From its beginnings early in this century until the First World War, Expressionism was understood as internationalist and modernist in Germany, and it was not until later, after the war and increasingly through the twenties, that it came to be seen, both within and beyond German borders, as a specifically German movement that should be distinguished from Dada and Vorticism, with which it has much in common, and Futurism, Cubism, and Surrealism, from which it differs in important ways. And yet, despite the progressive narrowing of Expressionism within national borders, many aspects of the expressionist vision proved eminently transportable to the New World. What was this vision? How did it first cross the Atlantic, and how does Expressionism compare with those other 'isms' with which it is so often confused?

Well before the war, self-styled prophets, theoreticians, and supporters of the new art, as well as the artists themselves, had begun to define what they understood by Expressionism. Their remarks are interesting for various reasons, not least for the light they throw on the differences among the various modern-isms. Moreover, the first step in coming to grips with Expressionism is to understand it in its own context and terms. In 1911 Kurt Hiller, a Berlin writer, moving spirit, and spokesman for Expressionism, proclaimed that the impressionists, who were 'only wax plates for impressions and machines for recording the minute details of descriptions,' were 'inferior to us': 'We are Expressionists. We are once more concerned with the contents, the intent, the ethos.'[19] Although one must always be wary of taking theoretical and partisan statements like this too seriously, manifestos, essays, and theoretical and political discussions were very much an ongoing part of Expressionism, not an after-the-fact rationalization, and Hiller's remarks highlight two important features of expressionist art: it thought of itself as a rebellion, and it insisted upon an ethical as well as an aesthetic revolt.

In the fine arts, literature, or theatre, artists were consciously revolting against the detailed mimetic reproduction of reality and the complementary materialist conception of human beings. For them, impressionism in painting, naturalism in literature, and realism on the stage were anathema because they depicted the surfaces, hence a superficial image, of life and because, in practice, they seemed mired in the *petit bourgeois* life of middle-class acquisitiveness and repressive social structures. The young expressionists (so often the disaffected sons of despised *bürgerliche* fathers who still supported them) thought of themselves as rebels and iconoclasts, and as is true of any self-consciously revolutionary movement, there were many who wasted their time in the cabarets, cafés, and bohemian excitement of Berlin and to a lesser extent Munich, and a few others who would produce lasting monuments to the expressionist – and modernist – spirit.[20] As Hiller's remark suggests, they were revolutionary in more than stylistic matters. They were also concerned with content, ethos, with what is usually referred to by the expressionists themselves as 'vision.'

By vision they meant the renewal of the human spirit and the brotherhood of man in the face of an increasingly industrialized, dehumanized capitalist world, and the redress of social injustices, the overthrow of the repressive Wilhelmine regime, and the search for and discovery of the 'New Man,' who, like Christ, would bring a new message of love and faith to the world. Woman played a very minor role in what was, with few exceptions, a deeply sexist vision. Most of the expressionists were either socialists or communists or were well to the political left of centre, while many initially supported the First World War as a way of purging contemporary social and political evils.[21] As the war dragged on, some became ardent pacifists, and when the war failed to change much, bringing instead inconceivable loss and suffering, others supported the German revolution of 1918 and the Spartacist uprisings early in 1919. Even when they refused to become actively involved in politics, their sentiments were clear, none more so than those of Beckmann or the Austrian who so impressed Canetti, Karl Kraus. Beckmann's *Hell* (*Die Hölle*, 1919) is a moving tribute to the suffering human spirit, an unsparing condemnation of the right-wing repression of the Sparticists and of human brutality in general (see Plate 7), and Kraus's *The Last Days of Mankind* (*Die letzten Tage der Menschheit, 1918–19*) is a monstrous vision of European apocalypse in fifty-five scenes that concludes with a baby's plea to be aborted rather than be born into this world.[22]

For the scholar Jost Hermand, Expressionism was defined by its 'deeply revolutionary character' and interdisciplinary nature, and it is on these grounds, especially the former, that he attempts to defend the movement against past and present charges from the left of failing in its sociopolitical program.[23] To all practical intents and purposes Expressionism did fail in its goals because the visionary ideals were just that – visionary. And yet the spirit of revolt and social criticism was still sufficiently potent in the thirties to draw the National Socialists' fire. Although it did not create the radical political revolution it called for, Expressionism did liberate human perception, feeling, and expression from the strait-jacket of realism; it did force many to acknowledge the dislocation, alienation, repression, and misery of contemporary society; above all, it did celebrate the free exercise of human passion and imagination. Looking back in 1921 on the first tumultuous phase of Expressionism, Ivan Goll described it as 'not the name of an artistic form, but that of a belief, a conviction. It was much more a sense of a world-view than the object of an artistic endeavor.'[24] Expressionism, its power and popularity within Germany and its image abroad, cannot be understood apart from this 'belief,' 'conviction,' or 'ethos.'

Nevertheless, what is usually identified as Expressionism is a particular style, subject-matter, and subjective emotionalism in painting, poetry, drama, fiction, music, dance, and film. In his now famous 1917 lecture on expressionist writing, novelist and theorist Kasimir Edschmid (actually Eduard Schmid) exclaimed that the expressionist artist 'does not see, he looks. He does not depict, he lives. He does not reproduce, he creates. He does not select, he searches. Today we no longer have a chain of data: factories, buildings, illness, whores, outcry, and hunger. We have them in visionary form.'[25] Again and again in expressionist literature, theory, and criticism one encounters the term 'vision' with its co-ordinates, 'Soul,' 'Self,' subjective emotion or 'inner necessity,' and while they are accurate names for the source of expressionist art, they are also rather vague and misleading. For example, although the expressionist vision derives from the innermost emotions and deepest feelings of the artist, it does not necessarily constitute an exclusively private response to the world. To think of Expressionism as merely *self*-expression is, in fact, a distortion of much expressionist art and a misreading of the theory developing alongside it. What this art attempts to express – that is, to press out from inside the individual artist, speaker, or character – is the emotionally intuited essences of life within Man and within the external world of nature, cities, or, in some instances, the cosmos. The Self of the expressionist visionary, whether artist or fictional character, is not the particularized individual ego anatomized in realist literature but the particular embodiment of general human essences and the mediator between the individual soul, with its intense feelings and spiritual longings, and the cosmic Soul, or the essences of animals, things, and other human beings.

It is no accident that the painters, for example, spoke of their art as a bridge (*Brücke*). Thus, Beckmann could say that what he wanted to show in his work 'is the idea which hides itself behind so-called reality. I am seeking for the bridge which leads from the visible to the invisible,' and Franz Marc could write, in a 1912 article on the new painting, that 'today we search behind the veil of appearances for the hidden things in nature which seem to us more important than the discoveries of the Impressionists ... We seek and we paint the inner, spiritual side of nature.'[26] With this vision of the soul and of essences in mind Hermann Bahr, another of the early theorists, could claim that in Expressionism, 'Man screams from the depths of his soul. The whole age becomes one single, piercing shriek. Art screams too, into the deep darkness, screams for help, for the spirit. That is Expressionism' (1916), or Kokoschka could say, in more measured terms, that it 'is not my trade to unmask society, but to seek in the portrait of an individual his inner life'[27] (see Plates 1 and 10).

To identify the expressionist vision too closely with self-expression is a distortion in another sense as well, because it implies that the artist (or voice, character, sitter, and so on) is speaking only to him or herself, whereas for the expressionist it was always important to communicate with others. Thus, Kokoschka insists that 'true Expressionism does not live in an ivory tower; it addresses itself to a fellow being, whom it awakens,' or as Georg Kaiser puts it in *Vision und Figur*: 'Of what type is the vision? There is only one: that of the renewal of Man' ('Von welcher Art ist die Vision? Es gibt nur eine: die von der Erneuerung des Menschen').[28] In the best expressionist plays, certainly those of Kaiser and Toller, who were the most influential abroad, playwrights used the theatre to speak out to their fellow human beings, not merely to indulge their private fantasies.

A number of valuable clarifying points about Expressionism can be made only by examining specific genres or, indeed, specific texts or the *oeuvre* of individual artists. To do this, however, leads further away from what characterized the movement as a whole, giving it its special force and character, but these general, common qualities are at least as important in understanding Expressionism, either as a German movement in the arts or as a leading modernist phenomenon that would deeply influence English-speaking artists in the New World. Expressionism as a whole was always deeply, deliberately, and self-consciously in revolt against accepted mimetic criteria for painting, literature, and theatre and seriously opposed to the social structures and assumptions of a complacent bourgeoisie. In the place of impressionist, realist, or naturalist art and the classical ideals of harmony and unity, the expressionists offered distorted, fragmented, violent images of humanity and the world or moved on towards an ever-increasing abstraction of reality. They experimented freely with colour, language, narrative structure, and theatrical forms in order to find new methods for expressing not only their opposition to a restrictive, dead tradition and a repressive society but also their vision of rebirth, of imaginative freedom, of spiritual and/or social transformation.

With its neo-romantic belief in the powers of the artist, Expressionism was perhaps the last example of an artistic movement that actually believed that art and imagination could effect such a transformation. The naïveté, confidence, hope, and idealism of Expressionism are nowhere more apparent than in Kandinsky's famous 1912 essay *Concerning the Spiritual in Art* (*Über das Geistige in der Kunst*). This essay is a crucial expressionist document and, together with Worringer's *Abstraktion und Einfühlung* (which is discussed in detail below), is of value for the light it sheds on the sense of 'awakening' (*Aufbruch*) to a new religion, on the value of emotion, and on the belief in artistic mission that permeates expressionist thought and art. Speaking of the problems facing the contemporary artist, Kandinsky explains that,

> only just now awakening after years of materialism, our soul is infected with the despair born of unbelief, of lack of purpose and aim. The night-mare of materialism, which turned life into an evil, senseless game, is not yet passed; it still darkens the awakening soul ... But someone always comes to the rescue – someone like ourselves in everything, but with a secretly implanted power of 'vision' ... If the emotional power of the artist can overwhelm the 'how' and give free scope to his feelings, then art has started on the path by which she will not fail to find the 'what' she lost, the 'what' which forms the spiritual necessity of the nascent awaken-ing. This 'what' will no longer be the material, objective 'what' of a stag-nant period, but an artistic substance, the soul of art, without which the body ... can never be healthy, whether an individual or a whole people ... That which has no material existence cannot be materially crystallized. That which belongs to the spirit of the future can only be realized in feel-ing, and the talent of the artist is the only road to feeling.[29]

The artist will only find the way to express his or her 'feeling,' to create the forms that will embody and communicate this spiritually uplifting emotion, by heeding the demands of 'internal necessity,' to which Kandinsky devoted several pages of explanation in *Concerning the Spiritual in Art*. He defined this concept as '*the purposive vibration of the human soul*' (47) and pinned enormous hopes on this rather vague, at once mystical and troublingly deterministic, notion. What Kandinsky described in complex and abstract terms, Max Pechstein captured visually in his cover illustration for the 1919 revolutionary pamphlet *An alle Künstler!* (*To All Artists!*), which shows the artist reaching out to others and up to the heavens, setting the world on fire with the burning zeal of his inner vision (Plate 8), and Reinhard Sorge's poet in *The Beggar* (*Der Bettler*, 1912) proclaims in an ecstatic outburst:

> I want to show you images
> Of coming things which have in me arisen
> In all splendour, visions that have led me on
> To where I am today ...
> Just listen now: this will become
> The heart of art: from all the continents,
> To this source of health, people will stream
> To be restored and saved.[30]

Although the socialist or communist politics of expressionists like Pechstein were not readily exportable, and indeed were crushed in Germany only months after the revolution itself (in Berlin in January 1919, with the repression and assassinations so powerfully depicted by Beckmann in *Hell*, and in Munich in April 1919, with Toller's arrest for treason and Kurt Eisner's murder), the artistic and aesthetic revolt was infectious. Painters as different as Lawren Harris (in Canada) and Marsden Hartley (in the United States) had already taken up the German challenge, Hartley in his 1913 Berlin paintings and Harris in works such as *In the Ward* (1916) and *Miners' Houses, Glace Bay* (1921). Both men were deeply influenced by *Concerning the Spiritual in Art*. As early as 1922 a book appeared in the United States that proved influential in spreading the expressionist vision in North America: Kenneth Macgowan's *Continental Stagecraft*, with splendid illustrations by set designer Robert Edmond Jones of performances seen on their 1921 European tour.

For Macgowan, Expressionism was nothing less than a 'blinding storm of illumination' that would lead the American theatre out of the 'bog' of realism.[31] While frankly critical of some of the extreme expressionist excesses and bizarre morbidity, Macgowan and Jones felt that Expressionism was the main hope for a spiritual, non-realistic theatre of the future. They had the highest praise for Max Reinhardt, his use of chorus and light as a 'Life Force,' and his support for 'presentational' as opposed to 'representational' acting, and for the director, Leopold Jessner, then head of Berlin's Schauspielhaus, whose famous steps and platforms transformed the stage from an interior minus its fourth wall to a highly stylized, formal space with depth, fluidity, and symbolic significance. Macgowan and Jones, however, reserved their highest praise for Jürgen Fehling's September 1921 Berlin Volksbühne production of Toller's *Masse*

Mensch (translated as *Masses and Man*). Macgowan devoted a chapter to discussing it, and Jones provided five illustrations of the full expressionist production (see Plate 21).

In his impassioned final chapter Macgowan called for a new theatre in the United States, an expressionist theatre that would once again reveal 'the sense of god-head in man which is art and life together.' In the crass materialism of America, Macgowan concluded, this could only be achieved through 'vision,' and the playwright with this vision was already hard at work. Eugene O'Neill, a close friend of Macgowan's, may also have been influenced by Ashley Dukes's translation of Kaiser's play *From Morn to Midnight* (*Von Morgens bis Mitternachts*), which appeared first in *Poet Lore* in 1920 and two years later in book form. Dukes's *The Youngest Drama*, published in London in 1923, was an apology for expressionist theatre; he, like Macgowan, believed that this new vision held the key to the theatre of the future.[32]

Two years later another American voice was raised in praise of German Expressionism and the lessons it could provide, the model it could be for a new, revolutionary, truly American art. Herman Scheffauer's *The New Vision in the German Arts*, first published in 1924, offered analyses of space in the expressionist film classics *The Cabinet of Dr Caligari* and *From Morn to Midnight* (based on Kaiser's play), of language in the poetry of Rudolf Blümner, and of the expressionistic film music of Walter Ruttmann. Scheffauer devoted two chapters to Toller and the Volksbühne productions of his plays, and singled out Kaiser as the correct American ideal. (O'Neill would soon be called the Georg Kaiser of American drama.) In his first chapter, 'The Essence of Expressionism,' he described the movement as 'a system, a method, a cult and even a *Weltanschauung*' that had 'spiritualized and given new life' to the arts.[33] Scheffauer fervently believed that 'our art' needed to be liberated from the shackles of Greece, Rome, Paris, and the British Academy and that only German Expressionism could 'teach us the lesson of a spiritual-aesthetic contemplation so intense, pure and sacrificial that all ties and husks are cast off' (39). Sheldon Cheney's influential *A Primer of Modern Art* also appeared in 1924; like Scheffauer, Cheney, who began writing about Expressionism in 1914, believed it was the most vigorous form of contemporary art and that it was leading the way into the future in America.

Similar voices were raised in Canada, though there the response to messianic expressionist pronouncements tended to be more moderate, slower to develop, and much more resistant to calls for revolt. Unlike the United States, Canada is a nation unsympathetic to the revolutionary spirit, its first true proletarian revolt being quickly and typically suppressed by British troops in 1837.[34] None the less, eight years after Macgowan and Jones's *Continental Stagecraft* and in part inspired by that book, a young Toronto playwright, director, and O'Neill scholar, Herman Voaden, published what was, in effect, a manifesto in his introduction (discussed in chapter 5) to a collection of new plays entitled *Six Canadian Plays* (1930). Like Macgowan and Jones, Voaden had visited Germany, seen what was happening there in theatre, dance, music, and painting, and returned to North America convinced that his new vision would lead to the spiritual awakening of mankind through a new, vitally expressive, 'theatral' art. While he did not renounce realist and historical dramaturgy, Voaden praised Expressionism as a liberating force: 'In revolt against [realist and mechanistic] types of production, the expressionist makes the stage instrument secondary to his personal vision. He discards non-essentials, he seeks a richer orchestration. He aims to express himself [and defines a] peculiarly intense vision of modern life.'[35]

In 1931 the Canadian painter Charles Comfort published a clear, sensible, even eloquent defence of Expressionism against the ignorance and prejudice of an American reviewer who had criticized Picasso's *The Painter and His Model* (1927) for having no model, no painter, no modelling, no taste, and for taking liberties with the spectator. To Comfort, Picasso's painting 'is simply a convenient example of an approach to expressionism,' and the reviewer's diatribe provides him with an opportunity to examine the limitations of mimesis. Comfort suggests that, for the 'rational man,' his euphemistic term for the literal-minded critic, 'the expressionist theory is unsubstantial, chaotic, obscure, and immoral,' whereas for the 'liberal thinker ... realism limits the means of art expression by the very inadequacy of imitative means.'[36]

To all intents and purposes, the expressionist seed had crossed the Atlantic and sprung up on North American soil. What would grow there is the subject of following chapters, and it is, as we shall see, a double variant on the original German model, a hybrid plant combining the essential features of an expressionist vision with the indigenous materials of North American life. What Expressionism everywhere holds in common, no less in Canada and the United States than in Germany, is the sense of aesthetic revolt against a stultifying past, a superficial realism, and a de-spiritualizing materialism that denies the 'godhead' in mankind and blocks rebirth. Expressionism in North America survived its severance from active political ideals – as it did in Germany – by concentrating on art, on stylistic experiment, on language as an end in itself, and on pictorial or verbal abstraction.

As the timing of Expressionism proper (1905–25) suggests, the movement overlapped with all the other major 'isms' of the modernist period: Futurism, Vorticism, Cubism, Surrealism, and Dada. Although it has a great deal in common with each of these contemporaneous movements – in fact, Vorticism can be thought of as English Expressionism – it differs from them in some important respects. The starting point for distinguishing Expressionism from all the other isms is its conscious revolt against the ideals of representation and mimetic techniques, which seemed to have been exhausted by the impressionists. To be sure, the modes of representation and expressive abstraction are not the mutually exclusive opposites they are often felt to be (or that many expressionists, in the heat of debate, made them seem). As is demonstrated in my synchronic model (Figure 2), they are useful ways of distinguishing the interrelated tendencies governing artistic conception, and all expressionist art, whether verbal or pictorial, maintains some element of representation, either of objects or of speech. An expressionist, however, regardless of medium or genre, begins with subjective emotion and inner necessity, and from these impulses he or she struggles to express those feelings within him or herself, within a subject (such as a sitter or character), within external reality (in the form of landscape or animals), or within the cosmos. The surfaces of objective reality and their faithful imitation are never as important as the emotional response to or spiritual essence of the subject. Thus, when Henri Gaudier-Brzeska, the vorticist sculptor, was creating his 'Hieratic Head of Ezra Pound' in 1913, he could insist to Pound: 'You understand it will not look like you, it *will ... not ... look ...* like you. It will be the expression of certain emotions which I get from your character.'[37]

To the degree that cubist painting deals with surfaces seen from several angles simultaneously, it is epistemologically as well as aesthetically quite distinct from Expressionism. Despite its fundamental acceptance of a relative and indeterminate reality, cubist art is conceptually and perceptually more realist than Impressionism; it begins and ends with the object as seen. This distinction is quite clear if we compare, for example, Picasso's *Portrait of Daniel-Henry Kahnweiler* (1910) with Ludwig Meidner's 1913 self-portrait *The City and I* or one of Kokoschka's famous portraits, say of Adolf Loos (1909), Professor Forel (1910), or Herwarth Walden (1910) (see Plates 9, 10, 22). In the Picasso the subject is broken down into relations and facets that constitute the picture-plane and the reality of painting as object; representation of the subject – Kahnweiler – is reduced to the barest abstract suggestion of eye, nose, and hand; figure-ground distinction is completely ignored. The Meidner or Kokoschka, however, is a detailed likeness in which the retention of figure-ground distinction, and the distortion of specific features (hands are a striking feature of Kokoschka's work) are indexical signs that express the subject's inner being. The viewer's response, like the artist's perception, is distanced, intellectual appreciation in the one, emotional and intimate recognition in the other.

Similar comparative points can be made about Gertrude Stein's cubist literary portraits and the expressive work of Djuna Barnes. In *Exact Resemblance to Exact Resemblance: The Literary Portraiture of Gertrude Stein*, for example, Wendy Steiner demonstrates how realist Stein's literary Cubism is and how closely she modelled her work on Cézanne.[38] And yet, just as cubist painting can be highly expressive, as the work of Henri Le Fauconnier and Delaunay or a painting like the *Guernica* (1937) illustrates, so expressionist painting can resemble Cubism, can draw on the lessons of the cubists, as is clearly the case with Franz Marc, August Macke, Lionel Feininger, and Heinrich Campendonk. When speaking of modern art, it is impossible to make an absolute distinction between a northern (specifically German) spiritual and emotional tendency culminating in Expressionism and a southern (specifically French) materialist and rational one culminating in Cubism, although Wilhelm Worringer tried to do just that. At the same time, however, it is true that Expressionism flourished in Germany, while only a few minor French painters, such as Gromaire, de la Patellière, Fautrier, and Georg, all influenced by Le Fauconnier, are thought of as expressionist.[39] Prior to 1945 the international art scene was dominated by Paris, and the tastes and standards of an essentially realist (whether impressionist or cubist) art prevailed, but even when they did learn from the cubists, the German expressionist painters never shifted the expressive basis of their art or adopted the cerebral and analytical extremes of Cubism.

Expressionism differs even more sharply from Futurism, which Ezra Pound described with contempt as 'a sort of accelerated impressionism.'[40] Although the flamboyant Italian poet-impressario F.T. Marinetti was well known in avant-garde circles in Germany, and Armin Arnold makes a convincing case for the influence of *Mafarka le futuriste* (1909) on expressionist fiction, Expressionism differs from Futurism in the stress it places on humanitarian and idealistic goals and the spiritual or emotional sources of life and art.[41] Where the futurist values technology, the expressionist privileges the human soul; where most expressionists always were or, with the First World War, quickly became pacifists, Marinetti glorified war as 'the only health giver of the world.'[42] In his 1910 manifesto Marinetti proclaimed that all previous art must give way to 'Our Whirling Life Of Steel, Of Pride, Of Fever And Of Speed,' and his writings are characterized by his hatred for women, his glorification of violence and war, and his celebration of the machine.[43] The point at which Futurism most closely touches Expressionism is language. Marinetti advocated an economy and energy in language that recalls Imagism and a concept of 'words-in-freedom' that is closely linked to dadist practice, with which several expressionist writers were allied.[44] Hugo Ball, Richard Huelsenbeck, and other expressionists helped to create Dada in Zurich's Cabaret Voltaire in 1916, together with Tristan Tzara and Hans Arp. But like the cubists and futurists, expressionist writers seldom adopted the violent, absurd extremes of the dadists, nor were they tempted by dadist laughter or by the reliance on chance and spontaneity that would lead Tzara to explore automatic writing, which was later developed by the surrealists.[45] On the whole expressionists wanted to communicate with their audience and, if possible, to reform Mankind, and such social and ethical ideals were incompatible with Dada; indeed, from the dadist perspective they were quite ridiculous.

Vorticism is discussed further in chapter 8 because it is an important link between Expressionism and Sheila Watson's fiction, but the affinities between the much stronger German movement and the short-lived British one (1910–17) should be noted at this point. The British philosopher T.E. Hulme met Worringer on a trip to Berlin in 1912–13 and as a result was the first to introduce London's avant-garde to Worringer's views on abstraction in art or to apply Worringer's distinctions to the contemporary art scene. But Vorticism, as it appeared in the early work of Wyndham Lewis (1910–12), was already deeply expressive, even before Hulme's championing of Worringer, so that it was not surprising that the vorticists – so christened by Pound, and including Epstein, Gaudier-Brzeska, Lewis, and Pound – would pronounce their alignment with Expressionism: 'The Manifesto of the Vorticists. The English Parallel Movement to Cubism and Expressionism ... Death Blow to Impressionism and Futurism and all the Refuse of naif science.'[46] Vorticist painting aims at expressing essential forms in a violent juxtaposition of abstract, geometrical, or distorted shapes that are full of internal energy on the one hand and yet are static, rigid, and almost calm on the other, and it is in this stillness and rigidity that it differs from much expressionist art. It is closest to the Expressionism of the *blaue Reiter* group in its abstraction, and yet Lewis, unlike Pound, rejected the extreme abstraction of Kandinsky, believing with the *Brücke* artists that the human subject was always important in the work of art. Vorticist writing, at least as it is represented by *Blast 1* and some of Lewis's prose, resembles Expressionism in its fragmented stylistics, its explosive juxtapositions of typeface, text, and illustration, its extreme, violent characters and disrupted structures, and vorticist aesthetics, with its stress on energy, essences, and the spiritual importance of the new art (particularly for Hulme), closely parallels the German vision while never carrying the cry for rebirth to comparable extremes.

Despite the parallels that can be found between Expressionism and Futurism, Dada, Cubism, or Vorticism, and the fact that it pre-dates the French movement by several years, more often than not Expressionism is linked to Surrealism, which was not born until 1922 in Paris.[47] However, there are many distinctions to be made between Surrealism and Expressionism, and these are every bit as important as any overlap between the two movements. Both draw upon images and structures from a dream world, but where the surrealists transcribe a private dream world with relevance only for the dreamer and as an end in itself, the expressionist seldom *relies* on dream images, and when he uses dreams they are meant to express the soul of Man and to link the dreaming character to a collective mythos. The dream-like subjectivity of some expressionists is part of a larger social, political point and often has allegorical overtones, whereas the dream-like subjectivity of the surrealist lays bare a psychologically analysable and positivistically conceived mind. Automatism came to be an important principle in surrealist art, especially for Breton, and it evokes an image of the artist as essentially passive, transcribing the subconscious or responding to psychic forces beyond his or her conscious control.[48] In sharp contrast, Expressionism is always conscious, active, purposeful, indeed violent and aggressive, and although such distinctions are impossible to establish absolutely, Expressionism appeals directly to the emotions, whereas Surrealism invites the reader or spectator to contemplate or analyse the relations among the strange images before him or her.

Both Surrealism and Expressionism distort the reality presented in the work of art, and yet surrealist and expressionist paintings, for example, *look* very different; surrealist and expressionist texts *read* differently. The differences in the uses and type of distortion arise from a basic difference in the attitude towards objective reality. For the expressionist the world itself, its objects, phenomena, inhabitants are distorted because the artist fights against material reality, with its demanding surfaces, causality, determinism, and psychology, in order to express the visionary, mystical, and spiritual essences of life. Surrealism, however, accepts the 'real-ness' of dreams, of objects seen or presented, and achieves its distortion by disrupting the relations between and among things: not the things themselves but their context is bizarre. Thus, Dali can 'explain' what is happening in his *One Second before Awakening from a Dream Caused by the Flight of a Bee around a Pomegranate* ... (1944): 'Putting into an image for the first time Freud's discovery of the typical dream involving a long story argument, resulting from the instantaneity of an accident causing awakening. Just as the dropping of a rod on the neck of a sleeper gives rise simultaneously to his awakening and to a very long dream ending with the descent of the guillotine blade, here the sound of the bee provokes the sensation of the sting that awakens Gala.'[49] Where the surrealist distinguishes between dreams and waking, the expressionist conflates the two.

Finally, expressionist art is actively concerned with expressing not only its sense of dis-ease with the world or the individual's subjective sense of despair but also its desire to change the world, however impossible or even contradictory its idealistic goals may be. By contrast, the surrealist (with the important exception of the post–Second World War Quebec movement, more properly known as 'surrational automatism') is less likely to make the violent social protests or emotional upheavals of his or her characters the subject of poetry, painting, or fiction. Instead, he or she will concentrate upon a certain '*justesse* du rapport a-logique' because, in the words of Pierre Reverdy, whose definition of the image André Breton accepted as surrealist: 'L'image est une création pure de l'esprit' ('The image is a pure creation of the mind').[50] No expressionist (or vorticist, for that matter) would speak of images created by the *mind*; emotion, instinct, intuition, Soul – these give shape to Expressionism.

'The more horrifying this world becomes ... the more art becomes abstract; while a world at peace produces realistic art.'[51] So said Paul Klee in 1915, and it is a remark that summarizes succinctly what Wilhelm Worringer had been saying since 1908. Worringer is usually seen as a kind of prophet of German Expressionism, but it would be an error to think of him as a critic of the movement. He does not use the term at all in *Abstraktion und Einfühlung (Abstraction and Empathy)*, which was first published in 1908, and by 1921 he had grown disillusioned with this new art, which he felt had betrayed its spiritual ideals.[52] Worringer was more properly a part of the movement, albeit a leading theoretical part. His ideas were especially influential for Kandinsky, whom he had met as early as 1908, and for Franz Marc and T.E. Hulme, whom he met in Berlin in 1912, and they should be viewed as a guide to expressionist aesthetics.

Since 1908 it has become almost commonplace to describe Expressionism in terms of its internal contradictions or the opposing tendencies that Worringer first formulated. Frequently, the contradictions are used to condemn the artists for political emptiness or social reaction, or to defend them against such charges,[53] while at other times, as with Klee, these contradictions become a way of explaining a personal response to the world. For Worringer, however, the opposites of 'abstraction' and 'empathy' are the fixed parameters of all art: together they constitute diachronic and synchronic systems for understanding art history, and an expressionist poetics can be located at the conjunction of these tendencies.

In his effort to free art history from the blinkers of Aristotelian thinking and classical standards, Worringer adopts the basic premise of the nineteenth-century Austrian scholar Alois Riegl, who had argued that art must not be seen as the development of skill or technical means but as the history of volition, *Kunstwollen*, or the will to form, which was not always the same in different countries or eras. As a first step towards understanding why artistic volition differs from period to period or culture to culture, Worringer rejects naturalism as the goal of artistic production and challenges the hegemony of mimesis as the sole evaluative criterion of art: the human 'elemental need to imitate or copy nature,' writes Worringer, 'stands outside aesthetics' and 'has nothing to do with art' (11). Because Worringer believed in the psychic need for art, he set out to reconceive art history and to outline a new psychological approach to style that would undermine the dominant, established view that the best art is mimetic, classical, harmonious, and somehow beautiful, while all other styles or periods are either precursors of great things to come or examples of decline and decadence.

Worringer's argument rests on various assumptions such as the concept of volition, the belief that art is an index to society and human psychology, the validity of racial and cultural distinctions, and the questionable notion of 'empathy' (the usual, though unsatisfactory, translation of *Einfühlung*), but since it is not the accuracy of Worringer's assumptions that interests me here, I shall pass over these problems in order to concentrate on his explanation of style as the interaction of empathy and abstraction.[54]

Worringer explained both the work of art and the artist's (or culture's) motives in terms of these contrary yet potentially balanced impulses. Empathy he understood as the desire to represent and preserve the physical world; the empathetic artistic volition occurs when the artist feels happy or comfortable within the natural world, unthreatened by space, and willing to lose the self in that physical reality. Empathy with the material world and normal social experience produce what Worringer sees as essentially realist art: he speaks throughout *Abstraction and Empathy* of 'naturalism':

> The urge to empathy can become free only where a certain relationship of
> confidence between man and the external world has developed, as the
> result of innate disposition, evolution, climatic and other propitious

circumstances. Amongst a people with such a predisposition, this sensuous assurance, this complete confidence in the external world, will lead, in
a religious respect, to a naïve anthropomorphic pantheism, and in respect
of art to a happy world-revering naturalism.   (45)

Abstraction, or the impulse to abstract from physical, objective reality,
springs from the feeling of dis-ease with this reality, what Worringer
considers a form of alienation from the external world manifested in an
extreme dread of space: 'Whereas the precondition for the urge to
empathy is a happy pantheistic relationship of confidence between man
and the phenomena of the external world, the urge to abstraction is the
outcome of a great inner unrest inspired in man by the phenomena of the
outside world; in a religious respect it corresponds to a strongly transcendental tinge to all notions. We might describe this state as an immense
spiritual dread of space' (15).

For Worringer, the impulse to abstract is anti-mimetic because the
artist longs to transcend this world and lose the self in some metaphysical
dimension. Worringer describes abstract art rather clumsily as 'Stil'
(style), suggesting stylized or stylization but unfortunately implying that
its opposite, naturalism, is not stylized and is, therefore, less artistic. But
the most important aspect of this concept of abstraction is not so much the
stylized (that is, for Worringer the non-representational), geometric
nature of the art it gives rise to as the double-edged nature of the impulse
to abstract. Abstraction is both negative and positive, destructive and
creative according to Worringer; at the same time as it responds to a deep
dissatisfaction with the world, it strives for a means of overcoming that
world; it rejects a slavish mimesis, destroys the harmony of relations
characteristic of 'naturalism,' and replaces these with a subjective,
emotional intuition of essences.

Diachronically, Worringer's view of art history suggests that early
twentieth-century art manifests a revival of the 'exalted hysteria' of the
gothic spirit, but synchronically his system permits a potentially constant
interaction of factors (see Figure 1) that describe not only art but religion
and social relations – *Kultur* in the broadest sense. Although he does not
speak of twentieth-century art in *Abstraction and Empathy*, his synchronic paradigm identifies the conflicting impulses, the tension and
ambiguity, as well as the dynamic, iconoclastic energy of Expressionism.
He equates redemption with the concept of transcendence and consequently with abstract art (more precisely with non-iconic abstraction,
which is discussed below), thus revealing his own desire to see this art as
superior (spiritually and artistically) to naturalism. Therefore, although

FIGURE 1
WORRINGER'S POLES OF 'ARTISTIC VOLITION'

Empathy (Einfühlung)	*Abstraction*
Greek	Egyptian
man at home in the world	man & world at odds
immanence	transcendence
desire to lose self in nature	desire to escape nature
pantheistic	monotheistic
rationalist	spiritual, mystic
individualist	group or mass oriented
personal expression	personal transcendence
acceptance of space (& time)	fear of space (& time)
urge to represent natural world in art	urge to deny & abstract from natural world
organic harmony	disharmony & dualism
perspective & illusion of three dimensions	relations of plane & negation of figure / ground
'classical' art	'primitive' art

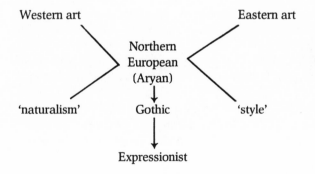

Western art   Eastern art

Northern European (Aryan)

'naturalism'   Gothic   'style'

Expressionist

gothic art partook of both impulses, its true value lay in its style, and the logical conclusion to draw from Worringer's theory is that the more abstract (that is, non-iconic or geometrized) an art becomes, the more desirable, because spiritually transcendent, it will be. The revival he hoped for in contemporary art would entail the destruction of mimetic standards and limitations and the freeing of the will to abstraction, a kind of rebirth of the gothic spirit leading to a new, spiritually redemptive art. It is small wonder, then, that Worringer grew disillusioned with Expressionism because, with a few notable exceptions like Kandinsky, it always remained iconic; it retained a recognizable, represented, or depicted subject; it privileged *Naturalismus* over *Stil*. To avoid Worringer's misunderstanding of Expressionism today, the critic must find some way to explain and make sense of the many divergent tendencies – such as the conflicting pull towards abstraction and 'empathy' – within what remained an essentially representational art.

In *The Revolution in German Theatre, 1900–1933*, Michael Patterson alters Worringer's terminology slightly (albeit significantly) and shifts attention from the psychology of style to theatre history and stage design. He outlines two distinct twentieth-century theatre traditions that stem from the dual impulse of Expressionism towards what he calls 'Abstractionism' and 'Primitivism': 'Abstractionism sought to replace mimesis by the autonomous constructs of the human mind. It was an attempt to establish the primacy of form. By contrast, "primitivism" in its revolt against civilization distrusted all form and sought to replace it by primitive, visceral expression.'[55]

From a slightly different perspective, Worringer's abstraction-empathy dichotomy becomes Walter Sokel's naïve and sophisticated Expressionism or Frederick Levine's 'apocalyptic regression.'[56] This dichotomy – and critics' attempts to adapt it – addresses the epistemological and ontological contradictions of the more representational expressionist works – those of Kirchner and Nolde, for example, and the majority of novels and films. Only by acknowledging and working with the dual impulses of Expressionism can the critic hope to illuminate such fundamental questions as: Do these works distort reality because the artist believes he or she can thereby reveal essences beyond the surfaces of life, or because the distorted image reflects the inner anxiety, or even madness, of the artist or character? When does such distortion cease to be the mirror of the soul or of a deranged world and become a step towards a more spiritual, because abstract, vision? What, finally, is meant by abstraction in this context?

To examine these questions thoroughly here would involve a lengthy aside, but some distinctions must be made before I go on to my synchronic model of Expressionism or attempt to discuss specific texts. In *Abstraction and Artifice in Twentieth-Century Art*, Harold Osborne argues that painting can be classified in two ways: as iconic (Osborne uses the term 'semantic,' but I prefer iconic, which seems consistent with his intention and avoids confusion in subsequent classifications) or non-iconic.[57] To be iconic a painting must contain some trace, however minimal, of representation; it must refer beyond itself to something that exists in the world – a person, inanimate object, scene, or even a spiritual essence or truth (which is why Kandinsky is often, though not here, described as iconic) – through the effort to depict that subject. By contrast, non-iconic forms 'do not depict' or represent anything recognizable from the external world (Osborne, 97). Of course, non-iconic art, such as the paintings of the New York Abstract expressionists, the constructivists, the famous geometrical figures of suprematists like Malevich, and the neo-plasticism of Mondriaan, have frequently been labelled abstract. But to describe paintings without referential depicted subjects as abstract is purely a matter of convention. To be abstract, in a precise sense, a painting must abstract *from* something while retaining enough of the image for the abstraction to signify, and the process of abstraction can be carried out in a number of ways and to greatly varying degrees: for example, in works as different and increasingly abstract as Kirchner's *Girl Circus Rider* (1912), Heckel's *Glassy Day* (1913), Schmidt-Rottluff's *Rising Moon* (1912), Franz Marc's *The Fate of the Animals* (1913), and lastly, Kandinsky's *Small Pleasures* (1913), at which point it becomes very difficult to draw the line between iconic and non-iconic abstraction or between expressive abstraction and Abstract Expressionism (see Plates 2–6). Thus, as Osborne points out, abstraction in its primary sense is a characteristic of all art (28), but it has been a privileged characteristic in most twentieth-century painting, where it impinges forcibly upon each of the three basic properties of art: semantic, syntactic, and expressive.

For Osborne's purposes the semantics of a painting are synonymous with its representational significance, and 'semantic abstraction' is achieved through such means as the reduction or elimination of detail, the overdetermination of detail (as in the physiognomic stress of Toulouse-Lautrec), selection, stylization, distortion, and so on (28–41). The other half of this familiar content-form equation is, in Osborne's terms, 'non-iconic abstraction,' or what I shall describe as syntactic abstraction. Here it is the formal, structural qualities of the painting – its syntax of line, colour, plane, and virtual space – that are stressed until, properly speaking, the form becomes its own subject and a painting is entirely without referential meaning – that is, without representational significance.

The process by which we perceive expressive qualities as a property of the work of art rather than as an aspect of the work inferred by us is a complex and little-understood aesthetic and psychological phenomenon. Osborne argues that the appreciation of expressive characteristics is a function of our 'physiognomic perception,' by which we attribute feelings and aesthetic qualities to animate and inanimate objects.[58] The point to stress here is that expressivity is achieved by semantic *and* syntactic means, especially by the abstraction of the subject and / or the foregrounding of structural and formal properties. Thus, the intense expressivity of Expressionism derives from both semantic and syntactic abstraction and from the successful *Gestalt* of the work. Clearly, 'physiognomic perception' will not explain the expressive qualities of language (although it plays a key role in the theatre), but our attention to the semiotic properties of discourse, to rhythms and to syntactic disruption (which can be described as syntactic distortion and abstraction), constitutes a parallel mode of perception appropriate to verbal art.[59]

For the most part Osborne's study is a lucid and convincing one, and if I retain his terminology (with some modifications) here it is because it facilitates the shifts between painting and literature entailed by my study and because it is compatible with Rudolf Arnheim's view, in *Visual Thinking*, of language as isomorphic with painting and with the semiotic position of Wendy Steiner, for whom the 'work of art is a sign, not a thing, and both arts – visual and verbal – establish some degree of tension between the semiotic and the object world.'[60] This basic homology permits interartistic comparisons and suggests many parallels that can be drawn between the visual and verbal arts of this century as they move more and more towards what we think of as expressionistic and abstract forms. The crucial point to remember through the following pages is that Expressionism as a movement and expressionistic techniques and subjects are only in rare instances, such as the Abstract Expressionism of Kandinsky, non-iconic; expressionist art, whether visual or verbal, is to some degree tied to the external world and to the artist's feelings about that world. Its expressive force arises from a distortion of and abstraction from the semantic and syntactic properties of the work. I will take up the question of literary abstraction in detail in chapter 8 in order to demonstrate why Sheila Watson's novel must be seen as expressive abstraction instead of as a literary analogue of Abstract Expressionism.

In my adaptation of Worringer's synchronic paradigm (see Figure 2), I have changed the focus from his psychology of style and artistic volition to one of *Gestalt* and hermeneutics in order to suggest how expressionist art vacillates between extremes of regression and apocalypse, which are both

FIGURE 2
SYNCHRONIC MODEL OF EXPRESSIONISM

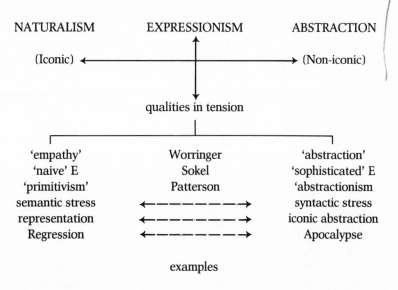

NATURALISM   EXPRESSIONISM   ABSTRACTION

(Iconic) ←——————————————→ (Non-iconic)

qualities in tension

'empathy'	Worringer	'abstraction'
'naive' E	Sokel	'sophisticated' E
'primitivism'	Patterson	'abstractionism
semantic stress	←————————→	syntactic stress
representation	←————————→	iconic abstraction
Regression	←————————→	Apocalypse

examples

Die Brücke
The Cabinet of Dr Caligari
Toller's *Masses and Man*
Kokoschka
Kafka

Der blaue Reiter
Metropolis
Kaiser's *From Morn to Midnight* or *Gas II*
Kandinsky
Döblin

formal and thematic codes for understanding these texts. Works tending towards regression are characterized by topoi of inversion, whereas the more apocalyptic works exploit topoi of explosion to inscribe their vision of the world, and I discuss these topoi further below (66–7). By thematic regression I mean what Levine describes as 'the sense of profound yearning, a longing to return to the distant echoes of the animal past, a past free of moral restriction and restraint.'[61] At its extreme it articulates the profoundly atavistic desire to be reunited with primitive, instinctual forces and it expresses, as Freud recognized in *Beyond the Pleasure Principle*, a longing for death. In a less extreme form regression images a joyful human identification with nature, as in Kirchner's paintings of naked bathers. By contrast, to the expressionist, apocalypse signifies a cataclysmic, purgative destruction that should lead to regeneration and spiritual rebirth for mankind as well as the individual. Although the concept of apocalypse is open to varying interpretations, some secular, others religious, some predictive and literal, others allegorical and ethical, expressionist literature *generally* favours the romantic or visionary sense of apocalypse as a secular, allegorical, and ethical event leading to personal growth or transfiguration and symbolizing socio-political upheavals that may reveal the hitherto hidden perfection of the world.[62] In some cases, however, specifically religious echoes drawing on the Book of Daniel or Revelation are present, while in others apocalyptic images and events signify annihilation followed by the void. Although for a variety of complex scientific and historical reasons the early twentieth century manifests an obsessive attraction to apocalyptic thinking, expressionist artists responded to the idea with profound ambivalence. As a result the secular visions of apocalypse in expressionist texts all too easily tip over into regression when the energy and hopes of the former are spent and the peace of unself-consciousness or death seems preferable to the bitterness of defeat.

In Figure 2, beneath Worringer's 'empathy' (which conflates viewer response and the artist's motivation with the syntactic properties of the work of art) and abstraction, the terms 'iconic' and 'representation' are used because they preserve the basic idea of reference to an external, natural world while signifying a semiotic condition of the art-object that includes the concept of abstraction. But the term 'abstraction' must be understood to include both iconic (Osborne's semantic) abstraction *from* and non-iconic abstraction, with the former being the mode of Expressionism. Instead of claiming that one style, response, subject, and so on is intrinsically superior to another, I wish to stress that regressive elements in some of the more representational expressionist works constitute no more negative a vision than the straining towards apocalypse in more abstract works. Either vision can image human despair and annihilation. Certainly there is nothing to be gained by arguing that one *form* is inferior, or in some way lesser art – the exact charge from which Worringer wished to rescue abstraction, and a bias that contemporary realists, in literature and painting, must confront.

Expressionist art in all media, regardless of its position within some broader historical framework, displays and argues out the tensions between regression and apocalypse, between the pull towards representation in the retention of the human figure or the reproduction of nature and the pull towards greater and greater abstraction from these depicted subjects, between the need to document the ugliness and dehumanization of bourgeois society and express personal feelings of anxiety or hostility and the desire to express the essences of things or proclaim ideals of love and brotherhood. On the one hand, expressionist art is subject-centred, primarily concerned with the artist's own emotions and the existential situation of the individual, while on the other it is object-centred, focused upon transcendent spiritual forces, what Franz Marc spoke of as 'Man's existential relationship to the cosmos.'[63] It can be either passionately political and acute in its social commentary or aloof, apolitical, turning its back on the sordid realities of life. The celebration of personal emotion, instinct, and eroticism that frequently leads to an atavistic union with nature or an aggressive assertion of sexual power is balanced by the rejection of such emotion in favour of an ascetic, mystical vision, just as a language that reproduces the jarring disintegration of life often gives way to flights of lyrical rhetoric. Above all expressionist art is anti-mimetic; even the most iconic examples employ marked distortion and abstraction. Furthermore, the tensions outlined in Figure 2 usually coexist in the same work, so that regression and apocalypse, representation and abstraction, subjective emotion and ecstatic ideals must be seen as two sides of the same coin.

To see subjective emotion as the obverse of ecstatic ideals, however, is to fall prey to what Hal Foster has called the 'expressive fallacy.'[64] Because this dilemma is central to Expressionism and must be grappled with by each of the writers examined in subsequent chapters, a brief consideration of it here will be useful. The problem arises from the artist's attitude towards his or her medium and the essentialist, romantic belief that the *real*, inner Self or Soul can be captured and authentically expressed in art. Concomitant with this idea is the belief in a transcendental subject, a Logos or ultimate Truth beyond the language used to inscribe such concepts, that can, nevertheless, be *re*-presented in art. As

Foster explains, Expressionism privileges the subjective or inner world as *prior* – prior to the objective, material world, but prior also to all codes and systems of signification (language, paint, music, and so on): 'Expressionism not only conforms to this metaphysics of presence, it celebrates it ... Indeed, the old metaphysical opposition of inside versus outside, soul versus body, is the very basis of expressionism – and of all its oppositions' (61).

Having subscribed to 'the metaphysics of presence,' the expressionist artist is then trapped in the vicious circle of the 'expressive fallacy': desperately needing to believe that the Soul can be revealed, healed, and transformed through expression, the artist, on some level usually recognizes the impossibility, indeed absurdity, of the enterprise:

> Such is the pathos of the expressionist self: alienated, it would be made whole through expression, only to find there another sign of its alienation ... its utterance is less an expression of its being than an address, or plea to an other ... for *even as expressionism insists on the primary, originary, interior self, it reveals that this self is never anterior to its traces, its gestures*, its 'body'. Whether unconscious drives or social signs, these mediated expressions 'precede' the artist: they speak him rather more than he expresses them.   (Foster 62, emphasis added)

The irony of the 'expressive fallacy,' according to the Derridean and Lacanian position sketched here by Foster, is that the artist can never escape codes and conventions. As a consequence, personal anguish or metaphysical doubt characterize the drama and fiction of expressionists, and the 'expressive fallacy' defines the agonistic ground on which the artist struggles with conflicting (though equally fallible) impulses towards representation and abstraction, regression and apocalpyse.

Nevertheless, from my examination of expressionist art, it becomes increasingly clear that this art is often – in the terminology of Mikhail Bakhtin – strikingly dialogistic and carnivalesque. And herein lies the power of its resistance to convention and repression. By 'dialogism' Bakhtin means the condition of full interplay among independent multiple meanings (of words, points of view, consciousnesses) in a work of art, in sharp distinction from a single, authoritative – hence monologistic – one. And he designates as carnivalesque those artistic forms that (like the European phenomenon whose name they bear) destabilize and subvert repressive norms and conventions, and release or free imaginative, sexual, and verbal energies.[65]

Although Bakhtin deals primarily with literary discourse, he derives his theories of texts not only from linguistics and political theory but also from German aesthetics, most importantly from Worringer.[66] It is possible, therefore, to speak of dialogism and the carnivalesque in painting, drama, and film when we consider these forms as semiotic systems isomorphic with discourse and limit our descriptions to the level of the total work that we are reading. (Bakhtin preferred to speak of meta- or translinguistics instead of linguistics for this very reason.) While fundamental to all language, dialogism can, in fact, be heightened (stressed, foregrounded) or buried (silenced, repressed) by the artist, depending upon how (and why) he or she uses the medium in question and the socio-political conditions under which it is produced. According to Bakhtin, the more realistic the work, the more monologistic it becomes, and as a result the more orderly, classical, homophonic, causal, harmoniously unified – in short, Aristotelian – it is. Thus, monologism is authoritarian, logocentric, and hierarchic (*PDP* 80–3). Paradoxically, the same can be said of extreme abstraction in the arts, especially in non-iconic abstract painting, where what at first *seems* a rebellious gesture of an avant-garde often reveals itself to be reified, dead, closed to any dialogue with a viewer: pushed to its extreme, as Kandinsky realized, abstraction rejoins realism. Dialogistic art, by contrast, resists and subverts official truths, whether they be sacred conventions of an art form or the socially sanctioned mores of a particular culture. It allows us to see and hear ambivalence (in Bakhtin's sense of the word, *PDP* 126), multiplicity, and polyphony: rather than a single, unified, causal form, a work of art is produced that creates its 'wholeness' out of interpenetrating, contradictory fragments. A Bakhtinian poetics, outlined in Figure 3, demonstrates the distinctions that in turn support my description of Expressionism as dialogistic.

Speaking only of Bakhtin's theory of the novel, Julia Kristeva notes that 'the multi-stylism and multi-tonality of this discourse and the dialogical status of its word explain why it has been impossible for classicism, or for any other authoritarian society, to express itself in a novel descended from Menippean discourse.'[67] Such carnivalesque art (Rabelais and Dostoevsky are Bakhtin's examples; I would add Sterne, Joyce, Kafka, and, to varying degrees, each of the authors considered in this study) shatters rational concepts of human identity, disrupts order, causality, spatial and temporal norms, and resorts to distortion of reality and to fantastic or grotesque images that unsettle and throw into doubt our epistemological and ontological categories.

Bakhtin felt that, although the expressionists 'correctly understood' Dostoevsky's dialogizing of self-consciousness (*PDP* 54), they failed – in the drama, at least, since his examples are Kornfeld and Werfel – to be artistically convincing. But in practice expressionist art is often highly dialogized and carnivalesque; it commonly depicts an ambivalent world of conflicting voices, a world made strange, made to stand on its head. By its very nature such art opposes a totalitarian state and returns synchronic, totalizing systems to diachrony, to the contexts and processes of history. When we see Expressionism poised between the opposing tendencies of empathy and abstraction, articulating the tension between regression and apocalypse, and thereby as dialogistic and carnivalesque, it is not difficult to understand why Hitler labelled it 'degenerate' and expended such effort in trying to destroy it.

FIGURE 3

Monologism	*Dialogism*
Aristotelian principles	Heraclitean, Nietzschean
aesthetic unity of whole	whole in relationships
classical art	anti-classical
pure forms (tragedy, comedy, allegory, realism in painting & literature)	mixed forms (Menippean satire, gothic, Expressionism)
affirms representation	resists representation
epic logic	carnival logic
non-iconic abstraction	iconic abstraction
homogeneity	heterogeneity
images order, sanity, & coherent identity	images pathological soul-states, madness
results in catharsis, harmony	ambivalence: regression / apocalypse

German Expressionism in the Arts

Expressionism in Germany touched all the arts. Although the painters are usually credited with initiating the revolt, proto-expressionistic novels such as Heinrich Mann's *Professor Unrat* and Jakob Wassermann's *Alexander in Babylon* appeared in 1905; expressionist plays began to be written as early as 1908, when the Vienna performance of *Murder, Hope of Women* (*Mörder, Hoffnung der Frauen*) caused a small riot, and distinctly expressionist poetry could be heard in the Berlin cafés by at least 1910. My purpose in the following pages is to look more closely at the individual media and genres and the dramatic shattering of conventions demanded by this new art. It is safe to say that theatre, painting, sculpture, dance, and music have not been the same since the advent of Expressionism, which also left its mark on the cinema and on that most amorphous of literary genres, the novel.

Two groups of painters, *Die Brücke* – begun in Dresden in 1905 by Ernst Ludwig Kirchner, Fritz Bleyl, Erich Heckel, and Karl Schmidt-Rottluff – and *Der blaue Reiter*, which gathered around Kandinsky and Franz Marc in Munich in 1911, form the focal points of expressionist painting and clearly demonstrate the opposing tendencies of all expressionist art. There were, of course, many other important painters who never belonged to, or were only briefly associated with any group, painters such as Emil Nolde, Oskar Kokoschka, and Max Beckmann, and these painters also display the pervasive concerns and deep-seated tensions of the expressionist vision.[1]

The *Brücke* artists were particularly noted for their stunning woodcuts of distorted, angular, and fragmented shapes defined by roughly cut areas of black and white. Erich Heckel's *Standing Nude* (1908) or *Woman Praying* (1908), his *Squatting Woman* (1913) and his *Portrait of a Man*, a coloured woodcut from 1919, are among the most expressively powerful works of modern art. There is a primitive, violent and immediate quality about these and many other expressionist graphics (see Plate 12), whether they depict conventional subjects like the nude or the portrait in startling, unconventional ways or are devoted to frankly erotic subjects (as is so often the case with Kirchner) or religious suffering and ecstasy.

Although it is difficult to generalize about any group, even one as closely knit as the *Brücke*, certain features were shared by many of the artists, including those like Max Pechstein and Otto Mueller, who joined at a later date, or Nolde, who left in 1907, only eighteen months after joining. They were preoccupied with the human figure and face and with man's primitive and freely instinctual existence within nature. To express their imaginative understanding of this interpenetrating human and natural essence, they employed brilliant, almost screaming colours – pure reds, greens, and yellows – in sharply contrasting planes and angular, broken, or distorted forms that, though still recognizable, are primarily expressive. Pechstein's *Beach at Nidden* (1911) and Mueller's *Bathing Women* (1912) are good examples of this theme and treatment, as is Kirchner's *Naked People Playing under the Tree* (*Spielende nackte Menschen unter Baum*, 1910), which depicts uninhibited sexuality in a natural setting through its bright greens, reds and oranges and its focus upon the flame-coloured, aroused male.[2] Over and over again in these works, particularly those by Nolde, such as *Dance around the Golden Calf* (Plate 11), Pechstein, and Kirchner, the viewer confronts images of ecstasy, eroticism, and an atavistic longing for a merging of man in nature or a spontaneous absorption of man by his instincts and desires. If these paintings express the essence of man, then the essence is a seductively simple, deeply disturbing, and regressive one in that it appears to submerge the mind and spirit in a wave of intense colour and primitive feeling.[3]

By 1911 most of the *Brücke* artists had left Dresden for Berlin, where they held their major exhibits. While some, like Heckel, continued to be primarily concerned with the nude figure in nature, Kirchner became obsessed with the city, and between 1911 and 1917 he painted some astonishingly vivid, frightening and frenetic scenes of the whirling, sophisticated, yet alienating metropolitan scene. In works like *The Street* (1913) and *Five Women on the Street* (1913) his people are pointed, tainted by a disconcerting green light, their faces twisted into mask-like leers; space is crowded, and the figures seem to sweep forward from the picture-plane, as if to engulf the viewer in their jarring, hurried movement. Brush stroke, diagonal line, and exaggerated perspective accentuate this sense of crowding and movement. This is not the city of futurist fantasy, a modern spectacle of speed and power. Kirchner's urban world is cruel, aggressive, charged with psychic tension. Its people are dehumanized types, the sophistication of their clothes and surroundings emphasizing their basic greed and sensuality. They recall the characters in Döblin's *Berlin Alexanderplatz*, the figures in Kaiser's *From Morn to Midnight*, or the marionette-like New Yorkers in O'Neill's *The Hairy Ape*. The Expressionism of these Berlin scenes is not a romantic celebration of man's liberated instincts but, like the still more terrible urban scenes of Meidner, Beckmann, and Dix, a glimpse into the violent, bestial essence of modern life. Perhaps Kirchner's most impressive and prophetic work from these years is his four-colour woodcut illustration for A. von Chamisso's *Peter Schlemihl*, done in 1916 (see Plate 12). Bisected by the white diagonals cutting across the dying woman's body and the man's distorted face, and broken by splotches of bright red, this powerful image fixes the violent sexuality and spiritual *Angst* not only of Kirchner's personal situation but also of the expressionist generation. Kirchner suffered a complete breakdown in 1917, when he had to leave Berlin for good in order to recuperate. The later shame of being persecuted as 'degenerate' and grief over the confiscation of his work drove him to suicide in 1938.

By the time the *Brücke* artists had disbanded as a group in 1913, the *blaue Reiter* was not only well established but had held two controversial and successful exhibits (their last joint show would be at Herwarth Walden's Berlin *Sturm* gallery in 1914) and had published their famous *Blaue Reiter Almanac* in May of 1912, the same year that Kandinsky's *Concerning the Spiritual in Art* finally appeared in print. The *blaue Reiter* is inseparable from the views and goals of Kandinsky and Marc, for both painters believed that art must free itself of superficial representational constraints and a cumbersome classical tradition in order to transcend mere matter, to penetrate beyond physical reality and express the spiritual in mankind and cosmos.

The *Blaue Reiter Almanac* is a fascinating document. The common goals of its editors, Marc and Kandinsky, are everywhere apparent – in the extraordinarily wide choice of contributors, in the visual dynamics of the illustrations and reproductions, and in essays.[4] Kandinsky and Marc each contributed several essays, the most important among them being Kandinsky's 'Über die Formfrage' ('Concerning Questions of Form') and Marc's discussions of the *Brücke* and other German movements, called

'Die Wilden Deutschlands' ('The German Wild Ones' – or expressionists – a title that anticipates the 'neuen Wilden' of the eighties), but there were many other essays on art, music, and theatre by Arnold Schönberg, August Macke, and others. The volume was truly interdisciplinary, and this was part of its main point. What Marc, Kandinsky, and their contributors were anxious to show was the extent of these new developments in the arts, how they touched and transformed all artistic expression. At the same time, the *Almanac* demonstrated the existence of an international tradition for this new vision, which cut through conventional criteria and academic categories to place so-called primitive art from Africa or Alaska beside Japanese woodcuts and medieval manuscript illuminations, or Bavarian behind-glass painting, children's drawings, and Russian folk art beside works by Cézanne, Matisse, and Picasso. An El Greco was included, together with Chinese masks and Easter Island sculpture, and the major expressionists were well represented with work by Kirchner and other *Brücke* artists, by Nolde and Kokoschka, and by members of the *blaue Reiter*, such as August Macke, Gabriele Münter, Heinrich Campendonk, and the Russians Burliuk and Goncharova. Interestingly, they included six examples of Henri Rousseau (*le douanier*), a painter who was virtually unknown in Germany at the time.

Leafing through the *Almanac* today, one is still struck by the visual stylization and abstraction, the absence of perspective and naturalistic colour of the illustrations; all these works display a simple, primitive force and power. The *Blaue Reiter Almanac* was a revolutionary document and a monument to the expressionist belief in the principle of 'inner necessity' that leads an artist to express the Soul, or spiritual essence, of things, regardless of his or her nationality, medium, or historical period. It provided a manifesto, an alternate tradition, and a catalogue for the new expressionist art.

Where the *Brücke* artists rejoiced in sensuous humanity at play in nature, Marc and Kandinsky rejected the human figure in favour of an ascetic and increasingly abstract art. During his short lifetime as a painter (he was killed in 1916 at only thirty-six) Marc did not achieve the full non-iconic abstraction that Kandinsky would develop after his series of *Improvisations* (1909 to 1913), but in many ways Marc best typifies those expressionists who sought transcendence through art while maintaining their ties with the physical world. In a note he made *circa* 1912, Marc explained: 'Art is metaphysical ... it will free itself from man's purposes and desires. We will no longer paint the forest or the horse as they please us or appear to us, but as they really are, as the forest or the horse feel themselves – their absolute being – which lies behind the appearance that

we see.'[5] Marc's feelings about nature and what he called the 'animalization of art,' through which he strove to capture the essential rhythms,
spirit, mystery, and unity of life, were first ignited by Van Gogh, whose
painting he saw in Paris in 1907, but it was only a short, though
important, step from this position and significant canvases like *Horse in
Landscape* (1910), *Red Horses* (1911), or *Yellow Cow* (1911) to the highly
abstracted *Birds* (1914) or *Fate of the Animals* (1913) (see Plate 5).[6]

In *Yellow Cow*, for instance, the large animal dances through a blue,
orange, purple, and yellow landscape whose curves repeat the lines of the
animal's body. Though perfectly recognizable, neither the movement nor
the colour is realistic, and both creature and natural world seem free of
human intervention or manipulation. By 1913 the influence of the futurists
(whom Marc praised highly) and the Cubism of Delaunay helped Marc
towards the greater power of prismatic forms and refracting colour that
make *Fate of the Animals* such a haunting painting. Here the animals are
fully integrated with their environment through the splintered forms and
shafts of colour and light that break the picture down into a new unity of
spirit and energy. Given the limitations of the 'expressive fallacy,' in this
painting Marc comes as close as possible to the 'metaphysical' art that
reveals the forest and its animals in 'their absolute being – which lies
behind the appearances which we see.'[7]

To compare a Kirchner or Pechstein canvas with one by Marc, to
juxtapose the work of the *Brücke* with that of the *blaue Reiter*, is to see
how dramatically different expressionist painters could be. Unlike the
surrealists, futurists, or cubists, among the expressionists there is no
clear, all-embracing, or unified style. What unites them is their common
revolt against what they saw as the superficiality of Impressionism, the
weight of a repressive pictorial tradition that demanded the formal
harmonies and representational detail of nineteenth-century romanticism,
and the materialist view of life in which humanity is determined by an
increasingly commodity-oriented system. They all sought to free their art
from these constraints and, in doing so, to free the human imagination,
which could then re-establish contact with spiritual longings and essential
instincts. What united them inextricably was the expressionist vision.
Furthermore, all expressionist artists employ a degree of distortion and
abstraction in their art through the free use of colour in painting and line
in graphics and drawing, and this distortion is the most immediate visual
quality of expressionist work. However, it is here that the two divergent
tendencies of Expressionism begin to emerge: whereas the *blaue Reiter*,
at least in the person of Kandinsky, was prepared to carry abstraction to
the extreme of a fully non-iconic painting, the *Brücke* artists retained the

object, especially the human figure, and with it a considerable degree of representation or what Worringer called 'empathy.'

Expressionism in music and dance are well beyond the scope of this study, but they should be mentioned both for the light they throw on the interdisciplinary scope of the movement and because they were sources of expressionist influence for both Lowry and Voaden. In his study of New German Dance, Manfred Kuxdorf points out that the New Dance taught by Mary Wigman at her Dresden Institute, founded in 1920, was devoted to her concept of dance as an expressive 'symmetrics' that revealed human instincts in touch with primordial forces.[8] Wigman toured England in 1928 and the United States in 1930, and a Wigman school opened in New York soon after. She wore masks, stark costumes, and danced to percussive rhythms (see Plate 13). Isadora Duncan, though more a proto-expressionist dancer, is another figure who, with Wigman and Rudolf von Laban, helped to free the dance from stultifying conventions. By the time of her death in 1927 Duncan had become famous for her solo dancing in simple white robes, through which she attempted to express the Soul. Her theories had a decided influence on Edward Gordon Craig, who in his turn provided crucial inspiration for the producers of expressionist plays.[9]

By 1932 the lessons of the New German Dance movement had been absorbed by Kurt Jooss in ballets such as *The Green Table* (*Der grüne Tisch*). On a trip to Europe in the spring of 1933 the young Herman Voaden, who would integrate dance into his 'symphonic expressionism,' studied dance at the Kurt Jooss School in Essen and was profoundly impressed by this ballet, which he described as the 'finest example of the new theatrical dance' with its 'synthesis of music, dance, and light.'[10] *Der grüne Tisch* has many expressionistic qualities, such as the sequencing of eight scenes, character-types, its stylized, often violently expressive movement, and the use of masks, but its most significant feature is its criticism of war and of the cynical diplomats who cause wars while pretending to call for peace. The ballet has been called 'a twentieth-century dance of death,' and it is as powerful and portentous today as it was in 1932, when Jooss himself danced the role of Death (see Plates 14, 15).

Some of the major figures in twentieth-century music were very much a part of the expressionist movement. Arnold Schönberg (1874–1951), who was closely associated with the *blaue Reiter*, Alban Berg (1885–1935), and Anton Webern (1883–1945) all composed expressionist music that is characterized by its unresolved dissonance, atonality, 'emotional extravagance, formal freedom, and an atmosphere of existential anxiety,' and the roots of expressionist music have been traced backwards from Mahler and Strauss (notably in *Salomé* and *Elektra*) to Wagner.[11] According to Henry A. Lea, Gustav Mahler (1860–1911) anticipated many features of this music in his marches, several of which are 'apocalyptic processions' that suggest fateful events (317), and in major works like *The Song of the Earth* (*Das Lied von der Erde*). But a fully fledged Expressionism is best found in Schönberg's dissonant monodrama *Expectation* (*Erwartung*, 1909), his 'drama with music' *The Hand of Fate* (*Die glückliche Hand*, 1910–13), and in Berg's well-known opera *Woyzeck*, which was completed in 1921 but did not receive its Berlin première until 1925. *Woyzeck*, based on Georg Büchner's play, is a powerful drama of a poor soldier who endures abuse and mockery from his superiors, suffers from tormenting visions and violent, apocalyptic hallucinations, kills his girlfriend when she betrays him, and finally drowns (see Plate 16). Much of the libretto is declaimed in an emotional *parlando* voice (Woyzeck's monologues are especially effective instances of this), and Lea describes the music as 'a classic example of the dissociative aspect of Expressionism' (327) because it brings together wildly disparate musical forms. Both the disparate forms and the violent subjects of Schönberg and Berg appealed to Lowry, who saw parallels between them and his own work, notably his strangely co-ordinated collection of stories called *Hear us O Lord from heaven thy dwelling place*.

Generally speaking (and with the partial exception of *Woyzeck*, which is more dramatically accessible), expressionist music is highly esoteric and sophisticated. Its overthrowing of tonality, paralleling the resistance to realist conventions in literature and naturalism in painting, is a sign of its formal abstraction and its successful revolt against musical conventions. But to listen to this music is to hear the disturbing, discordant sounds of human anguish, of the expressionist *Schrei* that lies beyond the power of language to communicate and reaches through intellectual difficulty. In the words of Arnold Schönberg: 'A work of art can achieve no finer effect than when it transmits to the beholder the emotions that raged in the creator in such a way that they rage and storm in him.'[12]

In retrospect, 1913 seems to mark the beginning of the German silent film's rise to fame as one of the most powerful media of Expressionism. In 1913 Max Reinhardt made his first film; Paul Wegener, one of the best known of expressionist actors, appeared in Robert Wiene's *The Student of Prague* (a *Doppelgänger* adventure about a young man who sells his soul to the devil), and Kurt Pinthus published *Das Kinobuch*, with screenplays by some of the most prominent expressionist writers. Pinthus, himself an expressionist writer and theorist, predicted that in film the ordinary facts of reality would be replaced by an idealized, fantastic reality released from causality and the ponderousness of things.[13] The German silent film was born at precisely that moment when the revolt against realism and the formulation of an expressionist vision reached their first intense peak, and for a short while, primarily between 1919 and 1925, the screen mirrored the torments of the human soul.

The story of expressionist film is inseparable from the careers of three major directors, Robert Wiene, F.W. (Friedrich Wilhelm) Murnau, and Fritz Lang, the acting style of Paul Wegener, Werner Krauss, Rudolf Klein-Rogge, and Conrad Veidt, and films such as Karl Heinz Martin's *From Morn to Midnight* (1920, based on Kaiser's play and starring Ernst Deutsch as the Cashier), Wiene's *The Cabinet of Dr Caligari* (1919), *Raskolnikow* (1923), and *The Hands of Orlac* (1924), Stellan Rye's 1913 *The Student of Prague* (revised in 1926 by Henrik Galeen), Murnau's *Nosferatu* (1922) and *Sunrise* (1927), Arthur Robison's *Warning Shadows* (1923), Paul Leni's *Waxworks* (1924), Karl Grune's *The Street* (1923), and Lang's *Metropolis* (1927), *Dr Mabuse* (1922), *Die Niebelungen* (1922–24), and *M* (1930), his first sound film, with Peter Lorre as the schizophrenic murderer.[14] Perhaps the most striking feature of all these films is their distortion; in each the so-called normal surfaces of life (details of social context, spatio-temporal relationships, psychological plausibility, and so on) are replaced by wildly distorted perspectives, violent eruptions of passion, and grotesque, almost demonic behaviour. These films create their own world, a kind of dark opposite to the everyday one, which obeys its own mysterious and frightening laws. Dramatic chiaroscuro, geometric, stylized sets (the most celebrated being those in *Caligari* – see Plates 17, 18), whirling fairgrounds, mirrors that seem to reflect the depths of madness, jealousy, or fear, and flights of stairs that wind and climb, split and double back on themselves contribute to the expressionist vocabulary of these films.

Expressionist acting, of course, is the perfect complement to the style and subject-matter of these films, and many of the actors were trained on the stage, where ecstatic speech and exaggerated gestures were demanded. Even today Veidt's staring eyes and raised, claw-like hands as he contemplates his murderous skill in *The Hands of Orlac* (see Plate 19) or moves towards his next victim in *Caligari*, and the hysterical gestures of Klein-Rogge as the raving Attila in *Die Niebelungen* or the mad Rotwang in *Metropolis*, impress the viewer as images of the darkest corners of the human soul.

The influence of expressionist films such as *Caligari*, *The Hands of Orlac*, or those by Lang, is noted at various points in the following discussion. For earlier modernists like O'Neill and Lowry these works seemed to be examples of what could be achieved in their own rebellion against realist conventions, whereas for postmodernists like Aquin and Pynchon, these films become crucial texts that can be used for a variety of parodic purposes. *Caligari*, after all, is much more than a stylistic *tour de force* because in its dramatic framing device – placing the young hero's story about Dr Caligari's use of the somnambulist Cesare to carry out his murderous designs within the context of an insane asylum – it draws into question all our assumptions about sanity and madness, abusive, manipulative authority, and a necessary social order. It is a deeply ambiguous film that, by refusing to say whether or not the hero, a quite ordinary young man, is paranoid and whether or not his revelations about the doctor are the truth or the fantastic imaginings of a persecution complex, reveals the innermost tensions of the expressionist vision. If Francis is right and Caligari is a monster, then his incarceration under the doctor's care only underlines his failure to liberate himself and mankind from a double-faced tyranny, either during the dramatic events in his hometown of Holstenwall or in the narrative present of his retelling. If, however, Caligari really is the good-natured man of medicine that he appears to be at the end, then the young man's story is little more than a violent, subjective fantasy – unless this fantasy is itself an accurate reflection of the true essence of social order and patriarchal authority. Either way, the film leaves us with the image of Francis, together with the other figures in his story, withdrawn into escapist dreams, lost in a fog of mad imaginings, removed from any contact with the real world of action, politics, and history. The primitive violence unleashed by Caligari remains unaccounted for, and this final image is regressive.

By contrast, Lang's *Metropolis* offers an image of apocalyptic revolt that succeeds in re-establishing a new social order. Here the hero, a bona fide expressionist New Man, the only son of a wealthy industrialist and leader of the capitalist city, rebels against his decadent surroundings and all-powerful father and takes sides with the workers who slave underground to maintain his extravagant, sophisticated world. After a cataclysmic flood that almost destroys the entire city (and a variety of lesser but equally dramatic catastrophes), Freder, together with Maria, the woman who has opened his eyes to the workers' enslavement, convinces the father to reform: Head (Herr Frederson), Heart (Freder and Maria), and Hands (the workers represented by their leader) join in a highly symbolic, sentimentalized scene of reconciliation.[15] *Caligari* and *Metropolis* are excellent examples of the two dominant tendencies that recur throughout the plays and fiction of the movement. (See Figure 2, p 37 above.)

J.L. Styan is certainly correct in claiming that the 'lively conventions of expressionism' have become the accepted stock-in-trade of the contemporary playwright and are quite familiar to today's theatre-goers.[16] Nevertheless, Expressionism in the German theatre between 1908 and the early twenties was more than a stylistic breakthrough to new conventions. It was often a violent expression of sexual and generational hostility, pitting male against female, father against son; for some playwrights, like Kaiser and Toller, it was the best way to portray the conflicts within the human soul and between the representative individual struggling for rebirth and the economic and political forces within a hostile, repressive society. Toller defined expressionist drama in such a way as to stress the link between aesthetic and ethical concerns. Looking back on the writing of his plays, he explained that

> today many people smile at Expressionism: at that time it was a necessary
> artistic form. It took a stand against that kind of art which was satisfied
> with lining up impressions side by side, asking no questions about the
> essence, the responsibility, the idea. The Expressionist wanted to do more
> than take photographs. Realizing that the artist's environment, as it were,
> penetrates him and is reflected in the mirror of his soul, he wanted to
> recreate this environment in its very essence. For it was the intention of
> Expressionism to influence this environment ... In the Expressionist
> drama, man was no incidental private person. He was a type, applying to
> many by leaving out their superficial features. By skinning the human
> being one hoped to find his soul under the skin.[17]

Once more we have the revolt against a realist tradition in art; once more the expressionist stresses the importance of soul and vision and the artist's responsibility to depict the innermost essences of life.

Among the early influences on the German theatre, Strindberg was possibly the most decisive. There were no fewer than 1,035 performances of twenty-four Strindberg plays staged in Germany between 1913 and 1915,[18] and *To Damascus* (1898), one of the most popular of these, is highly expressionistic, with characters who represent the human condition and a general longing for spiritual transformation. *A Dream Play* (1901) was also extremely popular, and the influence of its 'polyphonic' dialogue, intimate staging, and tormented inner world is apparent in many later expressionist plays. What limits the Expressionism of this play is that it presents Strindberg's own private nightmare instead of a symbolic expression of Man's troubled soul, as is the case in Toller's *Masses and Man*, Hasenclever's *Humanity*, and, to a lesser extent, Kaiser's *From Morn to Midnight*. Frank Wedekind was also an important forerunner of Expressionism, but more for his subject-matter and critical revolt against the tastes and mores of the establishment than for any revolutionary break with theatrical convention. A play such as *Spring Awakening* (1891) – an unsentimental treatment of puberty and its tragic consequences within a repressive, prudish environment in school and at home – shocked its audiences in 1906, when it was finally produced in abridged form for the first time, and Wedekind's famous Lulu plays – *Earth Spirit* and *Pandora's Box* – introduced the problem of sexual freedom and appetite to the stage in a cynical yet powerful portrayal of human instinct.[19] A long line of expressionist plays exploring sexual violence and the revolt of the young against their parents can be traced to these Wedekind plays.

Reinhard Sorge's *The Beggar* (1912), subtitled *A Dramatic Mission*, is one of the earliest and in many ways one of the more interesting and complex of expressionist plays.[20] The hero is the Poet, whose revolutionary new plays meet with little support from a condescending Patron, who recommends conservative evolution instead of early performances that will take the young man's vision directly to the people. His friends and family are also of little help. In fact, the poet poisons his mad Father and exhausted Mother in an ecstatic scene at the end of the play, thereby freeing them from their suffering and himself from their complaints and demands. Now his only companion is a young prostitute, the Girl, who will abandon all, including her illegitimate child, to nourish his soul. The play has three acts, one at the theatre, two at home, and each act consists of a sequence of scenes, at times fairly realistic, at others highly abstract and stylized, that flow one into the next without curtain or scenic division. Sorge's stage instructions call for highly expressionist visual effects: at one point 'a floodlight falls slantwise across the left half of the stage' (33), dividing the set into sharply constrasting areas of light and dark; at another Sorge calls for a group of prostitutes and lovers to 'posture as a monument' (36); the second act opens with the mad Father beating a drum, and as the stage becomes visible, the drumbeats grow faster until they 'finally merge in a furious roll' (47).

One further noteworthy point about this play is that with his contrasting scenes of near realism and extreme expressionist abstraction (made especially dramatic through the use of light and sound), Sorge has contrasted two types of drama and two sharply opposed ways of living and creating. By rejecting the complacent world of the bourgeois Patron and ridding himself of the burdens posed by filial obligations, Sorge's Poet has made his expressionist vision possible; he is now free to develop the vision that appeared in the ecstatic monologues and symbolic scenes (for example, between the Youth and the Girl in act 2) of the play. *The Beggar* thus juxtaposes two visions of art and life – the realist (and certainly bourgeois) and expressionist – and dramatizes the overthrow of the one by the other. As Styan claims, it is a 'metatheatrical' play about the search for a new theatre – hence the subtitle – and a statement about how such a theatre could be achieved.[21]

Many of the same expressionist features can be found in Kaiser's *From Morn to Midnight* and Toller's *Masses and Man*, both of which were more influential and better plays than *The Beggar*. *Masses and Man* was written while Toller was in prison and was first produced in the fortress of Niederschönenfeld in October 1919. Its subtitle, *A Fragment of the Social Revolution of the Twentieth Century*, indicates Toller's wide political scope. The play consists of seven 'Pictures,' four of which Toller calls 'visionary abstracts of reality,' while the other three are dream pictures, almost separate visions.[22] The characters are unnamed types: the Woman (also called Sonia), Her Husband, Working Men and Women, and so on. In this portrayal of the ideological struggle between the masses and the state Toller uses a woman as a symbol of his belief in peaceful social change, but she becomes a martyr who chooses death rather than return to her bourgeois husband or compromise with the violent rebel leader when her message of peace and love fails and the masses begin to revolt. Thus, she carries the visionary burden of the play, and her death represents a transfiguration. The many expressionist techniques of *Masses and Man*, such as the double structure of 'realistic' and dream pictures, the contrasting styles of staccato dialogue and lyrical monologues, the abstractions of character, and the effective massing of choruses to represent the people, together with Jürgen Fehling's remarkable expressionist production at the Berlin Volksbühne in 1921, made *Masses and Man* one of the best-known, most highly praised plays of the expressionist repertoire (see Plate 21). This is the play that moved Macgowan and Jones so deeply and inspired Herman Voaden.

Kaiser's play is a still finer example of expressionist dramaturgy in that it is more tightly structured and economically focused on the ordeals of one man. It is closer to Sorge's *The Beggar* than to *Masses and Man* because it avoids any direct reference to the masses of mankind who, like the Cashier, suffer a dehumanizing existence and long for release. Instead, mankind is portrayed through the figure of a single pathetic little man, whose mechanical existence at work and *petit bourgeois* home-life are shattered by the appearance of a beautiful woman who arouses his instincts and his desire for rebirth. After embezzling sixty thousand marks from the bank, he rushes forth to encounter a series of crushing defeats in

Ludwig Meidner, *The City and I*, 1913

his search for a new life and finally ends up committing suicide when he is betrayed to the police by the Salvation Army girl who has urged him to confess his crime.

From Morn to Midnight is an expressionist *Stationendrama*, consisting of two acts in seven stations, or loosely connected parts, that portray separate events in the man's day, from his morning revolt to his death at midnight. It provides a clear dramatic instance of the *Aufbruch* (a breaking free or sudden starting forth) so characteristic of expressionist plays, when the Cashier awakens abruptly from his semi-catatonic existence and rushes violently from the bank. It also provides an interesting example of the kind of cynical ambiguity typical of Kaiser, to be sure, but also found in much expressionist literature. Although the Cashier does not provide an attractive image of mankind, his death is none the less disturbing because at every turn he is frustrated or defeated by a society that is worse than he is. Whether they are the stultifying members of his family, the gamblers at the cycle races, prostitutes at a cabaret, or fellow refugees from the lonely night in the Salvation Army hall, the creatures he encounters in his 'stations' all exhibit a selfishness, lethargy, and stupidity more debilitating than his own. His suicide is an act of despair, not the truly transfiguring martyrdom of a Christ-figure (see Plate 18) or of Toller's Sonia in *Masses and Man*, and his final gasped 'Ecce Homo!' only underscores this irony.[23]

Several common features emerge from these three plays, and together they illustrate what is distinctive about expressionist theatre. First of all, plot and structure no longer follow the dictates of the classical unities. The play is broken into episodes, contrasting scenes, or loosely, symbolically connected tableaux. At some point, usually early in the play, the protagonist will experience his *Aufbruch* and from there set forth on his journey in search of rebirth. This search will sometimes carry him forward, stage by stage, towards his *Erlösung*, a favorite expressionist term suggesting deliverance and redemption and thus combining secular and religious possibilities for release from suffering, repression, guilt, or, more generally, the normal restrictions of this life. As Douglas Kellner explains, *Erlösung* could be individual in focus or an image of communal salvation.[24] It is the former type that Sorge's Poet achieves at the end of *The Beggar*, but it is the latter ethical vision that Toller's hero experiences in *Transfiguration* (*Die Wandlung*, 1918, Plate 20) or Sonia undergoes in *Masses and Man* and that Kaiser depicts in the transfiguring, sacrificial suicide of his heroic New Man, Eustache de Saint-Pierre, in *The Burghers of Calais* (*Die Bürgers von Calais*, 1917). In a final scene closely foreshadowing similar moments in plays by Voaden and O'Neill, Kaiser has Eustache's body carried into the church and placed before a floodlit deposition from the cross and resurrection. However, despite the attractions of a dramatic *Erlösung*, only a few expressionist plays end with this vision of the Christ-like New Man and his hopeful message for mankind. More often the *Aufbruch* leads only to an ambiguous, ironic death, as in *From Morn to Midnight* (see Plate 18), a celebration of violent sexuality, as in Kokoschka's *Murder, Hope of Women* or Werfel's *Goat Song*, or to regression and despair, most tellingly, perhaps, in Kaiser's *The Raft of the Medusa* (*Das Floss der Medusa*, 1940–43).

Second, the characters lose their individuality; they are types, nameless figures, such as the Poet, the Woman, the Cashier, rather than specific personalities, and they are often exaggerated or grotesque embodiments of essential human qualities or of groups within society. As far as psychological development or consistent, believable behaviour is concerned, they are quite unreal, and their ecstatic monologues are signs of their symbolic rather than realistic function. These monologues, like the dialogue, which is often very close to a monologue mode, tend to fall into two distinct types. Sometimes they are lyrical and rhapsodic, as, for example, in Sonia's lyrical outburst towards the end of *Masses and Man* or the Poet's monologue in *The Beggar*, part of which was quoted above. At others they take the form of the famous 'staccato' or 'telegraph' style associated with expressionist writing (whether in plays, poetry, or fiction), consisting of short, abrupt outbursts, broken phrases, expletives, abundant punctuation and parataxis. This is Kaiser's Cashier:

> Here I stand. I stand above you. Two are too many. There's space for one only. Loneliness is space; space is loneliness. Coldness is sun. Sun is coldness. The fevered body bleeds. The fevered body shivers. Bare fields. Ice spreading. Who can escape? Where is the way out?[25]

While technically a monologue, of course, a speech like this should not be confused with monologism in Bakhtin's sense. Here the Cashier, with his rhetorical questions and his newly discovered need to speak *with* others in order to exist, sounds very like Dostoevsky's Underground Man.

As would be expected, the acting style called for in these plays was highly stylized. The claw-like hands, wildly staring eyes, violent gestures, and jerky movements are familiar from the acting in expressionist films (though the film medium itself is responsible for some of the effect), and masks were often used to distort reality, to heighten the sense of alienation and horror experienced by the protagonist, or to stress the spiritual and symbolic truths being presented (see Plates 14, 15, 18, 19, and 20). The mask, said Yvan Goll, in his 1918 preface to *The Immortals*, is 'the primary symbol of the theatre'; it is 'rigid, unique, and impressive. It is unchangeable, inescapable; it is Fate'; in the mask 'non-reality becomes fact.'[26] And within a few short years Eugene O'Neill would begin exploring the potential of the mask to suggest an inescapable fate. But one of the most important statements on expressionist acting was Paul Kornfeld's 'Epilogue to the Actor' appended to his 1913 play *The Seduction* (*Die Verführung*). It was Kornfeld who coined the term *Seelendrama* (drama of souls); like Edward Gordon Craig, he demanded acting that was unashamedly non-realistic and utterly subservient to the essences of character and reality: 'Let [the actor] therefore pick out the essential attributes of reality and be nothing but a representative of thought, feeling, or Fate! The melody of a great gesture says more than the highest consummation of what is called naturalness.'[27]

If 'naturalness' was an evil to be avoided in acting, speech, and characterization, it was still more strenuously avoided on the stage itself. Available evidence suggests that the sets and staging for these plays were tremendously innovative and that the Germans were years ahead of their French or British counterparts. Stripped down to the most basic elements, the stage expressed the play through flights of steps and platforms (for which Leopold Jessner was famous) or through bizarre, distorted shapes (like the skeletal tree that blocks the Cashier's way) reminiscent of expressionist painting; and through bold colour contrasts and imaginative lighting the stage became a projection of the characters' minds and souls (see Plates 20 and 21). In fact, lighting became an active force in the drama and a vital way of revealing the characters' inner torments, their manipulations by fate or their spiritual transfiguration. Because the world presented on stage was often either an inner one or else an image of the world distorted by the frenzied vision of the protagonist (and thereby seen in its essential hostility and corruption), spotlighting or chiaroscuro were effective means for suggesting the intensity of this vision and for distinguishing between those sufficiently awake to experience it and those still trapped in a mechanical, blind routine.

Perhaps the chief inspiration for these innovations on the expressionist stage was the Englishman Edward Gordon Craig, who had begun to publish his views by 1908 and was well known in Europe (though rejected at home) for his revolutionary ideas by 1912.[28] Craig, who abhorred realism, wanted a visionary theatre of light and motion that would express the soul and mankind's spiritual longings, but it was the Germans – Reinhardt, Jessner, Martin, and Fehling – who realized these dreams through the plays of the expressionists. At the end of the war in 1918, when German expressionist theatre was about to reach its peak, Kurt Pinthus predicted that the drama would be the most 'passionate and effective form' of expressionist writing because 'there Man explodes in front of Man.'[29] The plays of Sorge, Kokoschka, Kaiser, Toller, Werfel, Hasenclever, and others, brought to life by a generation of brilliant directors, suggest that Pinthus was right.

Speaking of expressionist literature in 1925, the literary critic Albert Soergel correctly pointed out that 'Expressionism is lyric outcry, dramatic stress, not epic action' ('Expressionismus ist lyrischer Zwang, dramatischer Drang, nicht epischer Gang').[30] This terse comment identifies the basic tendencies of expressionist literature, but it implies that expressionists will encounter difficulties when they attempt the novel, and in this Soergel gives a somewhat false impression. In the theatre Expressionism proved highly effective, while expressionist poetry ran the gamut from apocalyptic despair to clinical horrors in a style ranging from exaggerated, emotional rhetoric to revolutionary linguistic experimentation that merged, at its extreme, with the dadist movement in Zurich and Berlin.[31] But several hundred expressionist novels and fictional prose works were published in Germany between 1905 and 1925, and this body of literature, though extremely difficult to classify, provides a fascinating source of material for any study of the movement.[32]

Before embarking on a brief discussion of expressionist poetry and prose, however, it is important to note that as far as the English-speaking world is concerned, very little was known about this literature until after the Second World War. There were a few outstanding exceptions – Franz Kafka, Alfred Döblin and Gottfried Benn – but even their work was not known in English translation until 1930, for Kafka's *The Castle*, and 1931 for *Berlin Alexanderplatz* (*Metamorphosis* and the Muirs' translation of *The Trial* did not appear until 1937), or after the Second World War, when T.S. Eliot drew attention to Benn in his 1953 National Book League lecture on the voice of lyric poetry.[33] Expressionism was influential abroad because of theatre productions, art exhibitions, and films such as *Caligari* and *Metropolis*, which were extremely popular in avant-garde intellectual circles, because of proselytizers like Macgowan, Ashley Dukes, Scheffauer, and Cheney and because of the very real international interchange among artists. Expressionism began to be visually accessible and available in London at least as early as the spring of 1914, when woodcuts by Kandinsky, Marc, Pechstein, and other *Brücke* artists were exhibited at the Twenty-One Gallery (and warmly praised by Wyndham Lewis in his note for the exhibition catalogue) and 1913 in New York at the famous Armory Show, which stressed French painters but did include some Kirchner, Kandinsky, and a few others. But it was not until the twenties that expressionist plays were frequently performed in both centres, and *Caligari*, released early in 1921, quickly became a sensation.[34]

Although it does not seem especially startling now, Jakob van Hoddis's poem 'Weltende' created quite a stir when it was recited in the Berlin cafés of 1911. It was not the poem's language or style (there are a mere eight tidily rhyming lines) that appealed so much as his images of apparent apocalypse: a hat flies off the burgher's pointed head, roofs collapse, floods rage, trains tumble from railway trestles, and a storm engulfs everyone. In its theme this little poem set one of the keynotes of expressionist literature because for many expressionist writers before and after the First World War the world seemed to be on the brink of some cataclysm; indeed, many felt that massive destruction was necessary in order to cleanse society. Georg Heym, a contemporary of van Hoddis, also wrote formally conventional poems that are nevertheless early examples of expressionist poetry because of their despairing cries, violent imagery, and visionary treatment of destruction.

But conventional form and language do not characterize the most interesting expressionist poetry, which shatters syntax, resorts to neologism, and exploits grotesque imagery or develops rhythmic patterns appropriate to the embodiment of the expressionist *Schrei*. The opening lines of August Stramm's long poem 'Die Menschheit' ('Mankind') provide a fine, if difficult to translate, example of these qualities:

> Tränen kreist der Raum!
> Tränen Tränen
> Dunkle Tränen
> Goldne Tränen
> Lichte Tränen
> Wellen krieseln
> Glasten stumpfen
> Tränen Tränen
> Tränen
> Funken
> Springen auf und quirlen
> Quirlen quirlen
> Wirbeln glitzen
> Wirbeln sinken
> Wirbeln springen
> Zeugen
> Neu und neu und neu

Vertausendfacht
Zermilliont
Im Licht![35]

Space circles tears! / Tears tears / Dark tears / gold tears / bright tears / Undulating spinning / Glassy dull / Tears tears / Tears / Sparks / Springing up and twirling / Twirling twirling / Whirling glistening / Whirling sinking / Whirling leaping / Generating / New anew renewed / By the thousands / The millions / In the light!

Gottfried Benn is primarily of interest in the present context for his 'monologue' poems, which have been frequently anthologized. His 'The Lost I' or 'Fragments,' for example, present devastating images of modern man lost in a mechanical, spiritually meaningless world, speaking only to himself because in such a world communication is impossible. Benn's monologues echo the cries for mankind or for the lost self so often heard in expressionist plays and express in words the anguish depicted in Munch's *Geschrei* or Ludwig Meidner's *The City and I* (*Ich und die Stadt*, 1913; see Plates 22 and 29). Like the hallucinatory monologues in expressionist plays and fictions, these poems are essentially the verbal counterpart to the painter's obsession with the soul (whether his own or his human subject's) and as such constitute one of the most important features of Expressionism.[36]

Comparatively speaking, expressionist fiction has been neglected by historians and critics of the movement in favour of the fine arts, drama and theatre production, poetry, and even film. As a result the general criteria and definitions of Expressionism have been derived from other literary genres or other media and in their details apply less well, or only metaphorically, to the novel. According to A.P. Dierick, irony is often considered incompatible with Expressionism simply because it is less tangible in the poetry and plays that take their anguished cry for humanity and the ideals of rebirth and brotherhood so seriously and because it seems irrelevant to the vocabulary of expressionist painting. But irony is an important structural and thematic element in most narratives, and expressionist fiction is no exception. Indeed, as Dierick suggests, irony is an essential vehicle for mediating between expressionist extremes of ecstasy and despair and for supplying some critical perspective on the New Man, whose *Erlösung* may or may not be particularly successful in a given text.[37] Not surprisingly, then, there are some important differences between expressionist novels and other forms of Expressionism.

Two major attempts to chart expressionist prose have already been made, one by Walter H. Sokel in *The Writer in Extremis: Expressionism in Twentieth-Century German Literature* and the other by Armin Arnold in *Prosa des Expressionismus*. Because their approaches are so different, Sokel and Arnold provide complementary and useful ways to think about Expressionism in fiction. Sokel approaches the problem from a philosophical and psychological perspective, tracing the movement back to roots in Kant's theory of the anti-mimetic basis of art and the idea of an 'inexorable estrangement between man and nature,' and suggesting some of the paths by which Expressionism leads to existentialism.[38] He perceives two quite distinct (and opposed) tendencies in expressionist literature that cut synchronically across the expressionist field regardless of genre. The first he describes as naïve, subjective and rhetorical, the other as sophisticated, intellectual, and experimental; the first is closer to Surrealism because it is 'subjective, dreamlike, visionary' – though Sokel is quick to point out that it differs from Surrealism because of its 'existential seriousness and consistency' – whereas the second, he suggests, is closer to Cubism because it is object-centred.[39] Kafka is an example of the former type; Kaiser, Benn, and Döblin of the latter. Unlike Sokel, Arnold places expressionist fiction within a detailed socio-historical context. He traces a number of foreign influences on the expressionist novel, among them Flaubert's *Salammbô*, Marinetti's *Mafarka le futuriste*, and Jack London's *The Sea Wolf*, and explains why and to what extent the Germans were fascinated with these foreign and exotic writers.[40] He warns against loose thematic or stylistic definitions of this fiction, and yet, through his focus on a few particular and largely forgotten writers, such as Franz Jung and Curt Corrinth, and his constant attention to the dozens of other stories and novels being published between 1905 and 1925, a clear sense of what constitutes Expressionism in narrative fiction gradually emerges from his study. Where Sokel is helpful in establishing certain limits and extremes within Expressionism, Arnold provides an essential context and overview that is at once flexible and clear.

By considering the observations of Sokel and Arnold together with some recognized expressionist novelists such as Döblin, Kafka, and Robert Walser,[41] it is possible to isolate certain characteristics that are not only present in the German novel but are also distinguishing features of the English-language novels examined in subsequent chapters.

First, character in expressionist fiction is not understood or developed in a rational, psychologically consistent manner; human motivation is seldom explained or even apparent. Instead, character is a function of instinct, will, or governing idea, and the 'figures' (a term used by Kaiser in *Vision und Figur* to distinguish his 'characters' from realistic ones) in a narrative are often grotesque, eccentric abstractions from reality or quasi-allegorical images of mankind. Although this tendency towards abstraction is less pronounced in most novels than it is – indeed, than it can be – in the drama, the characters in an expressionist novel tend to be representative types rather than fully rounded individuals. They are not depicted as determined by and responding to a social context of which they form a part; therefore, in many instances they do not appear to learn from their experiences in a logical, deductive manner; they do not grow. Their behaviour is unpredictable, often inexplicable both to the characters themselves and to others (including the reader), and the characters act from obscure impulses, intense emotions of jealousy, anger, desire, or despair, and vague ideals. For a writer like Döblin, as for Lowry, who had read and admired *Berlin Alexanderplatz* in translation, conventional realist psychology and character etiology were irrelevant and boring. In addition, characters in an expressionist text frequently seem undifferentiated from each other (or even from the narrating voice) because the idiom they use and the language used about them, if there is a third-person narrator, is the same. This is a problem of narrative voice and language that will receive detailed attention and qualification in other chapters, but for the time being Sokel's general explanation of this phenomenon will suffice. He suggests that this 'sameness of idiom among all characters does not, as in the classical drama, reflect the cohesion of an idealized social-cultural elite, but underlines the fact that the characters ... are fragments of a single mind.'[42] It should be added, moreover, that the reunification of a single consciousness is seldom sought or achieved in expressionist writing and that this fragmentation contributes to the dialogistic quality of this fiction.

Second, settings in expressionist novels are either exotic – that is, far removed from the everyday world of Europe – or else bizarre in some way: the ordinary world of home, city streets, school is distorted and made unreal by the absence of a social context that would help to establish spatio-temporal relations among people, places, and events, and through the concentration upon a dislocated, partial, and at times hallucinatory perspective or the creation of unusual and freakish minor characters. Gregor Samsa could scarcely be in a more ordinary place than his own bedroom, and yet he wakes one morning to find he is *ein Ungeziefer* (a vermin or bug). Of course, by removing characters and action from familiar locales or by disrupting our sense of what is familiar and safe, the expressionist writer forces us to see not what is simply unreal but what lies beyond or beneath the surface realities of life. These settings are usually expressions of a character's innermost terrors – an image of the state of his soul – or of what the world is actually like beneath its fashionable surfaces. The exoticism and / or distortion serves a crucial epistemological and anti-mimetic purpose. Moreover, such settings and states as the condition of Gregor or the jungle in O'Neill's *The Emperor Jones* are literalized metaphors: the self or the external world *becomes* (in the text, on the stage) what is oppressive or feared. These metaphors are among the most striking and common features of expressionist texts.

Third, the action in this fiction parallels the characterization: it is fragmented, episodic, and lacking in logical cause and effect. Sometimes it is dream-like, unified, yet illogical; often disjunct episodes that seem complete in themselves follow each other paratactically, without any spatio-temporal narrative connections or explanations. Even when there is a clear diegetic thread (as there usually must be in an extended fiction), it is the intensity of the moment rather than a developing, unified believable story that is of primary importance. Again, Kafka is a fine example of the former mode, which is apparent as well in Ralph Ellison's *Invisible Man* (see chapter 4), and Döblin of the latter. For Döblin, as for Barnes, Lowry, and Watson, the first goal of the novelist was not to tell but to build ('Nicht erzählen, sondern bauen'); hence his primary concern was with structure instead of character.[43] He wanted his novels to live in their individual parts. Where the expressionist dramatist often used a *Stationendrama* structure, thereby unifying a play through the controlling metaphors of ordeal and journey, the novelist was driven to discover new, dynamic ways of organizing, or *building*, and unifying his or her text.

Fourth, of the various techniques used by expressionist writers either to abstract their stories or to express the soul-states of their characters, only two need be mentioned at this point because an extended discussion of technique must be situated within the analysis of a specific text. Frequently scenes are juxtaposed in a kind of montage so that they relate to each other in terms of repeated images and motifs or as a series of partial and fragmented perspectives. Although a governing metaphor, such as that of the journey, may provide thematic or symbolic unity for the story, individual chapters, scenes or episodes, indeed the overall narrative structure, are constituted through relations of parataxis and metonymy.[44] Also of special importance in expressionist fiction is the monologue, which must be distinguished from *monologue intérieur* and by no means confused with narrated monologue (*erlebte Rede*) or stream of consciousness.[45] Like the monologues in expressionist plays, these long, ecstatic 'speeches' are expressions of inner emotional states, not of thought processes, and they are addressed less to any specified listener or interlocutor within the text than to the cosmos, to the self, to empty space, or perhaps to Man ('O Mensch!') in the guise of the reader. I call them expressionist monologues and discuss them in detail when they occur.

Thematic concerns form a fifth characteristic of this fiction, and there are some extremely powerful themes common to all forms of Expressionism. But one must be careful not to exaggerate the uniqueness of any one theme; bitter conflict between the generations, which seems almost synonymous with expressionist literature, is scarcely a discovery of the expressionists. More often than not, what makes a theme expressionist is the obsessive or distorted way it is handled, so that while sexual aberrance and atavism and an interest in eroticism, jealousy, and betrayal and in violent sexual crime are age-old subjects, they do occur with remarkable frequency and emphasis in the literature, film, and painting of Expressionism. With qualifications, this type of subject-matter could be said to characterize much expressionist fiction. Two themes, however, do seem to be especially important: the first is the conflicting pull towards apocalypse or regression basic to the expressionist vision; the second is what Sokel calls 'the impotence of the heart.' In point of fact, they are overlapping themes, but because I discuss regression and apocalypse in another context, some further attention should be given to the theme of impotence here.

According to Sokel, the failure of love is a quintessential expressionist subject and is intimately related to the frequent doubling of characters. Because of his 'emotional impotence,' the hero (often the artist *him*self, because the German expressionist only depicts the artist as male) 'long[s] to be different, to be his opposite, the strong simple man of action who is fully alive to the world around him and, therefore, capable of genuine feelings and love.'[46] His situation is full of unresolvable tension and paradox because, on the one hand, the hero longs to be his opposite, even if it is the recognition of his own soul-state that occasions his insight into reality, while on the other he is often seen (most notably if he is an artist figure) as attempting to bring the message of his expressionist vision to others, those others whom he cannot love or reach. Whether his impotence is physical, spiritual, emotional, or all three, this version of the expressionist self is tragically divided and rendered useless by its own agonizing incapacity. Sokel suggests the heroes of Kafka, René Schickele, and Kaiser as examples of this dilemma, but many others come to mind, such as Professor Unrat in Heinrich Mann's 1905 novel by that name (*not* the pathetic little man of von Sternberg's film *The Blue Angel*), young Jakob in Walser's *Jakob von Gunten* (1908), or the heroes of Franz Jung's novels, where, as Arnold points out, 'the best Man can do is to sit in a corner with a beer and switch off his mind [und den Verstand auszuschalten].'[47]

Sixth, no expressionist work, whether play, film, or novel, is complete without the expressionist 'hero' (Wedekind's Lulu and Toller's Sonia are female exceptions to the masculine norm, but they follow the general pattern of the male protagonist), and typically he can be of two distinct, extreme types. In either case he must be alien in some way, different, other, outside the social pale, extraordinary. Arnold distinguishes sharply between the Christ-like New Man of Expressionism and the Nietzschean *Übermensch* (though Nietzsche himself characterized the Superman as a Caesar with the soul of Christ), and he finds the expressionist novelists showing greater interest in the superman as 'macho' leader because, with few exceptions – Döblin's Franz Biberkopf in *Berlin Alexanderplatz* is the most substantial – they could not believe in the ideal of the New Man.[48] The heroes in novels like Jakob Wassermann's *Alexander in Babylon* (1905) are violent, rebellious, self-centred, and amoral men of action descended from Nietzsche via Gabriele D'Annunzio, Marinetti, and Jack London. Lang's Dr Mabuse is, perhaps, the most charismatic and powerful of all these Supermen, who, weighed down by a further debilitating ambiguity, haunt O'Neill's imagination and spring to new, alarming life in contemporary works by Aquin and Pynchon. Nevertheless, the hero usually associated with expressionist literature is the New Man who represents a Christ-like ideal of rebirth in all men, a rebirth generated from within, from the inner man or soul and directed towards inspiring a parallel rejuvenation in others and in society as a whole. The New Man's message is quite familiar: love within a spiritually revitalized individual will lead to the brotherhood of Man. But such an ideal is fraught with obvious, unresolvable, inner contradictions and was often invoked, as in Kaiser's case, for example, more as an evasion of reality than as a valid means of transforming it. In practice the New Man appeared to advocate a kind of mystical union with the cosmos or an atavistic lapse back into nature; both possibilities appealed strongly to Voaden and go a long way towards explaining Barnes's enigmatic Robin Vote in *Nightwood.* It is no wonder that the expressionist dream could effect little in the way of practical change, for, as Douglas Kellner observes, the 'vision was extremely flawed, weakened by an excessive individualism, or messianic-rhetorical moralism, which tried to recycle old ideas of heart, spirit, love and brotherhood ... when war, political upheavals and ... capitalist and Stalinist industrialization were destroying bourgeois culture.'[49]

There are few efficacious New Men in the expressionist canon: Eustache de Saint-Pierre in Kaiser's *The Burghers of Calais*, Friedrich in Toller's *Transfiguration*, possibly Döblin's Biberkopf, and certainly the fully idealized – and unconvincing – son, Freder, in Lang's *Metropolis* are exceptions. In the literature about to be examined, Sheila Watson comes closest to creating a Superman who is transformed into a New Man. More often the expressionist hero is a failure, and even his success sometimes necessitates his death (often by suicide); frequently, he is little more than an absurd, pathetic figure, his message collapsing into some atavistic gesture. The other side of the expressionist New Man is not the Superman, who is his opposite, but the fool, an anti-heroic figure depicted ironically as degenerate, as a passive victim of fate or of his own violent desires and self-destructive impulses. With some qualifications, this is O'Neill's 'hero,' Lowry's Consul, and Barnes's Dr O'Connor.

Two more characteristics of expressionist literature should be mentioned briefly at this point because they are central to my analysis of expressionist plays and novels. In the first place, expressionist texts develop through complementary codes of inversion and explosion that inscribe aspects of regression and apocalypse respectively; either the ordinary world of human relations, of cause and effect, of daytime reality is turned inside-out or upside-down, or else it explodes because of some internal conflict or pressure. What we think of as normalcy is displaced, thrust aside by the eruption of a dark vision stemming from a mythic underworld, a suppressed trauma, a forgotten yet universal, instinctual realm, or by a violent outburst of destructive energy; either it is a carnivalesque vision, at once liberating and regressive, or a shattering, apocalyptic one. Furthermore, these codes are often mirrored in a dominant image or character – a topos of inversion or explosion – within the text. Obvious examples from painting are Egon Schiele's doubled self-portraits or Kirchner's *Girl Circus Rider*, where the spectator's eye is held by the upside-down central body (see Plate 2), and *Caligari* is a paradigm of this inversion. Pictorial topoi of explosion are clear in Meidner's *The City and I* (Plate 22), where lines and splashes of colour burst out around the centred human head, or in the abstract diagonals and blocks of colour surrounding the figure of a deer in Marc's *Fate of the Animals* (Plate 5). As we shall see, these topoi have much in common and thereby constitute an important key to the reading of expressionist texts. Secondly, as has often been remarked, the ambiguities and dichotomies of Expressionism are in themselves defining qualities of the expressionist style and vision.[50] It is a style characterized by extremes, fragmentation, disruption, rather than by a homogeneous, unified vocabulary. In its resistance to a monologic order it dialogizes utterance. It can be described as a subjective vision of the individual soul or as the intuitive expression of essences underlying the reality of objective forms. It pulls towards regression or apocalypse, towards 'empathy' or abstraction, towards 'primitivism' or 'abstractionism,' and its interest lies in these conflicting postures (see Figure 2, p 37 above).

In many ways expressionist art highlights the crisis of individual subjectivity in this century, and in its extreme visions of regression or apocalypse it registers the ambiguity and despair of this crisis. The works discussed in the following chapters, together with their German forerunners, share a vision of the world turned dark side up, where all normal surfaces and constraints are shattered to reveal the other side of existence, or one in which things explode from a centre under insupportable pressure. This inversion-explosion is both thematized and imaged in these texts – in O'Neill's bars and cages, in Lowry's Day of the Dead, in Barnes's nightworld, in Aquin's black snow, or in violent murders, cataclysmic fires, and images of blinding, transfiguring light – and because these topoi characterize expressionist art, they provide the lense through which to survey the territory covered by the moderns and to speculate about the neo-expressionist art of the present. To the degree that expressionist art constitutes a modern tradition that refuses classical unities, harmonies, and an ordered, monologistic vision of the world, then in its violently contradictory impulses, in its topoi of inversion and explosion, it epitomizes twentieth-century life and continues to be of relevance today.

PART TWO

Expressionism on the North American Stage

'The New Art of the Theatre' in New York and Toronto

This so called new art of the theatre is but a flash in the pan of inexperience. It is the cubism of the theatre – the waif of the incompetent and the degenerate.

DAVID BELLASCO, *New York Herald*, 7 January 1917

When Bellasco protested against experimental theatre productions in New York, it was already too late to stifle the new impulses shaping American theatre in this century. Things had begun to change as early as 1912, the year that, according to Floyd Dell, editor of *The Masses* and *The Liberator*, gave birth to a 'New Spirit ... in America.'[1] The same year also saw the performance of Wedekind's *Spring Awakening* by the New York German-language Irving Place Theatre. Between 1912 and 1921 – only nine short years – what we know today as modern American theatre was born.

The factors contributing to this upsurge of innovative activity were many, from mounting dissatisfaction with the tired melodramas of an earlier era to an increasing awareness of what was happening abroad, especially in Germany. The famous Armory Show of 1913 opened American eyes to European avant-garde painting; the ideas of Appia, Craig, and Reinhardt, for example, began to be endorsed by men like Cheney, Macgowan, and Jones; and in 1914 the seeds were sown for creating a new art of the theatre in the United States. When the Washington Square Players began their work in 1914, George 'Jig' Cook and Susan Glaspell were on hand, but Cook in particular was dissatisfied with the group, and by the summer of 1915 he and Glaspell had founded the Provincetown Players in the quiet summer retreat of Provincetown, Massachussetts. Cook and Glaspell wanted a theatre that was experimental and American. To all intents and purposes the following year marks the beginning of a truly experimental modern American theatre that from its beginnings was influenced by Expressionism. In 1916 Theodore Dreiser published his expressionist *Plays of the Natural and the Supernatural*; in 1916 the Provincetown Players performed one of Alfred Kreymborg's 'mildly expressionist' plays, *Lima Beans*; in 1916 Sheldon Cheney founded the progressive *Theater Arts Magazine*, with Kenneth Macgowan as his associate editor; and in 1916 Cook and Glaspell discovered Eugene O'Neill.

From this point, until their 1921–22 session, things moved quickly: ninety-three plays by forty-seven American playwrights were performed by the Provincetown Players (Bigsby, 20), including sixteen by O'Neill, with *Emperor Jones* (1920) providing the pinnacle of the Players' achievement, three by Djuna Barnes (*Three from the Earth, An Irish Triangle*, and *Kurzy from the Sea*), *Aria da Capo* by Edna St Vincent Millay, *Vote the New Moon* by Kreymborg, and eleven by Susan Glaspell, the most important of which, *The Verge*, is discussed below. After Cook left the Players for Greece, there was a year's hiatus before the triumvirate of Macgowan, Jones, and O'Neill started up again with plays by Strindberg, O'Neill, and others.[2] By the early twenties the American theatre had found the soul Cook had dreamt of discovering, and with it the playwright who would adapt Expressionism to his own highly personal and American ends.

But as this sketch of these years implies, O'Neill was not the only (or even the first) writer to introduce expressionistic qualities to the New York stage. According to Mardi Valgemae in *Accelerated Grimace*, Kreymborg was writing expressionistically as early as 1916, and Susan Glaspell, Elmer Rice, and John Howard Lawson also made significant contributions to an expressionist American theatre.[3] The context within which O'Neill grew to maturity can best be suggested in a brief examination of two of the best plays by his contemporaries: Glaspell's 1921 play *The Verge* and Rice's *The Adding Machine*, first produced at the Garrick Theater by the Theater Guild on 19 March 1923.

Glaspell's play, with sets designed by Cleon Throckmorton, was considered an 'expressionistic' *tour de force* by Macgowan in 1921, and it still proves to be a moving and interesting play to read today. Despite its conventional three-act structure *The Verge* is a strong example of expressionist theatre because of its sets, symbolism, theme, and its exceptionally forceful expressionist New Woman. Claire Archer, the botanist-visionary-feminist hero, is obsessed with the dream of creating a new form of life in her greenhouse-cum-laboratory. Part mad scientist and part modern woman, Claire searches for freedom and rebirth attained through a ruthless exclusion of family, ecstatic visions of 'otherness,' and the violent, apocalyptic murder of her male soul-mate. Thus summarized, *The Verge* sounds like a feminist response to Kokoschka's *Murder, Hope of Women*, but it is, in fact, much more.

The play opens on the darkened main floor of Claire's laboratory, with a light from a trapdoor in the floor creating menacing shadows from the leaves of a strange vine that twists across the stage. It is a deliberately claustrophobic set symbolizing Claire's withdrawal from and rejection of the bourgeois world of husband, child, home, and middle class, and intrusive patriarchal demands. The scene for act 2 describes a tower-room that recalls the sets in *The Cabinet of Dr Caligari*; a 'distorted' spiral staircase leads up to 'a tower which is thought to be round but does not complete the circle. The back is curved, then jagged lines break from that, and the front is a queer bulging window – in a curve that leans.'[4] Within this ambiguous, subjective world, part prison, part refuge, Claire struggles to preserve the purity of the environment needed for both her plants and her ideals: 'This place,' she tells us, 'is for the destruction that can get through' (*V*, III, 77).

The destructive act that Claire believes in is a truly apocalyptic one that will purge the world in a way that the last war failed to do, one that will clear the way for entirely new forms and undreamt-of possibilities. Not only does she profess her belief in the necessary violence of annihilation; she is prepared to act on this belief. Early in act 1, in the highly impassioned, staccato speech so typical of expressionist dramaturgy, she proclaims the value of 'the madness that breaks through': 'Mankind massed to kill. We have failed. We are through. We will destroy. Break this up – it can't go farther. In the air above – in the sea below – it is to kill! All we had thought we were – we aren't. We were shut in with what wasn't so ... Throw it in! Now? Ready? Break up. Push. Harder. Break up' (*V*, I, 29). Shortly after this outburst she tears her Edge Vine out by the roots because it 'is running back to what it broke out of,' and in the last moments of act 3 she strangles the man who, like the vine, tempts her to regress into the protection and safety of his identity and thereby to betray her vision.

Glaspell's *The Verge* is rich in ambiguities and tensions that are formal and linguistic as well as thematic. Her extraordinary expressionist hero is surrounded (rather like Sorge's Poet) by an infuriatingly mundane, *petit bourgeois* society, and yet her belief in Nietzschean forces of madness, destruction, and rebirth traps her within the bizarre tower and laboratory of her own mind. Although she loathes and mistrusts language, especially as it is wielded by those around her who hide behind the façades of convention and cliché, she must (as must the playwright) use language to communicate her vision, and she struggles painfully to do so; again, she seems trapped, this time by what Derrida describes as the 'détraquement' of apocalyptic discourse.[5] At the end the so-called real world of society, represented by her three men – Tom, Dick, and Harry – her self-righteous sister, and the neurologist, waits just off-stage to punish her for the murder, but Glaspell clearly wants us to see her New Woman transfigured and liberated by her act.[6] She refuses to reconcile the ambiguities of her play or soften the harshness of her uncompromising vision. In many ways, therefore, *The Verge* must be seen as carrying the emotional, visionary and apocalyptic excesses of Expressionism to their only logical conclusion. Her vision here far exceeds O'Neill's, in either *The Emperor Jones* or *The Hairy Ape*, and prefigures his later works such as *The Great God Brown* and *Days Without End*.

To turn from *The Verge* to Elmer Rice's *The Adding Machine* is like turning from the passionate heat of Sorge and Toller to the ironic chill of Kaiser and Sternheim. The differences between the two plays highlight the range of possibilities open to expressionist treatment. Rice's play has the *Stationen* structure found in Strindberg and the Germans, and many other expressionist touches, such as monologues, stylized sets, a revolving stage, and exaggerated sound and lighting effects, while the hero, Mr Zero, who is a bookkeeper for a department store, shares much with Kaiser's Cashier. Mr Zero is dominated by his ugly bourgeois wife and surroundings; his inner world, mirrored in the home and office walls, which are papered in foolscap bearing column upon column of numbers, is a mute reflection of his socio-economic condition. Again like the Cashier he is roused out of his silent automaton's condition by a sudden confrontation at the end of scene 2: his boss of twenty-five years fires him to make way for adding machines. Jolted out of his lethargy by this shock, Mr Zero murders the Boss in a scene so exaggerated as to seem a deliberate parody of the expressionist *Aufbruch*. Merry-go-round music is heard; the floor begins to revolve faster and faster; the Boss screams 'business – business – BUSINESS,' and Rice's stage instructions call for an extravagant climax:

> The platform is revolving now. Zero and the Boss face each other. They
> are entirely motionless save for the Boss's jaws, which open and close
> incessantly. But the words are inaudible. The music swells and swells. To

it is added every offstage effect of the theatre: the wind, the waves, the
galloping horses, the locomotive whistle, the sleigh bells, the automobile
siren, the glass-crash, New Year's Eve, Election Night, Armistice Day,
and Mardi Gras. The noise is deafening, maddening, unendurable. Suddenly it culminates in a terrific peal of thunder. For an instant there is a
flash of red and then everything is plunged in blackness.[7]

This apocalyptic climax, however, does not usher in a new dispensation. Instead, Mr Zero is tried, convicted, executed, and spends scenes 5
and 6 in the next world, only to learn in the final, seventh scene that he is
about to be recycled (reborn does not convey the sense of repetitive
illusion and increased meaninglessness that await him), having learned
precisely zero about life. Rice's irony and satire are heavy and bitter. His
expressionism is aimed at exposing the stupidity of humanity and the
corruption of bourgeois capitalist society. As a result the play is highly
stylized and parodic, and Rice's characters are two-dimensional types
through which he can project his message. Where Glaspell articulates a
complex vision of *Erlösung*, Rice presents a deeply pessimistic view of life
that is not seen again in American expressionist literature until Thomas
Pynchon.

The excitement shown about the possibility of a new art of the theatre
was by no means limited to New York. In 1928, little more than a decade
after Cook and Glaspell founded the Provincetown Players, Herman
Voaden arrived in Toronto to show audiences just what was possible on
the stage, and today theatre historians would generally agree that he was
'the most significant Canadian playwright in the first half of the twentieth
century.'[8] Voaden's plays are discussed separately in detail; what is
important here is the focus he supplied for the creation of a truly
avant-garde theatre in Toronto. As teacher, editor, advocate of a national
theatre, collaborator with other artists, but above all as a director in his
own theatre workshop, he encouraged others to break free from the
double handicap of a stultifying realism and a prevailing colonial reliance
on foreign materials.

Voaden was not entirely alone, and he was never without support from
other artists or from the city's leading arts journalists. The famous Group
of Seven painters, spearheaded by Lawren Harris and centred in Toronto,
had formed as early as 1920, and in 1926 F.B. Housser had published his
study of the Group, called *A Canadian Art Movement*, which proclaimed
the painters as the best examples of a truly modernist and Canadian art.
Roy Mitchell, doyen of the Arts and Letters Players of Toronto (founded in
1905), which was dedicated to experimental theatre, and first director of
the Hart House Theatre (opened in 1919), published his *Creative Theatre*

in 1929. For Mitchell, an avant-garde, non-realist theatre was the place where 'the living soul of man [swirls] out into a visible, plastic medium of revelation'; extolling the creative power of lighting over painted sets, he concluded that 'Expressionism in time is the art of the theatre.'[9]

By the mid-twenties the time was ripe for the creation of a Canadian theatre that combined precisely those qualities sought for Americans by 'Jig' Cook ten years before: innovation and native writers. What was in fact a first progress report appeared in Bertram Brooker's Yearbook of the Arts in Canada, 1928–1929, with essays by Mitchell, Harris, Brooker, and many others. In 1929 another contributor to this vital scene, Boris Volkoff, arrived in Toronto to establish his unusual ballet school, and in a matter of months he had attracted attention for his abstract and metaphysical work.[10] Like the Group of Seven, Voaden, and Brooker, Volkoff was keen to unite the methods of the new dance with a specifically Canadian vision, which he did in July 1936, when he took two highly expressionistic pieces, Mala and Mon-Ka-Ta, based on Indian and Inuit materials, to the Berlin International Tanzwettspiele, where his was one of five groups, including Mary Wigman's, singled out for special praise by the Germans. Later, in 1942, Volkoff would collaborate with Voaden in the production of the playwright's most ambitious example of his 'symphonic expressionism,' Ascend as the Sun.

By the late twenties Voaden was only beginning to put his plans into practice, but it was already clear to him that a traditional, realist drama was inadequate to the expression of a Canadian, northern experience. In 1929, after a trip to the north shore of Lake Superior (in emulation of the trips made by members of the Group of Seven), Voaden organized a competition for one-act plays using a northern setting. He suggested that the plays follow the mood and subjects expressed in recent Canadian landscape painting, and the three winning plays, published together with three other plays chosen by Voaden in Six Canadian Plays, convey this inspiration clearly.[11] But the book itself was more than a collection of uneven one-act plays. With its opening quotations from Brooker's essay 'When We Awake,' from the Yearbook, its explanatory preface and introductory manifesto, its plates of four paintings by Lismer, Harris, MacDonald, and Thomson, and several drawings by Lowrie Warrener, Six Canadian Plays offered a coherent and courageous program for the development of a Canadian theatre using plays that explore that crucial element in the Canadian psyche – the impact of vast northern spaces upon the lives of humans.

But as all these plays show, in order to dramatize the north, the playwright must bring the landscape alive so that it becomes an actor in the drama. Voaden knew that this must be done. In his own plays the north is an active force, and in the best of these plays, *Manitou Portage*, *Lake Doré*, and *Winds of Life*, the landscape dominates the people, driving them insane or to suicide or to an uneasy and hard-won reconciliation with its spirit.

To dramatize the north, however, required something more than the resources of realistic action and speech, and it was T.M. Morrow's *Manitou Portage*, Voaden's favourite of the six plays and by far the most experimental, that offered 'unique opportunities to the director [because] it [lent] itself to expressionistic production – the mobile play of light, rhythm, colour, and sound, combining with words and action to build an emotional crescendo of fear.'[12]

As Voaden realized, *Manitou Portage* bore many resemblances to O'Neill's *Emperor Jones* and *The Hairy Ape*. Essentially a one-character play, it is dominated by the Yank-like presence of Big Jack O'Connors, boss of a gang of lumbermen and boss of the river on which they run the logs. He is a boastful bully of a man, always itching for a fight and quick to threaten others, yet basically insecure in his place and identity. His constant questions and protestations – 'where do I come in?' – 'I'm the boss of the gang ... I can lick 'em all ... An don't yuh forget it!' (53) – seem closely modelled on Yank's. But in a manner more like *Emperor Jones*, O'Connors insists upon spending the dark, cold night alone in the forest, at the portage where no one else has ever stayed and survived to tell the tale. Manitou Portage is sacred to the Indians and a place where many rivermen have drowned. No sooner has night fallen than O'Connors begins to be haunted by 'all the spooks in the world' (61), represented by the ghostly figures of dead men, who move across the stage, or by the eerie Northern Lights. When the Old Boss Bully appears, O'Connors challenges him, only to be crushed to death in his embrace. As O'Connors lies dying, the grotesque and enormous mask of the Manitou rises up from the river to loom over the man, as if to verify the efficacy of its power, and the audience is left to believe either that O'Connors has been destroyed by his own inner fears, superstitions, and insecurities projected upon the landscape or that some malevolent spirit in nature has punished him for his arrogant trespass.

Manitou Portage is a slight piece, lacking in the complexity of *The Hairy Ape*, but staged by Voaden it must have been an effective example of expressionist dramaturgy used to bring an ominous landscape alive. Indeed, well staged and directed, it could be as effective as *The Emperor Jones*, which it so closely resembles, and with something of the same warning: human pride and strength are nothing compared to the primitive powers within nature. With the more realistic plays *Lake Doré* and *Winds of Life* Voaden dramatized the landscape through the sets and lighting, which depict, in *Lake Doré*, 'the bleak and austere feeling of the wilderness' where the heroine dies. Nothing about the set was representational; the stylized forms in silver grey 'with cold blue and green lights thrown on them' express the mystical, almost lyrical, union of the woman with the land and her dead husband. *Winds of Life* required a similar set in silver grey with the stylized rocks suggesting something of the characters' emotional response to a harsh and alienating land (see Plate 23).

Nineteen thirty-four marked the beginning of an important phase in Voaden's activities as a director because it was in the fall of that year that he began his Play Workshop at the Central High School of Commerce in Toronto, where he was head of the English Department. The Workshop was modelled on George Pierce Baker's famous graduate course at Yale, which Voaden had attended in 1930–31, and it enabled him to explore expressionist staging techniques with new, experimental scripts – such as two extraordinary one-act pieces by Bertram Brooker. At the time Brooker was best known, along with Kathleen Munn, as one of Canada's first abstract painters; his symbolic, metaphysical canvases revealed his affinities with Worringer and the later Kandinsky.[13] But he was also a writer – of novels, poetry, and plays.

Both *Within* and *The Dragon* were produced by Voaden on the stage of the Toronto Central High School of Commerce in 1935 and 1936 respectively, and in Voaden's words, 'the two plays he wrote for the Workshop [were] milestones in Canadian expressionistic theatre writing.'[14] *Within* is the more interesting of the two: in this play the man, whose mind we enter as the action begins, is dreaming of the woman he loves but suspects of betraying him. As the dream develops, his agitation increases until, in a frenzy, he almost murders her. The dream ends abruptly with the forces of the mind in revolt smashing the Will.[15]

This highly erotic and violent scenario is framed by the voices of the Author and an Angel in a manner reminiscent of quasi-expressionistic works like Pirandello's *Six Characters in Search of an Author* (1921) or Nikolai Evreinov's *The Theatre of the Soul: A One-Act Monodrama with Prologue* (1912). In response to the Angel's disorientation, the Author explains that they 'are only ideas that have entered his ... mind to observe it'; they have been drawn by his dream. But the Angel, troubled by the loss of his freedom, continues to question the Author: 'Is this one of the chambers of hell?' 'and these strange forms – what are they?' 'and what is under this dome?' The Will lurks under the dome, which will be smashed when the senses revolt; the strange forms are 'the organs of the senses,' and the man's mind *is* a hell because the senses and Reason insist upon measuring and labelling experience. 'Because of the counting,' the Author explains, 'we shut ourselves out of eternity – which is all around us in a colossal moment – now!'

Suddenly the light increases and the voice of Instinct announces that She is coming. At this point the senses, nerves, Reason, and Will all begin to speak, supported by a chorus of voices, which repeats the words of the principals. As anger and passion increase, Instinct and Reason begin to battle for control of the Will with an Antiphonal Chorus echoing their words in an emotional crescendo. Under the sway of Reason's doubts, the Will succumbs to hate and jealousy, and urges the body to rise up and kill the escaping woman. But Instinct calls for revolt: 'Smash this empty shell. Destroy forever this whispering myth of the will. Strike!' The dream play ends in a frenzy of destruction, with the Author running on stage calling for the curtain.

Not content to dramatize man's violence and helplessness or to illustrate an apocalyptic climax that purges the soul of its limitations in preparation for a spiritual renewal (and both possibilities hover over the ending of the play), Brooker returns his Angel to the stage to announce that man's misunderstanding of himself equals his misunderstanding of God, who is a flowing power instead of a controlling Divine Will. The play then ends in darkness, with a transfiguring light shining on the 'lifted face of the *angel*' (emphasis added) and the chorus chanting: 'For ever and ever and ever.' Brooker has used highly abstracted expressionist means to portray his 'ultimatist' belief in a vision of spiritual harmony and unity that lies beyond the rational limits of human understanding and, as the play seems to suggest, can only be achieved by a human being after, indeed as a result of, apocalypse.[16] In Brooker's play we have a fine example of Glaspell's 'destruction that can get through,' but in a symbolic form relying heavily upon semantic and syntactic abstraction.

Although no photographs of the Workshop production appear to have survived, an early fragment of the play, dated 7 November 1927, together with a pencil sketch, illustrate the abstract stage Brooker required. As in much of his painting he moved as close as possible to a fully non-iconic art without, of course, being able to realize that ideal on stage. In the fragment he calls for dancers, revolving discs in bright red light, and 'brain-figures' on cords. Instinct and Reason are enthroned at the top of the dome, or brain, and everything is in darkness at the beginning while the Author and Angel speak. Although there is a plot-line, it is of virtually no consequence, and there are no speaking parts written for the man and his lover, Eleanor, neither of whom appears on the stage. The entire play, including the set, employs Craig's concepts of abstraction, motion, and puppet-like acting in order to express warring inner forces; it is these forces that we see on the stage, acting out the drama 'within.'

Actual stage instructions by Brooker are sparse, and Voaden says nothing specific about his production of the play, but in his regular *Toronto Globe* column Lawrence Mason praised the 'choral speaking, massed groups, sculptural poses, shadow effects [and] contrasting voice-timbres.'[17] Clearly, Voaden applied his 'symphonic expressionism' to the play, for which it seems well suited. Its extreme abstraction, hybrid subject-matter combining themes of passion, betrayal, and violence with a kind of mystical moralizing, its focus upon instinct, sexuality, and inner turmoil, and its thrust towards apocalyptic vision could only be handled by an avant-garde director on an expressionist stage.

Despite the sincere praise and intelligent commentary that Voaden's Workshop productions invariably received from leading reviewers like Mason, these plays failed to establish a deep-rooted tradition for expressionistic drama in Canada. Resources were scarce, and Canadian taste was decidedly conservative. No truly experimental Canadian play won in the Dominion Drama Festivals, which began in 1932, and by the 1940s attention had turned to the war. After 1945 a return to realism stifled experimental theatre, anything at all Germanic in tone was suspect, and a conservative, realist style continued to dominate Canadian stages until the early seventies.

There is one exception to the prevailing conservatism of Canadian theatre that deserves brief mention, and that is Gwen Pharis Ringwood's *Still Stands the House*, a haunting one-act play about claustrophobia, incest, and murder that won first prize in the 1939 Drama Festival.[18] Though by no means an expressionist play – its three main characters are psychologically convincing prairie people, and its set is a recognizable farmhouse interior – the play exploits slight expressionistic touches as it moves towards its swift climax. These touches are used to project an atmosphere of hatred, fear, and jealousy and to express the madness of a woman who will resort to murder to stop her brother and sister-in-law from selling the family farm. The play ends with this woman absorbed in her inner, hallucinatory world conversing with the portrait of her dead father.

Clearly, Ringwood learned from O'Neill how to manipulate her dramaturgy to create effective theatre, but this is not Expressionism. A truly expressionist play by Ringwood would have to wait until 1969, when she wrote *The Deep Has Many Voices*, a play with the familiar expressionist subject of a character's search for freedom from bourgeois society and for rebirth into a new order. Using platforms, symbolic lighting, masked dancers, music, chant and other repetitive sound effects, and an abstract structure of lyrical moments or 'scenes,' Ringwood's young heroine in *The Deep Has Many Voices* progresses from a stultifying, puritanical home-life to a discovery of the self within 'the deep woods.'[19] That she does so without a violent *Aufbruch*, requiring ecstatic speeches or actions, underscores the great difference between Ringwood's more abstract, optimistic vision and Glaspell's; Ringwood's victory seems easy and unequivocal, whereas Glaspell's is ambiguous, teetering between regression and apocalypse, and hard-won.

These brief considerations of the theatre scene in New York and Toronto begin to suggest some of the distinctions between expressionism as it unfolded in the work of O'Neill and Voaden. To some extent these distinctions are greater than individual differences and seem to spring from the basic, if sometimes subtle, differences between the two countries. Expressionism in the American plays tends to be more violent and to mirror psychological states; by contrast, the Canadian works tend to be more abstract, lyrical, and symbolic, and expressionistic devices are employed to express external natural forces as much as inner soul-states. There is, in short, more *drama* in the American plays and more theatrical idea in the Canadian.

4 Eugene O'Neill: The American Georg Kaiser

When Eric Bentley began work on the German-language première of *The Iceman Cometh* in 1951, he faced a problem that has always confronted O'Neill directors, critics, and readers: he had to decide what to do with O'Neill's expressionism. In an article with the somewhat condescending title 'Trying to Like O'Neill,' Bentley concluded that *The Iceman Cometh* had 'a genuine and a non-genuine element, the former, which [he] regarded as the core, being realistic, the latter, which [he] took as inessential excrescence, being expressionistic.'[1] In order to preserve what he considered to be the 'essential – or at least better' O'Neill, Bentley decided to cut the expressionist elements and stress 'all that is realistic in the play' (Cargill, 335). But he was unable to do this successfully because, as he realized himself, expressionism is too important to the basic structure and intention of the play. Being unenthusiatic about expressionism and failing in his effort 'to like O'Neill,' Bentley went on in his essay to deliver an exasperated diatribe on O'Neill's efforts to escape realism and on the disastrous results for this play and the earlier *Mourning Becomes Electra*.

Bentley's response to *The Iceman Cometh* is of interest here for two reasons. Whether or not one agrees that O'Neill's expressionism is a weakness, he does underscore the fact that it was not merely an aberration of O'Neill's early to middle years: *The Iceman Cometh* (1939) is a late play and, along with *Long Day's Journey into Night* (1940–41), usually considered a masterpiece. Bentley also represents one side of what amounts to a critical debate over O'Neill, with the lines drawn firmly on this question of expressionism: there are those who approve his expressionism and those who dislike and reject it.

This divided response has characterized the production and reception of O'Neill plays from 1920 on. Several O'Neill critics avoid the issue altogether by placing him within an indigenous American tradition, while others, who feel that O'Neill lost his way artistically because of expressionistic experiments, stress his realism or 'super-naturalism.'[2] In order to do this, however, a critic must dismiss O'Neill's expressionism as superficial experimentation in a few plays and ignore his comments on expressionism, his criticisms of the contemporary American theatre, and the variety of important influences on his art from abroad. Most critics do acknowledge that O'Neill was deeply interested in German Expressionism, at least during the years 1920–34, but there is little agreement on the extent of this interest or the sources of influence that contributed to it.

Because O'Neill himself claimed Strindberg as his inspiration and denied any direct influence from Georg Kaiser or other German expressionist playwrights, several of his best critics concentrate upon parallels with Strindberg or stress the general influence of the Germans through Americans such as Sheldon Cheney, Kenneth Macgowan, and Robert Edmond Jones.[3] At the opposite extreme are those who argue that O'Neill was deeply and directly influenced by the Germans. Chief among these is Mardi Valgemae, who, in 'O'Neill and German Expressionism,' points out that many Americans take O'Neill at his word and dismiss a German connection too easily. This failure to consider 'the influence of the German expressionists in general and Georg Kaiser in particular,' writes Valgemae, 'makes it difficult to evaluate O'Neill's development as an experimenter with dramatic form.'[4] In 1929 Erik Reger went so far as to call O'Neill 'the Georg Kaiser of America' and to claim that '*The Hairy Ape* [was] unthinkable without Kaiser and Toller,' but this is overstating the case.[5] Although Valgemae is correct in suggesting that some American critics have distorted the plays by ignoring their wider, specifically German influence and context, some of his European admirers err in the opposite direction. If O'Neill is America's Kaiser, it is because of his stature and vision rather than of explicit models and direct influences.

The critics who come closest to a balanced view of O'Neill's expressionism are those who trace O'Neill's exposure to the expressionist mode to both Strindberg and the Germans, whether directly through the plays and films of German Expressionism or indirectly through the informed enthusiasm of Cheney, Macgowan, and Jones.[6] Furthermore, it seems clear from this critical debate that a close scrutiny of Expressionism (such as that offered here in chapters 1 and 2) allows one not only to see his overtly expressionist plays more clearly but also to appreciate the wider expressionistic aspects of his *oeuvre*. Despite his sharp impatience, Bentley recognized a permanent expressionist quality in O'Neill's abstract dramaturgy, but it is Catharine Mounier, writing from a greater sympathetic understanding of O'Neill, who puts the case for him as an expressionist most judiciously. She suggests that

> si l'expressionisme, considéré dans son ensemble, est avant tout ... un mouvement spirituel dont le but est la régénération de l'homme, la signification, sinon toujours la forme du théâtre d'O'Neill, est expressioniste, elle est tout entière un cri.   (340)
>
> If, on the whole, Expressionism is first and foremost a spiritual movement in which the regeneration of Man is the goal, then O'Neill's meaning, if not always his theatrical form, is Expressionist; it is in every sense a cry.

What Mounier singles out here is the thematic crux of O'Neill's vision, a concern that lies at the heart of everything he wrote and to one degree or another conditions the structure, style, settings, imagery, in fact, the entire semiosis of an O'Neill play. Although it is impossible to analyse the semiotic system of even one play in the present context, some steps can be made towards that end by exploring the codes (visual, thematic and linguistic, and characterological) across a segment of it. My primary concern is not with the system itself but with O'Neill's expressionism, which, once fully acknowledged and clearly elucidated, helps to reveal the system in a way that discussions of his realism or naturalism do not.[7]

The plays chosen for examination here were written between 1920 and 1934, and all, with the exception of *Strange Interlude*, display overt and multiple expressionist elements. They are *The Emperor Jones* (1920), *The Hairy Ape* (1921), *Welded* (1922–23), *All God's Chillun Got Wings* (1923), *The Great God Brown* (1925) – in many ways the quintessential O'Neill play – *Lazarus Laughed* (1925–26), *Strange Interlude* (1926–27), *Dynamo* (1928), and *Days Without End* (1931–34).[8] Although O'Neill employed a number of dramatic expressionist devices in the plays of this so-called middle or experimental period of his career, the more realistic plays of his earlier and especially his later period bear close resemblance to these plays. By the forties O'Neill was writing out of a profoundly expressionist vision, 'tout entière un cri,' without the experimental form and expressionist devices of the twenties and early thirties. He was, as he said, writing a 'drama of souls,' attempting to project on the stage the inner anguish and search for faith and purpose of twentieth-century humanity.

Each of his plays, from something as early and slight as *Before Breakfast* (1916) to a masterpiece like *The Iceman Cometh* (1939), portrays women and men 'in panic nailing Man's soul to the cross of their fear' (*LL*, 343), fear of death, fear of love, fear (and loathing) of self.

A reconsideration of O'Neill's expressionism illuminates the reasons for his expressionist vision and may help to explain his revival in the seventies and eighties by drawing attention to those universal qualities of his art that speak to today's audiences or readers. In his 1975 doctoral study of 'O'Neill's expressionistic grotesque' James Robinson maintained that a 'failure to recognize the thematic importance of the expressionistic plays [he is referring to nine plays from the middle years] is difficult to comprehend, for their grotesque techniques express a vision that is in many ways more contemporary than that of the late work.'[9] Robinson reminds one here of both the timeliness of O'Neill's dark vision and its essentially expressionist nature. The cry persists into *Iceman, Long Day's Journey,* and *A Moon for the Misbegotten* (1943), but the expressionist's characteristic hope and despair are proclaimed in the most emphatic, unmistakable tones in the great plays of the twenties, when O'Neill still believed in the possibility of *Aufbruch* and *Erlösung*.

It seems impossible to establish with absolute certainty which expressionist works O'Neill read or saw, when he may have done so, and as a consequence, whether or not certain texts influenced him directly. We do know, however, that he discovered Nietzsche, beginning with *Thus Spoke Zarathustra,* some time in 1908, and that by 1913–14 he was reading Strindberg, Dostoevsky, and Wedekind and studying German in order to read Nietzsche in the original.[10] At precisely the time he was finding himself as a playwright (1912–16), his imagination was fired and his vision informed by these four major precursors of German Expressionism.

During his year at George Pierce Baker's Harvard Drama Workshop, 1914, he had further exposure to contemporary theatre and dramaturgy. Although conservative, Baker was none the less conversant with contemporary developments in Germany. The period of 1915–16, from the completion of the Workshop up to his spring arrival in Provincetown, is an important one, but O'Neill's biographers do not provide many particulars about his activities or artistic acquaintances; we know that he saw Hauptmann's *The Weavers* six times, spent hours drinking at the six-day bicycle races in Madison Square Garden, and many more hours drinking at the 'Hell-Hole' (a Village establishment called The Golden Swan.) In fact, during these months O'Neill was on the verge of drinking himself to death with the blessing of a favoured crony, Terry Carlin. There is no record of his having seen the 1915 New York production of *He Who Married a Dull Wife*, with expressionist sets by Robert Edmond Jones, the young designer who had returned from Germany at the outbreak of the war and was soon to become a close friend and associate, but he did meet Mabel Dodge, probably through John Reed, and may also have met other members of the Village avant-garde through him.

In the summer of 1915 Cook, Glaspell, and Jones began the famous Provincetown Players' performances on the wharf, and in the spring of 1916 O'Neill went to Provincetown, where he met the three founders and the American expressionist painter Marsden Hartley, who, like Jones, had left Germany because of the war.[11] Thus began the friendship and collaboration that in so many ways *made* O'Neill and simultaneously gave birth to a strong native drama. Cook recognized O'Neill's potential by producing him immediately, both at Provincetown and later at his small New York Playwright's Theater, where the famous expressionist productions of *The Emperor Jones* and *The Hairy Ape* took place in 1920 and 1922. Sheldon Cheney, who began publication of *Theater Arts Magazine* in 1916, continued to advocate expressionism throughout these years. His *The New Movement in the Theater*, published in 1914, introduced Americans to contemporary developments in theatre, from Adolphe Appia and Edward Gordon Craig (of whom he was a special devotee) to the German expressionists, and in *The Art Theater* (1916) and *Modern Art and the Theater* (1921) he elaborated his ideas further. The line of theoretical thinking about experimental theatre runs directly from Cheney to Cook, Jones, Macgowan, and O'Neill.

In the three and one-half years between his arrival in Provincetown and his writing of *The Emperor Jones*, O'Neill continued to write realistic plays such as *Anna Christie* and *Beyond the Horizon* and a number of one-acters, but around him others such as Glaspell, Rice and Alfred Kreymborg were using new experimental methods. In 1920, for example, Cook produced Kreymborg's highly expressionist *Vote the New Moon*, which made an important contribution to experimental and expressionist theatre in America.[12] These influences were simply in the air, a part of the prevailing atmosphere for O'Neill that included his friendship with George Jean Nathan, the New York critic who was notorious for his attacks on Bellasco-style theatre, Alice Woods, a Provincetown writer and former member of the Stein circle in Paris, and Mary Heaton Vorse, an admirer of German theatre and supporter of the Provincetown group.

Early in 1920 he began what was to be a lifelong friendship with Kenneth Macgowan, and later that year Ashley Dukes's translation of *From Morn to Midnight* appeared in the autumn issue of *Poet-Lore: A*

Magazine of Letters.[13] *The Emperor Jones* was written in three intense weeks in October 1920, perhaps because of direct stimulation from Kaiser, whom O'Neill may have read in German before English translations appeared, but more likely because his idea for the play coincided with his growing exposure to experimental theatre in general. In 1921 Macgowan, now fully devoted to the development of expressionist theatre in America, published *The Theater of Tomorrow*, following Cheney's lead, and in the summer of that year O'Neill saw and was deeply impressed by the New York screening of *The Cabinet of Dr Caligari*. According to Louis Sheaffer, O'Neill still spoke highly of *Caligari* as late as 1943, and in 1922 he thought of filming *The Emperor Jones* 'along Expressionistic lines.'[14] By December of 1921, when he wrote his most expressionist play (and one of his best), *The Hairy Ape*, O'Neill was well informed about contemporary German theatre, well read, as he liked to boast, in modern drama, had first-hand knowledge of Kaiser in either German or English, was working closely with the two most articulate and active American champions of expressionist theatre, and had served the necessary apprenticeship to his craft that would make the writing of *The Hairy Ape* possible.

The question of influence and source is less problematic in the years following 1921 because, from *The Hairy Ape* on, O'Neill spoke openly about expressionism and continued to experiment widely with different aspects of the mode. By this time European Expressionism was in the New World air and O'Neill wanted to play a part in exposing audiences to it. *From Morn to Midnight* was produced by the Theater Guild in 1922, and O'Neill, who together with Macgowan and Jones took over the Provincetown Players in 1923, wanted to produce Wedekind, Hasenclever, Andreev, and Strindberg on the first bill. When this proved too ambitious, O'Neill settled for Strindberg's *The Ghost Sonata* (1907), which he called *The Spook Sonata*, and his own expressionistic arrangement of *The Ancient Mariner*.[15] The group premiered Hasenclever's *Beyond*, which O'Neill described as an 'example of essence of Expressionism in acting, scenic, everything'[16] in 1924, and produced Strindberg's *A Dream Play* in 1926 and Lajos Egris's *Rapid Transit* in 1927. There were other New York performances of the Germans as well: Toller's *Masses and Man* at the Theater Guild in 1924, Kaiser's *Gas* and Werfel's *Goat Song* (of which O'Neill spoke very highly) in 1926, and Toller's *The Machine Wreckers* in 1927, the same year that Fritz Lang's *Metropolis* was playing in New York. By 1925 the reorganized Provincetown Players were known by reviewers for their experimental, in particular, their expressionist productions. In addition to European plays, they produced expressionist plays by Edmund Wilson (with Caligarean sets designed by Cleon Throckmorton), Em Jo Basshe, and E. E. Cummings, as well as more O'Neill – notably *All God's Chillun Got Wings* (1924), designed by Throckmorton, and a reading in 1928 of *Lazarus Laughed*.[17]

Most discussions of O'Neill's expressionism focus on *The Hairy Ape* but note, at least in passing, the influence of the Germans – especially Kaiser – and/or Strindberg on several of his other plays, particularly *The Great God Brown*. O'Neill himself was emphatic about his intentions in *The Hairy Ape*, which remained one of his personal favorites, but he tried to distinguish the play from anything by Kaiser, or Strindberg for that matter. As far as he was concerned, the play grew directly out of his experiments in *The Emperor Jones*.

On 24 December 1921, shortly after completing a first draft of the play, O'Neill explained to Macgowan, 'It seems to run the whole gamut from extreme naturalism to extreme expressionism – with more of the latter than the former. I have tried to dig deep in it, to probe in the shadows of the soul of man bewildered by the disharmony of his primitive pride and individualism at war with the mechanistic developement [sic] of society.'[18] He wanted expressionistic sets, and these were designed by Jones and Throckmorton for the now famous production starring Louis Wollheim (see Plates 24 and 25).

Despite enthusiastic audiences and a long run, the reviewers were cool, and O'Neill felt that his play was being misunderstood: he complained that 'they don't understand that the whole play is expressionistic. Yank is really yourself, and myself. He is *every* human being.'[19] This claim for symbolic universality seems at odds with O'Neill's later attempt to free himself from comparisons with Kaiser by criticizing the German expressionist tendency to create mere abstractions. His example of this sort of expressionism is *From Morn to Midnight*, where, according to O'Neill, Kaiser's bank clerk is no more than a character abstraction. Yet, in spite of the pains he took to distinguish himself from Kaiser, and from expressionism generally, on the grounds of characterization, O'Neill's claim that 'Yank remains a man and everyone recognizes him as such' (Cargill, 111) is not entirely convincing; in *The Hairy Ape*, as in all his plays, O'Neill uses his characters to convey a few fundamental themes that troubled him all his life. Even if some allowance can be made for O'Neill's criticism of expressionist characterization, there are many other expressionist qualities – and signs of Kaiser's influence – in *The Hairy Ape*. Without doubt, O'Neill recognized the essential value of expressionism as 'the dynamic qualities ... that express something in modern life better than' realism could do (Cargill, 111).

One of the earliest, and still one of the best, examinations of O'Neill's debt to European Expressionism is Clara Blackburn's 1941 study 'Continental Influences on Eugene O'Neill's Expressionistic Dramas.'[20] Blackburn stresses O'Neill's indebtedness to Strindberg, locating it first in their 'supersubjective' personalities and then tracing it through certain features of O'Neill's plays. Although she finds resemblances between *From Morn to Midnight* and *The Emperor Jones*, her most important point is that both plays employ monologues and an *Ausstrahlungen des Ichs* (literally, radiation or emanation of the I, whole being, or self), and that both Kaiser and O'Neill were influenced by Strindberg's development of these methods for projecting subjective states in *To Damascus* (1898). In addition Blackburn finds a number of parallels between O'Neill's later plays such as *The Great God Brown* and *Dynamo* and Kaiser's *Gas* plays and *The Coral*, but she neglects the strong parallels between *Lazarus Laughed* and *The Burghers of Calais*, the plays in which Kaiser and O'Neill offer their most positive visions of the New Man and of humanity's potential for rebirth and salvation. Instead, she compares O'Neill's play with Werfel's *Mirror-Man* (*Spiegelmensch: Magische Trilogie*, 1920).

Mardi Valgemae carries the argument for Kaiser's influence a step further than Blackburn in his 1967 article 'O'Neill and German Expressionism.' He notes the use of cages in *The Hairy Ape* (see Plate 24) and *From Morn to Midnight*, the 'gaudy marionettes' in scene 5 of the play (see Plate 25) and a similar scene in Kaiser's *Hell, Road, Earth* (*Hölle Weg Erde*, 1919). He mentions several parallels between *The Hairy Ape* and *Gas I* and *The Coral*, and then traces O'Neill's frail heroine, the use of chiaroscuro, and the 'penseur' motif to *The Cabinet of Dr Caligari*. But perhaps Valgemae's most important contribution to this debate over who influenced O'Neill and how is his insistence that, unlike Strindberg, O'Neill projected the soul-states of invented characters and not of himself. The distinction is an important albeit a subtle one to make because, like Malcolm Lowry, O'Neill was an autobiographical writer obsessed with certain themes of painful significance to himself. In plays like *To Damascus* and *A Dream Play* (the two Strindberg works most often cited as influences on O'Neill) 'the consciousness of ... the author holds sway over the surreal action' (Valgemae, 122), but as his remarks above about Yank show, O'Neill prided himself on his ability to create characters who enact his passionate quarrel with life in their own tortured souls. Like so many of the Germans, including Kaiser, O'Neill struggled to dramatize cosmic, or universal truths – as he perceived them – *through* the characters, as well as through structure, dramaturgy, and subject-matter.

In the most recent treatment of O'Neill's debt to Kaiser, Horst Frenz assumes that O'Neill knew Kaiser's plays, especially *From Morn to Midnight*, very well indeed. Although Frenz adds little to our understanding of how O'Neill discovered Kaiser or of the precise influence of the German playwright, he does provide two thoughtful observations on the O'Neill-Kaiser comparison, observations that do not, in fact, depend upon O'Neill's first-hand knowledge of Kaiser's plays. First, he argues that the major conflict in O'Neill's *Emperor Jones* and *The Hairy Ape* and Kaiser's *From Morn to Midnight* arises from the confrontation between the individual and society and that the chief protagonist in each play progresses (or in my terms, as outlined in chapter 1, regresses) from a civilized to a so-called primitive state, dramatized by his gradual recognition of hitherto repressed instincts. Second, Frenz claims that the reformative impulse takes different forms in the two writers: Kaiser wished to better society, whereas O'Neill concentrates on liberating the individual soul.[21] Despite the qualifications that might be made to this view of Kaiser,[22] what Frenz highlights here is the general expressionist nature of both dramatists' visions; the expressionist vision contains within it the potential for both types of regeneration and liberation, with the individual, in particular the artist (a favourite among O'Neill's heroes), often providing the necessary example of the New Man. Frenz might have added that both O'Neill plays, and to a lesser extent the Kaiser, end in ironic failure for both their individual protagonists and for society. Jones and Yank do not progress (in the sense of learning to reintegrate themselves) so much as regress, their liberation an ironic comment on human isolation in a meaningless universe; Kaiser's Cashier is betrayed by the very society he hopes to awaken, his Christ-like death a bitter comment on those around him and a mocking reflection on his own reach for freedom.

Discussions of expressionism in *The Great God Brown* by Blackburn, Valgemae, and Frenz centre on the parallels with Kaiser's *The Coral* and O'Neill's use of masks. The similarities of the two plays are striking, although *The Great God Brown* marks an advance in O'Neill's personal exploration of his central expressionist theme. Both plays involve the struggle and murder or self-destruction of alter egos: in *The Coral* the two men are indistinguishable except for a small piece of coral that belongs to the secretary whom the Billionaire kills; in *The Great God Brown* the jealous friend takes on the identity of his dead rival, who thereby controls his destiny and drives him to his death. In Kaiser's play the coveted quality is happiness, represented by the secretary's simple home and peace of mind; in O'Neill's, Billy Brown covets Dion Anthony's creativity and his wife's love. In both plays the superficially successful businessman lacks something that makes his opposite happy, and in both this type of man, who represents the repressive forces of society, destroys the happiness he desires in the effort to possess it. The representatives of materialism destroy themselves by monopolizing the spiritual power that makes life possible.

In addition Blackburn, Valgemae, Frenz, and others note O'Neill's use of masks in this play, which, after *Lazarus Laughed*, represents O'Neill's most extensive use of the device.[23] Each of the four main protagonists wears a mask (Dion wears his from the start) that hides his or her inner self or soul while at the same time recording the ravages of time, age, and adversity on the outward personality and feeling of the character. When Brown usurps Anthony's identity, he does so by wearing his mask, which means that he superimposes Anthony's cynical outer self, from which vitality and creative energy are nearly drained, on his own rather single- and simple-minded self. O'Neill, however, was greatly disappointed by the use of masks in the original production of *The Great God Brown* because he felt they implied a kind of neurotic, split personality in his characters, especially Dion Anthony, whereas he intended them to convey 'the abstract drama of the forces behind the people.'[24] In his 'Memoranda on Masks' (Cargill, 116–22), a series of articles for the *American Spectator*, O'Neill explains that the mask symbolizes an inner reality and assists the dramatist in the presentation of 'a drama of souls.' His remarks about Noh and African masks suggest Macgowan's influence (his *Masks and Demons* appeared in 1923), and his reference to a masked *Hamlet* that would enable audiences to 'identify ... with the figure of Hamlet as a symbolic projection of a fate that is in each of us' recalls Edward Gordon Craig's concept of that play as a monodrama.

But perhaps most important of all, in the three brief articles constituting 'Memoranda on Masks,' all written between November 1932 and January 1933 (more than a decade after *Emperor Jones*, *The Hairy Ape*, and *All God's Chillun*, and while he was struggling with *Days Without End*), O'Neill links the mask unequivocally with expressionism. He goes on to state that, with the exception of the protagonists, he would now use masks throughout *The Emperor Jones*, *The Hairy Ape*, and *All God's Chillun Got Wings*: 'All save the seven leading characters should be masked; for all the secondary figures are part and parcel of the Expressionistic background of the play' (Cargill, 119). In this O'Neill is certainly following the expressionists' example. Kaiser had called for masks in *From Morn to Midnight*, and in his 1918 preface to *The Immortals* Yvan Goll proclaimed that the mask is 'the law of the drama' that makes 'non-reality' become 'fact.' In a remark prefiguring the efforts of O'Neill, he asks: 'Do not the greatest works of art, a Negro god or an Eygptian king, often appear to us as masks?'[25]

With few exceptions O'Neill's critics – those, at least, who are interested in his expressionism – have limited their remarks to an investigation of sources, parallels, and comparisons between O'Neill's plays and those of Strindberg, Kaiser, Werfel, and a few other German expressionists. Their research is invaluable because it demonstrates not only that O'Neill knew more about specific plays than he admitted but that he was deeply attuned to the anti-mimetic, experimental trends of his day. This began with a personal affinity for Nietzsche and Strindberg and, from there, extended to some first-hand knowledge of Kaiser, Werfel, Hasenclever, and others. But whatever his debt to European expressionists, Eugene O'Neill moved beyond 'the banality of surfaces' (Cargill, 109) because he had his own vision to express. After the distorted settings, the marionettes and masks, the chiaroscuro, choruses, and doubles in the plays from these middle years are abandoned, O'Neill projects this expressionist vision through the abstraction of his plots and his magnificent monologues. Whether we can like O'Neill or not, Eric Bentley's lesson is an important one: the essential O'Neill is inextricably bound up with the expressionist. As Mounier insists, his work is 'tout entière un cri.'

Beginning with *The Emperor Jones*, where his dramaturgical breakthrough was startling and sure, O'Neill drew increasingly upon expressionist methods in order to portray the human soul and the forces that convulse it. Most of the plays written in the twenties and early thirties provide numerous examples of O'Neill's expressionist techniques. Mention has already been made of his masks, while his monologues, which are the most significant aspect of his expressionism, are analysed in detail below, but there are other expressionist techniques that are worthy of note: *Stationen* structure, settings, use of lighting, rhythm, choruses, pantomime and marionettes, doubles, schematic character configurations, and symbolic characterization, in particular his negative and typically expressionist portrayal of women.

The *Stationen* structure of loosely connected scenes portraying stages in a hero's journey through life and search for faith usually commences with some form of abrupt awakening and culminates in transcendent vision or ironic defeat. This pattern is most apparent in *The Emperor Jones* and *The Hairy Ape*, each of which contains a sequence of scenes without formal or diegetic divisions into acts. Both plays are framed by their opening and closing scenes: in *The Emperor Jones* these situate the inner turmoil of Jones within an intransigent and completely hostile reality; in *The Hairy Ape* they stress the futility of Yank's search by replacing one type of imprisoning space, the stokehole, with a prison cell or a cage in the zoo, one kind of death-in-life existence with a literal and symbolic annihilation.[26] In several later plays where there is a clear division into acts, the scenic progression still carries the main forward thrust of the plot so that the three- or four-act divisions seem arbitrary and irrelevant. For example, in *Lazarus Laughed*, O'Neill called for four acts, each with two scenes, but the scenes, not the acts, carry the basic rhythm of the play, which captures the variations in Lazarus's impact on those around him, especially on Caligula, who vacillates between contempt and admiration for Lazarus and his vision. In *The Fountain* (1921–22), where there are three parts but eleven consecutive scenes, it is the scenes that structure the play.

Even in *Dynamo*, which uses a conventional three-act division, the return of the hero, Reuben Light, to his home after a violent awakening at the end of act 1 marks the shift in the play's dramatic structure to a series of incremental scenes depicting his step-by-step progression towards what he believes to be faith and salvation. O'Neill's insistence upon three acts, especially the break between acts 2 and 3, reflects his desire to retain a sense of temporal reality (act 3 begins four months after the end of act 2), but the extremely awkward conflation of expressionism and realism and of allegorical subject and *Bildungsroman*-type story seriously undermines the play. If *The Hairy Ape* is a more powerful play than *Dynamo*, which it surely is, this is in part because in the earlier play O'Neill stylized external reality in order to privilege the stages in Yank's inner drama, whereas in *Dynamo* he attempted to present the stages in his hero's spiritual rebellion and madness while at the same time maintaining a large degree of physical reality (in his characters' homes, as well as in the technical details of the dynamo) and in the temporal sequencing of the plot.

O'Neill's sets are one of the most interesting aspects of his expressionism. He always knew precisely what he wanted, and he retained the quality of rigid abstraction (as Bentley found to his annoyance) well after he had abandoned the obvious distortion and chiaroscuro of earlier plays. The story of 'Jig' Cook building the *Kuppelhorizont* for his 1920 production of *The Emperor Jones* is already part of theatre legend.[27] What he and O'Neill wanted to create was the sense of a claustrophobic space that would dramatize the forest walls closing in on the increasingly distraught Jones. The 'little formless fears' and 'dem ha'nts' that possess him perfectly complement this darkening, confining space, which finally coincides with the terrifying prison of his mind.

Pictures of famous productions of *The Hairy Ape* (see Plates 24, 25, and

26) and *All God's Chillun Got Wings* show the distorted or abstract, symbolic sets of both plays; the shops on Fifth Avenue, where Yank waits for a glimpse of the 'white-collar stiffs,' are an expressionist extravaganza – grotesque, distorted, exaggerated images of materialist greed – and the 'stiffs,' when they finally appear, are masked, marionette-like symbols of bourgeois capitalism, utterly oblivious to Yank.[28] The stark wedding scene in *All God's Chillun* is divided into black and white, light and dark, to stress and symbolize both the racial and the spiritual dichotomies of the play. The church, dominated by its large double doors, is flanked by tenements where the windows, with shades down, give 'an effect of staring, brutal eyes that pry callously at human beings without acknowledging them' (318); as the 'metallic clang' of the church-bell sounds, the neighbours 'form into two racial lines on each side of the gate, rigid and unyielding' (319), and the doors open to spit out Ella and Jim, who are thrust from darkness into glaring light.

However, the symbolic division with which their union and departure (an *Aufbruch* of sorts) begins, like the schematic split between Yank and the Fifth Avenue world of the 'stiffs,' achieves its most forceful expression in the claustrophobic interiors of subsequent scenes in both plays. The opening scene of the fireman's forecastle in *The Hairy Ape*, with its narrow, cramped space and imprisoning steel bars ('by no means naturalistic,' in O'Neill's instructions) gives way to the hellish distortion and inhuman, mechanical existence of the stokehole, which is later exchanged for a prison where 'the cells extend back diagonally from right front to left rear. They do not stop, but disappear in the dark background as if they ran on, numberless, into infinity' (239; see Plates 24 and 26). O'Neill embedded almost too many references to bars, prisons, and cages within the play in order to prepare for the most claustrophobic scene of all: Yank's death inside the gorilla's cage at the zoo. But his use of claustrophobia in *All God's Chillun* is handled more subtly and is possibly more horrifying as a result. As Ella slips deeper and deeper into paranoia in the second act of this compact two-act play, the walls close in on her and Jim, the ceiling barely clears their heads, and O'Neill calls for light to pick out the threatening Congo mask that Ella will soon attack. The significance of the black/white, light/dark contrasts of act 1 expands beyond racial hostility to include madness and sanity, love and hate, a vicious battle of the sexes, and the tragic perversion of hope (represented by Jim's law-books and Ella's bridal gown) into regression and despair.

This effective use of claustrophobic setting is one of the central features of O'Neill's plays, even when he calls for more realistic interiors in bars or homes. The tension in plays like *The Iceman Cometh* and *Long Day's*

Journey into Night, for example (although the same is true of *Desire Under the Elms* and *Mourning Becomes Electra*), arises less from dramatic conflict between protagonists than from a suffocating sense of being trapped in one place, situation, or mind. But no discussion of expressionist aspects of the sets is complete without some comment on the deadly technology of *Dynamo* and the cross that concludes *Days Without End.* O'Neill was anxious to capture the sense of power of an actual dynamo, and yet his stage instructions suggest an expressionist monster recalling the terrible machinery in Lang's *Metropolis.* Although the room housing the dynamo is described as complete with switch galleries and double busses, the dynamo itself, 'brilliantly lighted by a row of powerful bulbs in white globes,' is 'huge and black, with something of a massive female idol about it, the exciter set on the main structure like a head with blank, oblong eyes above a gross, rounded torso' (*D*, 473). Before the play is over, of course, Reuben will have sacrificed the real woman who loves him to this black female idol and electrocuted himself. Such an ecstatic ending seems only slightly less preposterous than Lang's optimistic vision of heart uniting head and hands in *Metropolis.*

The cross in the final scene of *Days Without End* is by no means the only expressionist aspect of the play, but it is the key symbolic component of the set; in an important sense it is the object towards which the entire play moves. Here as in *Dynamo* O'Neill strove to overlay a basically abstract image of faith with realistic detail. The diagonal division of the stage and the high, narrow windows suggest the interior of a church, but in a slightly distorted and highly simplified way. The cross itself, with a life-sized Christ, is enormous, and it stands out from its dark surroundings because of the dim light that falls directly on it. As Loving expires and John achieves his triumphant *Erlösung,* the light reaches a 'brilliant intensity' on the cross, which shines with radiance. The life-and-death struggle that takes place between John and Loving at the foot of this cross may not be convincing or satisfying to contemporary readers and audiences, but it is nevertheless visually reminiscent of Kaiser's cross at the end of *From Morn to Midnight* (see Plate 18) or, what is more to the point, the vision of resurrection that ends *The Burghers of Calais.* In fact, this type of religious symbolism, using distorted or exaggerated images of the cross and dramatic lighting effects, is fairly common in expressionist theatre, from Strindberg's *To Damascus* (1898) to Toller's *Transfiguration* (1918), and foreshadows Herman Voaden's later attempt to project images of spiritual transcendence in his plays.[29]

Other subsidiary techniques, which none the less contribute effectively to O'Neill's expressionism, are his use of rhythm, both of sounds and movement, choruses, and massed groups. The most famous example of rhythmic sound is the drum in *The Emperor Jones*, which begins softly at the pace of a normal heartbeat and increases in volume and speed until Jones is shot. The crescendo of the drum parallels Jones's rising frenzy and externalizes his inner state. Because of this double function, it is possible to see Jones driven to madness and death either by the spiritual powers of the natives or by the terror in his own soul. The mechanical, rhythmic movements of the stokers in *The Hairy Ape*, like their staccato, hoarse barking throughout scene 4, are equally successful dramatic touches that emphasize the distortion and dehumanization of their, and Yank's, existence. Both *Lazarus Laughed* and *Dynamo* draw heavily on rhythmic sounds with obvious symbolic functions, though how one could successfully stage the constant laughter of the former or the 'harsh, throaty, metallic purr' of the latter is not easy to imagine. A more subtle internal rhythm, arising from the constant shifting back and forth between dialogue and forms of monologue, aside, and externalized debate, is also apparent in *Welded*, *Dynamo*, *Strange Interlude*, *The Great God Brown*, and *Days Without End*, and although this rhythm is not necessarily expressionist, in O'Neill's plays it contributes to the emotional tension and schematic patterning of the action. Examples of the use of choruses and massed groups abound in expressionist plays, Toller's *Masses and Man* being only the most famous example, and O'Neill employs the same technique on a massive scale in *Lazarus Laughed*, which calls for no fewer than eight choruses, all masked according to age and character-type; only Lazarus, who no longer fears death, wears no mask.

One of the most powerful of expressionist literary techniques is the monologue. Although the form seems intrinsically tied to the theatre, where one expects to find speech, novelists have found a variety of ways to portray characters speaking to themselves, to the reader, or even to external forces and God, and monologues in novels must be described precisely in order to distinguish the *monologue intérieur* from so-called stream-of-consciousness, narrated monologue, and expressionist mono-logue. A similar problem of nomenclature and typology arises with the drama, especially with a playwright like O'Neill, who experimented with soliloquy, monologue, thought-asides, and a variety of other related speech-forms (choral chants, for example) and even antiphonal dialogue, where characters speak past each other, as if to themselves. Kenneth Macgowan was the first to remark upon the importance of O'Neill's monologues, which he saw as directly related to his ransacking of expressionist methods for digging beneath 'the banality of surfaces.'[30] Macgowan also saw these great speeches as O'Neill's 'outstanding contribution to modern dramaturgy' (Cargill, 449). Many others, of course, have commented upon the monologues, some noting their expressionistic qualities, but most recently Michael Hinden has returned to Macgowan's early evaluation and gone on to show where and how O'Neill's expressionist monologues come to life again in the anguished soliloquies of Peter Shaffer's characters.[31]

Among the most important distinguishing features of the expressionist monologue, as it was developed by the Germans and later by Glaspell in *The Verge* and by O'Neill, is its anti-realist purpose. This type of speech is the *Ausstrahlungen des Ichs*, an outpouring of the soul, a projection of the innermost, subjective feelings of the speaker. As a consequence, the language is usually extreme, exaggerated, intense, and the style is either dramatically fragmented and incoherent or intensely lyrical and ecstatic. In addition, the truly expressionist monologue is both extended (often very long indeed) and, unlike Shakespearean soliloquy, central to the 'action' of the play; at times it *is* the dramatic action, because the play expresses a central character's inner turmoil and *Aufbruch*. Furthermore, the expressionist monologue – and this is true as well of novelists like Barnes and Lowry – almost invariably represents a character's desperate struggle to constitute the self through words. Language here becomes not only a means of self-expression but a kind of ontological imperative for an individual who lacks a reason to exist and is, moreover, terrified of silence, of being silenced.[32] O'Neill's famous thought-asides in *Strange Interlude* and *Dynamo* do not manifest these qualities, and therefore they should not be confused or conflated with the expressionist monologues in *The Emperor Jones*, *The Hairy Ape*, *All God's Chillun*, *The Great God Brown*, *Lazarus Laughed*, *Days Without End*, and, to a lesser degree, *Welded*.

Even after a detailed examination of the style and syntax of the asides in *Strange Interlude*, Liisa Dahl is forced to conclude that O'Neill's vocabulary and word-order differ very little from normal dialogue. In *Dynamo* Reuben's thoughts are spoken aloud in perfectly clear, usually complete sentences, without any of the stylization and emotional exaggeration of the expressionist monologues. For example, as he sits contemplating the dynamo, he thinks: 'It's like a great dark idol ... like the old stone statues of gods people prayed to' (474). Or later, at the climax of his panic, he thinks: 'Mother! ... have mercy on me! ... I hate her now!' (487). These asides sound so ordinary because O'Neill's chief purpose in them is to capture realistically the unexpressed but quite conscious and coherent *thoughts* of his characters.[33] O'Neill's thought-asides bear closer resemblance to narrated monologue or *erlebte Rede* in fiction than to expressionist monologue.

Apart from the first and last scenes, which frame the central ordeal of *The Emperor Jones*, scenes 2 through 7 constitute one long monologue in a kind of psychodrama where the hero (and speaker) will gradually lose control of coherent language until he is reduced to whimpers and final silence. In this early play, however, O'Neill does not fully exploit grammatical and syntactic possibilities for a thoroughly expressionistic speech. Jones's accent, colloquialisms, and sentence structure are, in fact, a realistically effective representation of a man of his race and class, and O'Neill's chief means for expressing Jones's rising terror and confusion are screams, gestures, scenic effects, silence, and the drum beat. However, Jones's speech does alter, becoming slightly more fragmented in syntax and more exclamatory as his long night progresses. Throughout these scenes Jones is physically alone on the stage (in the forest) and in the metaphysical present of the play – a situation that brings *Before Breakfast* to mind – but O'Neill's expressionist monologues are just as likely to occur when others are physically present yet oblivious to the hero's cry. Ostensibly, the hero speaks by turns to himself or to another presence, and beyond that person or thing (for example, the mask in *All God's Chillun* or the apes in *The Hairy Ape*) to the empty universe with its silent or absent God.

Ella in *All God's Chillun* has two fine expressionist monologues to demonstrate her encroaching madness (act 2, scenes 1 and 3), but Jim's speech, as they are leaving the church at the end of act 1, is an excellent example of O'Neill's use of the form to express degrees of emotion within the speaker at the same time as he reveals the symbolic ramifications of the scene (and of his theme), and to prefigure the tragic dilemma of act 2. Jim may be surrounded by people at this point and holding his new wife by the hand, but in a radical sense he is and will remain alone, striving to fill the void around and within him with words. He begins calmly enough as he tries to reassure Ella, but as she slips into a somnambulistic state, a 'hysteric quality of ecstasy ... breaks into his voice':

> And look at the sky! Ain't it kind and blue! Blue for hope. Don't they say blue's for hope? Hope! That's for us, Honey. All those blessings in the sky! What's it the Bible says? Falls on just and unjust alike? No, that's the sweet rain. Pshaw, what am I saying? All mixed up. There's no unjust about it. We're all the same – equally just – under the sky – under the sun – under God – sailing over the sea – to the other side of the world – the side where Christ was born – the kind side that takes count of the soul – over the sea – the sea's blue, too –   (320)

By the end 'he is on the verge of collapse, his face twitching, his eyes staring' (321), and this anguish is reflected in the repeated questions, followed by sentence fragments, and climaxing in the long exfoliating, exclamatory sentence beginning: 'We're all the same.' This sentence opens in a typical O'Neill manner with straightforward subject, verb, object formation, and right-branching clauses and modifiers but rapidly collapses under the string of disjointed and unconnected (at least grammatically) modifiers to give extremely effective lyric expression to Jim's pain.

According to Jean Chothia, in her fine study of his language, O'Neill not only 'ceased to use low-colloquial forms' after 1924, but he adopted a 'monotonous,' 'abstract,' 'curiously neutral' speech that she describes as a 'failure of language in the middle years.'[34] Chothia is particularly critical of *Lazarus Laughed* (though she sees *Days Without End* as suffering from a similar verbal malaise), but *Lazarus Laughed* none the less provides some of the more extravagant and, in themselves, successful examples of the expressionist monologue in the O'Neill canon. As Chothia points out, the play is extremely wordy, but I cannot agree that the superfluity of words is necessarily inconsistent with the heavy reliance upon sound and movement throughout the play. The very wordiness, the frequent speech-ifying, are part of the straining after extreme expression attempted everywhere in the play, from the complicated system of masks to the ubiquitous laughter. The characters, with the notable exception of Lazarus, are continually struggling to assert themselves – to exist – *in language*. When they relinquish that struggle, they lapse either into laughter or into silence. Caligula's long, crazed speech at the end is just such an example of expressionist monologue, but there is an equally effective, and shorter, example in act 2. In a frenzy, Caligula strains to overpower the sound of Lazarus's laughter, to affirm his own existence against Lazarus's monopolizing presence. He is not physically alone on the stage, to be sure, but no one is really listening, no one acknowledges or responds to his outburst:

> I hear the legions, Lazarus! They are laughing with them! You are playing me false, Lazarus! You are trying to evade death! You are trying to spare your people! You are small and weak like other men when the test comes! You give way to pity! Your great laughter becomes pitiful! You are a traitor, Lazarus! You betray Caesar! Have you forgotten I will be Caesar? You betray me, Lazarus! You on the wall! Sentry! It is I, Caligula! Kill! Kill! Kill laughter! Kill those who deny Caesar! I will be Caesar! Kill those who deny death! I will be death! My face will be bright with blood! My

laughing face, Lazarus! Laughing because men fear me! My face of victorious Fear! Look at me! I am laughing, Lazarus! *My* laughter! Laughter of
Gods and Caesars! Ha-ha-ha-ha!   (319)

You. Me. My. I. Through the obsessive repetition of these pronouns and
through the relentlessly repetitive short staccato sentences, the increasing
parataxis and exclamation, O'Neill lifts the maniacal Caligula through
several shifts in mood and emotional pitch to the point of collapse,
followed by complete silence.

Speaking of the double in German expressionist film, Lotte Eisner notes
that 'for the Germans the demoniac side to an individual always had a
middle-class counterpart,'[35] but the figure of the *Doppelgänger* by no
means originated in films. The double was a popular image in literature
from the Romantics on, and O'Neill might well have acquired an interest
in the figure from Poe's *William Wilson* or Wilde's *The Picture of Dorian
Gray*, which he knew well. The popularity of the double reached particular heights with the expressionists, however, because of its inherent gothic
and romantic qualities and because it was such an effective means of
objectifying the soul or inner self, of literalizing metaphor. For artists
obsessed with soul-states and influenced by the contemporary discoveries
of Freud and Jung, the double was of obvious value for portraying inner
conflict in a visually effective and dramatic manner, for exploring what
R.D. Laing would today call a 'divided self,' and for moralizing about the
destructive effects of a materialistic, bourgeois society that alienated the
individual from his or her true nature or identity. At times the double is
diabolical, as in Henrik Galeen's film *The Student of Prague* (1926); at
others he seems a distraught mirror image of the self, victim of some
unidentified power, as in the many doubled self-portraits of the Austrian
expressionist painter Egon Schiele, while at others he represents the
better, or at least more desirable, aspects of an individual divided against
himself: Poe's William Wilson is the classic example, but Kaiser's hero in
The Coral provides a dramatic example of the type in a play that many
feel was an influence on O'Neill.

Whatever his sources, in *The Great God Brown* and *Days Without End*
O'Neill created two extremely powerful texts by using the figure of the
double in a bold, extended manner to serve his own purposes. In many
ways these two plays are companion texts, to some extent mirroring but
also paralleling and contradicting each other. They are discussed further
in connection with O'Neill's central expressionist theme; however, a few
preliminary observations about the doubles in each play should be made
at this point.

In *Days Without End* the Loving half of John Loving is the most nearly evil double that O'Neill created. He is opposed to bourgeois social constraints, especially marital fidelity, but also to the Christian God of love and faith, towards which John longs to return. The play is reminiscent of Marlowe's *Doctor Faustus* in its reductive allegory of good and evil warring within the soul of man. *The Great God Brown*, which prepares the way for the later, more schematic struggle, is both more complex and much more interesting. Dion Anthony and Billy Brown turn out to be doubles, but only after the climactic scene of Dion's death at the end of act 2, when Dion 'wills' Brown his Mephistophelean Pan self. In other words, Dion Anthony was doubled *before* Brown became his *Doppelgänger* (though clues that they are 'brothers' are present from the beginning of the play). Through his use of the mask of the Great God Pan, which covers Dion's highly sensitive, spiritual 'St Anthony' inner self, O'Neill projects an image of the artist as man divided against himself. He also mines one of the richest veins of nineteenth- and early twentieth-century mythology – the myth of Pan.[36]

O'Neill could well have inherited the image of a physically and symbolically double Pan, at once a Christ-like figure and a potentially demonic pagan force, or he may have known Pan more simply as Christ's dramatic opposite, a god whose death, proclaimed originally by Plutarch and loudly lamented by the Victorians, is a direct result of Christ's supremacy. Certainly, as Travis Bogard suggests, O'Neill's goat-god is not truly Dionysian at all (Bogard, 272–8). However, in his ambiguous conflation of a Nietzschean Dionysus and Swinburnean Pan with a Christian Anthony, O'Neill does dramatize the wider struggle between the disruptive creative (and sexual) energy of the pagan goat-god and/or Dionysus and the orderly but repressive spiritual dictates of a bourgeois Christianity. Because his Dionysian artistic Pan-self can co-exist neither with his inner spiritual Christ-like self nor with the outer world, where conservative businessmen like Brown flourish, he is fatally divided against himself. His revenge on life is to bequeath his torment to the envious Brown, who then becomes Dion's 'murderer and his murdered' (320).

Dion-Brown's only other legacy is the architectural plan for a new Capitol building. The original plans designed by Dion are made respectable by hiding 'old Silenus on the cupola' (312) so only those of Dionysian energy will be able to detect 'the wearily ironic grin of Pan' behind the 'pompous façade' (313). The death that Dion-Brown finds at the end of the play is ambiguous, if not simply confused, because it appears to negate utterly both the male energy typified by Pan the goat-god and the rational order of the Logos in favour of a pantheistic god of love and the cycles of

Mother Earth. The Great God Pan is, indeed, dead, but O'Neill's efforts to transcend the energizing dichotomies he presents with a quasi-mystical, lyrical invocation to the earth do not ring true.[37] Like so many expressionist works; the ending is atavistic, imaging release from inner divisions and social alienation as a lapse back into unconsciousness and death.

A complaint frequently lodged against O'Neill is that his characters are types, closer to bloodless abstractions and mechanical vehicles for his thematic concerns than he realized. O'Neill, of course, was very anxious to distance himself from the German expressionists on precisely these grounds, and yet, as his handling of doubles suggests, he did use his characters in the service of his ideas: Dion and Brown, like John Loving, Jones, Yank, Lazarus, Reuben, and many others, are abstract, almost puppet-like figures through which we watch the play of forces in the human soul or within the seemingly absurd universe they inhabit. Despite their proper names, they closely resemble the *Figuren* of Kaiser's plays. At his death, for example, we are told that Dion-Brown's name is 'Man!' (*GGB*, 323) *Ecce Homo*! If this is the case, as I believe it is even for earlier plays like *Beyond the Horizon* and *Desire Under the Elms* and later plays like *Iceman*, it should be evident from an examination of O'Neill's central theme: his search for faith and rebirth in a spiritually bankrupt age.

> The playwright today must dig at the roots of the sickness of today as he feels it – the death of the Old God and the failure of science and material-ism to give any satisfying new One for the surviving primitive religious instinct to find a meaning for life in, and to comfort its fears of death with. It seems to me that anyone trying to do big work nowadays must have this big subject behind all the little subjects of his plays or novels, or he is simply scribbling around on the surface of things and has no more real status than a parlour entertainer.   (Cargill, 115)

Thus spoke Eugene O'Neill in a letter to George Jean Nathan, and for all his pompous earnestness O'Neill put his finger on the nerve-centre of his art. Throughout his plays, but especially in the nine under study here, O'Neill portrays man searching for something to believe in, some faith, and some purpose or meaning beyond the banal and vicious surfaces of life. In the course of this search O'Neill's characters long for spiritual rebirth or death, pit themselves against opposing forces within themselves or the world around them, and cry out in anguished monologues against a silence that always threatens to engulf them. When the hostile forces exist primarily within the soul or psyche, O'Neill objectifies these forces through 'ha'nts,' doubles, masks, or emotional and spiritual succubae. When these forces are external to the hero, whether social, political, scientific, or religious, O'Neill usually embodies the obstacle in the person of a woman – mother, wife, whore.

If we examine O'Neill's plays in terms of character configurations and codes, in most we find the male struggling against a negative woman: Eleanor Cape in *Welded*, Ella in *All God's Chillun*, Margaret in *The Great God Brown*, Nina in *Strange Interlude*, and Elsa in *Days Without End* (later, there is Evelyn in *Iceman* and Mary in *Long Day's Journey*). Even in plays like *The Hairy Ape, Dynamo*, and *Lazarus Laughed*, where specific social, scientific, and religious forces obstruct the hero's path, it is a woman who represents those forces – for example, Mildred in *The Hairy Ape*, Reuben's mother and Ada in *Dynamo* (not to mention the dynamo herself), and Miriam and Pompeia in *Lazarus Laughed*. O'Neill's heroes are all much alike – dark, brooding, sensitive, artistic men, striving to find themselves in an uncaring world where they do not seem to belong. When they divide against themselves and turn bad, becoming Mephistophelean cynics, drunks, murderers, and suicides, it is because they have failed to achieve transfiguration. His women are equally type-cast, doomed to play the devouring female within O'Neill's narrowly sexist conception of human relations and cosmic forces.[38] That O'Neill inherited his vision of woman and of sexual relations from Schopenhauer, Nietzsche, Strindberg, Munch, Otto Weininger, and the German expressionists is easy to see; that he was drawn to it so deeply is a function of his own temperament and biography.

If, however, we examine O'Neill's plays from the perspective of result, conclusion, or ultimate answer to the big question he is asking, then we find a different but complementary binary pattern emerging. Of the nine plays examined here, *The Emperor Jones, The Hairy Ape, All God's Chillun Got Wings, The Great God Brown*, and *Strange Interlude* conclude with regression, and the remaining four with a leap towards a kind of apocalyptic purging and rebirth. O'Neill once said that the 'birth-cry of the higher men' would only 'come at the command of the imagination and will' (Cargill, 107), but in these four plays he was unable to imagine a truly convincing birth-cry: the ecstatic transfiguration of *Welded* seems undercut by the title of the play, if not by what we have seen of the husband and wife; *Dynamo* and *Lazarus Laughed* can both be viewed as ironic or insincere forcings of the apocalyptic vision, and *Days Without End* suggests a desperate effort to reaffirm a Catholic vision of rebirth.[39] Before the vision grew faint and died with Josie's dreams in *A*

Moon for the Misbegotten, O'Neill teetered back and forth between these two polar extremes of regression and apocalyptic transfiguration, and each of his heroes is drawn to the silence of annihilation even as he gropes towards an assertion of self and an affirmation of belief that will announce the New Man.

Throughout the following consideration of O'Neill's most expressionistic plays, there are three elements in his dramatization of this search for faith that must constantly be kept in mind: the stages in the hero's search, the type of 'God' he seeks or believes he needs, and the consequences of his search. Even when the hero is successful in locating his god, he is seldom better off than when he first realized his need.

For all its brevity, *The Emperor Jones* remains one of O'Neill's most theatrical and thought-provoking plays. It has not gone out of style or out of date. The play raises a host of moral, social, and ideological issues, but it resolves few. For example, Jones is clearly a greedy, violent, ambitious man, but he has seized power and wealth through means frequently condoned by so-called civilized society, and yet the other members of Jones's world, from Smithers (a kind of cynical, envious white Crusoe to Jones's rebellious Man Friday) to the primitive, vengeful Lem, provide no foil for Jones and no superior moral perspective. Once we see his past and that of his people, it is not hard to pity 'dis po' sinner' as a man more sinned against than sinning. As a consequence it is difficult to locate the source of wrongdoing in *The Emperor Jones*, and this vagueness, together with Jones's suffering and disintegration, is typical of expressionism. (Toller's clarity on social issues, such as it is, is more the exception than the rule.)

In fact, what finally seems at issue here is less a matter of capitalist greed, racism, or crime than a generalized picture of man's inhumanity and the terrible consequences of his desire to make the self outwardly god-like in a world where other gods are false, inadequate, or absent. When Jones shoots the crocodile-god with the silver bullet that he was reserving for his own death, he is actually shooting at the primitive godhead in the racial unconscious, at the projection of a force within himself. Without realizing it, Jones has committed psychological suicide here by killing the god within, while ironically calling on the Jesus of his Baptist upbringing. The conflict in *The Emperor Jones* is not really man against social injustice or even man against man (Lem's men merely finish off what Jones has, in fact, accomplished). It is man against himself, in a drama of self-betrayal within an individual who cannot bridge the gap between the outer trappings of reality in a deceiving world where he thought he could be king by playing the part and an inner reality, projected as layers of the subconscious and unconscious, that he cannot comprehend. He is an image of Man caught by the 'expressive fallacy.' The irony of the drums that beat throughout the play and come to an abrupt halt with Jones's death is that they conflate the inner reality of Jones's terror and the outer form of that terror in one ambiguous sound.

If there is any message in *The Emperor Jones*, it is quite simply that man does not know himself and that the externals of life, be they the emperor's clothes or the language of conventional Christian faith – 'Lawd Jesus' – are worthless. However, O'Neill provides no sense of Jones's having understood this or of any general renewal arising either from the violent death of this man or from the exposure of his misconceptions. O'Neill presents us, instead, with an image of regression on all levels. With each scene the stage becomes increasingly dark and the forest walls close in. Jones's physical deterioration, effectively portrayed through his torn, discarded clothes, is closely paralleled by his psychological collapse. From his entrance as a large, handsome man in regal attire, he reverts to a naked creature grovelling on his knees until, in scene 7, he lies completely prostrate 'with his face to the ground, his arms out-stretched, whimpering with fear' (202). This whimpering signals his collapse in status, from a highly articulate being at the beginning of the play to a creature who, step by step, loses his ability to speak at all. The sharp retort of each gunshot is followed by increasing silence. For Brutus (betrayer of his inner self) Jones there is no hope of rebirth, not even a meaningful *Aufbruch*; when he sets out it is only on a journey into a dark night of the soul. Certainly his death is a pointless sacrifice, unless the primitive gods of the soul or unconscious have been somehow appeased.

The Emperor Jones ends with the silence of an unanswered question, but O'Neill put the question again in *The Hairy Ape*. Because this is one of O'Neill's most often discussed plays, there are only a few points about its expressionism that need to be stressed here. Critics of the play err, I think, if they place too much emphasis on its socio-political theme. To be sure, there is a very real class and economic conflict in the play, and O'Neill was more concerned about such matters, especially in his earlier work, than is usually allowed. Moreover, both these issues are represented in Mildred and her horrified encounter with Yank. But Mildred's cry, 'Oh, the filthy beast,' initiates a true *Aufbruch* for Yank, the central thrust of which will not be for him to challenge social inequality and economic exploitation but to find himself and to know where he belongs. This *Aufbruch* reaches consolidation in scene 4 with Yank's newly formed resolution: 'Hairy ape! So dat's me, huh? ... Ain't she de same as me? Hairy ape, huh? I'll show her I'm better'n her, if she on'y knew it. I belong and she don't, see!' (230–1)

The remaining four scenes chart his search for an image of himself to replace the one Mildred conjured up, and with each scene the play becomes increasingly expressionist. The chorus of stokers in scene 4 with black Caligari circles of coal dust around their eyes 'like black make-up, giving them a queer, sinister expression' (226), with their mechanical repetition of words like 'Love,' 'Law,' and 'God,' gives way to the masked marionette-like figures of scene 5, to the disembodied 'Voices' of 'the unseen occupants of the cells' in scene 6, and finally to the 'chattering, whimpering wail' of the monkeys at the end of the play. Yank himself changes from a normal stoker to an unwashed, 'blackened, brooding figure,' to a bandaged and bruised Rodin 'Thinker,' to a crumpled heap on the floor of a cage. Both the external world and the figure of individual man are increasingly abstracted in order to focus upon the struggle of the soul in its search for self-expression and identity. One might almost say that Yank's individuality is a matter of surfaces and that the more aware he becomes of his inner life or soul, the less he cares for the world around him. Thus, the quarrel of an individual stoker called Robert Smith with the daughter of his capitalist boss is quickly submerged in a deeper human dilemma. What Yank longs for is not political reform. He categorically rejects the idea: 'Gimme a dollar more a day and make me happy! Three square a day, and cauliflowers in de front yard – ekal rights – a woman and kids – a lousy vote – and I'm all fixed for Jesus, huh? Aw, hell! What does dat get yuh? Dis ting's in your inside, but it ain't your belly … It's way down – at de bottom' (250). As he comes to see, his problem is being human: 'I was born, see? Sure, dat's de charge' (251).

Prior to meeting Mildred, Yank unquestioningly worshipped the great furnaces whose energy he served. In facing the fact of his humanity he has also faced the falsity of his previous god and the absence of purpose or meaning in his life. Worst of all, he has faced the burdens of consciousness and language without any external power, Logos or Divine Word, that can shape reality for him. Here, in Yank's fear and trembling, O'Neill explores for the first time an aspect of his big theme that he would continue to wrestle with. Lacking belief, man is not only at the mercy of 'primitive religious instinct' (as was Jones) and without protection against death, he is also, and perhaps most painfully, without the Word, and when his own words fail him, he is left with silence in a void. This, it seems to me, is the real centre of *The Hairy Ape*, and all other aspects of Yank's search fall into place around it. In order to escape someone else's label – 'a hairy ape' – he must find the words to say himself. He must speak, and speak he does, in long, incoherent, rambling monologues punctuated with exclamations, rhetorical questions, and sentence frag-

ments, which are an increasingly desperate effort to fight off the approaching silence of a meaningless, un-speakable death. From this perspective
the climax of scene 8, which is one long monologue, is Yank's realization
that it is man's fate to fail. Unlike the animal he addresses, Yank 'kin
make a bluff at talkin' and tinkin' – a'most get away wit it – a'most! – and
dat's where de joker comes in' (253). In *The Hairy Ape* Yank's *Aufbruch*
leads only to silence after he has regressed, like Jones, from a stammering
consciousness back to an animal state that lies even further beyond the
working, howling, quasi-conscious creature of the first three scenes.
O'Neill's vision here is deeply nihilistic. Being born, symbolized by a
brutal awakening into consciousness, is the source of pain from which the
only release is the silence of death, and the play ends with the questions
still unanswered and the forces of darkness and unreason loose in the
world.[40]

Welded is by no means O'Neill's first play to present the proverbial
Strindbergian and expressionist battle between the sexes, but it is the first
in which he tries to reverse the catastrophic results of the battle portrayed
in each of *Before Breakfast* (1916), *Beyond the Horizon* (1917–18), and
Desire Under the Elms (1924). Here for the first time O'Neill uses the
ecstatic, lyric qualities of expressionism to overcome a marital and sexual
deadlock. There are a number of expressionistic features to this play, such
as the use of light on each character 'like auras of egoism' (*w*, 443), the
somnambulistic movements of Eleanor (for example, when there is
knocking at the door), and the speeches in which husband and wife sit
separately, talking past one another as if to themselves, but the end of the
play is a kind of expressionist extravaganza of speech, gesture, and
symbolism.

Briefly, what O'Neill has done here is to explore an ideal of marriage as
the religion of the chosen few, chief among them Michael Cape, who
insists that his wife replace God's mercy in a painful world where 'life
lives.' What he desires is faith in an almost mystical union that 'reveals a
beginning in unity that I may have faith in the unity of the end' (488).
When she resists this role, which threatens her own identity, their
relationship degenerates into vicious quarreling. When she accepts this
role in his play of life (she is an actress; he is the playwright), she has
acquiesced in his vision of her as a totally pliable mother-lover-wife. In the
final moments of the play husband and wife move together in the shape of
a cross to which she is praying, and then, in the penultimate image, 'they
form together one cross' (489). Presumably they are transfigured by this
love that gives unity and meaning to his life, and yet there is an
unintentional irony in this scene. By sacrificing themselves on this cross /

altar of conjugal love, they are actually withdrawing from reality into *Michael's* 'old dreams.' What looks like transfiguration is, in fact, regression on his part and abdication on hers, and she becomes the first in a collection of willess, passive females in O'Neill's plays. Although O'Neill has disguised the fact behind the breathless pseudo-mystical rhetoric of this scene, Eleanor and Michael are on their way to bed, where, like the artist in Kirchner's *Self-portrait with model* (1910), Cape will consummate the victory of his will and creative energy over her submissive female flesh.[41] What he will achieve by doing so is unclear. What O'Neill achieved by the bald portrayal of his 'tortured' hero's sexual and creative crisis is a strident, unconvincing play that lyric expressionist outbursts could not save.

All God's Chillun Got Wings is a much more complex and rewarding play than *Welded*, but it explores a similar situation and attempts to replace an ineffectual, indifferent Christian God with an ideal of marriage. (The indifference of this god could not be more clear than in O'Neill's instructions for the wedding in scene 4 of act 1.) This time the hero is genuinely sympathetic and his fate tragic. The woman, however, is a jealous, voracious monster whose very madness images her destructive nature while providing the plot with its necessary causality. Beginning from the relatively high point of Jim and Ella's childhood affection and Jim's desire to succeed at a white profession in order to be worthy of the girl he worships, the play slips steadily into failure, estrangement, madness, and despair. Jim is the increasingly familiar O'Neill hero in his sensitivity and need for faith; Ella is a disturbing figure, a kind of atavistic throwback to Bertha in *Jane Eyre*, a projection of deep-seated fears.[42]

Although *All God's Chillun* seems to be about the social evil of racism, as with *The Hairy Ape* the social question masks a deeper problem. Why should Ella go mad in the first place? Why should she want Jim to fail? Miscegenation and prejudice are not entirely convincing answers. What O'Neill has created in Ella is a type of vampire who draws the male into a regressive childhood dream and who, by making him a child again, emasculates him in order to use his power – sexual and creative (or perhaps, since Jim wants to be a lawyer, one should say intellectual) – to support her own parasitic existence. Jim's tragic error is to worship a false god in the form of this woman, and his final exalted prayer to the Christian God strikes an ironic note. In his confusion he mistakes Ella's desires for a divinely sanctioned mission, but the only god in this play lies within the Congo mask that Ella destroys. The search for faith in *All God's Chillun* fails because God is absent or dead and the 'chillun' are slaves to a 'white devil woman.' The outcome of the struggle between male and female principles in *Welded* allowed O'Neill to attempt a transfiguring conclusion. In this play, however, it is the female who wins, and the result is unqualified regression.

Up to this point O'Neill had explored man's search for faith within himself (in *Emperor Jones* and *The Hairy Ape*) and within a perverse ideal of marriage, and in doing so he had probed the psychic wounds caused by unacknowledged inner truth, by the burden of human consciousness, and by the emotional cannibalism resulting from the battle of the sexes. In *The Great God Brown* he brings these elements together to create perhaps the most complex portrayal of his big theme. Here, however, all the gods are dead – the god of self, the Christian God, even the Great God Pan – except the most problematic one of all: the Earth Mother who, as O'Neill envisages her, invites man to forget his ambitions and creative energies in death. When the creative imagination dies, in the person of Dion, all that is left for Man (Brown) is to 'devote his life to renovating the house of [his] Cybel into a home for [his] Margaret' (297). The effort rapidly destroys him.

Dion Anthony, that image of the tormented, self-divided artist, lives a life of one long *Schrei* because no one understands what he really is and because he fails in his 'endeavor to see God' through his art. The two sources of pain – one psychological, the other spiritual – are closely related early in the play, and at the interface between them stands O'Neill's Munch-like Woman: Mother/Wife/Whore. (Dion links the first two explicitly in a long speech from act 1, scene 3, shortly after the two men have left Cybel's.) O'Neill's play is by no means as fragmented and dream-like as Sorge's *The Beggar*, but both plays portray the passionate, rebellious, anti-bourgeois expressionist artist struggling to survive in a hostile world where he is plagued by mother, father, conservative friend and patron, and turning in desperation to a 'Girl.' Where Sorge's poet kills his parents in a bid for creative freedom, Dion Anthony kills himself or, more precisely, is destroyed by Woman, who, on the one hand, rejects his totality and, on the other, offers him a kind of unity with her in death.

Dion Anthony experiences his one brief, illusive moment of *Aufbruch* in an important speech in the prologue to the play. Removing his mask, he reveals a face 'torn and transfigured by joy,' and stammers ecstatically: 'O God in the moon, did you hear? She loves me! I am not afraid! I am strong! I can love! She protects me! Her arms are softly around me! She is my skin! She is my armour! Now I am born – I – the I! one and indivisible – I who love Margaret!' (266) This speech is important for several reasons, not least its typically expressionist exaggerated language and staccato style. The crucial point to note, however, is that this moment of rebirth, which should start Dion forth on a new life, is abortive because Margaret recoils immediately from the maskless Dion. The entire situation of the play is contained in this one moment – ecstatic expression of the artistic *Ich* seeking faith and transfiguration through a woman who denies and betrays – and the four acts that follow trace man's fate to its inevitable conclusion. The action of the play does not so much develop or progress as unfold and reveal what was there beneath the surface from the beginning. As might be expected, Billy Brown also has a parallel moment of *Aufbruch* in act 2, scene 3, after Dion's death and before the full horror of consciousness and suffering descends on him too and he becomes divided and unacknowledged in his turn.

Through the Dion-Brown brotherhood, O'Neill is saying that man's only release from psychological and spiritual pain in this world is unconsciousness; we can either be like Brown, a complacent, superficial, higher-class Yank, or we can die. To experience *Aufbruch*, to awake into full consciousness is to acknowledge one's creative and spiritual longings (the two are virtually synonymous for O'Neill); and yet to be defeated on the very threshold of one's quest, before the search has properly begun, is to be defeated by one's humanity, which, as O'Neill once again predicts, is to be defeated by Woman.

I would suggest that both endings of *The Great God Brown* are profoundly pessimistic and regressive. In the first the dying Brown nestles against the whore and 'idol of earth,' Cybel, like a child returning to its mother's protective body, while she intones 'with calm exultance': 'Our Father Who Art!' (322) Although O'Neill strains to make their final speeches convey a transfiguring joy and love, it is impossible to forget that in this tableau we have the death of this naked man-child and the erasure of a Father in *Heaven*. (Cybel's prayer does not include Logos.) The male principle, within Man and God the Father, is completely overwhelmed by a seductive Earth Mother whose only answer to the 'intolerable chalice of life' is 'death and peace again!' (322) Why strive to find faith, why create or change anything, if the cycles of life and death are so all-consuming?

What Woman offers in her manifestation as Wife is scarcely more appealing, and yet it is the possessive, shallow Margaret who has the final words of the play. Margaret offers Dion immortality, but on her own terms, and, of course, only through his death: '*I want* to feel the moon at peace in the sea! *I want* Dion to leave the sky for me! *I want* him to sleep in the tides of my heart! *My* lover! *My* husband! *My* boy!' (325, emphasis added) Despite the seductive tones of this speech, this is 'still the same Margaret,' still the woman who could not see, and what she offers is death. The Dion/Pan/male creative principle she wants must fall and drown, submerging his identity and energy in her.

The endings of *The Great God Brown* are troubling and unsatisfactory for two reasons. In the first place, O'Neill seems to believe what his Brown, Cybel, and Margaret are saying; there is no clear ironic cue to imply that the spirit and energy of the Great God Pan has been betrayed; the author appears to accept and endorse this passive conclusion. In the second place, O'Neill has once again failed to envision a female power that is not in direct opposition to a male god and is not jealous of his energy. Cybel and Margaret are little more than the attractive side of the devouring female depicted in Ella and Nina. They are emasculating presences, awesome in their need to absorb and smother. This schematic dichotomy of male/female, creation/destruction, spiritual longing/physical annihilation, apocalypse/regression is not far removed from Kokoschka's *Murder, Hope of Women*, however much more flesh O'Neill has put on the bones of his characters and plot. The tragedy for O'Neill is that, although he saw the negative aspects of God the Father and desired another type of divine presence, he was unable to envisage a fully satisfying, creative female deity; he was trapped by the very patriarchal thinking that he, at least in part, sought to escape.

Like *Welded, Lazarus Laughed* reverses the outcome of the male/female struggle and provides O'Neill's one truly apocalyptic vision. Women of any kind are peripheral in this play, which focuses consistently upon Lazarus and Caligula. In choosing Lazarus as his hero, O'Neill chose a pre-eminent symbol of rebirth and *Aufbruch*, a figure who, furthermore, unites the qualities of renewal and life associated with Dionysus and Christ. When Lazarus dies at the end in a climax of sacrificial flame, ecstatic laughter, and the rhythmic chanting of a chorus, it is possible to see Caligula as purged and ready for rebirth. From this perspective, Lazarus becomes definitive proof that apocalypse is both an end and a new beginning and that the fear of death and the lust to kill can be destroyed to make way for the laughter of new life. Moreover, the god whom Lazarus serves defies Miriam and her weeping mothers; he is a male god of energy, pride, and laughter, who insists that his creature believe enough to risk all: 'Away with such cowardice of spirit,' says Lazarus, chastizing his wife. 'We will to die! We will to change! ... This must Man will as his end and his new beginning' (LL, 324).

Despite their many differences, *Lazarus Laughed* bears comparison with *The Great God Brown* and the later *Days Without End* because the underlying issue in all three plays is the same. *Lazarus Laughed* almost seems a response to and contradiction of the conclusion reached in the earlier play. By dismissing Woman (Miriam withers away into increasing silence, old age, and death, and Pompeia throws herself on Lazarus's funeral pyre) and the deceptive ideal of marriage that Michael Cape controls so precariously in *Welded*, Lazarus is free to discover God and to pass this apocalyptic vision on in his laughter and death. *Days Without End* also relegates Woman to a secondary, nurturing role that does not rival male authority. John Loving's struggle is a simplified version of the Dion Anthony dilemma, and its resolution is apocalyptic, but in greatly subdued and private terms. But before he could imagine a return to conventional Christian *Erlösung*, O'Neill tackled the 'white devil woman' twice more, in Nina Leeds and the mother/whore machine of *Dynamo*.

Strange Interlude is the least expressionistic of these plays. There are no abstracted sets, no masks or stylized acting, no clear hero to pass through the stations of his ordeal, and the thought-asides are dramatic adaptations of realist *erlebte Rede*, not the expressionist *Ausstrahlungen des Ichs*. Most important is the lack of a hero for the expressionist ordeal, because O'Neill, unlike Susan Glaspell in *The Verge*, could not create an expressionist New Woman. Nevertheless, the subject of the play is closely related to the expressionist search for God, rebirth, and creative energy in the preceding plays. In *Strange Interlude* O'Neill pauses to confront the whore/mother/wife female that has gradually emerged in plays like *All God's Chillun* and *The Great God Brown*, to expose her sexual voraciousness and then to erode her power, leaving her to 'rot away in peace' (*SI*, 197) at the end. This play is not a celebration of womanhood; it is a nightmarish vision of what a domineering female can do to the men around her.

In her grief over Gordon's death, Nina longs for a Mother God because she could make death natural and dispense peace and comfort (*SI*, 42–3), and then she does her best to become that female God. The results are not pleasant. Distraught over her failure to possess Gordon, who escapes her in a fiery airman's death in the war, she prostitutes herself before achieving power through her role as mother. At the apogee of her career she delivers her 'my three men' speech, and the scene, with Nina standing, dominating the lives and thoughts of the seated men, Darrell, Evans, and Marsden, is chilling:

> My three men! ... I feel their desires converge in me! ... to form one complete beautiful male desire which I absorb ... and am whole ... they dissolve in me, their life is my life ... I am pregnant with the three! husband! ... lover! ... father! ... and the fourth man! ... little man! ... little Gordon! ... he is mine too! ... that makes it perfect! (135)

Nina suppresses 'hysterical triumphant laughter' after these thoughts because she knows she is hoodwinking 'God the father,' and her laughter, unlike Lazarus's, is utterly self-centred. Her men, at this moment, are in no such exultant state: Darrell's brilliant career is ruined, his mind and soul warped by envy and frustration; Evans is betrayed and rendered superfluous – his child bears Nina's past lover's name and has been fathered by her present lover, Darrell. Marsden, however, is the most disturbing of the three, because he suspects what has happened but is too weak to interfere. Marsden is a 'mama's boy,' an emasculated writer of second-rate novels who will stay with Nina when the others finally leave her because he is good for little else – and in any case, her power over males vanishes with her sexuality.

Quite consistent with the Mother God mythos he has developed so far, O'Neill will reduce Nina to a child-like state at the end, return her to her paternal home, and leave her with the most mothered man in the play. Like Billy Brown, Sam Evans will have died from the effort of pleasing her, but Darrell and young Gordon will escape her final clutching at their lives. Darrell will flee to the freedom and self-assertion of his work, and, most significantly, Gordon will soar beyond her reach in a plane. Male/female, sky/earth, moon/sea (as in Margaret's closing speech) – O'Neill concludes this play with the same dichotomies as the earlier ones. The only difference is that this time God the Father unequivocally reasserts his claim to power and leaves Nina to her life-in-death fate. Marsden provides the final, stunning image of the play: it is one of a sterile, regressive peace in death where life is no more than a 'strange interlude' of 'trial and preparation ... in which our souls have been scraped clean of impure flesh and made worthy to bleach in peace' (199).

Although God the Mother is anatomized and defeated in this play, O'Neill is not able to dismiss her altogether. The awesome Mother God could even be said to control the action from the wings in *The Iceman Cometh* and to cripple the lives of three more men in *Long Day's Journey into Night*. Certainly, she returns, more deadly than ever, in *Dynamo*, where the belief in self, ideal marriage, the Great God Pan, and the Earth Mother are replaced by the worship of technology. As theatre *Dynamo* is an unwieldy play, and many of its characters' speeches would sound ridiculous today (if they did not, in fact, do so in the twenties), but it does return to the struggle of a typical expressionist hero who breaks free from a hated, repressive father and a possessive mother in an *Aufbruch* at the end of act 1. His departure in search of faith and self-expression are suitably accompanied by a violent, if not quite apocalyptic, storm that heralds the break-up of the family and of approaching death.

The new Reuben who returns in act 2 is familiar from plays by Kaiser, Sorge, and Toller; he seeks new gods to replace the hated Christian God of his father; he insists upon self-expression, in lengthy, ecstatic monologues, and he ruthlessly asserts his sexuality. He is at his peak of self-confidence throughout act 2, until, in the last moments of that act, he approaches the dynamo. The attraction he begins to feel for this 'great, dark mother' (D, 474) quickly drives him from frenzied adoration, when he thinks he will be the new saviour, into the madness, murder, and suicide that dominate act 3. Despite the embarassing infantilism of the last scene, it is interesting to look briefly at what O'Neill does with his mad hero and mother-machine in the play's last moments because he seems to intend Reuben's immolation as an ironic comment on the illusion of rebirth and misplaced faith and as a melodramatic warning against the monstrous Mother God of his imagination. What is horrifying in this scene is not that the dynamo is a machine but that Reuben thinks of it as a mother with whose body he can be reunited. Reuben's murder of Ada and violent suicide may have some of the drama of a twentieth-century apocalypse, but the final vision is completely regressive. According to the stage instructions (which are more like exposition in fiction), 'Reuben's voice rises in a moan that is a mingling of pain and loving consummation, and this cry dies into a sound that is like the crooning of a baby and merges and is lost in the dynamo's hum' (488).

In *Days Without End* O'Neill schematizes the split within his tormented hero, John Loving, in such a way as to make a choice between the two parts of his psyche not only possible but necessary, if John is to save his marriage and his soul. Unlike *Welded* or *All God's Chillun*, the marriage provides only a superficial battleground for a struggle that fundamentally resides *within* the hero. John represents the good artist figure (though he is also in business), and Loving represents his evil *Doppelgänger*, a projection of the spiritual nihilism and cruelty within the man's soul. John Loving is a conflation of Dion Anthony and Billy Brown, but in this play the Anthony/Brown qualities will be victorious, presumably with John's creative abilities still intact. Throughout the play John is torn between his love for his wife and his unacknowledged longing for God, on the one hand, and the temptation to sin and despair, cynically supported by the articulate Loving, on the other.

Elsa's near-death and final forgiveness of the sins he committed under Loving's guidance provide the catalyst for the simultaneous death and rebirth of the hero, but as has already been noted, the ending of the play is unconvincing. Killing off the evil Loving, while John enjoys an ecstatic vision of God's transfiguring love, leaves several issues unanswered. How, for example, will this rebirth affect John's creative energies? Can this 'ideal marriage' of John's creation (524) really be reborn, or is this couple doomed to an existence like the Capes' in *Welded*? We are simply expected to believe that, unlike the Capes, the Lovings are reinforced by divine love, which somehow transforms and safeguards their earthly lives. Within the expressionist frame of reference, of course, there are many examples of this kind of appeal to Christ – Toller's *Transfiguration*, Kaiser's *The Burghers of Calais*, the paintings of Beckmann and Marc, and the sculpture and woodcuts of Barlach, artists all haunted by Christianity – but that does not save this play nor ensure that its creator would be free of the threatening female forces always there to pull him back towards 'easeful Death.' The apocalyptic collapse of Loving is too easy, and the *Erlösung* of John is, on the one hand, an inadequate response to the pain of consciousness and, on the other, a fragile bulwark against the Woman at home.

After *Days Without End* (1931–34) O'Neill completed only four more full-length plays before his death in 1953 – *The Iceman Cometh* (1939), *A Touch of the Poet* (ca 1940), *Long Day's Journey into Night* (1940–41), and *A Moon for the Misbegotten* (1943).[43] Several major projects were never brought to fruition or, in some instances, even begun, and the last ten years of his life were spent in ill health and increasing darkness of spirit. In retrospect, *Days Without End* appears to mark the end of O'Neill's capacity to struggle towards a positive vision of hope and rebirth. There are no New Men in the last plays. If Hofmannsthal was justified in saying that the expressionism of *The Hairy Ape* is qualified by its passive, acquiescent ending,[44] then the same could be said of the last plays, where life and hope are crushed and the characters remain trapped in an existence so painful and meaningless that escape into drugs, alcohol, silence, and death is all that is left. Like the boy Allan in Kaiser's last play, *The Raft of the Medusa*, O'Neill's last protagonists, Hickey, the Tyrones, Jaimie, and Con Melody, reject life because their creator had rejected 'the possibility of regeneration.'[45]

And yet, as Catharine Mounier suggests, the expressionist *Schrei* of pain and longing, if not also of rebellion, can still be heard in the late plays. They are, in fact, best understood as a culmination of the turbulent, experimental years between 1920 and 1934 when O'Neill was writing his expressionistic plays. During these years O'Neill learned how to probe beneath the banal surfaces of life and, therefore, how to express his big theme. He vacillated between a vision of hope, containing the possibility for rebirth, and a bleak vision of failure and regression, and he developed a mythology, albeit rather crude, to convey this ambivalence. In his search for faith, rebirth, and an ideal by which to guide his life and make sense of existence, O'Neill confronted his heroes with virtually insurmountable odds, sometimes social and economic, sometimes familial and racial, and very frequently psychological and sexual. He invariably saw the desire for spiritual ascendance, the capacity for artistic vision and creative energy, and the need to rebel against repressive bourgeois forces as a male enterprise. With very few exceptions (Lavinia in *Mourning Becomes Electra* or Josie in *A Moon for the Misbegotten*, for example) the insupportable pain of full human consciousness is also a male problem. Woman provides O'Neill with his chief antagonist. As mother/whore/lover she holds out a vision of peace that demands the abnegation of self and the abandonment of a search for ascendance and creativity. The ideal she offers is the essentially regressive one of surrender to silence and death. As wife she either merges with a mother-type or stands apart from the man, refusing to believe in his search, denying the reality of his true self and sapping his vital energy.

The polarities that emerge in these expressionist plays are fundamental to the system that informs and shapes all of O'Neill's work. Man searches for meaning, for the self, for God, and time and again his cry is swallowed up or erased by the surrounding silence. Because he was incapable of imagining apocalypse followed by a convincing vision of rebirth, his plays end in a strained, possibly ironic ecstasy or in regression and annihilation. But the measure of O'Neill's greatness or of the degree he can be said to be America's Georg Kaiser does not depend upon his failure to achieve a vision of transfiguration; for that vision we must turn to the Canadian Herman Voaden. O'Neill's greatness lies in the fact that he insisted on breaking the silence, on finding the words that say so much about being human and alive in this century.

5 Herman Voaden's 'Symphonic Expressionism'

The 'symphonic expressionism' of Herman Voaden stands, for the most part, in sharp contrast to the expressionist plays of O'Neill. Where O'Neill's work always retains a strong sense of represented human subject, considerable sexual tension and violence, and a predominantly pessimistic and regressive vision, Voaden's work, at its most typical, is a highly abstract, lyrical, and apocalyptic form of *Gesamtkunstwerk*. In large part, of course, this is a result of temperament. From the start Voaden was basically a more optimistic, idealistic and socio-politically involved individual than O'Neill. Like a number of the Germans – perhaps most strikingly Toller, whom he admired – Voaden *believed* in the possibility of the New Man and the regeneration of mankind. It was the artist's task, he felt, nowhere more so than in the theatre, to bring this renewal to pass.

It would be a mistake, however, to attempt some overly neat classification of O'Neill's or Voaden's work, to speak too quickly of empathy and regression in the one, abstraction and apocalypse in the other, because, as I stressed in chapter 1, Expressionism inscribes the opposing tendencies of these polarities. Although Voaden shares much, philosophically and aesthetically, with the *blaue Reiter*, his emphasis on northern landscape and on the human response to landscape reveals some intriguing parallels with Heckel, in particular, but also with Nolde and, beyond him, Scandinavians like Munch. The reasons for the tension and ambiguity in his 'symphonic expressionism' can be traced back to their roots in his influences and to the gradual articulation of his vision.

Born in 1903, Voaden was too young to fight in the first war but not too young to experience the sense of alienation and disillusionment with life so common among writers of his generation.[1] At fourteen he contemplated suicide in response to a crisis in his beliefs, and his subsequent need to locate, indeed create for himself, religious roots and faith characterized his dramatic work and fuelled his development of 'symphonic expressionism.' By the mid-twenties the twin pursuits of his life were in place: he had graduated from Queen's University with a degree in English and History in 1924, after taking courses on the contemporary theatre (which included works by Toller, Kaiser, Hasenclever, and Werfel), completed a master's thesis on O'Neill, begun teaching, and performed in *From Morn to Midnight* and O'Neill's *Beyond the Horizon* and *The Dreamy Kid*. From then until his retirement in 1964 Voaden divided his time between the theatre and the classroom.

The three years from 1927 to 1930 were charged with activity, and they were the years when Voaden's ideas about the theatre were cohering. For all his reservations about O'Neill – and he had many – the American remained for him a great playwright and a shining example of what could be done for the modern theatre in North America. After considerable preparatory work towards a PhD on O'Neill, he dropped scholarly research to direct, to write his first play, and to teach. He also undertook the first of three (in 1927–28, 1932–33, and 1937) important trips to Europe, where he was profoundly moved by Wagner, by Reinhardt's *Everyman* at Salzburg, and by a stunning performance of Toller's *Masses and Man*. When he returned from this journey, not only had he experienced some of the best that German theatres could offer, but he had also discovered his own attachment to Canada, which would be reinforced by the paintings of the Group of Seven. Between 1928 and 1930 he tried twice more (in plays discussed below) to write the type of play that expressed his vision of the northern landscape on the one hand and his passionate belief in the New Man on the other; he wanted to bring these two aspects of his own emerging philosophy together in such a way as to liberate Canadian theatre from its ties to a colonial and realist drama, and he wanted, above all, to express what he felt in his own soul.

For four distinct reasons 1930 marked the turning point in his career: he spent the year 1930–31 at Baker's Yale drama course, where, though not exactly encouraged to write experimentally, he was exposed to stimulation, discussion, and example; he wrote his only fully realistic play, called *Western Wolf*, a dramatization of actual social and courtship conditions in a small northern Ontario community (Baker liked it, but Voaden never again wrote this type of play); he travelled across the country to the

Rockies in order to write one of the most unusual expressionist pieces created in Canada prior to the seventies, *Symphony: A Drama of Motion and Light for a New Theatre*; and he published his first book.

In his 6 December 1930 column in the *Toronto Globe*, Lawrence Mason claimed that the book he was reviewing was an 'epoch-making ... point of departure in Canada's artistic history.'[2] The book was *Six Canadian Plays*, edited and with an introductory manifesto by Voaden. From here on Mason proved to be an enthusiastic supporter of Voaden's work, and if the collection failed to have the impact Mason desired, it none the less signalled the first serious attempt to write plays about what Brian Parker has described as the great 'antidramatic' Canadian myth of civilized man's confrontation with a vast, primitive, northern landscape.[3]

Beginning in 1930, then, Voaden deliberately set out to express Canada's non-dramatic myth of the north as an integral part of his deeply personal, religious vision, and because he realized that new dramatic forms and theatrical conventions would be needed, he turned for his formal models to the most innovative theories, dramaturgy, and stage-craft of the time – those of expressionism. Voaden called his theatre 'symphonic expressionism' because, as he explained in 1932, 'the expressionist artist has reached out to embrace other artistic media, to draw them into the theatre. Music, light and design are no longer incidental to the production: they are woven into its very movement and being ... In the emotion, movement and rhythm of the play, a new voice speaks ... [and] the theatre at last gains its utter freedom in a new and independent medium.'[4] As he saw it, expressionism released the artist from realism, that *bête noire* of the avant-garde in the early twentieth century, and what he was advocating was a drama that would avoid banal realism and narrow parochialism by embodying universal forces in a particular vision and by expressing that conjunction through an appropriate form.

Briefly, Voaden's vision was a highly idealistic, subjective, and neo-romantic one, influenced by Blake, Nietzsche, and Whitman, and accentuating the role of the artist/hero as the New Man who could show mankind the way to transfiguration and what Voaden called 'godhood.' He transmuted his personal search for faith into a type of mythopoeic journey leading, usually through death, to an individual's transfiguring union with nature: apocalyptic illumination for Voaden led to the discovery of a stern yet paradisal order within a northern nature and an exalted revelation of godhood. 'Symphonic expressionism' (originally called 'lyric expressionism') evolved from Voaden's effort to express this vision, which lay, to a considerable degree, beyond the power of words to convey. Like O'Neill, Voaden did not possess the gift of poetic language; his strength lay in his ability to orchestrate a symphonic expressionist experience in which the word plays only one part in a larger system.

Beginning with *Symphony*, Voaden created a highly semiotic theatre using light (especially white light to symbolize intense illumination), choruses, dancers, massed groups, pantomime, stylized sets, and music in an orchestrated, hence 'symphonic' total work. In certain ways his theatre experiments of the thirties recall *Lazarus Laughed* and point forward to the large-scale, outdoor performances of the American Paul Green, or to the multi-dimensional theatre of the Canadian writer-director James Reaney. Praising Voaden's work in his introduction to the playwright's article 'Toward a New Theatre,' Lawrence Mason called him 'the prophet of a new art of the theatre which offers playgoers an altogether novel kind of experience. Herman Voaden is keeping Canada abreast of the most advanced European development in this field by his fascinating experiments in presenting dramatic productions which utilize the whole range of artistic resources open to the modern regisseur.'[5]

In a sense expressionist theatre flourished in Germany when it did because the stage had already been set between 1890 and 1910 by Adolphe Appia and Edward Gordon Craig. Craig was a visionary who called for a renewed art of the theatre in the hands of a few great 'Artist-Directors,' and his disgust with realism permeates everything he wrote. Although he did not use the term expressionism, his theories clearly prefigure such art because he called for a new theatre that would be truly theatrical and predominantly visual in order to express symbolic and spiritual truths. Craig explains in his afterword to *Towards a New Theatre* (first published in 1913) that only a non-realist theatre could awaken in man 'the divine essence – the spirit – the beauty of life,' and in order to do this he advocated the use of platforms and flights of steps, an emphasis on gesture and movement, and the dramatic, symbolic use of light as an integral theatrical element. (See Plate 21 for an example of this type of staging.) The influence of Craig's vision and stagecraft, first on Roy Mitchell, then on the young Voaden, was profound.[6]

But while Craig may have been the single most important European influence on Voaden's thinking, there were many others whose work and theories are not so much influences as a part of the environment that nourished many North Americans of Voaden's generation. That Voaden was well-informed and discriminating about German expressionist theatre is clear, for he disliked their excesses and greatly admired plays by Toller or Kaiser and Reinhardt's powerful production of Büchner's *The Death of Danton* (*Dantons Tod*), which he saw in Berlin in 1928.[7] He was familiar with contemporary German films, particularly Wiene's *The*

Cabinet of Dr Caligari and Lang's *Metropolis*, and during one visit to
Germany, in 1933, he studied dance with Kurt Jooss, whose ballet *The
Green Table* (see chapter 2 and Plates 14 and 15) achieved 'a synthesis of
music, dance, and light' that, according to Voaden, exemplified the way
the modern arts were drawing upon each other and working together to
create 'symphonic art.'[8] Not long after seeing *The Green Table* he
adapted Jooss's Death figure for two of his plays, *Hill-Land* and *Ascend
as the Sun*. Perhaps the outstanding characteristic of the time, and the
phenomenon that most appealed to Voaden, was the degree to which the
arts were working together, and by its very nature such a tendency places
art above life, expression before representation.

During the twenties, three Americans had a considerable impact on his
thinking – Macgowan, O'Neill, and Whitman. Macgowan's *Continental
Stagecraft*, with its illustrations by Robert Edmund Jones (see chapter 1
and Plate 21) was an important source of information and inspiration.[9] To
a critic like Macgowan, Expressionism struck in a 'blinding storm of
illumination,' showing the way through the 'bog' of realism, and he was
able to define, analyse, and evaluate the expressionist movement, to
pinpoint its excesses and limits and to perceive, in expressionist plays
such as O'Neill's *The Hairy Ape*, its potential for a future rebirth of the
theatre. Macgowan likened expressionist drama to music in terms that
must have appealed strongly to Voaden; an expressionist play, he
claimed, eschews representation and soars 'toward direct expression of
spiritual reality. Expressionism in the theatre has to seek the way of
music, the way toward beauty and ecstasy.'[10] Macgowan called for a
new, truly American theatre that would draw upon personal vision (as
opposed to borrowed models or superficial trivia), and by 1930 Voaden
was making a similarly impassioned, nationalist statement with a comparable ideal in mind.

O'Neill and Whitman were of even greater importance to Voaden,
O'Neill for specific dramatic reasons and Whitman for more general
philosophic and possibly nationalist reasons. Although Voaden was
sensitive to limitations in O'Neill's vision, in particular to the absence of
that double sense of beauty and transcendence that were crucial elements
in his own work,[11] O'Neill's triumph remained twofold in Voaden's eyes:
first, he led the attack against realism in North America with dynamic
expressionist plays such as *The Hairy Ape*, *The Emperor Jones*, and *The
Great God Brown*, and second, he was a truly American playwright
whose work, as Voaden concluded in his thesis, was 'informed with the
moral earnestness and idealism, the vast troubled energy, of a new
land.'[12]

This ability to capture the sense of a new land was a Whitmanesque ideal shared by Voaden. Indeed, Whitman's influence permeated the first twenty-five years of this century, not only in North America, where one might expect the Whitmanesque poetic rhythms and rhetoric to appeal, but in Germany as well, where painters, poets, and playwrights knew his work through a series of translations. Certainly, Whitman's messianic idealism, his exultant praise of man, and his love for the grandeur of his native landscape all appealed deeply to Voaden, as they did to many of the Group of Seven painters and others of Voaden's generation. Moreover, his ardent nationalism, so clearly articulated in his 1888 essay 'A Backward Glance o'er Travelled Roads,' could scarcely help but strike a sympathetic note for Canadians: 'as long as the States continue to absorb and be dominated by the poetry of the Old World, and remain unsupplied with autochthonous song,' Whitman declaimed, 'so long will they stop short of first-class Nationality and remain defective.'[13] Change 'the States' to Canada and 'poetry' and 'song' to theatre and drama, and the remark could be Voaden's in 1929 or 1930.

There remains one further source of influence and inspiration for Voaden's thinking, and it is the most crucial. The impact of Lawren Harris and the Group of Seven on several Canadian writers during the twenties and thirties was profound. As Sandra Djwa points out in her article '"A New Soil and a Sharp Sun": The Landscape of Modern Canadian Poetry,' the landscape of the Group 'provided a resonant symbolic language'[14] for poets such as Frank Scott, A.J.M. Smith, and W.W.E. Ross, and this same landscape, together with the idealism and ardent nationalism of Lawren Harris, inspired the themes of Voaden's plays, particularly *Wilderness* (later *Rocks*) and *Murder Pattern*, which are inseparable from their northern settings.

As Voaden himself has remarked, Frederick B. Housser's *A Canadian Art Movement*, published in 1926, was instrumental in educating Canadians about the Group, their aims and methods, and their potential.[15] Housser predicted the development of a literature shaped by the natural forces expressed in the canvases of Harris, MacDonald (who was one of the three judges for Voaden's 1929 play competition), Thomson, and the others, and in a perceptive comment on Harris's 'Above Lake Superior' remarked that this painting 'embodies a philosophy of the north. It judges us as individuals and as a people. If we feel its bleakness and hate it, it is our own inner bleakness that hates, the finite part of us that dares not meet that infinite unfathomable thing, – the wilderness.'[16] It is this very dilemma that faces the women in Voaden's *Wilderness* and the farmers in his play *Murder Pattern*. Moreover, Harris's 'philosophy of the north,' with its emphasis on survival through transcendence and spiritual ideals (conveyed through his handling of light; see Plate 28) find their parallels in Voaden's themes and stagecraft.

When Harris described the Canadian artists' northern vision as one that transmutes and shapes 'our souls into its own spiritual expressiveness,' he singled out the central concept of Canadian modernism, one that the poets and playwrights – to a lesser degree the novelists – would have to structure in their own ways.[17] The search would be, as it had already been for the painters, a search for the forms, the language, to express such a vision. For Harris the stress was always on 'new creative vision':

> The creative artist in every productive age has always made the styles of his day and place. EXPRESSIONISM, however, is not a style, like impressionism, cubism, magic realism, or geometrical abstraction. It is ... a new realm of art wherein every modern artist creates his own style – and it has thus revivified representational painting because of the evocative demands of new creative vision. So we have today new creations of experiences of nature, of ideas and intimations and perceptions of the inner world of man, of inner motivations and reactions to life on all levels, given life by pictorial means.[18]

Although Harris, like Kandinsky, articulated his vision more thoroughly than did other painters, his expressionist stress on emotion, intensity, colour, rhythm, and inner spiritual experience was shared by many contemporary Canadian modernists, most notably by Voaden's close friend Lowrie Warrener but also by Kathleen Munn, Frederick Varley, Emily Carr, and Samuel Borenstein, each of whom has strong expressionist qualities.

To translate such a vision on to the stage, however, required a dramatist sensitive to the vision and able to move beyond realism to expressive form. Voaden's first attempt to describe what was needed appeared in the introduction to *Six Canadian Plays*. Quoting Whitman at length and calling for an idealism and dedication typified by Harris and the Group, Voaden presents his plea for a Canadian art of the theatre. Beginning with our painters, he explains, we are 'making the journey that Whitman made' by discovering the grandeur and inspiration of this land and the new forms and 'unfettered' style needed to express that experience. Therefore, he announces, 'this volume is dedicated to the north' because the northern spirit differentiates and defines us: 'It has a "spiritual clarity" which flows into our lives and makes them clearer and richer, giving distinction and national character to our idealism.'[19] But Voaden does not stop with this statement of faith. He goes on to explain how we can create 'a tradition in the staging of plays that will be an expression of the atmosphere and character of our land' (xxi). Although there should always be realist and historical Canadian plays, the best way to write about the 'spiritual clarity' and idealism of the north is in expressionist plays; therefore, according to Voaden, we must embark on a 'search for new forms' using dance, music, and the visual arts, which allow our 'innate ideality [to] force itself on our art' (xxiii). His example of what can be done with movement, light, design, and speech in order to stage a play is Toller's *Masses and Man*.

Until 1930 Voaden had tried to express his ideas in three different plays. *The White Kingdom* (1928), *Northern Storm: A Drama in Three Scenes* (1929), and *Northern Song: A Play of the North in Three Scenes* (1930) clearly demonstrate the steps he took in forging a theatre language suited to his evolving sense of northern nationality and subjective vision.[20] *The White Kingdom* is a slight piece portraying a vaguely symbolic but autobiographical quest for meaning on the part of a disillusioned yet idealistic young hero, and it is in many ways the thematic prototype of Voaden's later plays. *Northern Storm* is Voaden's first attempt to grapple with a northern setting that mirrors the inner turmoil of the characters. Although it is not expressionist, let alone symphonic, it illustrates very well the deeply ambiguous feelings about the north expressed in Voaden's work; this mysterious northland is at once powerful, beautiful, terrifying, and ruthlessly destructive. The play ends with suicide and defeat. And although Voaden struggles to transform defeat into the spiritual victory of transfiguration in subsequent plays, the presence of death and a brooding, ominous nature persist. *Northern Song* (the two plays are entirely different except for the use of a northern setting) demonstrates Voaden beginning to work with an expressionist monologue strategy, but the play remains theoretical and chatty; it is a statement of ideas about the north by an artist and his friend, not a play. The real breakthrough for Voaden came in the summer of 1930.

During a transcontinental trip with Lowrie Warrener, the two men co-authored what would be Voaden's first attempt at 'symphonic expressionism,' the expressionist *tour de force* in five movements called *Symphony: A Drama of Motion and Light for a New Theatre*. In letters and diaries written over the course of the trip, Voaden explained excitedly what they were trying to do: 'I think of expressionistic symphonic action – someone mad or dreaming – these great forms [around the North Shore of

Lake Superior] pulsing and sweeping by.' A few days later he wrote, 'Lowrie has just done the first drawing for the expressionistic drama ... It's fine.'[21] But both men were fully aware of the terrible side of the natural world around them, as is clear from Voaden's diary note: 'Do not carry too far the emotional intimacy with nature: it will make you mad.'

This stunning work, which Voaden called 'a painter's ballet,' is without dialogue and consists of brief story synopses for each of its five 'movements' and instructions for setting, music, dancers' movements, and light. The story is to be 'sung by chorus, or solo voice, or spoken' as a recitative before each movement. The actors, simply called Man, Woman, and Child act out the hero's pilgrimage from a Moloch-like metropolis, reminiscent of Lang's film or of the infernal, whirling cities of expressionist paintings such as Meidner's *The City and I* (see Plate 22). Voaden's characters meet with personal tragedy amidst a northern lake scene when the Child drowns and the Woman dies, and later when Man meets death amidst a terrifying mountain scene in the final movement. Like Kaiser's Cashier, Man breaks free from the madness and brutality of the city in a dramatic *Aufbruch* at the end of the first movement, only to find death beneath a great white cross of mist, recalling the Salvation Army cross in *From Morn to Midnight*. The northern scenes are extraordinary, especially in the second movement when Man encounters the wilderness, and his fears, very like Emperor Jones's, spring to life, or in the final visionary, quasi-Christian death scene. Here as in his subsequent plays, the harsh 'spiritual clarity' of the north and the final scene of light-filled transfiguration (recalling the symbolic light in a Harris canvas; see Plate 28) express the intensity of Voaden's idealism. Here there is no ironic undercutting of Man's journey, as occurs with the power shortage at the end of Kaiser's play, because in Voaden's play *nature's* radiant light images affirmation.

Symphony was first published in 1982, one year before Warrener's death, and despite several attempts by Voaden to interest composers and choreographers in Canada, England, and the United States, it has never been produced.[22] No final judgments can be made of any play based on the text alone, but this is even more the case with a work like *Symphony*. Very possibly the use of light and music at the end of the drama would succeed in projecting the type of affirmative, celebratory vision that Voaden sought. Nevertheless, as written, the apocalyptic ending, with Man plunging to his death and a radiant morning sun flooding the mountain peak, leaves the reader with the impression that the hero's union with a formidable nature in death, rather than leading to his rebirth or attainment of vision, is his only route to peace after a life's journey of acute pain, suffering, madness, and loss. The closing gesture of Man's reaching up before he drops 'out of sight into the mist below,' followed by 'appalling silence. Sudden darkness' (83), is regressive; Man succumbs and nature triumphs. The expressionist New Man is defeated.

In order to preserve the work from labels such as 'gloomy' and 'morbid,' Voaden later revised the ending to depict a triumphant hero waking from sleep to worship the sun, but this conclusion contradicts the dramatic logic of the play, and in its published version the original closing scene is retained. That dramatic logic is developed through the rich semiotic texture of the orchestration, which is without doubt the most innovative and complex aspect of the work. From the outset words play a minor role in *Symphony* because the story is both temporally and spatially separated from the diegesis: a chorus or solo voice introduces the subsequent action. The heart and soul of this 'play' is its orchestration of light, music, dance movement by a trained ballet, and gesture and pantomime to express emotion, conflict, and event. A brief 'reading' of the light/colour signs will, perhaps, suggest what the overall impact of the work would be.

Throughout, the emphasis is on an intense chiaroscuro, with sharply contrasting areas of light and shadow used to evoke fear, despair, and menace. For example, in the second movement, which takes place in a northern wilderness, 'shadowy black shapes' emerge from the 'complete darkness' in the wings and at the back of the stage (77). Then, 'as shadows and forms twist and glide, vague lights appear and disappear, enhancing the effect of weird terror ... in the face of Man' (77). Effective as the use of chiaroscuro would be on the stage, the use of coloured light is still more fascinating. With the exception of the fourth movement on the prairies, where a somewhat uninspired and naturalistic use of browns and greens is called for, three highly symbolic colour-codes are manipulated, almost like visual motifs, to express the characters' feelings and to convey symbolic meaning. Reds and oranges dominate the hellish metropolis: 'Dim red lights appear in the apartment silhouetting a line of dark shapes which make a distorted shadow pattern against the walls' (76), and then a great whirling disk, rising above a flight of steps at centre-stage to suggest both the demonic soul of the city and the mechanical, dehumanized existence of the inhabitants, 'flames into a red ball of fire' that seems to suck up the figures before it and fling them into the dark, surrounding void.

Grey light is used at several points as a sign with seemingly different indexical and iconic values, depending on its tone. Thus, 'grey-blue' light is used to spot-light Man in the city with 'hair dishevelled, face drawn and haggard, and the eyes of a madman' (75). The cold grey-blue will at once locate and differentiate the Man from his red context and express his inner dread at the encroaching threat of a mechanical existence. At the end of the second movement, when Man comes closest to *Erlösung* amidst the northern wilderness, Voaden calls for his silhouette to rise against 'the clear light of the sky' and the entire scene to be bathed 'in a mysterious sheen of silver-grey light' (78): the closer grey comes to white, the greater its spiritually positive and visionary semantic burden. Pure white is reserved for the light at the closing moments of the play, after Man's death, when the radiant mountain peak towers free of shadow and mist.

Yellow is the most interesting of the colours in *Symphony* because every time it appears, it signifies distress or disaster, from the 'ghastly yellow-grey' (76) of the city to the 'dim yellow light' (79) that picks out the coffin in the third movement and the 'yellow light playing about' the Man at the end of the fourth movement, when he stands 'in a drooping crucified posture' (82), utterly defeated by the prairie. In the last glimpse of Man, before he plunges to his death, he is virtually obliterated by shadow and mist until a 'violent lightning flash' illuminates him in what would probably be a sharp yellowish-white light, just as he sways and falls. Clearly, Voaden and Warrener were using a psychological colour theory in *Symphony*, one that closely parallels, if it is not directly influenced by, that of Kandinsky, for whom yellow is 'earthly' or 'sickly' and represents 'the manic aspect of madness,' while white is a great spiritual silence 'pregnant with possibilities.'[23]

The consistent use of light throughout the play leads me to conclude that the rhetoric of colour in *Symphony* signifies an annihilating defeat for Man in the *Stationen* of his life. Though he can escape the orange-red inferno of the city, he cannot free himself from matter, death, and decay, signified by yellow, to achieve for himself the spiritual purity inherent in nature and signified by white. The kinesics and musical language of *Symphony*, such as these can be imagined from a written text, *seem* to reinforce this colour-sign system with, in the final movement, for example, violent, agitated, and threatening music preceding Man's death, shifting to mournful, austere phrases which then give way to a 'tumultuous and triumphant' (83) finale with the white light shining on the mountain. Dance and gesture motifs from earlier scenes are repeated at the end by the accompanying dance figures, perhaps to suggest the projection of Man's continuous fears and memories of the past. But the last movements seen on the stage are the vertical gestures of luminous 'dream figures,' which precede the closing vision of sunlight on mountain peak, thereby suggesting the glorification of nature, not of Man, who has fallen from sight into the void.

Although Voaden never again attempted anything quite so ambitious and unusual, many of the symphonic expressionist techniques developed for *Symphony* recur in the later plays. This essential vision is articulated clearly here for the first time and in the full realization that his new abstract, emotional art of the theatre, like that total art combining music, image, words, and gesture sought by Kandinsky, must express the 'inner necessity' of the soul.

Voaden's first full-scale symphonic expressionist *play*, the 1932 *Rocks*, was based upon the earlier *Wilderness*, a starkly realist text depicting the responses of two women to the wilderness that claims the man they love. In *Wilderness* Ella Martin, the mother, resents and resists the land to the bitter end: 'Too much woods – too much rock.'[24] However, Mary, the dead man's fiancée, finally accepts its indomitable spirit and embraces its mysterious beauty as the young man had done: 'I too shall hear the wilderness calling, calling my life into a great adventure. It will be my land. I'll belong to it. I'll be part of its winds and woods and rocks' (96). To create *Rocks*, Voaden 'abstracted' *Wilderness* by replacing realistic sets with stylized platforms and rocks (see Plate 27), by making the characters more symbolic through ritualized movement and speech, and by adding music (for violin and cello), drum-beats, dancers, and 'light-colour orchestration.'

As the title-page of the original typescript shows (see Figure 4), Voaden divided the stage into symmetrically balanced playing areas defined by lighting, and he reserved centre-stage for the Jessner-like platform, steps, and stool where key moments of crisis and transfiguration would occur. Page fifteen of the typescript illustrates how carefully Voaden orchestrated the elements of voice, dancers' movements, music, space, and coloured light to achieve his effects: spots express the intensity of the women's emotions; cello and violin convey their moods and carry the mood-themes of the play; the dancers mime the unspoken thoughts, memories, or dreams of the women (in a kind of literal because physical stream of consciousness), and the shifting light on the cyclorama evokes the menace or the beauty of nature. Throughout, Voaden employs a 'sinister drum beat' (reminiscent of *The Emperor Jones*) to suggest a unity between subjective and objective forces.

As he explained in a 1932 *Globe* article, the result was the 'symphonic expressionism' needed to embody his personal vision of the north:

> The North is viewed as a participant in the action, an unseen actor. To present this theme effectively every means has been utilized. The lighting constantly varies in intensity as the moods of the characters change. The whole stage has been rigorously divided into areas, each of which has a

separate emotional or mood tone. Through these the characters move as
their emotions change. To secure clarity the movements have been stylized
and completely simplified. The areas have been arranged geometrically
and in balance, with only formal screens framing the proscenium to local-
ize the action. The cyclorama lighting, which is also a constant variant
in both intensity and color, expresses the North. The whole movement of
the lighting is symphonic. It should be considered as an actor, the personi-
fied North. [25]

Clearly, Voaden's symphonic technique here is at the service of his
conception of art, which in turn provides one mode, possibly the most
effective one, for expressing the north and the conflict created *within*
human beings who inhabit, and to a great extent internalize, a northern
landscape.

Judging by reviews, contemporary audiences were deeply moved by
what they saw. [26] Although it is difficult to visualize *Rocks* today or to
comment upon what a symphonic expressionist production would achieve,
at least a few observations can be made. What Voaden wanted in this and
subsequent plays was an orchestral, not a dramatic statement, so that in
spite of the amount of movement by the actors, dancers, and light, the
ultimate effect would be one of an almost plastic or architectural stasis.
The simplicity of the acausal story – it is scarcely a plot – reinforces the
static nature of the play because the fundamental situation of death and
loss is present from the outset, instead of developing from character
interaction or sequences of events. The two women intoning their lines
from opposite sides of the stage represent the eternal opposites of age and
youth, darkness and light, despair and hope central to the timeless
structure of myth. Indeed, Voaden captures something of this archetypal
opposition in the almost antiphonal dialogue; for example, in the two
speeches quoted above the old woman speaks in short, abrupt, laconic
phrases while Mary responds in a more lyrical, impassioned language.
The theme of the play, like the theme of Sheila Watson's novel *The
Double Hook*, is neither the darkness nor the glory of this northern life but
man's acceptance of its duality and balance; hence, the light at the end of
the play is an important symbol of the young woman's mystical experience
of unity with the land.

Of Voaden's four remaining plays, *Earth Song* (1932), *Hill-Land* (1935),
Murder Pattern (1936), and *Ascend as the Sun* (1942), only *Ascend as the
Sun* has not been published to date. [27] With the exception of *Murder
Pattern*, in which Voaden was tied to an actual event, the other three
plays all exemplify, to one degree or another, Voaden's idealistic and

<u>ROCKS</u>

A Play of Northern Ontario

Text of symphonic production with setting, music,
movements for actors and dancers, and light-colour
orchestration

Characters

Ella Martin

Mary Brown

Maxwell.....the station agent

Ed and Bill Keenan..lumbermen

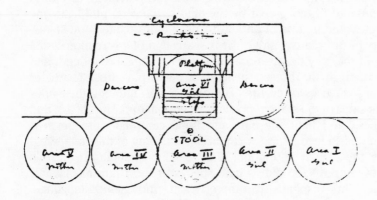

Note: Areas II and IV are further upstage,
in the line between the outer areas and the stool.

FIGURE 4

Title page and page fifteen of Herman Voaden's typescript for the 'symphonic
expressionist' production of *Rocks* (1932)

the likes", then dims to 2/8 on "neither".)

MRS. MARTIN (With this second outcry, her light builds to 6/8
on "never love you", dropping to 3/8 on "him" and
holding through the second sentence.) He'd never
love you the way y'love him. An' the years 'd only
make it worse. (Her light flares up to 7/8 on
"bush-crazy" then drops to 4/8 on "was", builds to
full on "mad" and drops to 3/8 at the end of the sentence.)
Bush-crazy he was! Strange an' mad as them hills out
there. (Her dancers lift higher as they remember
Blake's strangeness.) He liked the woods more'n
he liked you 'r me. (The cyclorama lights change to
a low menacing green. One the first "never've belonged"
MRS. MARTIN's light builds to 5/8, dropping back to
2/8 on "us". On the second it flares to 7/8 again,
dimming to 2/8. Her dancers are less wild, but bitter
still, following the same rhythm as the lights. A slow
sinister drum beat increases to a climax on "belonged".)
He'd never've belonged to either of us. He'd never've
belonged!

(As the cello theme is played the cyclorama sky
changes to a low blue. The light on the rocks dims.
MRS. MARTIN's dancers are old and wise, but MARY's
dancers sense the hope and belief of Blake.)

MRS. MARTIN It's a lonely land. It's as lonely now as it was a
thousand years ago. We come and go. Only the rocks
remain.

(The blue sky brightens while the violin theme is
played. The dancers echo the light-dark confrontation.)

romantic vision of Man's search for and discovery of godhead through a mystical union with the divine spirit in nature. Adam's words in *Earth Song* – 'New meanings flash upon me. New purposes are born. The sky is flooded with light. The sun will soon rise. The sun of a new life'[28] – while sharply reminiscent of the language used by the German expressionists' New Man, has a lyrical optimism and unequivocal affirmation distinct from the rest of his work, possibly because here Voaden is openly using symbols of man and woman instead of invented dramatis personae in order to express his idea. One interesting feature should be noted, however. In *Earth Song* Voaden displaces the full expressionist *Angst* so familiar from the hero's search and ordeal in the German plays, and in *Symphony*, by having his heroine, Eve, see what is happening to her Adam during his search, in visions reflected in the pool before her. Staring horrified at the image of his ordeal, she cries: 'A blinding vortex of light swallows you up. You emerge helpless, staggering, to plunge into another. You stumble and fall' (17). Neither Adam nor the audience directly experiences the torments that assail him because they are merely reported in the conventional, symbolic terms used by Eve. As a result the prime focus of the work remains the recurrent apocalypse of nature, and attention is never diverted from the movement towards ritual reunion, renewal, and rebirth that *Earth Song* enacts.

Structured around the cycle of the seasons, the play seems static and stylized well beyond dramatic interest, but in performance it may well have met Craig's demand for a theatre of divine beauty and spiritualism. Certainly, *Earth Song* stands at the very opposite extreme from that other primitive expressionist ritual, Kokoschka's *Murder, Hope of Women*. And the differences between these two extraordinary plays serve as reminders of the parameters of expressionist theatre.

Although it has a plot – a young man's acceptance through personal tragedy of the eternal processes of renewal and the transfiguring power of the north – *Hill-Land* is marred by too many lyrical passages about the 'rapture of the north-land' and the 'godhood' of the young lovers.[29] The play uneasily straddles the two tendencies in Voaden's work – the expression of a highly autobiographical and romantic vision and the struggle of believable characters for an understanding of their land. While the first lends itself to poetry and lyrical monodrama, the second gives wider scope to dramatic expressive form. In *Hill-Land* the two tendencies do not mesh, and the play as a whole, while requiring the full symphonic treatment of light, movement, music, and a chorus of voices in addition to the actors, seems for the most part closer to the idealized abstraction of *Earth Song* than to the more powerful iconic expressionism of *Rocks*.

Murder Pattern, first produced in 1936, is Voaden's best-written play because it represents his most successful fusion of traditional action with symphonic expressionist dramaturgy. The story is based on an actual murder in the Haliburton area north of Toronto and on the murderer's subsequent release from prison just before his death from consumption. But the 'pattern' of the play is not the sequence of events leading up to the murder, or even the series of events after it, so much as the pattern of loneliness and terror created by a majestic yet alienating environment that slowly drives men mad. Once again, as in *Rocks* and *Hill-Land*, Voaden's real protagonist is the north, and in order to evoke the spirit of the land he draws on all the resources of his expressionist method.[30]

Because it is a sequence of brief scenes punctuated only by shifts in lighting or by drum-beats and music, the visual and emotional effect of the play is one of a sustained moment in which the opening murder prefigures and balances the closing death scene. Although there are two named characters, Jack Davis the murderer and Steven Doan his victim, the other characters are not particularized beyond their roles as farmer, reporter, attorney, or narrator. The most impressive actors in the play are the various voices, especially the hooded Earth Voices, who personify the land, and their stylized movements and lyrical speech provide the important sense of hope and transcendent peace that concludes the play. At one point other accusing and friendly voices seem to close in upon the sleeping Davis in a typical expressionistic nightmare scene using a telegraph style:

> FRIENDLY ONE: *Both are moving steadily close to the sleeper.* Lost! Lost!
> ACCUSING ONE: Nearer, nearer! Coming to get you!
> FRIENDLY ONE: No! No!
> ACCUSING ONE: Almost at the door. Yes. Quick! Jump! Ah!
> FRIENDLY ONE: *At the same moment.* Gone, saved!   (110)

Voaden handles language and voice effectively throughout *Murder Pattern*, creating a rough colloquial speech for his farmers and a clipped, objective speech (heavy in passive verbals) for his reporters and narrators. These voices provide an effective contrast to the lyricism of the Earth Voices, and together the voices create tonal and emotional breadth:

> SECOND EARTH VOICE: The fear of death possesses the land. No wind stirs, the clouds press close upon the hills. The vast plains of water are still and dark, the black swamps are breathless, and the forests are silent as the grave. *Music.*

THIRD FARMER: I don't care what he done. There's no excuse for any man doin' away with another.

SECOND FARMER: You're wrong there. Whoever it was done the country a service.

SECOND REPORTER: The murderer is still at large, but the police are pressing the search, and arrests are expected within the next few days. From one source it is learned that feuds have existed within the Doan family circle for several years. (107)

Voice and language, even dialogue in *Murder Pattern*, are not used primarily to develop character or forward plot but to express the fluctuating moods of the land and its people, the patterns of loneliness, fear, hope, and peace that shape existence. Through this variety in voice and language Voaden suggests the conjunction of timelessness with the particular moment, of the vastness of space with a small, isolated existence, and of the objective reality of facts with the subjective reality of emotion. In fact, he has gone a considerable way towards expressing that essentially non-dramatic Canadian myth of the north.

Murder Pattern does not conclude with the spiritual affirmation symbolized by light in the other plays, but Voaden does use the Earth Voices to create a symbolic and moving conclusion. Their lines are among his very best, and the sets for his original production suggest that the scene with Davis on his stylized bier must have been impressive in its formal balance and severity.[31] However, expressionist *Erlösung* cannot belong to this character, as it does to Mary in *Rocks*, Adam and Eve in *Earth Song*, and the young heroes in *Hill-Land* and *Ascend as the Sun*; instead, it is articulated and visualized for us through the final image of Davis and the closing words of the Earth Voice: 'Your dreams shall blow steadily in the eternal winds. In them your spirit shall brood and pass endlessly among the hills ... lonely and enduring as the hills' (117).

Ascend as the Sun (1942) is Voaden's last completed play. Here he uses both light and musical phrases in a leitmotiv manner very much influenced by Wagner, whose subjects and musical structure he had in mind when creating *Ascend*. The staging called for in this play is also of considerable interest, and in its combination of realism and expressionism it recalls O'Neill's efforts with *Dynamo*. Voaden locates a realistic interior for the hero's home at the front of the stage, while above and behind it, on elevated platforms, he places dancers and figures that express the dreams and subconscious of the characters as well as the wider cosmic forces intersecting with their lives. When *Ascend as the Sun* was produced at the Hart House Theatre in Toronto, 13–16 April 1942, Voaden was able to do, for the first time, what had proved impossible with *Symphony*; he engaged a professional composer, Godfrey Ridout, for the score and Boris Volkoff's dancers for the choreography. Voaden's symphonic expressionist drama was well received by most reviewers, who seemed to feel that this complex semiotic mixture of words, gestures, music, dance, mime and light, together with a combined realistic and expressionistic staging, constituted an effective theatrical experience.[32]

Although overburdened by too much philosophical statement and obvious Christian symbolism, *Ascend* has some powerful expressionist scenes in which the young man, newly set out on life's journey, encounters the terrifying forces of spiritual and sexual doubt. The play is structured in eighteen scenes or vignettes that, like the *Stationen* of the German plays, bear little causal relation to each other; instead they portray the stages of development, at times the soul-states, of the young hero. (Elements of Christian allegory and pilgrimage recall Strindberg's *To Damascus*, and *Ascend* was originally intended as part one of a trilogy.) After a harrowing struggle with the temptation to commit suicide, expressed through the symphonic means of dancers, music, and choral accompaniment and during which voices of good and evil babble conflicting advice and 'immense groping shadows' surround him, David achieves an affirmation of life in which he proclaims: 'I believe in myself.' The play ends in a flood of light 'pulsing, invading, affirming; victorious over the retreating shadows,' and the chorus announces 'the birth of a new man, the making of a nobler man.'[33]

The title of the play, as the narrator-figure the Biographer tells us, comes from Whitman: 'We also ascend, dazzling and tremendous as the sun,' but 1942 was a difficult year in which to complete this portrait of the New Man, and Voaden could not sustain belief in his optimistic vision. Rather than breaking new ground either thematically or formally, *Ascend as the Sun* looks backwards and marks a recapitulation of Voaden's deeply autobiographical concerns and a further refinement of his symphonic expressionist techniques. As a restatement of his faith in the New Man, *Ascend as the Sun* had, emphatically if ironically, outlived its own relevance. When he realized this, he turned his energies from creating original plays to adaptations, collaborative efforts, teaching and editing, and active politics and arts lobbying. Only one work from the post-1942 period warrants mention in this context, and that is his documentary-expressionist play based on the life of Canadian painter Emily Carr. *Emily Carr: A Stage Biography with Pictures*, begun in 1951 and not completed until 1958, is a fascinating interpretation of an artist with whom Voaden identified, and he hoped to give it a symphonic expressionist production with slide projections and music. In Voaden's hands Carr becomes the very figure of the suffering expressionist artist who struggles to express her soul through her vibrant images of a powerful, at times demonic-seeming, natural world.[34] Whether or not he is fair to Carr in his somewhat patriarchal view of her life, Voaden recognized and responded to the expressionistic qualities of Carr's art, and for that reason comes closer than anyone else to capturing the visionary quality of her work.[35]

Voaden's 'symphonic expressionism' was a complex aesthetic, a powerful method, and a religious vision. It was expressionist in theme and epistemology, in its portrayal of the soul-states of an autobiographical *Ich* or of the dreams and nightmares of characters and in its ecstatic expression of a mystic vision of union between the individual and a cosmic soul. It was symphonic in its orchestration of all the arts, and through this orchestration Voaden expressed his moments of vision. Most important, Voaden's symphonic expressionist plays represented a playwright's response to the northern challenge faced by all Canadian modernists.

Unfortunately, however, the impact of Voaden's 'epoch-making' theories on a future Canadian theatre was negligible. Only recently, and apparently without his influence, have we begun to have a drama that approaches the mythic concerns of Voaden by using some degree of orchestration and expressionism – as, for example, in Cook's *Jacob's Wake* (1975) and Ryga's *The Ecstasy of Rita Joe* (1970).[36] And in both these plays (especially in *Rita Joe*) encounter with northern landscape – whether of sea or mountains – is secondary to human conflict. It would seem that contemporary playwrights are wary of attempting to dramatize the experience of *North*, and if poets and novelists or a critic like Brian Parker are right, the playwrights are indeed wise: not only is the myth of the north 'antidramatic,' but the appropriate response to *North* is *silence*: the northern story resists its telling, refuses enactment.[37]

And yet ... Voaden's endeavour commands our attention because of its integrity and courage and because the results of his method and vision in the theatre were considerable. Despite the problems involved in assessing these plays as texts instead of as performances, some tentative observations about the nature of these symphonic expressionist plays can be made. Perhaps their most striking quality is an emotional expressiveness that arises less from language – our need to break the silence with words – than from a direct appeal to our sensitivity to sight, sound, colour, light, and rhythm. Such a theatre is at a far remove from both realism and Brechtian epic. Because of the stylization of the architectural sets and non-representational acting, Voaden's theatre is static; it is not an enactment of conflicts or dynamic process but the expression of man's search for a 'spiritual clarity' in harmony with his landscape.

To criticize these plays for lacking the traditional dramatic action of human conflict may be legitimate, but it neglects the central philosophic and religious thrust of so much expressionist art, which strives to penetrate through the shifting realities of a phenomenal world to illumination.[38] The cycles of nature, so important a symbol in Voaden's work, represent not the flux but the eternal return of life and rebirth, a reality transcending daily existence and a type of apocalyptic renewal. Furthermore, they correspond with the soul's inner truth in those ecstatic moments of vision that plays like *Symphony, Rocks, Earth-Song, Hill-Land, Ascend as the Sun,* and, in a more limited sense, *Murder Pattern* celebrate. Voaden's mythopoeic subject is the timeless, repetitive one of a hero's search for enlightenment, and his characters, for the most part, resemble god-like symbols who move through a northern landscape that mirrors their souls and controls their destinies.

PART THREE

Expressionism and the
Modern Novel

The Dark Night of the Soul: Djuna Barnes's Nightwood

Like the woman in the *douanier* Rousseau's *The Dream* (1910) with whom Robin Vote is compared, a reader of *Nightwood* may also feel bewitched, or trapped in 'the set, the property of an unseen *dompteur*, half lord, half promoter.'[1] The most unsettling thing for the reader of Djuna Barnes's extraordinary 1936 novel is that the *dompteur* is 'unseen' and that with every page he or she becomes less and less certain about the show. Indeed, few texts have sustained as many conflicting interpretations or caused so many genuine problems for their readers. Where is the centre of *Nightwood*, which chapter, which character or consciousness, which issue or theme? Who is Robin anyway, and what is the significance of the chapel scene at the end, with Robin on her hands and knees beside Nora's dog and before an altar? How does one make sense of, or even respond to, the apparently disordered and proliferating images, not only in Dr O'Connor's monologues, where the linguistic flights could be attributed to his drunkenness or inspiration, but also in passages of third-person narration? Of course, these kinds of questions reflect the reader's desire to order the text, to make sense of it, to explain either what it means or how it works, and this desire, problematic as it may be, is at least more legitimate than cursory dismissals of the novel as incoherent or degenerate. Yet *Nightwood* resists (I think, successfully defies) all *dompteurs*; even the narrator refuses to order or explain or privilege a character who can do so, and furthermore, the text transgresses our familiar codes for reading and writing novels.

Nightwood cannot, should not, be tamed. To attempt such a rational controlling is to reduce and explain away the power of the work; it is also to miss the point, because to read *Nightwood* is to experience a scream of pain, loss, dislocation, and repression (with perhaps a moment of *Erlösung* in the chapel scene). *Nightwood* is the expression of that suffering and indirectly a profound criticism of those aspects of modern society and human nature that cause such pain. It is important to stress that *Nightwood* expresses suffering rather than being *about* pain and its social, sexual, and psychological causes, because to persist in thinking of a modernist work of art like this one as if it were *about* something is to perpetuate a misconception about its aesthetic intention, its style, and its fictional mode. *Nightwood* is an essentially expressionist work of art; only by treating it as such can we see how it achieves its expressiveness and what that expressiveness signifies, without taming its terrible energy.

Because expressionism presents intense personal emotion as well as social protest in forms that resist representation, that use distortion and varying degrees of abstraction, and that stress themes of degeneration, disintegration, and apocalypse, it provides a frame of reference for *Nightwood* that is less static and narrow than surrealism and more illuminating than labels such as 'grotesque,' 'subjective feminine,' 'apprehended tableau,' and so on.[2] To see *Nightwood* as expressionist is also to see it within a modernist context, together with, for example, the plays of Strindberg and early O'Neill, or a later work like *Under the Volcano*. Finally, to see *Nightwood* as expressionist is to shed new light on its iconography, particularly in the portraits of its women, and to raise the whole issue of the place of the female artist within the expressionist movement.

There are many extrinsic and intrinsic reasons for thinking of *Nightwood* in expressionist terms. Certainly Barnes was familiar with Expressionism in painting, theatre, and very likely film (by the early twenties 'le caligarisme' was already in vogue in Paris). Born in 1892 on a farm at Hudson-on-Cornwall, New York, Barnes moved to New York City sometime between 1911 and 1912 to study painting, and by 1915 she had begun to gain a reputation in artistic and intellectual circles for her journalism, her early poems (*The Book of Repulsive Women*, 1915), and her personal style. She frequented Mabel Dodge's salon and Alfred Stieglitz's gallery '291' from 1914 on, and in both places she would have been able to discuss art with New York's avant-garde and to see the work of Cézanne, Matisse, Picasso, and the American expressionist painters Max Weber and Marsden Hartley, with whom, according to her biographer, Andrew Field, Barnes became very close friends. Hartley was a painter of reputation and notoriety during the early part of the century;

some of his *Dark Landscape* paintings were exhibited in New York in the spring of 1911, and in the fall of 1912 Hartley held his second one-man show at '291.' Later, in 1914, 1915, and 1916 there were exhibits of his German paintings and his 1909 *Dark Landscapes* at various New York galleries where Barnes would have had ample opportunity to see them.[3]

Barnes and Hartley remained friends, and she spent several months with him and his circle of German friends in Berlin in 1921, where she visited Herwarth Walden's Sturm gallery. On her frequent theatre outings she must have seen expressionistic productions by Jessner and Reinhardt (for example, the 1921 production of *A Dream Play*) and the plays of German expressionists such as the famous Berlin Volksbühne's 29 September 1921 première of Toller's *Masses and Man*. The early twenties marked the high point of Expressionism in Berlin theatres and elsewhere in Germany, and Barnes, with her intimate knowledge of the theatre, its styles, personalities, and avant-garde repertoire, described the German theatre (and cinema) as 'marvellous ... better than the theaters in France.'[4]

These interests in theatre and painting are of particular importance to a reading of Barnes, not only because they point to possible influences and are part of her milieu in New York, Paris, and Berlin, but also because she painted at several points in her life (two portraits of friends are highly expressionistic)[5] and illustrated many of her articles, poems, and fictions with grotesque, Art Nouveau sketches or with miniatures that have striking similarities to expressionist woodcuts. She owned a copy of August L. Mayer's 1918 *Expressionistische Miniaturen des deutschen Mittelalters*, and even if she could not read Mayer's essay explaining the links between these miniatures and Expressionism, the illustrations speak for themselves, and some of Barnes's work resembles them in subject and style.[6] The images of vampire-like women in *The Book of Repulsive Women* and of *Doppelgänger*, as in the illustration of Una and Lena for her short story 'The Earth,' an illustration that recalls Egon Schiele, begin to appear early in her work and are developed verbally in *Nightwood* and *The Antiphon*.

Three writers closely associated with Expressionism, Strindberg, Dostoevsky, and Synge, were of special importance to her during the twenties (she cites Strindberg's *Miss Julie* as inspiration for 'A Night Among the Horses'), and, given her close connection with the Provincetown group and O'Neill, she may have known Wedekind's plays (*Spring Awakening* and *Lulu* bear certain affinities with *Nightwood*) before leaving for Paris in 1920.[7] During the twenties and thirties she was following the newest publications of her contemporaries in the *Little Review* and *transition*, where Joyce's 'Work in Progress,' the bizarre dadist-expressionist work of Kurt Schwitters, and the unusual ideas of Eugene Jolas on dreams expressing the soul were appearing. It is clear from some of her earlier journalism that she attended the cinema, and in view of her intellectual circle it would be surprising if she had missed *The Cabinet of Dr Caligari*, which is in so many ways the archetype of Expressionism and of the anti-representational tendencies of the early modern period.

Barnes's biography and milieu, however, only permit speculations about influences and models. To examine *Nightwood* itself is to return to the problem of fictional mode. Diegesis and discourse pull in two quite opposite directions in *Nightwood*, and the resultant tension is in large part responsible for the power and energy of the work, as well as for the problems readers face in coming to terms with it. The more one reads the novel, the more apparent is the story – a simple 'realistic' story of doomed love in a particular time and place. There are also five vivid characters who *at times* seem as realistic as the characters in Flaubert, Hardy, or Bennett. But these representational qualities, so familiar from traditional narrative, are frequently subsumed and finally overwhelmed by the abstracting pressure of the discourse and the way in which the characters are presented and the story told. For example, there is no definite hero or centre of consciousness (some critics favour the doctor, while others focus on Robin or Nora). Instead, Barnes gives us a web or constellation of interrelationships that centres upon the bewildering double image of Robin and Dr O'Connor, who oppose and yet complement each other, who never interact directly (except perhaps when he wakes her from her faint) and yet, like some fatal lodestone, draw all the others, Felix, Nora and Jenny, towards them.

To see the characters patterned in this way is to preserve their realistic

FIGURE 5

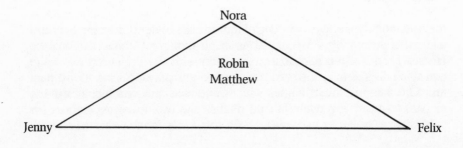

qualities – their separate, named identities, which point beyond them to briefly sketched biographies and pasts – while tracing an abstract design of their lives (see Figure 5). And it is this abstraction in presenting characters and story that bewilders the reader, who is searching for familiar realistic markers and representational codes. Barnes's use of abstraction is a function of her focus upon the inner life of the characters, an inner life presented not as a mimetic stream of consciousness but as the projection of these inner states through language, vivid scenes, and a patterning of human relationships. The vital tension she creates between representation and abstraction is perhaps the pivotal quality of *Nightwood* and of other successful expressionist works that, like Kaiser's *From Morn to Midnight*, *Caligari*, Kirchner's and Kokoschka's paintings, Barlach's woodcuts, and O'Neill's early plays, abstract and distort reality without losing touch with the human predicament that they express. Moreover, the distortion and abstraction of reality characteristic of expressionism in all the arts enables the artist to circumvent the 'banalities of surface' (which O'Neill deplored) that detract from the intense expression of the soul, that familiarize and tame the very forces that the expressionist believes must be acknowledged.

It will be necessary to return to this question of abstraction when considering narrative structure and characterization, but perhaps the most obvious expressionist quality of *Nightwood* is its subject matter, from its broadest themes to smaller touches of motif and allusion. T.S. Eliot was anxious to point out in his 1937 introduction to the novel that it is wrong to 'regard this group of people as a horrid sideshow of freaks' (6), and yet it is also important to recognize just how central the image of the circus is to *Nightwood*. Felix Volkbein seeks out circus performers as his special companions; indeed, it is Frau Mann, the trapeze artist, who initiates him into the infernal circus of his life: 'She looked at the Baron derisively. "Wir setzen an dieser stelle über den Fluss –" she said' (29). Nora comes to Paris because she is working for a circus company, and she and Robin, that wild thing caught in a woman's skin, finally meet back in New York at a circus. And Dr O'Connor has many circus attributes, from his prestidigitation at Robin's bedside to his clownish transvestism and extravagant rhetoric. Even as his ordinary self, stooped and in black, he recalls Caligari, that most infamous of Expressionism's quack doctors, the travelling *dompteur* of a somnambulist in his circus side-show at the local fair who uses the night for his acts of madness and murder. In fact the circus provides, together with the night, one of the key metaphors for setting and characterization in *Nightwood*. It is an important link with many other expressionist works (see Plate 2) where, in association with fairground settings and circle imagery, it images a world gone mad, out of control, bestial, licentious and grotesque.[8] Perhaps most significantly, the nightworld, whether on the streets of Paris or in rural New England, is increasingly established as an inner world, that dark side of the soul or psyche within each of us.

However, Eliot was right to warn against dismissing these characters as mere aberrations. The central thrust of the discourse is not to display freakishness but to reveal a terrible failure of love, what Walter Sokel sees as a major expressionist concern: the impotence of the heart.[9] Every one of the characters, not just Robin, is alienated from his or her time and place, living in a kind of perpetual exile from any kind of spiritual or physical home, constantly on the move and searching for 'permission to live' (168). That there are sociological and psychological reasons for this impotence and exile is true: Felix is a victim of his race, Nora of her narcissism. But more to the point, these characters suffer their despair and loss before us, and we are obliged to experience the full force of their outcry. If we can accept this assault, then, as Eliot suggests, we will realize that we are all 'eaten by the same worm' (6), that what looks like morbid abnormality or extreme distortion is an expression of a 'universal malady,' a sickness, or more neutrally, a suffering of the human soul.

Because sexuality and bestiality are so often linked in discussions of *Nightwood*, usually to explain the collapse and failure of its characters, it is especially important to point out how these two ideas, often but not always linked, are treated in expressionist works (and I shall return to this point when considering Robin).[10] The cult of the primitive and its associations with the human psyche were scarcely new ideas in the thirties; the theories of Freud and Jung were followed avidly in intellectual circles; Rousseau's last great 'primitive' canvas, *The Dream*, was exhibited in 1910; the violent colour and subject matter of the Fauves (in particular of Rouault and Matisse) had long since contributed to the expressionist movement in Germany, and Stravinsky's *Rite of Spring* (1913) was already twenty years old when *Nightwood* was being written. But the idea of mankind's being caught between the spiritual and the bestial is an especially common one in Expressionism, where the closer men and women come to the beasts, the greater their potentially destructive energy and sexuality will be. As Theodor Daubler remarked in his 1916 essay 'The New Standpoint': 'To return to the beast through art is our commitment to Expressionism,' and in his savage play *The Wolves* (1922) Alfred Brust gave explicit dramatic treatment to the idea.[11]

This split between the bourgeois, socially acceptable, ordered surfaces of life and the powerful, instinctual depths is one of the most seductive and ambiguous aspects of German Expressionism. In the hands of artists like Marc, Kokoschka, Toller, and Döblin and of numerous theorists it becomes the crucial dualism fuelling their protest against society. Or as Carol Duncan says of these artists: 'In their eyes, to exercise and express one's unfettered instinctual powers was to strike a blow against, to subvert, the established order.'[12]

For the expressionists, the sexual (and bestial) basis of human nature was the source of tremendous creative energy, which was being repressed (or so they felt) by contemporary society, and this in turn meant that people lived in exile either from themselves, their own souls or inner nature, or from a society that rejected them as dangerous because depraved – Hitler's adjective was 'entartete.' Franz Marc took this obsession with primitive animal energy a step further by portraying in painting after painting his idealistic view of the animal as symbolic of a harmonious natural world. Marc's 'animalization,' as he called it, represents his longing to return to a life free of crippling bourgeois constraints, to liberate the instinctual life, and to escape a degenerate society. As Frederick Levine stresses in his study of Marc, the animal and its associations with an irrational, pre-cognitive state had become an increasingly positive symbol by the early twentieth century, and this view, as well as Marc's striking example, should be kept in mind when assessing the conclusion of *Nightwood*.[13]

It has been said that expressionists in America shared a deep sense of alienation and exile, that they were either literally or spiritually (or both) living in exile, and the idea has special appeal in any attempt to understand Djuna Barnes and why she was drawn, like Marsden Hartley before her, to expressionist methods.[14] In a sense living in exile all her life, but particularly during the writing of *Nightwood*, Barnes has expressed that feeling of being exiled from one's inner life – the soul – with all the ambiguity implicit in German Expressionism. Throughout her work, but especially in *Nightwood* and *The Antiphon*, Barnes shows us that, on the one hand, we can deny those instinctual urges and, by driving them underground, destroy them, while on the other hand they remain hard to destroy and once let loose may threaten the individual and society. Either way these instincts cannot be tamed into placid co-existence with our rational strivings or domestic orderings; instead they must be accepted as part of us in a gesture that risks everything. All the people in *Nightwood* fail in their taming attempts and remain trapped in what Barnes calls 'the halt position of the damned' because, in her vision of life, the instinctual forces manifest in our affinities with animals or in our sexuality are the source of our suffering and damnation as well as of our joy and salvation.

In *Nightwood* Barnes has given full expression to that profound paradox: sexuality and a closeness to animals (to speak of bestiality is to speak pejoratively) is both an expression of a more complete humanity and an annihilation of what makes us distinctly human. Consider that final scene. What does Nora see from the chapel door on that night? An image of final degradation (she certainly does not see attempted intercourse, as some critics suggest) in the *lowering* of human to animal, a collapse into madness, an evil ritual or sort of black mass from which she draws back in horror and disgust? Or a primitive, sacred ritual, an ecstatic, celebratory rite in honour of a life-force running through all things, an expressed desire for worship, an image of ultimate humility and fellowship that enables her to understand herself and Robin? *Nightwood* leaves us with no simple, rational answer, only (and it is all) the exhausting experience of its emotion.

On more than one occasion *Nightwood* has been compared with the drama, but to speak loosely of its tragic or dramatic qualities is to say no more than can be said of many great novels, and to attempt to force it into a classic five-act mould is to do obvious violence to the text.[15] While the mood of the novel resembles that of Jacobean tragedy, and its rich language, like Lowry's in *Under the Volcano*, echoes the Elizabethans, the text has a highly fragmented structure of disjunct scenes. The chapters are not primarily associated through plot in an ongoing sequence of events (although the basic plot-line does exist and runs through each chapter). Instead, each is a separate expression of inner need, an exploding out of emotion rather than a probing into it that leads to increased understanding of pain, as Joseph Frank suggests.[16] Each chapter is like the others in this way, and each adds to the cumulative impact of the text. There is definitely a sense of building climax in the narrative, which splits at the end into the sound and fury of Matthew's collapse in chapter 7 and the silent ordeal of Robin in chapter 8, but there is no resolution, no dénouement, no return to the orderly surfaces of life.

If we are to compare the structure of *Nightwood* with the drama at all, then it should be with the famous *Stationen* of expressionist plays, where instead of the conventional three- or five-act form the playwright uses a series of loosely connected, vividly realized scenes. *The Emperor Jones* and *The Hairy Ape*, or Kaiser's *From Morn to Midnight*, Hasenclever's *Mankind*, and Strindberg's *To Damascus* are all fine examples of the form. Like them, *Nightwood*'s paratactic structure allows Barnes to do two related things: to disrupt the plot, and thereby weaken our grasp upon the superficial elements of a fairly realistic story and to focus attention on the language, imagery, and monologues that carry the expressive power of each separate scene. Typically, expressionist plays end with a violent outburst of emotion, with a death or a quasi-apocalyptic moment of vision, but not with a sense of evil purged and a restoration of order.

One further point might be made about the structure of *Nightwood*, and that has to do with Barnes's handling of time. Although there are dates that the reader can use to establish a chronology for the story, sequential, chronological time is not of particular importance in *Nightwood*, especially after the stage is set in chapter 1. The increasing disregard for causality and temporal specificity is yet another result of the abstraction of the story by the discourse. Nevertheless, there is one point in time, one night to be exact, that has pre-eminence, and each of chapters 3, 4, and 5 comes to rest on that night. This is 'the night' Matthew expatiates on in 'Watchman, What of the Night?' – the night we saw from the narrator's objective perspective in 'The "Squatter"' and the night we suffered through with Nora in 'Night-Watch.' It is the night that the doctor, Jenny, Robin, and the child, Sylvia, go riding in the Bois de Boulogne and Jenny attacks Robin in the carriage, only to embrace her later in the garden of Nora's home on the rue du Cherche-Midi as Nora watches. It is the night of multiple betrayals glimpsed again and again, but only in parts, as if in a nightmare. Not until and unless we place the three chapters together so that they overlap in retrospect are we able to unravel the events of that night. By presenting a rather simple sequence of events detailing jealousy, love, and betrayal in this fragmented way and from three points of view, Barnes can concentrate her efforts and our attention upon the emotional impact of the events instead of the events themselves.

No discussion of *Nightwood* can advance very far without considering the language. It is unusually rich, allusive, evocative and visual, and perhaps most important, it is highly sensuous, appealing directly to our senses through its imagery and frequently baffling any logical attempt to understand. *Nightwood* is a primarily metaphoric text, and this is fully consistent with its fragmented structure, its patterning of character and event, and its expressionism. A charge often levelled at the text is that its extreme metaphoricity is confusing and incoherent because Barnes's metaphors do not behave in the ways we have come to expect, even in poetry. Although this is an accurate observation, the proliferating images are not a weakness in the writing. Barnes's images are expressionist because her metaphors are characteristically destabilized through catachresis.

In his discussion of imagery in expressionist writing, R.S. Furness makes some excellent points about the predominance of the image and the behaviour of metaphors, which tend 'to become more and more independent and increasingly "absolute"' until facts and events disappear behind proliferating associations and an 'extreme subjectivity' is created, either for a speaker (such as the character in a monologue) or for a presented character whose inner world erupts before us. 'The metaphor (or image),' Furness continues, 'becomes *expressive* rather than imitative, existing as a powerful, autonomous figure of speech from which radiate a host of evocative meanings.'[17] A number of problems surround the status and function of the expressionist image, and these can be taken up with a specific passage, but the point to stress now is that the expressionist writer foregrounds imagery in order to evoke emotion in the reader and to express the turbulent inner states or essences of the characters rather than to represent or imitate objective reality or to establish rational connections among disparate ideas and things. Expressionist fiction typically uses monologues instead of the mimetic stream of consciousness (or *monologue intérieur*) to express a character's subjectivity.

Furthermore, imagery, especially metaphor, in expressionist writing proliferates instead of organizing and stabilizing associations, so that the result for the reader can be either confusion or excitement, depending on individual response. In a perceptive close analysis of Barnes's style, Alan Singer claims that her figurative language makes representation highly ambiguous, and although he does not link his discussion to any concept of fictional mode or governing aesthetic intention, his points are directly relevant to expressionism in *Nightwood*. He begins by pointing out that in general Barnes's metaphors are digressive, independent of narrative logic (that is, the diegesis or story), and juxtapose 'wildly disparate contexts.' They constitute a catachrestic discourse in which contextual relevance and clear tenor/vehicle substitutions are ignored. Within what he calls Barnes's' 'destabilized trope' Singer finds that

> the complementarity of tenor and vehicle is undermined. The vehicle is
> no longer comfortably assimilable within the scope of the originally pre-
> figured tenor. Thus, instead of nourishing the literal intentionality of
> the tenor, this vehicle declares its own purpose within the discourse. The
> vehicle usurps the contextual ground of the trope by proliferating itself,
> and so the univocality of the generating sign is lost in the multiplicity of its
> dissemination.[18]

Singer has identified here what Furness described as the 'independent and increasingly "absolute"' quality of the expressionist image, and it coincides with the way Barnes uses metaphor to fragment, distort, and disrupt objective reality. These destabilized tropes, when experienced together with the long cumulative sentences and unusual verbs and syntax of Barnes's prose, constitute an expressionist style and release what Kristeva calls 'desire in language.'[19] The highly 'poetic' quality of key passages in *Nightwood* is a direct result of Barnes's stress upon the semiotic processes in language as opposed to its principal functions of nomination and predication. Because of this semiotic stress, her language can be said to reactivate (as Kristeva argues) repressed instinctual drives, including incest and bestiality; certainly it is an appropriate vehicle for the subject of *Nightwood*.

This semiotic, rhythmic language also coincides closely with the expressionistic theories of Eugene Jolas, theories with which Barnes must have been familiar from the pages of *transition*. According to Jolas, creative literature could only be reformed when language itself was freed from the constraints of pragmatism and materialism, which corrupt intuitive vision, and he saw this reform initiated by the expressionist's and dadist's 'violent onslaught on academic language.'[20] Among the Germans, he particularly praised the expressionists August Stramm (see pages 59–60 above), Gottfried Benn, Carl Einstein, and the 'primitive stammerings' of Kurt Schwitters (whose work he translated for *transition*), and with a few exceptions he criticized the linguistic and stylistic conventionality of French surrealists and English imagists. He praised Joyce, whose 'Work in Progress' he was publishing in *transition*, as the pre-eminent coiner of new words, but this stress upon neologism was only one aspect of the new, expressive 'language of night' that he championed. Words, for Jolas, were sacred, hallucinatory, giving shape to the primal 'matriarchal images' of the unconscious and pre-conscious 'night-mind' of the writer, whose task was to express, not to communicate. In a rather ecstatic passage from *The Language of Night*, Jolas chastises the utilitarianism of the age, and in a *style* echoing that of Nietzsche and the German expressionists, he concludes that the writer 'is no longer interested in the language of the nerves celebrated by the post-war epoch. The physical world collapses around him. He faces eternity. From the underworld, the tenebrous depths of his soul, he tries to emerge towards a Paradise of his own fashioning. He is not interested in changing the world. He only wants to change himself. His form is in movement. He struggles against nothingness. He composes the vision he suffers' (56).

According to Jolas, in order to compose this vision, the writer must draw upon the night-world of dream and hallucination (which he clearly saw in Jungian terms as the source of chthonic, primordial, telluric images) and be prepared to subvert the laws of grammar and syntax.

Whether deliberately or not, Barnes appears to have developed many of Jolas's ideas in *Nightwood* – even her title seems to gesture towards his monograph – and to have been particularly sensitive to his call for the expression of an inner vision through the primordial images of the imagination and a subversive rhetoric. Jolas's rather clumsy description of the 'primal man' within us as a 'visionary of nature' with a 'somnambulistic mind' is transformed by Barnes into the unforgettable Robin.

One of the most interesting moments in the text is that point in chapter 2, 'La Somnambule,' when we first see Robin. The introduction is unsettling because we do not learn who she is or what is wrong with her. Instead, the sensuous images present her primitive essence:

> On a bed, surrounded by a confusion of potted plants, exotic palms and cut flowers, faintly oversung by the notes of unseen birds, which seemed to have been forgotten – left without the usual silencing cover, which, like cloaks on funeral urns, are cast over their cages at night by good housewives – half flung off the support of the cushions from which, in a moment of threatened consciousness she had turned her head, lay the young woman, heavy and dishevelled. Her legs, in white flannel trousers, were spread as in a dance, the thick lacquered pumps looking too lively for the arrested step. Her hands, long and beautiful, lay on either side of her face.
>
> The perfume that her body exhaled was of the quality of that earth-flesh, fungi, which smells of captured dampness and yet is so dry, overcast with the odour of oil of amber, which is an inner malady of the sea, making her seem as if she had invaded a sleep incautious and entire. Her flesh was the texture of plant life, and beneath it one sensed a frame, broad, porous and sleep-worn, as if sleep were a decay fishing her beneath the visible surface. About her head there was an effulgence as of phosphorus glowing about the circumference of a body of water – as if her life lay through her in ungainly luminous deteriorations – the troubling structure of the born somnambule, who lives in two worlds – meet of child and desperado. (55–6)

There are two immediately conspicuous and disconcerting stylistic features of these paragraphs: first, the syntax is unusual because of the interrupted and complex predication and the considerable delay in naming the subject – 'the young woman' – of the opening sentence (this woman will go literally unnamed for several more pages); second, images swarm here in an overwhelming superabundance of modifiers, metonymies, similes, and metaphors. Because our arrival at the subject is delayed, we are first introduced to exotic plants and flowers and the music of unseen birds as if the foliage and imagined song (there are no birds, no cages left uncovered) should somehow explain what is 'on the bed.' We are led by the inverted syntax to expect that we will arrive at an understanding, but even the relatively straightforward sentences that follow 'heavy and dishevelled' are of little help: legs, shoes, hands, and face remain incongruous fragments in a logical and realistic context that refuses to take shape, metonymies for which the literal and metaphoric context is unclear. The cumulative right-branching clauses are representative of Barnes's style and add further to the proliferating, destabilizing effect of the prose. Even if the opening sentence were reversed into a more familiar English word order – 'The young woman, heavy and dishevelled, lay on a bed' – the sentence would still be paratactic, arching well beyond the woman figuratively (from her to the setting) and conceptually (from the question of her surprising condition to the mundane activities of 'good housewives'), before 'her head' returned us to the subject herself. The total effect of such a sentence is at once disorienting and expressive. The familiar purposes of descriptive sentences – to set a scene or introduce a character – are subverted, and the reader is denied a metonymically organized context that would explain the woman's presence.

The imagery of the second paragraph provides an excellent example of what Singer means when he says that 'the univocality of the generating sign is lost in the multiplicity of its dissemination.' Her body seems to have a life of its own, a life partaking of death, drowning, decay. The multiple associations of her body's perfume, her flesh, and her head do not add up to a single clear image of her dual state of life-in-death, her somnambulism, but radiate a troubling ambiguity in evocative, repellent touches. How can the 'odour of oil of amber' (the very sound and rhythm of the phrase is disturbing, distracting) be 'an inner malady of the sea'? How does this odour relate to such a sleep – 'incautious and entire'? How can sleep be a decay, let alone one that 'fishes,' and how does this metaphor relate to the flesh that began the sentence? Or to put it differently, what do dying sperm whales, which produce ambergris, have to do with Robin?

To pose these questions is to realize how pointless they are and how successful Barnes has been in forestalling them. Yet it could scarcely be said that this paragraph fails to communicate. It is one of the most strangely beautiful and haunting passages in modern prose. The two paragraphs together express Robin Vote in a mirror reflection; the first suggests her surfaces – partial, disordered, inexplicable; the second evokes her depths and expresses Robin by imaging those depths. It is hard to conceive a language that could better express, at one and the same time, that strange presence that is Robin and those deep, instinctual recesses of the soul or psyche normally repressed and held in check by the grammatical and rhetorical constraints of 'a civilization dominated by transcendental rationality.'[21] This is a foretaste of that night language, what Kristeva means by 'poetic language' – semiotic, heterogeneous to meaning, maternal, and incestuous – that will erupt in Dr Matthew Mighty-Grain-of-Salt Dante O'Connor's monologues.

When Dr O'Connor begins speaking, the story of *Nightwood* stops; discourse appears to run rampant, filling up the void left by the impossibility of meaning or explanation, desperately proclaiming the existence of the self and denying the terrors of silence. *Nightwood* is, in fact, a novel filled with talking, and as long as Matthew, or any of the characters, can keep talking, they can stave off the final 'nothing' of 'wrath and weeping' (233). (There is no speech, reported or direct, in chapter 8, only the description of inarticulate sounds such as breathing, barking, crying, followed by silence.) Matthew's great monologues are in many ways the expressionist heart of the novel: stylistically they embody all those characteristics of image discussed above; thematically, they dramatize the essential human need for language, even when real communication is no longer possible. And in their length, extravagance, and increasing passion they convey the suffering of the individual who is trapped by the 'expressive fallacy.' Here, as Hermann Bahr said, 'der Mensche schreit aus seinem Schrei,' and we hear a universal cry.

It is important to remember that the doctor's speeches are monologues, closely resembling soliloquies and not passages of stream-of-consciousness or even narrated monologues.[22] They are directly quoted speech, and although they are mediated by a third-person narrator, that 'unseen' but omnipresent *dompteur*, their length and dramatic power is unusual in fiction; other examples, such as Bonaventura's *Nightwatches* (*Die Nachtwachen*), often seen as a precursor of Expressionism, and passages from Beckett, Faulkner, Lowry, Ellison, and Aquin also come to mind.[23] In other words, Barnes is not presenting Matthew's thoughts mimetically but using the fiction of the directly spoken word that permits him to express himself. Within a novel such monologues are fictive discourse because, unlike dramatic monologues, they are unspoken, and yet they can be compared with the monologues in expressionist plays – the pre-eminent English-language example being O'Neill – for their fragmentation, digressiveness, self-reflexivity, extravagant language, staggering length, and passion. What Hickey in *The Iceman Cometh* is for the stage, Dr Matthew Mighty-Grain-of-Salt Dante O'Connor is for the textual show of *Nightwood*. Moreover their function in *Nightwood* parallels the use of monologues in expressionist plays, where they present outbursts of the soul, sometimes lyric, sometimes staccato in style, in which the character expresses his or her suffering in a barrage of words directed out towards mankind (audience or reader), the universe, or God, but seldom towards other characters. These expressionist monologues intensify the isolation felt in much of the so-called dialogue, where characters often talk past one another (a style associated with Wedekind) in an obvious and painful autotelia.

For example, in the long interview of chapter 7, 'Go Down, Matthew,' Nora and the doctor seldom converse in anything like a credible dialogue. Instead, their speeches are antiphonal, with the doctor frequently seizing upon a word in Nora's remarks or questions to use as a kind of initiating idea for his next outburst:

> 'Jenny,' she said.
> 'It rots her sleep – Jenny is one of those who nip like a bird and void like an ox – the poor and lightly damned! That can be a torture also. None of us suffers as much as we should, or loves as much as we say. Love is the first lie; wisdom the last.' (196)

As his passion and despair increase before Nora's lamentation and frantic questions, the doctor's monologues become increasingly self-regarding and distorted by bewildering imagery, increasingly fragmented and rambling, yet dominated by his own rhetorical questions:

> 'And I was doing well enough', he snapped, 'until you came along and kicked my stone over, and out I came, all moss and eyes; and here I sit, as naked as only those things can be, whose houses have been torn away from them to make a holiday, and it my only skin – labouring to comfort you. Am I supposed to render up my paradise – that splendid acclimatization – for the comfort of weeping women and howling boys?' ... 'Ah, yes – I love my neighbour. Like a rotten apple to a rotten apple's breast affixed we go down together, nor is there a hesitation in that decay, for when I sense such, there I apply the breast the firmer, that he may rot as quickly as I, in which he stands in dire need or I miscalculate the cry. I, who am done sooner than any fruit!' ... 'Do you think there is no lament in this world, but your own? Is there not a forebearing saint somewhere? Is there no bread that does not come proffered with bitter butter? I, as good a Catholic as they make, have embraced every confection of hope, and yet I know well, for all our outcry and struggle, we shall be for the next generation not the massive dung fallen from the dinosaur, but the little speck left of a humming-bird.' (216–18)

Ostensibly the 'you' in these passages is Nora, but included with her are the reader, the world, God: anyone who will listen. When she interrupts him with *her* 'Listen ... You've got to listen' (219), he can only mutter, 'Christ!' (221), because his monologue arises from his own pain to be flung against an absent God in a silent universe.

Contrary to Charles Baxter, who sees these autotelic monologues as narcissistic, exhibitionistic, feverish, and characteristic of a text that illustrates 'the crisis of Modernism' and enacts the failure of its author as well as the characters,[24] I believe that these great monologues are the very life-spring of the novel, its source of energy, and, as the voice of the most articulate and experienced of the characters, the distorted mirror in which the reader sees him or herself. These monologues, more than anything else in *Nightwood*, allow us to share in human suffering, to identify with the act of crying out, and finally to feel the full weight of the lapse into silence. Abstract as they are (as far as the conventions of realist fiction are concerned), these monologues are also deeply moving reminders of our own humanity; they maintain that delicate balance between abstraction and representation that permits the reader or viewer to locate a recognizable human subject (and subjectivity) with whom he or she can identify and empathize, and they can be seen as the doctor's breaking free of a host of social and rational constraints through language and style.

Whether or not he achieves any kind of final release or deliverance – *Erlösung* – with his closing words is more ambiguous. In contemplating the final scene of the novel, I suggested above that Barnes deliberately leaves room for opposing interpretations, including a possible *Erlösung*, and the same is true of our final glimpse of the doctor: 'For Christ's sake!' he whispers, 'Now that you have all heard what you wanted to hear, can't you let me loose now, let me go?' [233] The silence following his drunken collapse is either a sign of his own failure ('I've not only lived my life for nothing, but I've told it for nothing' – 233) or his deliverance from the pain of trying to speak; it is either insensibility or the acknowledgment of that ultimate silence that only Robin can inhabit. And for Barnes there is something mysterious and sacred about such silence. Plenitude or void, it lies beyond the reach of Matthew's ejaculations.

'A man is only whole when he takes into account his shadow as well as himself' (171) the doctor tells Felix. But there is little hope that Felix will understand Guido as 'the shadow of [his own] anxiety' when he so patently failed to understand the boy's mother. Even the doctor's right to pronounce is undermined by his imminent collapse, for, like the others, who understand what Robin is even less than he does, he is incapable of merging with that otherness, of accepting the shadow of his own anxiety. And yet, as I suggested earlier, Robin complements O'Connor: to his tender consciousness she adds subconscious depths; she matches his volubility and articulateness with an almost total silence broken only by a few brief phrases, cries, or deranged laughter; as he is culture's supreme representative – wise man, medical man, priest – she is primitive nature; where he is cerebral, devoted to reason and Logos, she is emotional, acting according to her instincts and searching from church to chapel for a divinity she can worship.

To compare Matthew on his knees in church, clutching 'Tiny O'Toole' and calling upon 'my lord,' for solutions, with Robin on her knees beside Nora's dog in the chapel is to bring the relation of these two 'characters' and the expressionist dilemma they encode into sharp focus. In one sense Robin is his soul or, perhaps, the human soul for which mankind cries out. Lost, wandering from body to body, 'seeking permission to live,' Robin will not be reunited with the conscious self (in Matthew, Felix, Nora, or Jenny) by force, but neither can they abandon themselves to her chaotic power, and it is the doctor who attempts to explain away their and his anxiety before the force she embodies.

What I find especially interesting in the doubled image of Matthew/ Robin (conscious/unconscious, culture/nature, male/female) is the way that Barnes divides them, creating in Robin a separate vehicle for inner, subconscious soul-states. In most expressionist art the soul-states screaming for attention are within man; in releasing them (through *Aufbruch*) he seeks to shatter the constraints and civilized inhibitions that threaten that inner power and, possibly, to communicate with some transcendent cosmic Soul. When the expressionist playwright dramatizes these inner forces, he usually projects them in the form of a *Doppelgänger* (as in O'Neill's *Great God Brown*), of hallucinatory shapes (such as the formless fears in *The Emperor Jones*), or by having inanimate objects come to life (for example, the tree in *From Morn to Midnight*, the buildings in many expressionist paintings, the distorted sets in expressionist films), by using masks and marionettes (Strindberg and O'Neill), and by unusual lighting effects (Voaden).

Working within the novel form, Barnes has combined a degree of separate reality – in the story, after all, Robin Vote is a young American in Paris whose promiscuous, autistic nature hurts all those around her – with an iconography central to the depiction of women in expressionist and other art of the period in order to create an exceptionally powerful, ambiguous character whose very separateness is frightening. This separate existence, wandering, unattached, out of control, obeying some *other* principle, is reminiscent of the Golem or Frankenstein. Robin exists doubly for us, not only as a character whom we come to know through the conventional fictional means of what is said about her and her impact on the lives of others, but also as a visual projection, as an image or literalized metaphor of the 'woman who presents herself to the spectator as a "picture,"' a 'mirage,' a 'vision' (59), as 'an image and its reflection in a lake ... parted only by the hesitation in the hour' (60). Barnes achieves this sense of visual projection by manipulating point of view so that we always see Robin from the 'unseen *dompteur*'s' perspective, by the predominantly visual imagery used to present Robin, by that key establishing reference to Rousseau's painting, and, most important of all, because we classify her as a somnambulist. As a sleepwalker she evokes a host of visual images dramatically associated with the effeminate Cesare in *The Cabinet of Dr Caligari*, with the catatonic movements of innumerable characters in expressionist plays, paintings, and films (Munch's females are only the outstanding example), and more deeply with a basic human fear of sleep-walking and of the night.

In her pioneering study of sexuality, power, and the portrayal of women, 'Virility and Domination in Early Twentieth-Century Vanguard Painting,' Carol Duncan argues that the powerless, subhuman nudes of Kirchner, Van Dongen, Heckel, and Vlaminck embody the same sexist 'structure of thought' as the *femme fatale* of the symbolists or of Munch's female vampires: 'Women are depicted with none of the sense of self, none of the transcendent, spiritual autonomy that the men themselves experience ... The headless, faceless nudes, the dreamy looks of Gauguin's girls, the glaring mask of Kirchner's *Girl Under a Japanese Umbrella*, the somnambulism of the *femme fatales* – all of these equally deny the presence of a human consciousness that knows itself as separate from and opposed to the natural and biological world.'[25] Moreover, these negative and reductive images of women – with or without their dangerous power – dominate the art of the period and are given their most graphic, violent treatment in the literature and painting of Expressionism (see Plate 11). In drawing upon this iconography, Barnes is utilizing one of the most pervasive and disturbing paradigms available to her. Why? If that question can be answered, what Barnes intends in *Nightwood* and how she uses the misogynist vocabulary of Expressionism (and of symbolist, cubist, and fauvist art) might be clearer.

At first glance, Barnes seems to be using these female stereotypes uncritically: her women are mindless, greedy bitches (Jenny), incestuous narcissists (Nora), somnambulists with vampire-like qualities and uncontrollable instincts (Robin). Furthermore, these fatal women cause nothing but trouble for themselves and their men. (Jenny may not look like Lulu, but she has gone through four husbands.) And yet, if one looks further at *Nightwood*, especially in the context of her *oeuvre*, Barnes's portraits of 'repulsive women' reveal depth and sensitivity.[26] In her discussion of the images of women in early twentieth-century painting, Duncan makes an excellent point about the problem of depicting human sexuality faced by female artists of the period:

> The vogue for virility in early twentieth-century art is but one aspect of a total social, cultural and economic situation that women artists had to overcome ... It was not sexuality per se that was valued, but male sexuality. The problem for women ... was not to invert the existing social-sexual order, not to replace it with the domination of women; the new woman was struggling for her own autonomy as a psychological, social and political being. Her problem was also the woman problem. Her task was also to master her own image.   (301–2)

At the same time as they foregrounded the battle of the sexes, the expressionists equated primitive psychic energy and sexuality with creative power and innovative rebellion, and saw in nature (as natural instincts, primitive myth, and the natural world of plants and animals, all seen as synonymous with the female) the source of that energy. For the male artist (from Lawrence, Eliot, Joyce, and Pound through Stravinsky to Wedekind, Strindberg, and O'Neill) the problem became how to control the power that they saw looming up in woman and threatening them with castration, or a loss of identity and autonomy, and how to make that power serve and validate a male erotic energy. For the female artist the problem immediately folds back on itself. Because there is no 'other,' no distinct opposite to establish as a primitive source of power (nature and woman are equated, so tradition states, for better or worse), the energy, at once seductive and destructive, of the *femme fatale* and of the natural world is synonymous with oneself.

The female artist can resolve this predicament in one of two ways – in a kind of paralysing fear and self-loathing, or in a celebration of a female-generated energy and sexuality. Both responses are fraught with ambiguities and confusion: to wallow in self-loathing is self-defeating and psychologically crippling, and yet to affirm such female energy as codified in the dichotomies of nature/culture, and so on, is to place oneself outside culture, to abandon what society validates as distinctly human, to join Emil Nolde's bacchantes in *Dance around the Golden Calf* (see Plate 11), to accept the anonymity of multiplicity so dramatically imaged in what

Duncan calls the 'jungle-brothel' of Picasso's *Les Demoiselles d'Avignon* (1906–7).

Given this context and iconography, it is scarcely surprising that *Nightwood* refuses easy answers. For Djuna Barnes, the artist-heroine of her own ordeal (and here I refer not to biography but to the self-conscious position of the expressionist artist whose art is always about him or herself), the very creation of Robin represents her attempt 'to master her own image.' In the final scene Robin is both appalling and exciting, atavistic and yet strangely galvanizing. That Robin should be finally and, I feel, irrevocably separated from her conscious, articulate, culture-bound (and in the doctor, *male*) self is both thematically and symbolically appropriate. In Barnes's fiction men and women both fail in coming to terms with the dark otherness of the soul, but that energy persists within us – male and female – as a constant reminder of what we cannot tame, least of all with words. Dr Matthew Mighty-Grain-of-Salt Dante O'Connor must be silenced because Robin exists beyond his power to name her.

By ending *Nightwood* in this manner Barnes has gone past the iconography of somnambulist *femme fatale* to comment upon 'the woman problem.' With a backward glance at Rousseau's *The Dream*, her silencing of the doctor is tantamount to saying that the male artist deceives himself if he believes he has tamed the beast of his anxiety about nature and woman by containing her on his canvas, shaping her power to his own ends. It is, after all, the image of Robin that we are left with beyond the end he cries out for, an image compounded of beast and human, of passivity and power, of affirmation and denial, of the self as other. And it is an image only Nora has the courage to contemplate: she guides us to the chapel, she stumbles to the door, she watches the strange ritual. While I cannot agree entirely with Jane Marcus that '*Nightwood* is the sacred grove of Diana' and that the ending is a 'triumphant ... rite of female connection between the mythological Diana and the Madonna before whose altar Robin bows down' (7), I do think that Barnes has used the ambiguity of the somnambulistic *femme fatale* to express those contradictory forces in each of us that we dismiss at our peril. Indeed, her use of the image in *Nightwood* constitutes a recuperation of the iconography, a grasping and redirecting of its power. To reject Robin, or to tame and civilize her, is at best a self-deception, at worst a destruction of the soul.

In a 1931 article, Djuna Barnes wrote that she liked 'human experience served up with a little silence and restraint. Silence makes experience go further and, when it does die, gives it that dignity common to a thing one had touched and not ravished.'[28] Despite my emphasis here upon the screaming and suffering of *Nightwood*, there is a disconcerting restraint about this expressionist text; it is by no means as savage as *Murder, Hope of Women*, as hallucinatory as the 'Circe' episode in *Ulysses*, as flagrantly solipsistic as *To Damascus* and *A Dream Play*, or as hysterical as Einstein's *Bebuquin*. This quality of restraint contributes enormously to the power of the novel; it arises in part from the distanced narrative of the 'unseen *dompteur*' and in part from the brevity, simplicity (as compared with preceding chapters), and final silence of chapter 8. The dreadful outbursts of the doctor might almost be seen as a parody of the expressionist man's self-centred and self-aggrandizing suffering, and his silencing as an ironic comment upon the useless self-destruction of this 'inbreeding of pain.'

To suggest that there may be an element of parody or irony here is not, however, to imply that Matthew is without importance or that we should not empathize with him. A more interesting conjecture is that, in choosing to end with Robin Vote, Barnes is finally coming to the dark centre of her expressionist vision – a mystery before which we must be silent, an experience we can perhaps feel but never name or know, never ravish. That the experience includes horror, revulsion, perhaps a perverse fascination and dread, is certainly true, but it also embraces the most truly tender moment of communication in the entire novel: 'she gave up, lying out, her hands beside her, her face turned and weeping; and the dog too gave up then, and lay down, his eyes bloodshot, his head flat along her knees' (239). Leaving the floundering male behind with his drunken *Schrei*, Barnes moves on to the primitive, female source of the expressionist imagination – what Kokoschka called his 'Goddess.' In a revolutionary gesture Barnes removes the male – artist, wordsmith, medicine man, failed priest – from the centre of the stage, or canvas, where the male artist so emphatically placed him (only think of Kaiser's Cashier or Meidner's *The City and I*; see Plates 18 and 22),[29] to confront what contemporary iconography depicted as that underlying female force in the primitive human soul.

In doing this Barnes has achieved two things. Of course, she has used the most powerful iconography available to her, but in a fresh way: Robin is the *femme fatale*, the instinctual, unconscious female of male expressionist fantasy from Munch to O'Neill's Nina, but she is faced directly as an essential, terrible power. Barnes has also created a fiction remarkably different from that of her male contemporaries, expressionist and other, in that it rejects the centrality of the male ego paraded before us in the heroes of Strindberg, Kaiser, Döblin, O'Neill, and Lowry, and in the obsessive self-portraiture of its painters, for a web of interrelationships that share a universal need for Robin Vote. As we shall see, Sheila Watson builds her novel on an abstracted community without a soul and on a web of destructive relationships, and this de-centred quality of *Nightwood* and *The Double Hook* suggests that the expressionism of these female writers differs from that of contemporary males in much the same way that Käthe Kollwitz differs from Munch: the stress on personal suffering in the one shifts to a deeper 'universal wound' in the other. To be sure, both tendencies are present in most expressionist art, but the movement has been defined by its male theorists and practitioners by privileging the private pain of the individual artist and by treating Munch and Strindberg as the 'fathers' of Expressionism (its 'mothers' are often forgotten), and this has meant that its female artists have either been dismissed as peripheral or relegated, as has been the case with Barnes, to a kind of general category of subjective, hysterical, ornate and 'feminine' aberration. Reading *Nightwood* in the context of Expressionism does not make it possible to say that *this* is what Barnes means, but it does illuminate what the novel is doing and helps to reinstate it in its proper context as a superb, and revolutionary, example of expressive modernist art.

7 The Soul in Writhing Anguish: Malcolm Lowry's Under the Volcano

Everyone who knows *Under the Volcano* recognizes that it is a highly filmic novel; Stephen Spender said so in 1965, and as a direct consequence many directors flirted with the idea of filming it and many more screenplay writers attempted to adapt it for cinematic treatment.[1] The first response to *Volcano*'s challenge appeared in John Huston's 1984 realistic treatment of Lowry's masterpiece, with Albert Finney as the drunken Consul, Jacqueline Bisset as his estranged wife Yvonne, and Anthony Andrews as his shallow half-brother Hugh. What Huston proved, however, is true with many great literary works: they simply do not translate well into a cinematic vocabulary. But the reasons for this failure with *Under the Volcano* are especially interesting and should be pursued a little further.

Lowry, who was a true film *aficionado*, knew first-hand what such problems of translation could be. In 1949–50 he had struggled to make a film-script, indeed did create a script, of *Tender Is the Night* that provides many clues to his personal vision, to his approach to the aesthetics of film, and to the process of translating one medium into the other.[2] Essentially, Lowry wanted an expressionist treatment of Dick Diver's life, and his typescript and notes contain frequent references to expressionist films and explanations of his expressionistic intentions. What Lowry intended for Fitzgerald's novel might well be applied to his own. Perhaps a director like David Lynch will give *Volcano* an expressionist treatment one day, and when this happens the film will come much closer to the soul of Lowry's masterpiece than any meticulously representational style could do,[3] for Lowry was an expressionist artist, the greatest one working in the English language.

However, that claim is no sooner made than it must be qualified; a writer of Lowry's stature and complexity cannot be neatly labelled. What I am suggesting here is that Lowry is best seen as an expressionist artist who was at one and the same time able to see the flaws and dangers of his position and yet finally unable to abandon it, who was anxious to move beyond the dark, regressive side of his vision (and succeeded in doing so on occasions) and yet created one of this century's literary masterpieces from the very depths of that visionary abyss. Conventional Aristotelian character and plot were the last things he was interested in. 'There are a thousand writers,' he protested to Jonathan Cape in his magnificent apologia for the novel, 'who can draw adequate characters till all is blue for one who can tell you anything new about hell fire. And I am telling you something new about hell fire.'[4]

Like the expressionists, with whom he shares so much, Lowry was a deeply religious man, one who felt desperately humanity's precarious state in the twentieth century and loathed the dehumanization and mechanization of contemporary existence. Again like many of the young Germans in Berlin cafés or Herwarth Walden's gallery, he was the disaffected youngest son of a well-meaning but essentially unsympathetic bürgerlicher father.[5] The tragic ambivalence of his work (and his life) lies in the fact that, while drawn to the need for an apocalyptic purging and rebirth that would restore mankind to a lost paradise and while able to see with a ruthless clarity humanity's need for a New Man to show it the way, he, like his Consul, loved Hell and welcomed the damnation of this world. In most of his work, certainly in *Under the Volcano*, Lowry balances regression and apocalypse so that his readers, and his eponymous heroes, can weigh the seductive comfort yet horror of the one against the ecstatic promise of the other – before plunging into the abyss.

Malcolm Lowry (1909–57) began *Under the Volcano* shortly after arriving in Cuernavaca, Mexico, with his first wife, Jan Gabrial, in 1936. Before he left Mexico in July 1938 he had separated from Jan, failed to drink himself into total oblivion, generally experienced every horror associated with the dark night of the soul, and completed a first draft (there would be three more, and even then he was not satisfied) of the *Volcano*. Lowry returned to Cuernavaca seven years later, in December 1945, in order to show Margerie Bonner, his second wife, the scene of the novel with which she had helped him for more than six years, and it was there, while staying in the very house that was Laruelle's *zacuali* in the novel, that he received the letter from Jonathan Cape citing a reader's criticisms and apparently rejecting the manuscript. Lowry slashed his wrists in a half-hearted attempt at suicide, then sat down to compose his famous thirty-one-page letter to Cape explaining why *Under the Volcano* had to be as it was and what, in part at least, each of its twelve chapters meant (*Letters*, 57–88).

By the early forties Lowry knew that *Under the Volcano* should not stand alone. At first he thought it would be the *inferno* in a Dantean trilogy, with a massive opus called *In Ballast to the White Sea* as the *paradiso*. When this manuscript was lost in an actual *auto-da-fé* – the burning of his squatter's shack on Burrard Inlet, across from Vancouver, on 7 June 1944 – he was forced to reconceive the nature of his work-in-progress, which had, in any case, grown beyond the limits of the trilogy form. He described his evolving plans to Albert Erskine, his editor at Random House, in a 1951 'Work in Progress' statement: his masterwork was to consist of a sequence of at least seven novels, to be called *The Voyage That Never Ends*.[6] It would proceed thus:

> The Ordeal of Sigbjørn Wilderness I [fragment]
> Untitled Sea Novel [*Ultramarine*]
> *Lunar Caustic* [to be revised]
> *Under the Volcano*
> *Dark as the Grave Wherein My Friend Is Laid*
> Eridanus [mss published as *October Ferry to Gabriola*]
> La Mordida [mss]
> The Ordeal of Sigbjørn Wilderness II [fragment]

The *Voyage*, of course, was not completed, and only parts of it were published during Lowry's lifetime. The framing novella meant to introduce the primary persona/hero, Sigbjørn Wilderness, never got beyond some notes and preliminary drafts. But from this material it is clear that Sigbjørn, who lies near death in a hospital in the opening part, relives his past through the following novels and is restored to life, 'as if by a miracle,' in part 2.

The entire concept of this protagonist, who is also the central *Ich* in *Dark as the Grave Wherein My Friend Is Laid* (1968) and the novella 'Through the Panama' from *Hear us O Lord from heaven Thy dwelling place* (1961), is too complex to examine at length here. What makes this 'character' and the framing fragment relevant to Lowry's expressionism is the light they throw on his attempts to portray *Erlösung*. On the one hand, Lowry clearly envisaged rebirth and transcendence for his protagonist after a purgative, apocalyptic experience, but on the other that possibility never reached its final form in art ... with one stunning exception – 'The Forest Path to the Spring' – to which I shall return. The burden of Lowry's vision, therefore, is carried by *Ultramarine* (1933; 1962), *Lunar Caustic* (1963), *Under the Volcano* (1947), and the posthumous, heavily edited *Dark as the Grave* (1968) and *October Ferry to Gabriola* (1970). This vision is oppressively dark. One after the other, from the young Dana Hilliot in *Ultramarine* to the older Bill Plantagenet in *Lunar Caustic* and the middle-aged Geoffrey Firmin of *Volcano*, Lowry's men experience *Aufbruch*, followed by despair, defeat, and regression. Unbelievably, they rise from each regression in the spirit of the master persona of Wilderness, to struggle once more in the next novel; indeed, Sigbjørn in *Dark as the Grave* wins through to a modicum of hope and enlightenment at the end of his ordeal.[7] But the tension between regression and apocalypse in the *Voyage* is not (theoretically never can be) resolved.

Although one could argue on stylistic terms alone that *Volcano*, *Lunar Caustic*, and many passages from the other novels are expressionistic, there are extratextual reasons for doing so. The *Tender Is the Night* film-script is a case in point, but Lowry had some knowledge of and considerable interest in expressionist painting, theatre, music, and film. He knew the work of Munch, Schönberg, Berg, the writing of Rimbaud, Strindberg, Dostoevsky, Wedekind, and the plays of Toller, Kaiser, and O'Neill, whose *The Hairy Ape* and *Emperor Jones* were special favourites. He discovered O'Neill during his teens, and in 1925 he saw the London production of *From Morn to Midnight* starring Claude Rains. Years later, this expressionistic production would provide an interesting motif for *October Ferry to Gabriola*. During a stay in Bonn in 1928 (he was supposed to be studying German, but his knowledge of that language, as of French and Spanish, was limited), he became familiar with German expressionist theatre and film, and was deeply impressed by a Cologne production of O'Neill's *The Great God Brown*. Twenty-three years later, in 1951, Lowry wrote to Clemens ten Holder (the first German translator of *Under the Volcano*) in some detail about his time in Bonn and his respect for German theatre, and his recollections of those eight weeks when he was nineteen are worth quoting at length. He begins with affectionate memories of his teacher, Karlheinz Schmidthus, and a description of his reading skills in German – 'almost the only thing I learned at all in Bonn, outside the bar of the Hotel Rheinischer Hof' – then continues:

> One thing I shall always remember; I pleased him [Schmidthus] because I showed a true appreciation even at that age, which the other English boys of course didn't, of the triumphs of the German theatre – even modern

expressionist triumphs, and he was staggered that I even knew about 'George' Kaiser, and what was more knew that he had written about thirty plays, and not just *Vom Morgens bis Mitternachts* [sic], and set about righting (as you may right my rendering of *From Morn till Midnight*) my pronunciation immediately.

Gay-org Kaiser, Herr Lowry.

He didn't think as much of Gayorg as I did (I had just seen Claude Rains playing in *From Morn till Midnight* in England as I was later to have a minor hand in the production of the same at Cambridge, as also of Toller, whom I later came to know well, both in London and Mexico) but he was delighted just the same, as he was also delighted when I repeated to him that *Der Gross Gott Brown* [sic], by Eugene O'Neill then playing at the Schauspielhaus in Koln [sic] – by far the most imaginative wonderful production I have ever seen of O'Neill, incidentally, far better than the play itself, which it had leant over backwards to extract the last juices of meaning out of, and where there weren't any, had provided some of its own – could not have been written surely without the influence of the said Gayorg. Herr Schmidhus [sic] promised to look into these deep matters, but perhaps was more pleased when I showed some knowledge of Wedekind. (*Letters*, 238–9)

His interest in a group of writers less known for their links with Expressionism is more remarkable – Maeterlinck and Hermann Bang, Oscar Wilde and Poe are all considered to be forerunners of the movement – and he also knew Döblin (see chapter 2).[8] The most important influence, however, was the wonderful-horrible German expressionist film: *The Cabinet of Dr Caligari* (1919), *From Morn to Midnight* (1920, based upon Kaiser's play), *Waxworks* (1921), *Nosferatu* (1922), *Warning Shadows* (1922), *The Street* (1923), *The Hands of Orlac* (1924), *The Student of Prague* (1926). These, among others, provided Lowry with a cornucopia of effects, themes, and allusions.

As Ulrich Weisstein has noted, the 'bona fide Expressionist ... must reject the mimetic approach ... What Expressionist art seeks to render visible ... are soul states and the violent emotions welling up from the innermost recesses of the subconscious.'[9] In general, this is true. Expressionist art is not mimetic; it does reject the epistemological assumptions of realism. However, the actual dynamic of expressionism is complex. Although the mundane world of objective, material facts does not interest an expressionist artist, the physical world is not denied. Instead, either an inner reality of intense emotional response to that world (including a desire to be reunited with nature) or an inner perception of spiritual truths and transcendent universals becomes the primary focus of attention, and frequently a dynamic tension exists between these two possibilities. Either way, of course, the artist is attempting to superimpose his or her subjective reality upon accepted notions of an objective world. Hence the violent distortions and semantic abstraction of a basically iconic art. The more extreme the abstraction, the less representational (or, in Worringer's terms, 'empathetic') a work becomes. This tendency characterizes Kandinsky, is strong in Voaden's 'symphonic expressionism,' and is brought to a fine expressive abstraction in Sheila Watson's *The Double Hook*.

Lowry's personal aesthetic position and his formal endeavours clearly parallel this fundamental expressionist dualism. He makes it clear in his letters that he is 'in rebellion' against the realist novel: 'unquestionably what one is after is a new form, a new approach to reality itself.'[10] In Lowry's view, reality is dynamic and perpetually protean. Furthermore, although he ignored neither an external objective reality nor a possible spiritual realm of universals, his method for understanding, accommodating, or articulating these ontological categories was essentially solipsistic. He began with the perceptions of an *Ich* closely modelled on the autobiographical self, and with his own inner vision. Thus, his master-protagonist, Sigbjørn Wilderness, was to embody what Lowry believed to be the unconscious human urge to constantly create a self that would reflect the dynamic essence of life.[11]

In addition to these similarities in epistemology and vision, there are many generic, stylistic, and thematic parallels between Lowry's work and that of the German expressionists. One of the most interesting of these is the handling of character. In the letter to Cape, Lowry went to considerable lengths to clarify his use of character: 'The truth is that the character drawing is not only weak but virtually nonexistent ... the four main characters being intended, in one of the book's meanings, to be aspects of the same man' (*Letters*, 60). He goes on to explain that the characters represent the unconscious and that the novel is concerned 'with the forces in man which cause him to be terrified of himself.'

The expressionist artist is totally uninterested in the psychological, and therefore realistic, development of the individual character. Similarly, Lowry was not interested in offering an etiology for his heroes, who are three-dimensional only in so far as required for the 'superficial plane' of his work. Apparently Lowry felt that fiction could not entirely reject a certain recognizable reality without losing its readers, and this view seems to have been shared by many expressionist dramatists and most prose writers. Of foremost interest to the expressionist is the portrayal of individual soul-states that also embody collective or cosmic forces. According to Jan Joseph Lipski, 'it is characteristic for E. to depict reality as reduced to the "I". But the "I", which is the subject of Expressionist literature, tends to identify itself with communal values and values of a cosmic nature, with the universal soul acting as a cosmic force, etc. Thus the dialectics of extreme subjectivism pitted against universal tendencies is essential for the movement.'[12] Here again, Lowry's intention is comparable. Geoffrey Firmin embodies and represents the soul of modern Western man on the brink of the abyss. As his familiars remind us, Geoffrey is Faustian and we are watching the battle of good and evil within his dying soul.

Another aspect of this expressionist concern with self (or an 'I' who is both self and cosmic force) is the expressionist predilection for self-portraiture and split selves (*Doppelgänger*). Weisstein suggests that self-portraiture is important to the expressionist because 'it is precisely the soul ... especially the soul in writhing anguish' that he wishes to project.[13] The literary vehicle for this concern with self is autobiography, and few writers have been as intensely autobiographical as Lowry. The device of the split self in portraiture, or the *Doppelgänger* in literature, is a literalized metaphor and a way of projecting the image of the 'I' as both self and other (for example, cosmic or Faustian force). Wilde's *Dorian Gray*, O'Neill's *The Great God Brown*, and Galeen's film *The Student of Prague* offer 'characters' who can watch their inner destruction unfold in a *Doppelgänger*, but Lowry's use of the *Doppelgänger* device is more general and metaphoric. Although Hugh is Geoffrey's *Doppelgänger*, Geoffrey's tendency is to perceive whatever is external to the self as a fragment or reflection of the self. In his agony, he sees himself, 'surrounded in delirium by these phantoms of himself, the policemen, Fructuoso Sanabria, that other man who looked like a poet, the luminous skeleton, even the rabbit in the corner and the ash and sputum on the filthy floor – did not each correspond, in a way he couldn't understand yet obscurely recognized, to some fraction of his being?'[14] Here the emphasis falls upon the isolation and terrible alienation of the split self.

There are a number of stylistic elements common to expressionist painting, literature, and film that Lowry used to great effect. The first is deliberate disruption of spatial and temporal continuities, one of those qualities that facilitates a Bakhtinian analysis of expressionist texts. The spatial disruption is obvious in the grotesque distortions that are such a striking feature of all expressionist art. Inner and outer, real and fantastic, become confused and interchanged in the effort to superimpose subjective reality upon the objective world. As the human figure becomes less stable (in a realist sense), sets and landscapes become increasingly expressive or symbolic diagrams of emotional states. For example, in the woodcuts and paintings of Barlach or Schmidt-Rottluff, or in O'Neill's *Emperor Jones*, landscapes appear to be alive and menacing. In *Under the Volcano* the entire landscape mirrors Geoffrey's confusion as well as seeming to participate in his destruction in a manner similar to the disturbing figure / ground relationship in Meidner's *The City and I* and Munch's *The Scream* (see Plates 22 and 29). Popocatapetl becomes Moby Dick; a sunflower stares at Geoffrey 'like God'; his surroundings taunt: 'Why am I here, says the silence, what have I done echoes the emptiness, why have I ruined myself in this wilful manner, chuckles the money in the till, why have I been brought so low, wheedles the thoroughfare' (359). Part of Geoffrey's problem is this projection of inner confusion upon external reality.

The disruption of temporal continuities is even more important. For the expressionist time and historical process are dynamic: 'history past and present is regarded as a continual struggle between good and evil' while 'time and its dynamic unfolding [are] constitutive agents in the struggle.'[15] Lowry also believed that reality was a dynamic struggle and that time must flow for life and art to continue. In *Under the Volcano* he went to considerable lengths to break up the reader's sense of temporal continuity by constructing twelve self-enclosed chapters, and the impression of stasis that results from the temporal discontinuity of this paratactic structure mirrors the accidie of Geoffrey's soul. While the hypostasizing effect of parataxis and discontinuity is typical of much expressionist art (despite the often frenzied activity of the protagonists), in Lowry's case the stasis has an important thematic purpose: Geoffrey, like the world, has 'bogged down' forgetting Goethe's words, '*Wer immer strebend sich bemüht, den konnen wir erlösen.*' And for the consul, of course, there will be no *Erlösung.*

There are many features of expressionist writing, such as telegraph style, specific topoi (mirrors, staircases, asylums, and whirling fairgrounds, which are especially obvious in expressionist films), and monologues, that Lowry exploited throughout his *oeuvre*. The characteristic telegraph style of jerky, abrupt exclamation is most successful in poetry or drama and less common in prose, but some telling examples do exist, as in the following example from Hans Fallada's *Der junge Goedeschal* (1920): 'He staggered. Garishly lit houses loomed up out of the dark as if seen from a speeding train ... No resting place! Stumbling, falling forward, he began to run, brushed past walls whose pores seemed to exude a sweaty slime.'[16]

Similar examples of a telegraph style are found in Lowry. The most extensive use of this stylistic device is in *Ultramarine*, especially in chapter 3, where it contributes to our sense of Dana's disturbed, whirling perceptions. Even in *Under the Volcano*, where the dominant style is that of long, circling, convoluted sentences, clause piled on clause, Lowry uses brief telegraphic passages to suggest the confusion of Geoffrey's mind (for example, the fair scene in 7 and the toilet scene in 10). His most striking example of the telegraph style, however, comes in an early work, the story 'June the 30th, 1934.' Bill Goodyear, returning to England by boat and train, is pursued and disturbed by reports of Hitler's atrocities and the imminence of war, by his travelling companion (a man called Firmin), and by visions of his son. He feels himself undergoing a strange transformation. The final passages of the story dramatize the fusion of his disturbed mind with the rhythm of the train as it screams 'like a shell, through a metal world':

> His eyes returned to the window. A man digging, sharply illumined by a shower of sparks like red blossoms, slowly raised his spade ... It's never too late, never too late. To start again. You bore in the earth. Silver and copper. Man makes his cross. With crucible steel. Base metal; counterfeit; manganese; chromium; makes his iron cross; with crucible steel.
> ...
> The train took a hill. The boy fell in the fire. The knitting needles flashed like bayonets. Steel wool. The red lights flashed. Green lights. Knit. Socks! Knit. Shroud! Knit. Stab! Iron, steel, said the train. Iron, steel. Iron, tin, iron, tin. Steel and iron steel and iron steel and iron steel and iron steeeeeeeeel![17]

Lowry's use of mirrors, staircases, fairgrounds, and asylums constitutes a strategic set of what Bakhtin would describe as 'threshold' topoi, but these topoi should be distinguished from the important motifs in Lowry's work. Although, like motifs (such as clocks, bells, candles, and stars), they recur obsessively, they function as the setting or location of 'crisis' moments or scenes in a protagonist's ordeal. Describing the carnivalesque world of *Crime and Punishment* in *Problems of Dostoevsky's Poetics* (with specific reference to Raskolnikov's dream in part 3, chapter 6), Bakhtin notes that

> *space* assumes additional significance in the overall symbol-system of carnival. *Up*, *down*, the *stairway*, the *threshold*, the *foyer*, the *landing* take on the meaning of a 'point' where *crisis*, radical change, an unexpected turn of fate takes place, where decisions are made, where the forbidden

line is over-stepped, where one is renewed or perishes ... On the threshold
and on the square the only time possible is *crisis* time, in which a *moment*
is equal to years, decades.   (*PDP*, 169–70)

Being 'threshold' topoi, Lowry's mirrors, staircases, fairgrounds, and
asylums alert us to the unstable, conditional psychic or physical position
of the character and to the carnivalesque, heterogeneous, and dialogistic
possibilities of his (or her, in the single case of Yvonne) experience. It is no
mere accident that Geoffrey should recall Dostoevsky at one of the most
significant crisis moments in his own ordeal of carnivalesque decrowning –
the toilet scene of chapter 10, which is discussed in detail below – because,
like Raskolnikov, he too will soon perish.[18] Indeed, within the novel's
'trochal' structure he has already died, and is, in a sense, repeating these
events *for us*.

A mirror, or mirroring – be it in water, panes of window glass, or
bottles – often brings the character face to face with a sinister or
threatening aspect of his inner self; thus, the mirroring surface acts as the
locus for two shifting, interpenetrating realities. Staircases, more loosely
interpreted as means for ascent or descent, for movement between two
different places, appear as ships' ladders (*Ultramarine*), imagined mountains, actual stairs and steep paths (*Volcano*, *Dark as the Grave*, and
Hear us O Lord), and rotten ladders salvaged from the sea ('Forest Path
to the Spring'). By signifying a connection between two places, media
(land/water), or spiritual states, without occupying or being identified
with either, these *Treppen* actualize the transitional and precarious
condition of the Lowry protagonist who finds himself on such a threshold.
The significance of the whirling fairground in chapter 7 of *Volcano* and of
the madhouse setting of *Lunar Caustic* (with its deliberate echoing of
Caligari) as threshold topoi needs no belabouring. Perhaps the most
crucial of all these topoi for Lowry, however, is the threshold between life
and death, sleep and waking, that Sigbjørn Wilderness would have
occupied in 'The Ordeal of Sigbjørn Wilderness' and that he explores in
Dark as the Grave.[19]

In general, it would seem that threshold places or states are necessarily,
functionally ambivalent: two or more possibilities are available to the
character on a threshold. In Lowry's case these topoi signify the either/or
of regression or rebirth. When the former option is taken, for example,
Plantagenet flees the hospital only to seek asylum curled up like a foetus
at the back of a bar and Geoffrey stumbles off the whirling MÁQUINA INFER-
NAL (*Volcano*, 224–6) stripped of his identity and reduced to a soul in
torment in the threshold scene that most forcibly prefigures his position in

the terrible Farolito of chapter 12. A successful negotiation of the threshold, however, leads to happiness, renewal, even rebirth and an earthly paradise. Glimpses of this resolution occur in the novella 'Through the Panama,' *Dark as the Grave*, and *October Ferry*, but 'Forest Path to the Spring' constitutes Lowry's most emphatic vision of rebirth. Here he creates a miniature *Voyage* ordeal issuing in a deeply mystical, lyrical celebration of nature and a symbolic restoration of Adam and Eve (the first-person narrator and his wife) to their earthly paradise. One could even say that Geoffrey is reborn *for us* by the circular temporal structure of *Volcano*, and this conjoining of violent death, enacted in a grossly physical, grotesquely distorted fictional landscape, culminating in rebirth, renewal, a return from the dead, is quintessential to Bakhtinian carnival. The ambivalence of carnival suggests that, although Geoffrey is decrowned and destroyed, he is also reborn from the ashes of his apocalyptic death to 'tell us something new about hell fire.'

In many ways the concept of monologue is central to Lowry's writing, despite the fact that his typical narrative voice is actually a subtly controlled third person. More often than not he creates a *monologue intérieur* or a narrated consciousness (*erlebte Rede*) that is quite distinct from expressionist monologue. When he does employ a full expressionist monologue, it is a *tour de force*, as in chapter 10 of *Volcano*. This chapter is in every way the most difficult one in the text and, together with 'Through the Panama,' represents his most experimental and generically iconoclastic writing. Because chapter 10 contains the Consul's chief expressionist monologue, as well as providing the best example of the way Lowry deploys visually expressive typographic techniques and inter-textuality, it provides an excellent opportunity to explore Lowry's expressionistic writing at its most forceful. Set in the Salón Ofelia, where Geoffrey, Yvonne, and Hugh have gone after the bullfight in chapter 9, for what the consul slyly calls 'the supper at Emmaus' (292), the entire chapter is presented from the Consul's point of view. It opens with the most ominous of words – 'Mescal' – and in his notes for the chapter Lowry remarks that things must be 'largely expressionistic,' depending upon 'how it looks in print.'[20]

'Oozing alcohol from every pore' (*Volcano*, 286), the Consul experiences one set of horrors after another, beginning with the death-train hallucination that overwhelms him in the opening three and one-half pages and culminating in the 'whirling cerebral chaos' (309) that engulfs him at the end, driving him out into the gathering darkness and on to his death. As the train hallucination subsides – the assailing noises and persecuting voices coming to a halt with: 'A corpse will be transported by express' (286) – the three prepare to order their meal. This carnivalesque scene, complete with verbal nonsense, macaronics, salacious jokes, and innumerable echoes of real events and conversations from earlier in the day interspersed with Geoffrey's own thoughts, even manages to be comic in a grotesque, sinister way. German touches are never far off, with Lowry's Bonn German language teacher reappearing, slightly distorted, on the menu: 'Dr Moise von Schmidthaus's special soup' (292).

But the meal fails dismally when Geoffrey's drunken consciousness rises up to dominate reality. Abruptly, without explanation (or narratorial assistance of any kind), he finds himself in the toilet:

> Why was he here? Why was he always more or less, here? He would have
> been glad of a mirror, to ask himself that question. But there was no
> mirror. Nothing but stone. Perhaps there was no time either, in this stone
> retreat. Perhaps this was the eternity that he'd been making so much fuss
> about, eternity already of the Svidrigailov variety, only instead of a bath-
> house in the country full of spiders, here it turned out to be a stone monas-
> tic cell wherein sat – strange! – who but himself? (296)

For the next seven pages Lowry weaves an elaborate intertextual web of visual and aural notations: voices from snatches of overheard conversation, remembered voices, unidentifiable voices, the bartender, Cervantes' voice, and the Consul's own cry, interrupted by signs: VISITE VD. TLAXCALA! SANTUARIO OCOTLÁN IN TLAXCALA, and many others, each accompanied by passages of tourist-folder text and followed by a railroad and bus-service schedule. The cumulative effect is dizzying until one realizes, upon closer inspection, that every echo and word participates in the complex verbal/ visual codes of the text. This toilet scene *expresses* the turmoil within the Consul's soul, at the same time as it represents, most effectively, his drunken condition and thickens the novel's discourse, striking resonant, symbolic chords at every turn. Like the Consul, stationary in his 'Cave of the Winds … sanctuary bought for a penny or nothing' (295), the diegesis stops, the story goes nowhere, while the anguish of Geoffrey's position and of Lowry's vision sinks in. For all its verbal density and typographic complexity, this section of chapter 10 is static and claustrophobic, very like Beckmann's terrifying vision in *The Night* (see Plate 7).

Geoffrey's monologue begins shortly after his return to the table: '"See here, old bean," the Consul heard himself saying, "to have against you Franco, or Hitler, is one thing, but to have Actinium, Argon, Beryllium, Dysprosium, Nobium, Palladium, Praseodymium – "' (305–6). Although interrupted time and again by Hugh, and frequently shouting questions at

Cervantes, the Consul returns persistently to his obsessive harangue ('I always come back to the point, and take a thing up where it has been left off' 310), which climaxes in his desperate cry: 'I choose – Hell' (316). Lowry's handling of this expressionist monologue is interesting because it clearly demonstrates the rhetorical displacement of the mode when it is used within a novel instead of a play. The monologue here is represented discourse, not an actual delivered speech; therefore, the audience must be imagined, and Hugh, Yvonne, Cervantes, and the old guitar player hovering in the background provide the necessary uncomprehending witnesses to the Consul's *Schrei*. Although he turns upon them all with accusations, and Hugh and Yvonne even try to stop him, this is by no means a dialogue. Geoffrey is not listening but expressing the pain and anger erupting within him.

As I noted earlier, in the discussion of Barnes's imagery, the expressionist metaphor, or image, rather than functioning as a mirror of objective reality with a specific referent becomes independent, and through proliferating associations a world of subjective meaning emerges.[21] Such expressive, autonomous images with constantly expanding associations make *Under the Volcano* a challenge to some and a frustration to others, who prefer to tie down symbols. Lowry explained some of the associations of his wheels, of the number twelve, of the entire novel in his letter to Cape. The image of the volcano is a rich example: it is Popocatapetl with ancient Mexican associations; it is Mount Aetna with Tartarus at its base; it is Moby Dick, a great white whale pursuing and beckoning Geoffrey; it is the Mountain of Delight for Geoffrey the pilgrim; it is a type of Mecca (the small Mexican town of Amecameca lies at its base); it is 'the mighty mountain Himavat' that Geoffrey believes he is climbing as he dies. This volcano is at once the perfect Meidner-like apocalyptic image of Geoffrey's mind and soul and of 'the world itself ... bursting, bursting into black spouts of villages catapulted into space' (*Volcano*, 375). Fully in keeping with an expressionist aesthetic, this autonomous image embodies both the exploding 'I' and the universal forces of destruction loose in a pre–Second World War world. The volcano image may only be understood centripetally, through its development within the discourse, and always with attention to its expanding nature.

Expressionist parallels with Lowry's themes are so obvious as to need little comment. As we have seen, the world of Expressionism is one of madness and degeneration; mad doctors, megalomaniacs, and murderers abound. Despite a recurrent emphasis on apocalypse, the *Aufbruch* of the expressionist more often than not is without positive result. Much stronger is the love of death, especially self-destruction, in and for itself.

The apocalyptic but ironic ending of *Volcano*, with Geoffrey's scream recalling Munch, is a case in point. Equally important to expressionists is the theme of impotence, and their heroes predictably suffer from sexual impotence and/or a sexuality that is tortured and masochistic. Moreover, this impotence marks a general failure of love and of the spirit: 'No se puede vivir sin amar.' As Walter Sokel suggests, spiritual and emotional impotence involves the hero in a desperate longing to become his opposite, the direct man of action who is capable of love.[22] This same impotence also results in violent male-female struggles, with variations upon themes of adultery, castration, and vampirism. The characters embody universal warring male and female forces, with the female invariably threatening to overwhelm the male (for example, in Strindberg, Munch, Kokoschka, and the early Kaiser), and father-son conflicts frequently arise from the repressions of family life (for example, Hasenclever's *The Son* and Kaiser's *Gas*). In general, the dynamic energy of expressionism leads to images and themes of tension, conflict, violent awakening of the soul coupled with a splitting of the self, and above all wilful self-destruction, and this is essentially the world that one finds in *Ultramarine*, *Lunar Caustic*, and *Under the Volcano*.

There are at least three distinct types of film influence apparent in Lowry's work – thematic, stylistic, and epistemological. The first arises from the numerous allusions to particular expressionist films such as *Caligari*, *From Morn to Midnight*, *The Student of Prague*, *The Street*, *The Hands of Orlac*, *Sunrise*, *Warning Shadows*, *Metropolis*. There are a few notable exceptions to the predilection for expressionism – Griffith, and Epstein's *The Fall of the House of Usher*, to mention only two – but references to the German films dominate. When viewing these film classics, one is struck by the recurrence of settings, themes, and specific forms of conflict. Murder and suicide occur regularly. The murderers and suicides are invariably haunted, obsessed, and guilty souls tormented by their overweening desires and persecuted by forces around them. In his *Classics of the Horror Film* William Everson describes *Caligari* and *The Hands of Orlac* as 'Mad-Doctor' films. Troubled marriages or doomed love affairs are another popular subject, from Murnau's *Sunrise*, Robison's *Warning Shadows*, and Grune's *The Street* to, once again, *Caligari* and *Orlac*. Often the jealous husband or lover has a rival and is about to be betrayed. Other ingredients of these films are *Doppelgänger*, mirrors and threatening shadows, framing devices for the main story, circus scenes with whirling ferris wheels, constant hallucination and delirium for the protagonist, and distorted landscapes achieved with stylized studio sets and special lighting effects (see Plates 17, 18, and 19).

There are obvious parallels between the themes and settings in these films and the themes and certain scenes in Lowry's fiction. Sometimes the allusion is made clear in manuscript drafts where, for example, Laruelle's madhouse is likened to something from *The Cabinet of Dr Caligari*.[23] More often the allusion is oblique, only fully appreciated if one is lucky enough to have seen the film. In *October Ferry*, where he alludes to many films, Lowry may have been thinking of German expressionist films when he has Ethan see his face in the rear-view mirror as 'Its lips silently [form] the one word: "Murderer!"' (216) In Fritz Lang's *M* (1931), *Caligari*, and *The Street*, the word 'murderer' appears suddenly and ominously on signs in the centre of the screen, or as a subtitle. (See Plate 17.)

The technical influence of film upon Lowry's work brings two distinct aspects of his narrative to mind. There is first that visual, typographical quality that Stephen Spender noticed and attributed to silent film. Lowry uses signs, advertisements, and inserted documents in a way that recalls the captions and subtitles of silent films. The semiotic dynamic is obvious in *Under the Volcano*, most notably in chapter 10, but the most famous example is the ominous sign that suddenly appears in *Volcano* (132, 235) and that Lowry chose as *Volcano*'s epigraph:

¿LE GUSTA ESTE JARDÍN?

QUE ES SUYO?

EVITE QUE SUS HIJOS LO DESTRUYAN!

But this semiosis is equally dramatic in *October Ferry*, while in 'Through the Panama' it is the determining feature of the discourse.[24] By making narrative material visually distinct and emphatic on the space of the page, Lowry achieves two things: he spatializes his narrative, foregrounding the page and the word in the attempt to privilege diegesis over mimesis, and by thus abstracting his narrative he succeeds in bringing the perceptions of his characters alive as if they were autonomous, possibly universal, forces bristling with significance.

Second, in the German expressionist film, sets, lighting, acting, and camera work were used to create a private universe that supersedes a world of familiar, common, everyday existence. In Lowry's fiction this 'world' is usually a projection of the individual perceptions of his characters. For example, the fairground scene in chapter 7 of *Volcano*, like the fairground in *Caligari* and in several of these films, symbolizes not only a madly revolving world perceived by the protagonist but the helplessness of the individual soul caught up in superior whirling forces. Lowry's famous solipsism, seen from the point of view of expressionism and the German films, is closely allied to the dialectic of subjective and universal tendencies essential to an expressionist style.

In some of his pre-*Volcano* work Lowry does refer to films, but in *Lunar Caustic* he handles the thematic and stylistic influence of film in ways both more sophisticated and more integral to his purpose. The novella falls into three distinct sections. The first and last ones portray Plantagenet before and after the hospital experience, with the last section repeating several details such as the bar, the old lady, and the church from the first. Together they frame the central action, setting off and emphasizing the world of the insane. This framing technique casts an ironic note over the entire story, for Plantagenet gains nothing from his pilgrimage and the world outside appears as threatening as the hospital.

Within the hospital section, five separate scenes are presented from Plantagenet's uncertain point of view. First impressions of the ward, disturbed by hallucination and fantasy, gradually give way to the puppet show, followed by the episode at the piano and the discussion with Claggart. The fifth scene occurs at the hospital window, as Plantagenet watches the storm.

There may be several influences at work in Lowry's description of the puppet show, but one of particular interest is Robison's film *Warning Shadows* (1922), which introduces the characters in the film as shadows on a stage, placed there and removed by huge shadow hands. The atmosphere of mysterious control created by this device is ominous, and this sense of threat is closely paralleled in Lowry's handling of the puppet-show scene:

> As the hand plunged about reaching for Punch with a weird accelerated motion which cast glowering shadows on the wall, it struck Plantagenet that the drama was being diverted from its course by some sinister disposition of the puppeteer's ... Was it only his imagination, or was the puppeteer trying to deliberately frighten them? ... He had the curious feeling that he had made a sort of descent into the maelstrom, a maelstrom terrifying for the last reason one might have expected: that there was about it sometimes just this loathsome, patient calm.[25]

The central metaphor of *Lunar Caustic* is that of the madhouse. Depending upon one's perception, the entire world can seem more mad than an asylum. Certainly, a madhouse is the perfect expression of a confused consciousness and a distraught soul, and Lowry's use of both framing strategy and hospital setting in *Lunar Caustic* bears a striking resemblance to *The Cabinet of Dr Caligari*. The movie opens with two men talking in a garden. One begins the strange account of his life as the scene fades to a fairground in the distant town of Holstenwall, and the story of Caligari unfolds. At the end we return to these men, who turn out to be inmates of an asylum, where the director, now in white coat, looks exactly like the madman Caligari. Like the film, *Lunar Caustic* questions whether the story is merely the result of a diseased mind or an astute portrayal of the real nature of authority, whether the world really is a place of such horror or whether this madness is nothing more than the reflection of an obsessed soul? The distinction between madness and sanity, or between subjective and objective reality, is disturbingly blurred in both, so that it is no coincidence that, in the context of *Lunar Caustic*, Plantagenet says to Claggart: 'There are always two sides, *nicht wahr, Herr Doktor*, to a show like this?' (47)

Among the films of obvious thematic and stylistic relevance to *Under the Volcano* are *Caligari*, *The Hands of Orlac* (with *Mad Love*, 1935, the Hollywood remake starring Peter Lorre, central to *Volcano*), and *Sunrise*. Each of these films portrays the essentially expressionist subject of a cataclysmic struggle within a man's soul or mind, and the stories are invariably macabre: a mad mountebank-doctor unleashes a murderous somnambulist or a musician with the grafted hands of a murderer goes mad. The characters operate less as individuals, despite the projection of subjective states of dream, hallucination, and madness, than as symbols of universal problems, social ills, or disturbed psychic states. Mirrors, whirling fairgrounds, double and multiple exposures and chiaroscuro create the sensation of a landscape alive with menacing power.

Mad Love is both the 'hieroglyphic of the times' in its portrayal of power and obsession, and a thematic parallel for the story of Geoffrey and Yvonne. Apart from Peter Lorre's magnificent portrayal of Doctor Gogol, it is a weak film, but Lowry had also seen the original *Hands of Orlac* starring Conrad Veidt (see Plate 19). The story involves a mad Doctor Gogol who grafts a murderer's hands on to an injured pianist, Stephen Orlac. Under this terrible influence, Orlac kills his father. Gogol meanwhile is determined to possess Orlac's beautiful actress wife, Yvonne. After her repeated refusals to betray her husband, the doctor attempts to destroy the artist, and then tries to strangle Yvonne while the Wildean refrain 'Each man kills the thing he loves' echoes in his mind.[26] Gogol does not succeed with his evil intentions because Orlac arrives just in time to save his wife, but in *Under the Volcano* there is no such facile conclusion. Destruction and betrayal, once set in motion, grind out a tragic conclusion, and Geoffrey *does* kill the thing he loves.

In 1928 Lowry saw Fred Murnau's *Sunrise* (*Sonnenaufgang*), which he said had influenced him 'almost as much as any book [he] ever read' (*Letters*, 239). In chapter 11 of the 1940 version of *Volcano* there are several references to *Sunrise*. Although the overt references were cut, chapter 11 of the final version opens with the cryptic direction 'SUNSET,' and in chapter 7, as the Consul views El Farolito in his mind's eye, he remembers a sunrise he had watched from there, 'a slow bomb bursting over the Sierra Madre – *Sonnenaufgang!*' (214).

Although Murnau's *Sunrise* was not the only film to make its way into the *Volcano*, it is probably a more profound influence than either *Caligari* or *Orlac*. Murnau's subject is an adulterous marriage in which the Man – none of the characters has a name, thereby universalizing the theme – attempts to kill his unwanted Wife. Double exposures produce the effect of good and evil battling for possession of the Man's soul until his tortured form takes on symbolic proportions and the landscape comes to life via menacing lighting effects. The couple is reconciled after near disaster, and, while they gaze at wedding photographs in a window, there is a sequence that resembles Lowry's handling of double exposure in the chapter 2 scene with Yvonne. As she and Geoffrey pause outside the printer's shop, Yvonne perceives their reflected image:

> They stood, as once, looking in ... From the mirror within the window an ocean creature so drenched and coppered by sun and winnowed by sea-wind and spray looked back at her she seemed, even while making the fugitive motions of Yvonne's vanity, somewhere beyond human grief char-ioting the surf. But the sun turned grief to poison and a glowing body only mocked the sick heart, Yvonne knew, if the sun-darkened creature of waves and sea margins and windows did not! In the window itself, on either side of this abstracted gaze of her mirrored face, the same brave wedding invitations she remembered were ranged ... but this time there was some-thing she hadn't seen before, which the Consul now pointed out with a murmur of 'Strange.' (*Volcano*, 61)

The image of Yvonne in the present moment and in the near and more distant past is superimposed upon the photographs and invitations within the window. These in turn are seen against the enlargement of '*La Despedida*' – 'set behind and above the already spinning flywheel of the presses' (61). Reflected in the window, Yvonne sees Geoffrey and herself as they once were: 'They stood, as once, looking in.' She sees herself as she has recently been, 'coppered by sun and winnowed by sea-wind.' There is even the suggestion that a completely different Yvonne appears in the window, a Venus-like Yvonne 'somewhere beyond human grief charioting the surf.' But moving forward through these fragmented images of Yvonne's personality, or these other selves, there are further levels of present and past reality – the photographs and invitations linking past to present, the spinning flywheel that temporally precedes the invitations, the ancient glacial rock, at one time whole, now split by fire. This time Lowry employs the double-exposure technique to portray the expressionist dialectic of subjectivism and cosmic forces. '*La Despedida*' is an excellent image of the forces overwhelming the world, while the superimposition of the image of the split rock on the reflection of Yvonne and Geoffrey implies that it is an equally apt image of the internal forces destroying these two people.

The third influence of film on Lowry's art is epistemological in two senses. The first and most important of these is what I call the dramatizing of epistemological problems, but Lowry seems to have had an additional factor in mind. In *October Ferry* (61) Ethan describes films as having more reality than life and novels as having no reality at all. In his letters, Lowry calls for a new approach to reality, and in his 1951 'Work in Progress' statement he speaks of his novels as films. *Volcano* can be seen as a film of Geoffrey's life, with the *Voyage* as the all-encompassing film of Sigbjørn Wilderness's life. Lowry felt that films somehow captured reality better than novels, probably for the simple reason that they move and therefore present, better than other art forms do, the illusion of dynamic, ever-changing reality.

Any discussion of expressionist film, however, tends to focus upon epistemological problems. Moreover, this influence from film brings one back to the non-mimetic foundation of expressionism and to the foundation of Lowry's art. The epistemological question is especially significant for film because it is the nature of the medium to comment upon these problems. Early film-makers were well aware of the film's capacity to reproduce objective reality, to produce as well an alternate, independent, yet parallel reality, and they often exploited the tension between the two in order to explore the nature of the self and the ways in which we perceive ourselves and the external world. *The Cabinet of Dr Caligari* is a classic example because the asylum frame forces the viewer to question the reality of what has been seen. Thus, the film creates a commentary between text and subtext that dramatizes epistemological problems.

The dramatizing of epistemological problems, apparent throughout Lowry's work, is most comparable to film in *Under the Volcano*. Here we witness the movie of Geoffrey's life, not simply in terms of externals, and certainly not with a precise etiology, but as the expression of his soul, which becomes synonymous with Western man on the brink of the abyss. A highly charged dialectic is maintained between text and subtext, between outer and inner reality. The toilet scene in chapter 10 is a splendid example. Although one can scarcely speak of this scene as framed by the rest of the chapter (the scene is quite short), it is set off on either side by the objective reality of the Salón Ofelia and the meal with Yvonne and Hugh. Disruption of temporal and spatial continuities together with a jerky telegraph style create the sense of extreme distortion and confusion in the Consul's mescal-fogged mind. By this point in the novel, however, it is clear that Lowry is telling us 'something new about hell fire' as well as about dipsomania, because the scene is much more than a mimetic rendering of a drunken mind. Geoffrey is the suffering writer-artist figure; he is Christ, Faust, Prometheus, the failed expressionist New Man. The superimposition of his inner reality upon the outer reality of tourist folder, railway schedule, indeed of the entire day, expresses his agony and forces the reader to perceive his personal horror *and* the universal implications of his vision.

It is the mark of a truly great writer that no *single* source or influence should dominate his art, and so expressionism is only one aspect of Lowry's fictional world, together with the Cabbala, a stern Protestantism, and mescal. Expressionism may, however, be more important than these other factors. Certainly, it was a profound and lasting influence that shaped Lowry's vision and his technique. That he continued to measure artistic creation in terms of expressionism is clear from a letter of 11 January 1952 to his editor, Robert Giroux, in which he wondered if jazz (another of his lifelong enthusiasms) was not less a type of 'music perhaps ... [than] a form of expressionism, maybe actually more analogous to literature or poetry, than music.'[27] Clearly, Lowry was still thinking about expressionism in the post-*Volcano* years.

Even in as late a work as *October Ferry* we find a distraught Ethan questioning his perceptions; it seems to him 'as if the subjective world within ... [has] somehow turned itself inside out: as if the objective world without [has] itself caught a sort of hysteria' (116). This thought immediately evokes memories of *The Hairy Ape* and Claude Rains in *From Morn to Midnight*. Apart from such overt references, however, Lowry employs a deliberately expressionist style in many scenes of *October Ferry* (for example, in chapters 18 and 31) in order to portray the tumult within

Ethan's soul, and these scenes mark stages of distress, *Stationen*, in his journey towards spiritual and psychic rebirth.

The strong expressionism of *Under the Volcano* can be seen in a similar light. To be sure, Lowry created a truly expressionist hero in Geoffrey and provided, through his eyes, an expressionist vision, but *Volcano* is also a stage in a much longer journey – *The Voyage That Never Ends*. Geoffrey's failure to progress can in part be attributed to *his* expressionist vision and limitations. Unlike Ethan, who, even in the published version of *October Ferry*, demonstrates greater potential for balance, the Consul is trapped in the metaphysics of the 'expressive fallacy.'[28] Unable to distinguish between self and not-self, unable to act or to love, he wills his destruction. To an extent, then, Lowry used expressionism deliberately and critically to dramatize the cost of such confusion.

The question remains, however, whether Lowry himself managed to control and outgrow his own attraction to German Expressionism. Expressionism was definitely a movement for the young, and most artists associated with the movement developed other styles and themes after a period of intense involvement. With Lowry the case is less clear. While *Hear us O Lord* strives for a vision of harmony and *October Ferry* incorporates expressionist scenes within a larger whole, Lowry was unable to finish these works. In the last analysis he typifies an expressionist (and carnivalesque) position in that his work demonstrates the essentially ambiguous pull towards abstraction, transcendence of this world in moments of lyrical beauty and mystical vision (achieved exquisitely in 'The Forest Path to the Spring'), and a positive apocalypse leading to rebirth on the one hand and towards 'empathy,' identification with the filth and decay of this world, and a longing for regression and death on the other. Interestingly, Lowry's vision of rebirth in 'Forest Path' depends upon the speaker-hero's intimate relationship with the surrounding forces of nature; in this one case he uses empathy as a positive, guiding principle in life, and like Pechstein or other *Brücke* painters, or like Herman Voaden, he celebrates the transforming power of the natural world.

Nevertheless, the fact that his greatest work is *Under the Volcano*, a distorted vision of collapse, serves as a reminder that the expressionist vision of madness and degeneration appealed profoundly to Lowry. Like Geoffrey, he was finally incapable of achieving a new balance. At the same time, his use of expressionism explains why Lowry is no detached formalist like so many modernists. As a writer he puts his own soul on the line, and in so doing he displays the deep expressionist concern for humanity.[29] By understanding Lowry's expressionism, it is easier to appreciate his special blend of spirituality and gross physicality, solipsism and vision, autobiography and prophecy; this blend characterizes his method and his position as a modernist on the brink of becoming post-modern. Expressionism, then, provides the necessary context for an understanding of Lowry's art and for a *Gestalt* reading of that twentieth-century masterpiece that portrays, as Lowry so aptly put it, 'the forces in man which cause him to be terrified of himself ... [and] the ultimate fate of mankind.'

Sheila Watson and the 'Double Hook' of Expressive Abstraction

In 1935, two years after she graduated from the University of British Columbia with a masters degree in English and a teaching certificate, Sheila Watson (1909–) found herself 'put down as a stranger' in Dog Creek, a dry, isolated hamlet in the Cariboo district of the British Columbia interior where she would spend the next two years. Then as now, it is an enormous leap from Vancouver to Dog Creek, from reading Eliot, Pound, Lewis, Stein, and Lawrence to teaching a handful of Indian and white children in a place no one has heard of. 'I had no idea where it was when I left by train in Vancouver, except somewhere *there.*'[1]

Dog Creek: roughly 274 kilometres north of Vancouver as the crow flies, but 634 from Vancouver via Williams Lake or 491 by the Clinton route over gravel logging roads; north of Hope and Cache Creek, south of Quesnel and Alkali Lake; at an elevation of 3,370 feet on the Chilcotin Plateau rangeland, with a mean annual rainfall of less than 30 centimetres, where temperatures range from -51.1 to 38.9 degrees Celsius and you are lucky to have 90 days frost free. Dog Creek: 8 kilometres to Gang Ranch, 19 to Alkali, 47 to Riske Creek, 74 to Lone Bute, 68 to Painted Chasm, and 187 to Kleena Kleene: places in the middle of nowhere, names to conjure with, and a past woven out of legend, history, and myth. An important stop during the 1850s and 1860s on the first Gold Rush wagon road between Yale and Soda Creek, Dog Creek once claimed the Dog Creek Hotel (1856), with 'the finest wines, liquors and cigars,' stabling for twenty-five horses, and the headquarters for the stage line, and on the walls of the caves in the basaltic escarpment above the town you can still see the pictographs made by Indians who worshipped there.[2] But the gold in the rivers and mines to the north ran out, and the miners, speculators, adventurers went away. Dog Creek: today as in 1935 you arrive 'somewhere *there*' in a lonely wilderness of bleached colours and of parched, wrinkled hills, on a scale so immense that it dwarfs any horse and rider, or any car. Ancient, rounded hills covered in prickly pear and sage, dotted with clumps of cottonwood, and haunted by coyotes. A landscape so bare that little obstructs the eye from its startled perception of patterns – light and shadow, sky and undulating horizon, rutted road, winding creek bottom, cracked earth, willow roots – and a very few people: 'figures in a ground, from which they could not be separated.'[3]

Perhaps it was the isolation, or the concentration of a small community turned in upon itself, or the stark severity of the landscape, that unified these images and patterns in Watson's imagination so that several years later, in the mid-forties, and three thousand miles away on Bloor Street in Toronto, these images began to recur of 'the land ... humped against the sky' (*DH*, 53), of 'the folds of the hills' (19) with 'the raw skin of the sky drawn over them like a sack' (36) and of 'the padded imprint of a coyote's foot at the far edge of the moving water' (35).[4] Images: images and patterns, and the determination *not* to write *about* anything such as the west, Indians, murder, suicide, and childbirth. 'I'd been away for a long time,' Watson remembers, 'before I realised that if I had something I wanted to say, it was going to be said in these images. And there was something I wanted to say: about how people are driven, how if they have no art, how if they have no tradition, how if they have no ritual, they are driven in one of two ways, either towards violence or towards insensibility – if they have no mediating rituals which manifest themselves in what I suppose we call art forms. And so it was with this that the novel began'.[5]

But the writing itself did not begin until some time early in the fifties (c 1951–52), when the immediate experience of teaching, living, and riding in Dog Creek had settled into the potent images that could express, not one community's alienation, violence, and insensibility, but an entire civilization's *Angst*. She began in the thirties with a story called 'Rough Answer,' followed by a novel called 'Deep Hollow Creek' (the local name for Dog Creek), which was never published because, she tells us, 'I had to get the authorial voice out of the novel ... I didn't want a voice talking about something. I wanted voices ... a cry of voices – a *vox clamantis* – voices crying out in the wilderness.'[6] And what she finally wrote did not mirror external reality – British Columbia Cariboo country – but mapped an inner space, an inner voice. By what Doug Jones locates as her 'shift in mode, away from realism and towards myth,' Watson rendered 'the reality and intensity of inner experience, the shape and intensity of vision.'[7]

That *The Double Hook* did not finally appear until 1959 is another story, a consequence of the cautious conservatism of Canadian publishers, several of whom rejected the manuscript because it was unusual and experimental. In her 1968 article 'Canada and Wyndham Lewis the Artist' Watson noted, with a touch of wry irony, that as late as 1948 'modernists' in Canada were 'startled' by the canvases of Riopelle and Borduas and thought they had found 'in the work of Pollock and Rothko and in the birth of abstract expressionism in New York a wholly unheralded development.'[8] These modernists whom she so gently upbraids are the self-styled pundits and authorities, those whom Charles Comfort, Bertram Brooker, Kathleen Munn, Herman Voaden, Emily Carr, and Samuel Borenstein (to mention only a few of the truly aware and innovative) either had to face or ignore – and who, in turn, attacked or ignored them.

Although it is not true that *The Double Hook* has been ignored since it finally broke through a wall of resistance (from printers who 'altered the original ... to bring it more into line with "normal" prose punctuation,' editors who yanked out a seemingly explanatory passage to use as a prefatory quote, and academics keen to smooth the reader's way with helpful introductions),[9] it has been, until quite recently, Canada's most neglected and misread 'classic.' We know it, in the first place, because so many other more accessible writers have acclaimed the novel's mythic power and their debt to this power. Generally speaking, however, Watson, like Riopelle and Borduas (or other members of the avant-garde in Canada), like Pollock and Rothko, is still received with a certain 'startled' surprise as 'a wholly unheralded development.' But *The Double Hook* was not 'unheralded,' either within the context of Watson's own interests or (since her private interests cannot be widely known) within the context of twentieth-century art and literature.

Although Watson's literary output has been small – to date one novel, five stories, and a 1974 collection of essays from the sixties and early seventies – there has been a steadily increasing amount of serious critical attention to *The Double Hook*, and yet most critics seem unaware of the novel's roots in early modernist aesthetics. *The Double Hook*, however, is a work of expressive abstraction, one of the few and certainly one of the finest in the Canadian canon. The tension between story and discourse that pulls closer to empathy and representation in *Under the Volcano* or stretches taut and ambivalent in *Nightwood* reaches a fine degree of abstraction and stasis 'under Watson's eye.'

That training of the eye, which would culminate in the images of *The*

Double Hook, began with her university reading in literature during the early thirties, when the 'moderns' had to be smuggled into one's private curriculum, where their clandestine presence, of course, rendered them all the more important. During these years she was reading Yeats, Eliot, Joyce, Lewis, and Pound, and discovering lifetime favourites in Dostoyev-sky's *The Possessed* and Gogol's *Dead Souls*. She was also becoming familiar with modern art, including German Expressionism, and after the war purchased some of the earliest works available on the subject in English, such as Penguin's 1938 *Modern German Art*, written pseudony-mously by 'Peter Thoene.'[10]

Many years later her early passion for the moderns and a 1956 Paris exhibition of his painting led her to a serious consideration of Wyndham Lewis, whose double life as painter and writer became the subject of a doctoral thesis of more than five hundred pages. The formal work on the thesis began in 1957, after the year in Paris; however 'Wyndham Lewis and Expressionism' was only completed in 1965, the gleaning of over thirty years' exploration of modern art and aesthetics and of the short-lived vorticist movement in England. If this thesis, completed more than a decade after *The Double Hook*, is of interest to the novel's reconsidera-tion here, it is because of the light it sheds on the subtlety and depth of Watson's knowledge of Expressionism as a seminal modernist aesthetic and style. Watson, unlike most other Lewis scholars, sees his total *oeuvre* as a consistent system, instead of incoherent, conflicting fragments, that reveals itself most closely when Lewis is viewed within the context of Expressionism: 'Had Lewis not begun as an Expressionist he would not have understood the problems of Expressionism nor perhaps their rela-tionship to technology. But had he not moved beyond Expressionism he could hardly have created the multiplicity of characters which crowd and elbow in his pages.'[11] Of course, this is not the place to decide whether or not Lewis's Vorticism (a very brief phase in his life, from about 1912 to 1915, after all) is an aspect of a more general abstract aesthetic; nevertheless, it is very important to remember that Watson sees him this way and in doing so lifts him free of the vorticist label into a much more important context. Moreover, she precedes by a decade and more the other scholars who appreciate Lewis's expressionist qualities.[12] Only a mind already conversant with the expressionist position and interested in its history would perceive Lewis's *oeuvre* in these terms.

It seems impossible to disagree with her assessment of Lewis's *Enemy of the Stars* – with its violent subject, fragmented structure, jagged language, and *Doppelgänger* hero Arghol/Hanp – as an extravagantly expressionist play. *Enemy* was written at an early point in Lewis's exploration of expressionist art and aesthetics and at the enthusiastic beginning of the Rebel Art Centre (1913) and the vorticist movement (as Pound named it). It was published in *Blast 1* (1914), whose 'Vortices' and 'Blasts and Blesses' Ulrich Weisstein describes as 'patently Expressionist.'[13] But as Watson is careful to point out, Lewis soon became uneasy with the expressionist position, so that the novel *Tarr* (1914–15) already presents the 'implications of an expressionist way of life' *critically* in the figure of Otto Kreisler, a destructive Nietzschean madman-cum-artist. By the time he completed *Tarr* early in 1915, Vorticism was dead as a movement, and the war had usurped both public interest and artistic energy. Its most truly expressionist member, Henri Gaudier-Brzeska, would soon be killed in a charge at Neuville St Vaast (on 5 June 1915, aged twenty-three years), and Lewis had had time to reflect upon the consequences of *official* expressionist theory. His remark, as early as 1915 in the second and last issue of *Blast*, was as uncannily prophetic as it was perceptive: 'Unofficial Germany has done more for the movement that this paper was founded to propagate, and for all branches of contemporary activity in Science and Art than any other country. It would be the absurdist ingratitude on the part of artists to forget this ... We are debtors to a tribe of detached individuals.'[14] 'Unofficial Germany' was its artists, men like Marc, Pechstein, and Kandinsky, whose woodcuts Lewis had praised in an article for *Blast 1* – 'Notes on Some German Woodcuts at the Twenty-One Gallery' – for being 'permeated by Eternity' and expressing 'only the black core of Life.' 'Official Germany,' as far as the arts and culture generally were concerned, came to be represented by authorities like Karl Scheffler, Gustav Hartlaub, Heinrich Wölfflin, Wilhelm Worringer, Hermann Bahr, and Oswald Spengler. And one of the most valuable aspects of 'Wyndham Lewis and Expressionism,' whether it is Lewis or Watson we are considering, is the attention with which Watson traces the roots, assumptions, and developments of German expressionist theory as it is transformed from an active, creative, revolutionary impulse into a new dogmatism pronounced (and criticized) by a chorus of 'official' voices and vested interests.

The vorticists, after all, began by stridently proclaiming themselves opposed to Marinetti's Futurism (which Lewis disparagingly referred to as mere 'automobilism,' Hulme dismissed as 'the last efflorescence of impressionism,' and Pound labelled 'accelerated Impressionism'). They allied themselves emphatically with the anti-naturalist schools of Cubism and Expressionism, as their 1914 advertisement in the *Spectator* announced: 'The Manifesto of the Vorticists. The English Parallel Movement to Cubism and Expressionism. Imagisme in Poetry. Death Blow to Impres-

sionism and Futurism and all the Refuse of naif science.'[15] In sorting out
what Lewis understood by this 'parallel' position, Watson goes back to
Schopenhauer, Nietzsche, and the Austrian art historian Alois Riegl,
whose theory of will to form or inner necessity led directly to Worringer's
Abstraction and Empathy. The ideas of these philosophers and art historians are the inheritance of Lewis, who was one of the few in the
England of his day to have an intimate knowledge of contemporary German art. One other Englishman was also well informed, at least by 1913,
and that was T.E. Hulme, who had discovered Worringer, introduced his
work to English audiences in lectures, and applied Worringer's concept of
a dual *Kunstwollen* to the art of his contemporaries in London.[16]
Worringer's privileging of non-iconic abstraction coincided closely with
Lewis's practice, although Lewis also believed that art could be at once
expressive (that is, eliciting a degree of empathy from the viewer), iconic,
and abstract. (Worringer's example of just such an art was the Gothic.) As
late as 1938 Lewis was to describe Vorticism (*his* Vorticism) as that art in
which 'the direct and hot impressions of life are mated with Abstraction,
or the combinations of the Will.'[17]

Throughout chapter 1 of her thesis, entitled 'The Visual Revolution:
Inner Necessity and Significant Form,' Watson is at pains to describe
Lewis's expressive abstraction and to show where and why he rejected
the Expressionism of official Germany. Although clearly creating out of
some sense of inner necessity or artistic will, Lewis refused to grant that
necessity any absolute status as a *Zeitgeist* or as a principle of artistic
volition. Moreover, the extremes of feeling and subjectivity on the one
hand and Kandinsky's advance towards non-iconic abstraction on the
other repelled him equally. From *Blast 2*, Watson quotes Lewis – in a
remark fully applicable to *The Double Hook* – on the artist's duty to
'ENRICH abstraction till it is almost plain life, or rather to get deeply
immersed in material life to experience the shaping power amongst its
vibrations, and to accentuate and perpetuate these.' Herein lies the
essence of 'significant form,' which, as Watson notes (Thesis, 55), is not
Clive Bell's invention but a term formulated in the late nineteenth century
by Konrad Fiedler, who described the concept as the practical result of
'inner necessity' (*innere Notwendigkeit* – [see the discussion of Kandinsky
in chapter 1]). The 'shaping power' intuited or felt by the artist gives rise
to these patterns or essences, which he or she expresses as the significant
form of objects, *not* of the soul of the artist. As a consequence, these
forms, at once expressive and abstract, are hard, clear, and static. The
creating subject is implied, the subjective will to form transcended in the
work of art, which is 'a patterned energy made visible.'[18]

With a reading knowledge of German, Watson was not entirely reliant on English sources, but when she was writing her thesis, very little contemporary scholarly work had been done on German Expressionism, especially in English. Siegfried Kracauer (1947), Peter Selz (1957), and Walter Sokel (1959), all sources for her study, were among the earliest to introduce the once 'degenerate' German avant-garde to a post–Second World War English-speaking public. It is all the more noteworthy, therefore, that she lays bare the philosophical roots of the movement and focuses upon Worringer's 'official' role, which quite logically led him to believe that by the twenties the expressionists had betrayed the great non-iconic potential of a northern *Kunstwollen*.[19] Equally interesting is her description of Spengler's *Zeitgeist* as 'expressionist' (Thesis, 53) because he had expanded the theory of 'inner necessity' and *Kunstwollen* into cultural determinism (not a large step from Worringer's position in *Empathy and Abstraction.*) Spengler, of course, was one of Lewis's prime targets, the voice of a historically obsessed 'official' Germany at its worst, who called expressionist art an 'unabashed farce' in *Decline of the West* (Thesis, 108). Watson lays bare the expressionist context for Lewis's work with care, making distinctions and observations about the movement which have only recently become more commonly known and accepted. Her own reading lies primarily in art history and aesthetics (Toller and Kaiser are the only writers she cites); hence she frequently refers to the artists – to Kokoschka, Munch, Heckel, Barlach (a personal favourite of Watson's), and Marc, whose ability to make the inanimate animate is a measure of their (and like them, Lewis's) expressionism – in order to establish a salient point about Lewis's prose.

Working from this foundation, Watson articulates a vision of Lewis as abstract expressionist that reveals the significant form of his *oeuvre* and provides us with a clear frame of reference for her own work. The point is not that Watson's prose is *like* Lewis's or even that she was directly influenced by him – though like him she chose to write a 'mediating ritual,' to become a mythographer. It is more probable that she was in a position to see the figure of Lewis in abstract expressionist terms because she was already informed and sensitive to the ground from which he should not be separated. Just as Lewis was one of the few artists in England before the First World War to know German art, so Watson was one of the few in Canada to be interested in German Expressionism and its post–Second World War inheritor, Abstract Expressionism.[20]

When Watson turns from Lewis's aesthetics, criticism, and painting to discussion of his literary work – especially *The Childermass* – she does not apologize for retaining the term 'abstract expressionist' to describe his vision. And yet Abstract Expressionism is a term of fine-art criticism that denotes a particular type of fully non-iconic art that developed in New York after the war (see chapter 1). How can a writer be an *abstract* expressionist? From its first usage (probably in *Der Sturm*, 1919)[21] it signified a thoroughly non-iconic, rhythmic, patterned plastic art, but what Watson seems to identify in a Lewis canvas, and I prefer to speak of as expressive abstraction, is his combination of intensity (of colour, gesture, and line) with stasis, clarity, and control. Intensity combined with stasis seem to be the key terms in such a description, and they are as applicable, if not more so, to Watson's *Double Hook* as to Lewis's narratives – or, perhaps, Watson has succeeded in a way that Lewis did not. Certainly, the terms that have been used to describe the novel, such as symbolic, or mythic, are slippery in the extreme and in a sense testify to critical uncertainty about what to *do* with *The Double Hook*. Symbolic and mythic elements are unquestionably present in the text, but so they are as well in *Moby Dick* and *Lord Jim*, in *Wuthering Heights* and *Surfacing*. But it would be absurd to think of these novels as abstract or expressionist. There is something fundamental about the nature of *The Double Hook* that cannot be identified by reference to aspects or elements of its textuality, and elucidations of its sources in biblical or liturgical events or its debt to Amerindian mythology – pertinent as these may be – do not address the problem.

The unique and uniquely powerful nature of the text lies in its composition, in the way in which it has been built, its structural method. One clue to this method is apparent in Watson's stated purpose: not to write *about* the west or Indians or murder or whatever; in fact 'to get the about out' of her writing altogether.[22] Of course, to some degree she has failed in this – must fail – because literature, especially the novel, and language cannot escape reference and representation and still mean anything worth writing (about). Even MacLeish knew that the poem would have to mean. Nevertheless, Watson has achieved a remarkable degree of resistance to representation, hence of abstraction from the subject, while at the same time exploiting (and controlling) the inevitable *empathy* (with represented subject) that characters and story involve. My return to Worringer's word – *Einfühlung* – is deliberate here, for what Watson has done is to create a 'gothic' novel in the sense that Worringer would say a work of art is gothic when it arises from the *dual* artistic impulse of empathy and abstraction.[23]

The Double Hook is abstract in a way that Kandinsky's *Heavy Red*, Pollock's *Night Mist*, or De Kooning's *Gotham News* are not (though most of De Kooning's *Woman* paintings – for example, *Woman i, 1950–52* –

have the mythic power, violence, and representational flashes that invite comparison with Watson's figures), by virtue of the fact that it expresses something recognizable that is felt and shared by artist and reader – in short, and paradoxically, because of its represented subject and its empathy. It is on these grounds above all others that Watson differs so importantly from Gertrude Stein, the modernist writer most often thought of as abstract. But Stein's writing is an 'art by subtraction,' where not only the details of conventional realism but also characterization, action, and punctuation are cut, leaving (for example, in a work like *The Making of Americans*, where the narrating, describing subject recalls some of the New York Abstract Expressionists' theories, or in *Tender Buttons*) the 'verbal collage' of sounds and patterns that will suggest a cubist still-life.[24] Similarities between Stein and Watson, such as the reliance on repetition and temporal presentness (discussed below), are of minor significance. Stein's art is primarily cubist, deconstructive, and reistic, aiming to present only what is there as it is actually seen, but Watson wishes to 'ENRICH abstraction,' to release the meaningful 'shaping power' of life in the rituals, myths, and actions of a story.

'Mediating rituals which manifest themselves in ... art forms ...' – with these words Watson sums up her concept of art and of the role of the artist, and her expressive abstraction should be approached with these assumptions in mind. For Watson's purposes art is ritual, and as ritual it performs an intimate and vital function within a human community, a function close to those of religion and myth, a function capable of consolidating, preserving, even of redeeming humanity. The artist, like priest or shaman, mediates between the human community and the elemental, spiritual, or possibly cosmic forces impinging on it by expressing, while shaping and transforming, that energy. And as Pound said: 'Energy creates pattern.'[25] At the same time, the artist mediates among members of the group through the art-forms that safeguard them from extremes of 'violence or ... insensibility.' Although her remarks in 'What I Am Going To Do' only hint at what the necessary art-forms should be like, they do reveal the assumption underlying Watson's fiction – that humanity is 'space shy,' as Worringer would say, living alienated in ignorance and above all in fear of the environment. And *Angst* is the operative feeling of Watson's novel: 'Fear making mischief. Laying traps for men. The dog and his servants plaguing the earth. Fear skulking round. Fear walking round in the living shape of the dead. No stone was big enough, no pile of stones, to weigh down fear' (*DH*, 61).

Judging from the way the novel began – in voices, images, and patterns – and Watson's determination to refuse the 'about' of traditional storytelling, and judging from the text itself, art-forms that can fulfil their highest duty as mediating rituals are resolutely non-naturalistic; for Watson, they cannot arise from the desire to imitate or merely to represent. Furthermore, Watson's narratives are all highly objective. However much they spring from personal experience, there is no sense of an autobiographical self in the text and, emphatically in *The Double Hook*, little sense of a central perceiving and narrating 'I.' Here the artist really has refined herself out of existence (a point I shall return to), and if subjectivity can be spoken of at all in this novel, it is only with the most precise of qualifications. Watson's approach to art and the artist is, in part, explicable in terms of 'inner necessity' and 'significant form': the community must have myth, ritual – in short, art –if it is to survive, and the artist must express those needs in significant forms; human beings are figures in a ground, patterns in time and space. Like Eliot in *The Wasteland*, or Pound in *The Cantos*, both of which echo and reverberate through *The Double Hook*, Watson values tradition ('How if they have no art, how if they have no tradition') and is intent upon recuperating these precious fragments from the past (mythical, liturgical, and literary), which she needs to construct her text and carry out her ritual.

Instead of being acted upon by some ghostly *Zeitgeist*, she seizes what Frobenius calls the *paideuma* – in Kenner's words speaking of Pound, 'a people's whole congeries of patterned energies, from their "ideas" down to the things they know in their bones' – and through intensity and control finds its significant 'form-language.'[26] Her own tradition as active creator stretches back through Expressionism in painting and a devotion to the moderns, to Lewis, T.E. Hulme (indeed, his specific yoking of abstraction and redemption – like Worringer's – foreshadows Watson's vision), Kandinsky, and Worringer.[27] Her achievement in *The Double Hook* is no less than a resounding affirmation of the will to art, which promises to restructure a culture's inheritance in such a way as to revitalize the human community. Watson's *artist* does not rebel in despair and *Aufbruch*. Instead, that problem is society's (in *The Double Hook*, it is James's problem), and within its violent convulsions and fear she finds the patterns of apocalypse and redemption.

The story (and there *is* a simple story) begins with 'the characteristic gesture of expressionist art': a raised fist.[28] James Potter is murdering his mother, who seems somehow to stand in his way, blocking the stairs, resisting his will, denying his freedom. His sister, Greta, is at the stove 'grinding away James's voice' (*DH*, 19), seeing in this matricide her chance to rule in her mother's place, her chance to claim her brother for herself.

From here the rope spins out over the entire community, whose few members either become enmeshed in James's violence or deny it by refusing to acknowledge it, by hiding in insensibility.

But this is only the first of James's violent outbursts. He has made his neighbour's daughter, Lenchen, pregnant, and while he seems genuinely drawn to 'the girl,' he will not acknowledge his act or accept the responsibility of fatherhood until the final moments of the novel, when, lost, he circles and ends where he began. His day that begins in murder continues in smouldering rage until he turns on Lenchen, who has come to his door for help, with a whip and then savagely attacks and blinds Kip, the young man who has been his go-between with Lenchen. To make matters worse, his mother will not lie dead but haunts the community, fishing in the dried creek-bed, appearing and disappearing before the eyes of James, Kip, Ara and William (James's sister-in-law and brother), Lenchen's brother Heinrich and their mother, the Widow Wagner, and the useless Felix Prosper, whose gradual transformation from idle fiddler to priest and midwife symbolizes the rebirth of *communitas*. Fear, rage, and tension build until James breaks out: 'He crouched down between his horse's ears and pressed it into a full gallop. He wanted only one thing. To get away. To bolt noisily and violently out of the present. To leave the valley. To attach himself to another life which moved at a different rhythm.' (91). From James's perspective we are witnessing a familiar expressionist series of events: an abrupt awakening from a previously insensate, repressed condition, followed by violent acts of rebellion against social constraints in an effort to express the subjective individual will, and then *Aufbruch* – the breaking free, departure, and search for rebirth. We are not far from Kaiser's Cashier or O'Neill's Yank. And like theirs, James's immediate fate will not be pretty.

But *The Double Hook* is not merely James's story, and in its refusal to privilege the male hero it diverges sharply from the customary pattern of the German expressionists and of O'Neill, Voaden, or Lowry. While James is on his way to what he thinks of as a new life, Kip staggers to Felix Potter's place for help, and Lenchen seeks refuge there (her own mother having rejected her) to await the birth of her child. Suddenly Felix must act, which he does by seeking help from his estranged wife, Angel. Before Angel arrives with their children and the community can begin to regroup, one final act of violence occurs. Greta, maddened by fear, jealousy, and longing, locks the doors of her house, drenches her clothes in kerosene, and burns to death in an apocalyptic gesture of destruction.

In retrospect it is Greta's suicide and Felix's surprising ability to serve others, as much as James's disillusioning encounters with cheats and prostitutes in town, that turn an increasingly negative vision into 'a different rhythm.' James returns, penniless but prepared to accept and acknowledge. As he gapes at the 'blank smouldering space' (131) where the Potter house had stood and 'on the destruction of what his heart had wished destroyed,' he feels that he has 'been turned once more into the first pasture of things' (131). When Angel sees why Felix needs her – to bandage Kip, to assist Lenchen – she quickly dresses the man's wounds and goes to fetch the girl's mother. The wailing, denouncing Widow, however, has already repented her cruelty in rejecting Lenchen and accompanies Angel, carrying the baby's singlet she is finally making. The women return to find the baby delivered, with only Felix to help, and the community has gathered. Even James finds his way to Felix's door, and *The Double Hook* concludes with this nativity scene.

Such a summary of the plot, however, is entirely misleading and unfair: Watson, after all, is not interested in the 'about,' no matter how topical, credible, prurient, or potentially tragic; murder, suicide, incestuous desires, and sex are no more than the surface manifestations of the *Angst* and alienation at the heart of the novel. Only the most alert or forewarned of first-time readers will orient themselves quickly enough to the opening lines of this strange discourse to realize what James Potter is doing:

> In the folds of the hills
>
> under Coyote's eye
>
> lived
>
> the old lady, mother of William
> of James and of Greta
>
> lived James and Greta
> lived William and Ara his wife
> lived the Widow Wagner
> the Widow's girl Lenchen
> the Widow's boy
> lived Felix Prosper and Angel
> lived Theophil
> and Kip
>
> until one morning in July

> Greta was at the stove. Turning hotcakes. Reaching for the coffee beans. Grinding away James's voice.
>
> James was at the top of the stairs. His hand half-raised. His voice in the rafters.
>
> James walking away. The old lady falling. There under the jaw of the roof. In the vault of the bed loft. Into the shadow of death. Pushed by James's will. By James's hand. By James's words: This is my day. You'll not fish today.   (19)

Even before the voices and action begin, we experience these 'people' as an anaphoric patterning of words and images, as text, as figure/ground. If we are reminded of any genre at all, it will be of a play with its list of dramatis personae, and we may also be reminded of the divine liturgy by the anaphora (that part when the Eucharistic elements are offered as an oblation).

Such as they are, the events of the story are highly expressionist; to summarize them demonstrates that much. Although James does not command central attention throughout, he is none the less the expressionist rebel, and the rebirth, in which he shares (though unlike the expressionist New Man he cannot claim sole credit for it), signals the beginning of a new dispensation. Punishment for his crimes of murder and assault is irrelevant because the purpose of the text is general redemption, not individual indictment, patterned rhythm, not facts, discourse, not story, expressive abstraction, not realism.

The abstraction of feeling is immediately apparent. These 'people,' these 'figures in a ground' (recalling Kaiser's *Figuren*), like the characters in so many expressionist plays, are *types*, are the embodiments of larger forces, the expression both of cosmic and of soul-states. They all seem to haunt the dry landscape like Mrs Potter: James in his violence, Greta in her bitter desires, Ara, Lenchen, and the Widow in their varieties of fear, Kip in his interference, Felix and Theophil in their indifference. Despite their full names, these characters are not individuated personalities but presences and voices with which it is difficult to empathize (as we do more fully, say, with Jane, Rochester, and mad Bertha). This limitation to what Osborne calls 'semantic' aspects (see chapter 1) is a direct consequence of the fact that as characters they are depthless. Only rarely do we know their thoughts and never do we enter their subconscious or unconscious minds. They seem virtually without memories, although James will briefly remember making love with Lenchen, William will recall, with a phrase, their mother being hard on Greta, and the Widow Wagner's clothes-chest evokes the memory of her dead husband. Their remembering is stark statement, undeveloped. So Theophil complains of Angel, who has left Felix Prosper to live with him – 'I liked the look of you ... when you were out of my reach' (73) – and the Widow remembers her rejection of Lenchen – 'The girl chose to go' (61). Only Felix dreams, but his dreams are fragmented, and forgetfulness stalks his waking hours:

> Felix Prosper slept. He dreamed that Angel was riding through his gate on a sleek ass. He was pulling the scratchy white surplice over his uncombed head. It was early and the ground was wet with dew.
> I musn't forget, he thought. I musn't forget. (68)

Just as their memories are fleeting, oblique, and, for the reader, lacking in contextual embedding, so their reflections on their actions and their self-consciousness are ambiguous and aphoristic. It is the narrator who comments on James's position after his escape to town that 'all he'd done was scum rolled up to the top of a pot by the boiling motion beneath. Now the fire was out' (99). James may or may not realize this. His awareness at this point or later when he is robbed is not presented; his decision to return is unexplained. Like the others, he is afraid to think, reflect, or remember: 'He held memory like a knife in his hand. But he clasped it shut and rode on' (126–7).

What they lack in psychological depth of presentation, they also lack in temporal perspective. We are told almost nothing about who these people are, where they came from, or why they ended up in this isolated spot. Lacking a particularizing past, they exist primarily in a presentness that oppresses and threatens to overwhelm them. For the characters this amnesiac condition, uprooted from time itself in the hollow present of a parched landscape, is the outward sign of their spiritual, social, and psychological dread. For the reader, however, this minimalizing of context, consciousness, and temporal perspective serves to dehumanize and abstract these figures, enabling us to see them as ideas and soul- (or psychic) states that divide along a central axis or the shaft of a double hook: on one side are the life-deniers; on the other are the life-affirmers who struggle to resist an encroaching sterility. And there are degrees of regression in their make-up, just as there are degrees of resistance, so that Theophil persists in his insensibility and the Widow Wagner gradually welcomes a return to the glory and the darkness of life, so that Angel never denies the child, the man, and the responsibility of knowing, while Felix requires prodding to arouse him from his somnolence. Where Greta will conceive only fiery death as her consummation, Lenchen gives birth. Mrs. Potter and Kip, the murdered and blinded trouble-makers, are in a class by themselves. At the outset, the pattern is the 'double hook' of Figure 6. By the end this static pattern will have broken into a new ordering, with only Greta and Theophil adamant in refusal.

FIGURE 6

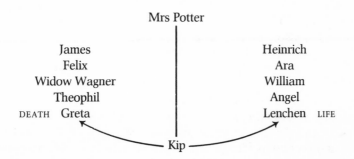

While the roles played or positions established by most of the characters are quite stunningly simple and clear, at least four of them invite closer observation. Greta is the most terrible and passionate of all the characters. Not only is her death foregrounded through powerful description and imagery; her passion is allowed to spill out in the strongest, most violent colours. She alone of all the characters is allowed something approaching the *Ausstrahlungen des Ichs*, but since this outburst is more appropriately examined later as a fine example of Watson's style, it is her death scene that I want to look at now.

The scene is short, and yet longer and more intense than most of the brief, staccato scenes of the text. Alone in the house now that James has gone, she bars the door against Ara and William, who have come to help. She hears their voices coaxing, questioning. She feels 'hands on the knob ... hands twisting her ribs. *Plucking* the flowers on her housecoat and *bruising* them. *Stripping* off the leaves until her branch lay naked as a bone on the dusty floor' (84, emphasis added). The violence of the participles at first disguises the fact that Greta is tearing her own clothes. In her madness, it is as if external forces assail her. The voices continue to hammer away as she stuffs her clothes into the stove and douses them in kerosene until the 'empty space' around her is filled with her abuse, her hatred, and her desire 'to shatter all memory of the girl who had stayed too long' (85). But Watson does not allow Greta to speak; she remains a figure, an object seen amidst violent colours – purple, green, gold, and flame – caught in the exploding space of her mind. Greta's suicide is like a scene from Strauss's *Elektra* (1909) or an expressionist painting – a detail from Nolde's *Dance Around the Golden Calf*, perhaps, or the naked woman in Erich Heckel's *The Glassy Day* (see Plates 4 and 11), where violence and aggression are held still in the impinging abstract shapes of land, water, and sky. The impact of this apocalyptic scene is visual and de-personalized. To speak of it at all is to move almost immediately from event to medium, from story to discourse. Not the woman, Greta, but the figure of rage consuming itself persists in the mind.

James is even more important and considerably less abstract than Greta because he has a larger role and interacts with other individuals both inside and outside his community. But his emotions and motivations are seldom touched upon and never explored in depth because he too is more important as a type. James's role is that of catalyst, for in two ways, at least, he breaks the imprisoning stasis of life, first by impregnating Lenchen and second by killing his mother. To a degree one can also think of him as a questor because his search for freedom brings him the knowledge prerequisite to a fruitful return home. What he is not is a Parsifal. Nothing he does directly renews him or the community. His grail is at Felix Potter's all the time, and the door, like his purged homestead transformed into the 'first pasture of things,' stands open 'by some generous gesture' (131). Moreover, the baby's name is Felix. In this important sense James Potter is not an expressionist New Man because his violence and *Aufbruch* are self-defeating; in his own right he achieves little more than the Cashier, or Toller's Sonia in *Masses and Man*. Through James, Watson states that the expressionist position seen in a violent assertion of self (James) or an outburst of inner torment (Greta) is inadequate and impotent. It is primarily in relation to Mrs Potter, Kip, and Lenchen that James signifies, but where Lenchen's function is clear and simple, Kip and Mrs Potter present many interesting complications.

Most readings of *The Double Hook* describe Mrs Potter in solely negative terms, as the representative of loss, sickness, sterility, and doom,[29] and there is little doubt that she is meant to be an ominous figure. Immediately after her death we begin to see her still fishing 'with a concentrated ferocity as if she were fishing for something she'd never found' (20). She fishes all along the stream in other people's pools, defying God's rebuke, 'fishing in the brown water for fish she'd never eat' (39). Everyone sees her and is afraid: to Ara she seems a sign of death at the sight of which even the herd cows turn away (21); to the Widow Wagner she is 'old ... wicked, fishing the fish of others' (25); after her death Greta is thought of by Ara, William, Heinrich, and perhaps the narrator (the context is deliberately vague) as having 'inherited destruction,' as having 'sat in her mother's doom as she sat in her chair' (113). But Mrs Potter also participates in the renewal of the community; Felix sees her at the end 'standing like a tree with its roots reaching out to water' (118), and she does other things besides fish.

Greta, who so deeply resents the old woman, complains because she must continually clean the lamps her mother blackens with her constant searching:

> I've seen Ma standing with the lamp by the fence, she said. Holding it up in broad daylight.
> I've seen her standing looking for something even the birds couldn't see. Something hid from every living thing. I've seen her defying. I've seen her take her hat off in the sun at noon, baring her head and asking for the sun to strike her. Holding the lamp and looking where there's nothing to be found. Nothing but dust. No person's got a right to keep looking. To keep looking and blackening lamp globes for others to clean.   (31)

If she haunts the landscape to fish and to search both before *and* after death, it is because something is wrong or lost or rejected: 'The whole world's got distemper,' James thinks; 'The ground's rotten with it' (43).

To describe Mrs Potter as the image of sterility comes close to implying that she is in some sense an evil force, the *cause* of the community's fear and regression. At first glance her murder by an avenging son might even substantiate such a reading. But to see Mrs Potter in this negative light is to miss the main pattern of the narrative. The old woman can be seen by everyone *after* her death because she is a projection of their soul-states; she is a literalized metaphor – 'Fear walking round in the living shape of the dead' (61); she is their fear made manifest before them; she forces them to think, remember, make associations. As such she is both a goad to their insensibility and a terrible warning against the dangers of their refusal to live, share, love, commune, and above all, see. Moreover, by projecting their *Angst* in her shape, they grant objective power to an inner state that could be transformed if it were not perceived as an external, hostile force. Mrs Potter fishes (the Christian symbolism is relevant here and elsewhere in the text) and searches until that moment when the community begins to see – that a child conceived must be born and acknowledged, that men and women overcome their isolation only by acting together, that ritual words and gestures such as fragments of prayer, preparation of swaddling clothes, catching and cooking of food for those gathered – still exist to consolidate reunion. The error and sterility of this community are not Mrs Potter's doing but her son's, her daughter's, and her neighbours'.

However, Mrs Potter has more than just the psychological force of a projected soul-state. The source of her mythic power can be located in the condition of those who fear and hate her most – Greta, James, the Widow Wagner, and Ara (though Ara comes around quickly under the loving influence of William). Each of these characters fears and/or denies sexuality and the rituals of human communion. Their sin is against the most primitive roots of life, against the *mother*. Mrs Potter haunts the dry, infertile landscape, fishing and searching because, like a type of Demeter, she mourns a shattered cathexis and defies the gods by wreaking her own kind of vengeance upon the earth. The Persephone on the Koré level of the narrative is the pregnant Lenchen, whose public acknowledgment and return to daylight, where she can be seen, initiates a restoration of fertility to all living things. Mrs Potter's living representative, the Widow Wagner, another 'old woman waiting,' can now be reconciled with her 'lost' daughter, and our last glimpse of Mrs Potter is of her chthonic transformation and participation in renewal: 'But she wasn't fishing, [Felix] said. Just standing like a tree with its roots reaching out to water' (118). Indeed, viewed from a Demetrian perspective, a line stretches through the text from her to the Widow Wagner, who embodies the life-denying dark side of the Great Mother, to Greta in her forced, sterile virginity, to her polar opposite Lenchen, a line that traces life and death in the positions of women, specifically in mother-daughter relations. It is Greta's purgative immolation, not James's matricide, that finally prepares the way for life. Furthermore, the pattern traced by these women is the double hook of existence, of life and death, as Kip knows best of all.

Kip is the most enigmatic of all the figures in the novel. Part Indian Trickster and spokesman for Coyote,[30] Kip knows what Mrs Potter is searching for, what the others reject and deny, that 'you can't catch the glory on a hook and hold on to it. That when you fish for the glory you catch the darkness too. That if you hook twice the glory you hook twice the fear' (61). He is like Mrs Potter in so far as he elicits strong responses from members of the community and stands as a warning to them of how vision can be abused. Like hers, his role is a psychological and mythic one; his blinding and consequent nursing permit them to see and to care. Both Kip and Mrs Potter stand apart from the others – hence my location of them on the vertical axis of Figure 6 beyond the forces straining towards violence and insensibility on the one hand and rebirth on the other – and yet each exerts a vital influence upon the sequence of events that brings a kind of redemption. Both Kip and Mrs Potter interfere, go where they are not wanted, cause extra work and trouble, but without them there would be only stasis. Where she is the presiding goddess (in her Crone phase) of the community, he is its scapegoat, his eyes the necessary sacrifice.

Although I have been speaking all along of *The Double Hook* as a novel, it is most certainly a novel with some unusual formal qualities. In fact, it looks as much like a play as a novel with its dramatis personae and five-part structure. Moreover, each of the five parts (Watson calls them parts, not chapters or acts) consists of a series of very brief, disconnected episodes or scenes presenting snatches of dialogue, fragments of description, incidents often unconnected with what immediately precedes or follows. Even the paragraphs from which these episodes are built are short, abruptly begun and ended, and intense in their visual and staccato effect. In a manner reminiscent of cinematic techniques, the perspective and focus shift constantly and without warning, from very close (James's murder of his mother, Greta's suicide) to distant (the glimpses of Mrs Potter, James's departure), from one interior and familiar point of view to another. The reader must make connections unassisted.

Because *The Double Hook* is a profoundly verbal text, comparisons with film form (be they Eisensteinian montage or German expressionist cinema techniques) can be misleading, but Watson's method of construction recalls Döblin's dictum: 'Nicht erzählen, sondern bauen.' Despite the comparative length of his novels, his narratives are built from brief, often discontinuous and disconnected scenes of highly objective presentation from which the author or narrator has withdrawn as completely as possible. The pattern that emerges from this type of 'building,' rather like the pattern in *Under the Volcano*, is primarily spatial, and as such disrupts the temporal flow traditional to storytelling. It is carried out in the prose style and image clusters as well.

The primary result of this patterned structure, composed of brief narrative units, is a crucial abstraction of the subject, which no longer exists as a temporal sequence of events but is read as one 'reads' an abstract painting, in blocks, planes of line and colour, intersecting and contrasting shapes. The story is preserved, of course, in the sequence of five parts, each in turn composed of many episodes. Stretched out this way from episode to episode within each part, the novel resembles many expressionist plays, with their *Stationen* plotting and paratactic structure. But here again, the qualifications that must be placed on James as an expressionist hero apply, because *The Double Hook* does not privilege one character who can experience the different stages of an ordeal and thereby unify the pattern. James's violent *Aufbruch* must be seen as an element moving across our field of vision, a dynamic plane joining the dominant picture plane.

Nicht erzählen, sondern bauen: the abstract structure of *The Double Hook* is inseparable from its highly objective, depersonalized *telling*, which seems an inappropriate term for such a narrative. Watson has gone off even further than Joyce, who may have been indifferently paring his fingernails but was at least visible from time to time – in irony, parody, or even pastiche and in the personal experience underlying so much of his fiction. Watson's novel seems to tell itself, even though the usual signs of a third-person omniscient narrator are clearly present, because so much is left unsaid and so little is felt. Coyote comments on events from the surrounding hills, but the narrator, like a camera's eye, is an observer, ostensibly setting down what is said, done, seen, but with almost no inflection of voice that encourages the reader to sympathize here, to judge harshly there.

In fact, Coyote's voice carries more overt authority than the narrator's. It is Coyote who calls from the rocks, 'In my mouth is forgetting / In my darkness is rest' (29), who comments, in the words of the Song of Solomon, on Greta's death – 'I've taken her where she stood / my left hand is on her head / my right hand embraces her' (85) – and, in the last lines of the text, cries 'down through the boulders' at the baby's birth:

> I have set his feet on soft ground;
> I have set his feet on the sloping shoulders
> of the world.   (134)

However, any tendency to empathize with or through Coyote is effectively blocked by the remote, mythic, and clearly symbolic status of this voice. Whether actual beast barking around the edges of the isolated community, chorus commenting on the near tragedy playing before us, or Trickster god of the Interior Salish Indians representing the combined mythic forces of glory and darkness, of life and death, this figure is enigmatic and alien, an unseen and inhuman presence that symbolizes the double hook of life.[31]

The further one moves away from the expressionist subject of *The Double Hook* and into the abstraction of the discourse, the paradigmatic character types, the highly patterned structure, and de-personalized narration, the closer one comes to what is, finally, the very nerve-centre of this extraordinary text: language and image. Here the active unit is the sentence or phrase, at most the short, emphatic paragraphs. All speech, whether dialogue or monologue, is presented visually as if it were a simple, unspoken prose, or an *un*represented speech. The constantly repeated, always unpunctuated 'he said' 'she said' quickly become part of the stylistic pattern. The normally foregrounded presence of represented speech conventionally signalled through rhetorical punctuation recedes into the background of the narrator's reporting, and the distinction between the reporting and representing blurs:

> Felix stood at the edge of his own brown pool. Kip sat on the bank beside him.
>
> When a house is full of women, Kip said, and one of them Angel, it's best for a man to take his rest among the willows.
>
> When a house is full of women and children, Felix said, a man has to get something for their mouths. (133)

What fades as well is the feeling that these are flesh and blood characters, so reliant are we as readers on the rhetorical punctuation to confer a sense of reality on represented speech. Instead, we respond to the words themselves, to their sounds, rhythms, and repeated patterns, as much as if not more than we do to their meaning.

Even an outcry as passionate as Greta's operates according to the same stylistic principles as the peaceful conversation quoted above. On the night of Kip's blinding and James's flight, the night before her own death, she suddenly blurts out her suffering before the uncomprehending Lenchen:

> Keep on looking, she said. And think what you want. I don't care. It's what I am, she said. It's what's driven him out into the creek bottom. Into the brush. Into the hogpen. A woman can stand so much, she said. A man can stand so much. A woman can stand what a man can't stand. To be scorned by others. Pitied. Scrimped. Put upon. Laughed at when no one has come for her, when there's no one to come. She can stand it when she knows she still has the power. When the air's stretched like a rope between her and someone else. It's emptiness that can't be borne. The pot-holes are filled with rain from time to time. I've seen them stiff with thirst. Ashed white and bitter at the edge. But the rain or the run-off fills them at last. The bitterness licked up. I tell you there was only James. I was never let run loose. I never had two to waste and spill, like Angel Prosper. (66)

Despite its brevity and economy the passage is powerful, one of the most powerful in the text. Its force derives chiefly from two stylistic features: repetition and sentence fragmentation. Of course, the repetition of sentence fragments, phrases, and right-branching modifiers ('It's what's driven him out into the creek bottom. Into the brush. Into the hogpen.') illustrates well how Watson can use these two devices together to create a sharp, aggressive style and to suggest the intense, staccato quality of Greta's bitterness. But repetition works separately as well; thus, the repetition of 'she said,' of 'A man,' 'A woman,' 'a man,' of 'can' or 'can't stand,' or of words like 'when,' 'bitter,' 'bitterness,' and 'never' establishes a rhythm that lifts the paragraph away from conventional prose towards poetry, controlling and unifying the rhetoric and above all abstracting it: this cannot be taken as so-called 'realist' speech. But repetition does not only function in this more obvious way. Sounds are repeated in alliterative clusters of dental consonants, long vowels, or sibilants, as in 'To be scorned by others. Pitied. Scrimped. Put upon' or 'But the rain or the run-off fills them at last.' Even the chiasmus of 'when no one has come for her, when there's no one to come' relies for its effect on repetition. And with the exception of two words, 'emptiness' and 'bitterness' (in themselves a pairing and grammatical repetition), the entire passage consists of mono- or disyllabic words. There is a delicate, calculated pattern to these lines, an exquisite precision to the positioning of words that recalls an imagist poem, but there is also, and above all, rhythm, what Kristeva calls semiosis that *expresses* the horror of sterility at the same time as the absence of conventional rhetorical markers and the repetition of specific words abstracts it, counteracting our desire to read this passage as the impassioned outpouring of a particular individual in a particular time and place.

But perhaps the most striking quality of Watson's prose is her imagery – hard, clear, highly visual, vital, and right. She often begins with a metaphor that animates the inanimate landscape or object (a quality she identified as expressionist in Lewis's work, and a constant feature of expressionist art, whether in Barlach's woodcuts, Schmidt-Rottluff's landscapes, Kaiser's or O'Neill's plays, or Lowry's Mexico). So the pot-holes Greta speaks of are 'stiff with thirst. Ashed white and bitter at the edge,' just as she is, although on parched ground in the Cariboo it is quite possible to see holes and sloughs baked dry and rimmed by a white crust of alkaline deposits. Or the flowers on the housecoat she has stuffed into the stove breathe 'out fragrance [from the kerosene] which filled the whole room ... [and raise] purple faces and [lift] green arms into the air above the stove' (85). At other points Watson creates an image directly paralleling an expressionist canvas (the green, purple, and gold bringing Nolde immediately to mind), with the aggressive, short strokes of repeated participles and syntactic fragments: 'Yet Greta stood almost full in the doorway like a tangle of wild flowers grown up between them. All green and gold and purple in the lamplight. Fat clinging clumps of purple flowers. Honey-tongued. Bursting from their green stems. Crowding against green leaves. Her face above. Fierce. Sharp. Sudden as a bird's swinging out on the topmost surge.' (63)

The Double Hook is built up from such intensely visual images and passages. Scenes succeed each other like tableaux sharply etched in contrasting areas of light and dark. We are exhorted to see by the light of a merciless sun, by the 'light stampeded together and bawling before the massed darkness' (36) of an approaching storm, and through the constant references to lamps and eyes: 'Eyes everywhere. In the cottonwoods the eyes of foolhens. Rats' eyes on the barn rafters. Steers herded together. Eyes multiplied. Eyes. Eyes and padded feet' (43). The text enacts a ritual (anaphora again) for right-seeing from its smallest units of description and image to its scenic structure and character configuration. Some of these people refuse to see; others see too much and abuse that power. But the meaning of Mrs Potter cannot be understood until what is hidden is acknowledged, until the darkness is accepted with the glory as death must be part of life, and the reader, too, must learn to look with new eyes at a novel that defies our literary or critical assumptions and challenges perception, forcing us to see not a sordid story about people in Dog Creek, British Columbia, but 'figures in a ground, from which they [cannot] be separated.'

Watson does not present her challenge in lexical inventiveness and neologism like Joyce, or in a willed deconstruction and demythologizing of a burdensome tradition like Stein. She is not rebelling against a language and a past that many modernists (especially dadists and some expressionists, like Schwitters) found to be intolerable constraints. Her inventiveness (in a sense, the difficulty of her text) springs from its expressive abstraction, visual immediacy, and what Joseph Frank would call its 'spatial form.'

If the Munch-like Mrs Potter is a *key* to the 'distemper' afflicting humanity in *The Double Hook,* she is so because of her mythic power to represent the community's sterility to itself and to goad it into the rituals necessary to its regeneration. But Mrs Potter is by no means the only mythic aspect of the text. The title stands as 'the proper and perfect symbol' ('the proper and perfect symbol is the natural object' according to Pound)[32] of the story's meaning: life is a double hook on which we must catch the darkness with the glory. Certainly, within the Canadian context *The Double Hook* has come to represent a quintessentially Canadian story of interdependent dualities, of isolated community coming together in endur-ance and renewal, of the hero ever-returning to wife, child, and home.[33] It would appear that this fiction strikes deep chords in Canadian readers and writers in as much as it isolates and shapes a vision recognizably 'at home' (though never 'regional') in Canada.

But the novel's mythic power only begins (or does it come to rest?) in a specific context, however loosely defined. The novel's universal mythic quality springs from its patterning of redemption, its rhythmic progress towards rebirth. Of the expressionist texts examined in this study (and of the many more German and other European examples of Expressionism that might be considered), *The Double Hook* is the only one to carry through the movement from violent *Aufbruch* to apocalyptic destruction (and a narrowly missed regression) and then on to rebirth and renewal. Although it would be false to say that the abstraction of the text in any way results from this upward swing, or is a sign of intrinsic superiority (as Hulme and Worringer thought), it does seem that the impulse to display an apocalyptic upheaval followed by rebirth has been well served by the abstraction of the discourse, and its mythic power is inseparable from the expressive abstraction of the characters, their setting and speech, the fragmented structure of the narrative, and the visual intensity, the aggressive angularity – in short, the expressionism – of imagery and style. Although Watson's apocalyptic vision does not follow the biblical pattern precisely, her apocalypse, more than those envisaged by any of the other novelists considered here, is a religious rather than a secular one. It is also a figure for personal, ethical growth within a cyclic and mythic conception of history: as the closing words of Coyote imply – 'I have set his feet on soft ground' – the process of degradation into violence and insensibility experienced by individuals like James and by the community, followed by destruction and renewal, will be repeated.

No matter how one turns *The Double Hook* in the light, as with a kaleidoscope each turn shakes out a different pattern, privileges a different figure, foregrounds a different narrative plane (or level). If we think of the spiritual aspects of the story held before us by the biblical echoes and snippets of Catholic liturgy, we must see Felix as pivotal, the priest and father-confessor with the community around him at the end in a fundamentally Christian vision of renewal. If we consider the novel as an exploration of human social and psychological alienation and *Angst*, then it is James we must attend to, for he expresses the community's as well as his own anger in his violent rebellion against the repression and 'distem-per' infecting all things. James's counterparts are the heroes of classical Greece, from Odysseus to Orestes, whose murder of a mother will not save a sister's sanity but will purge the community of evil.[34] The women of the novel comprise yet another pattern supported by the pervasive elemental imagery of fire, air, earth, and water. Greta, the Widow Wagner, Lenchen and Angel, Ara and Mrs Potter represent a web of symbolic associations and a complex mother-daughter cathexis that bind the group to a cyclic pattern of birth/death/rebirth and remind us of the enormous power of chthonic forces.[35] Here too, as on a spiritual or social level, the narrative rhythm achieves renewal after the apocalyptic purging by fire of the Potter household, but it is on this level that Watson is most emphatic about the necessary duality of life. To know Mrs Potter is to know death *and* life; to acknowledge Lenchen is to accept the cyclic nature of existence. The rebirth envisaged in the final tableau of the novel is *not* a transcendence, in either the Christian or the Kantian sense, of chthonic forces but a reminder that 'a person only escapes in circles no matter how far the rope spins' (132).

The presence of Coyote and his 'servant' Kip implies that there is a cosmological level to *The Double Hook*, one that reveals a universe governed by the Amerindian Trickster god who is 'at one and the same time, creator and destroyer, giver and negator,'[36] the embodiment of duality and ambiguity. But *The Double Hook* is not built upon this one level only. It shapes patterns of spiritual, social, psychological, and chthonic realities as well and then interweaves them so that one perspective invites another and each enriches the composition of the whole. As Lewis said the artist should, Watson has enriched abstraction; she has sought and found 'the shaping power amongst [life's] vibrations,' and has accentuated and perpetuated them. Her abstraction is enriched by an expressionism that, paradoxically (as Worringer saw), returns us to empathy, to her desire to feel with and for the material world and society, to our ability to identify with suffering and desire, with fear and desperation, through the violent gestures and colour of their expression, and to our shared need (as Derrida insists) to close the gap between loss and desire or words and deeds.[37] Like all expressionist art, this novel shows the signs of distortion, of the gothic and grotesque, of an abstract quality that assaults the complacent reader seeking a placid or conventional representation, but it carries its subject beyond the more typical contortions of expressionist self-destruction and regression into a vision of apocalypse, and it is the extended abstraction of its telling that controls this vision. Figure/ground, empathy/abstraction: *The Double Hook* is energy held in passionate stasis.

9 'The real soul-sickness': Self-Creation and the Expressionist Method in Ralph Ellison's Invisible Man

In the epilogue to his 1952 novel, Ralph Ellison's 'invisible' narrator looks back on the experiences that led to this telling of his story and succinctly diagnoses his condition: 'The fact is that you carry part of your sickness within you, at least I do as an invisible man. I carried my sickness and though for a long time I tried to place it in the outside world, the attempt to write it down shows me that at least half of it lay within me ... *That* is the real soul-sickness.'[1] With this admission he accomplishes two things: First, he fully acknowledges from his present position of hindsight what was so difficult for him to see before – that he was invisible to himself because he lacked self-consciousness. Second, he alerts the reader to both the subject and the method of his narrative; his writing-it-down has been a liberating act of self-expression and a healing act of self-creation. Moreover, it is one that we must read as a careful patterning of 'the chaos which lives within ... [our own] certainties' (*IM*, 502). On at least 'the lower frequencies' (503), Ellison's invisible man is the 'soul-sickness' within *us*, our collective dark double, the fear, passion, and imagination we refuse to see.

No doubt because of its social and historical density, the political urgency of its theme, the striking accuracy of its dialogue and the detailed precision in description, Ellison's novel has usually been praised as a moving, realistic portrayal of the identity-crisis faced by a young black American man in a deeply racist, urban society. And *Invisible Man* is rich in all these qualities. It has also been scrutinized for its debt to and use of folklore, jazz and blues, black oral and literary traditions, psychology, and social stereotyping.[2] A great debate about the social relevance of the story and the political motivations of its author sprang up around the novel almost immediately after its publication, and it is a debate that has continued to absorb much energy and attention. As a result, and despite Ellison's many protestations and explanations of its art, a serious consideration of style and fictional mode has not been undertaken. But questions of artistry are of prime importance here. Apart from the subject, what kind of novel is this? Or, more precisely, how does its form suit its subject? Why was it written this way?

To focus on the 'writerly' qualities of the text does not detract from its socio-political ramifications because, in the last analysis, we still read *Invisible Man* for its craft, without which its subject might have caused it to be quickly marginalized. From the earliest interviews Ellison insisted that he was not interested in social realism per se, in 'real characters,' 'case histories,' or autobiography. What he struggled towards during the seven years of writing the novel was a form to contain and express a 'deranged' reality that would reflect something essential about American consciousness as he understood it. What he created was a complex, shifting, mixed form, tightly framed and controlled by a cool, often reflective voice in a deceptively direct style. *Invisible Man* is, in a number of important ways, an expressionistic novel written by an artist who is both aware of and able to manipulate a variety of styles.

In an important interview, 'The Art of Fiction,' first published in 1955 and then reprinted in *Shadow and Act* (1964), Ellison stated categorically what he was doing and why. Since the passage is often overlooked or misunderstood and is crucial to my argument, I quote it in full:

> The Prologue was written afterwards, really – in terms of a shift in the hero's point of view. I wanted to throw the reader off balance – make him accept certain non-naturalistic effects. It was really a memoir written underground, and I wanted a foreshadowing through which I hoped the reader would view the actions which took place in the main body of the book. For another thing, the styles of life presented are different. In the South, where he was trying to fit into a traditional pattern and where his sense of certainty had not yet been challenged, I felt a more naturalistic treatment was adequate ... As the hero passes from the South to the North, from the relatively stable to the swiftly changing, his sense of certainty is lost and the style becomes expressionistic. Later on during his fall from grace in the Brotherhood it becomes somewhat surrealistic. The styles try to express both his state of consciousness and the state of society.[3]

The full import of this description has been obscured for at least two reasons. Ellison's terminology has not been taken seriously or, at least, not understood, so that critics have tossed off references – usually to the novel's surrealism – without closer scrutiny. In addition, the uproar over his portrayal of black-white relations and the communist 'Brotherhood' among black nationalist and/or leftist critics effectively distracted attention from artistic matters by concentrating narrowly on socio-political themes.

It is illuminating now to look back over three decades of response to this novel in order to see how readers have dealt with its style. One contemporary reviewer likened it, in general terms, to surrealist painting, while another recognized its 'expressionist passages' but condemned them as 'arty,' recommending that they be skipped.[4] Subsequent critics have quickly summed it up as surreal, naturalistic, or even as an 'impressionistic morass,' and as late as 1967 one critic described it as 'sprinkled throughout with dreams and symbols' and employing 'a combination of several techniques – realism, impressionism, and surrealism.'[5] Given the history of expressionism since 1933, it is perhaps not surprising that American readers and scholars would be so unfamiliar with the style as to mistake it for impressionism, or conflate it with a loosely understood notion of surrealism.

Ellison, however, was making important aesthetic and methodological distinctions when he used all three terms – naturalistic, expressionistic, 'somewhat surrealistic' – and his early training in the arts corroborates his ability to do so. Born in 1914, Ellison was from his college days at Tuskegee familiar with twentieth-century avant-garde music, fascinated by the artistry of Eliot's *The Waste Land*, and fully aware of the relationships among and between much classical music, Eliot's poetry, and jazz.[6] When he left Tuskegee for New York in 1936, he did so to study sculpture with Richmond Barthé, and although he soon shifted his activity to writing, he has never lost his interest in the visual arts. Ellison has only once published an essay on the visual arts, but on this occasion he chose the late collage work of Romare Beardon, a black American painter whose views on the role of the artist closely coincide with his own and whose work, influenced by George Grosz, Orozco, and Picasso, is highly personal, expressive, and intense.[7]

The influences he was experiencing were broad-ranging but deeply experimental; the choices he was making, even in the thirties, about what appealed to him and what he could *use*, as it were, were usually non-naturalistic and anti-conventional: Dostoevsky, Eliot, Stein, Joyce, Malraux, Hemingway (who has been called expressionist), and Yeats.

Dostoevsky, whose *Notes from Underground* is most often cited as a source for *Invisible Man*, was a key influence on developing expressionist thought and art in Germany, and the early Eliot of 'Preludes,' 'Rhapsody on a Windy Night,' and *The Waste Land* reveals a markedly expressionist perspective. In 'Preludes' (1917), for example, humanity projects its suffering on the cyclic round of day and night so that time, disjunct objects, fragments of a building or street, and pervasive smells take on a vaguely threatening life of their own, while a de-personalized voice describes an anonymous woman staring at her ceiling:

> You dozed, and watched the night revealing
> The thousand sordid images
> Of which your soul was constituted.[8]

And in 'Rhapsody on a Windy Night' (1917), Eliot again presents a highly distorted, deeply disturbing inner reality by depicting the empty streets, the street-lamps, and the moon through the emotions of an unnamed night wanderer and speaker. But here, even more than in 'Preludes,' he uses violent images, generated in part by striking synecdoches, and rhythm to evoke the despair of this existence. These manipulations of perspective and explorations of imagery and rhythm to express an inner, emotionally disturbed and distorted vision of external reality would provide Ellison with striking examples of expressionist writing.

The politics-versus-art controversy that has haunted Ellison and *Invisible Man* since its publication was probably inevitable. In response to the racial injustice and tension of American history, with their explosive intensification after the Second World War (Ellison actually reported on the Harlem riots that erupted in 1943), black American artists were expected to address themselves *directly* to these burning issues. *Invisible Man*, however, looked like a modernist sell-out to white literary prejudice and weak liberalism; not only did it flaunt degrading images of the Negro, it also offered no *clear* (that is, revolutionary, immediate) answers to real problems.[9]

It seems late in the day to raise these accusations again because today *Invisible Man* is so indisputably a profoundly black American book, whatever else it may be. But in the context of a discussion of Expressionism the virulent criticisms hurled at Ellison and his work from Marxist and black nationalist or neo-Marxist quarters carry an added poignancy. They are all too reminiscent of the debate waged by Lukács and Bloch over the German expressionists, with the socialist left accusing the artists of everything from bourgeois bad faith to incipient fascism and supporters of

Expressionism defending both the right of the artist to express his or her subjectivity and the socio-political value of the expressionist vision. Like the leading German artists discussed in chapters 1 and 2, Ellison has continued (most recently in his 1986 collection of essays, mainly from the sixties and seventies, *Going to the Territory*) to defend himself by articulating a poetics of the novel as an art of political protest in the widest sense of the term. To create, for Ellison, is to protest.[10]

There is, however, another sense in which the expressionism of *Invisible Man* and this vexed question of politics are linked. Beginning with 'The Art of Fiction,' Ellison has repeatedly stated that he consciously rejected the social-realist methods that were popular in the thirties and identified with both proletarian and black American writing, because his vision required less limiting, non-realist methods, and his governing desire was to explore universal truths through a shaping of particular realities. It is even possible to see his rejection of the accepted conventions as his way of saying no (just as his hero must learn to do) to other people's versions of his reality. John Reilly has suggested that Ellison's rejection of realist modes may have an even wider significance than the merely individual because, according to Reilly, there is something 'appropriate ... to the description of being black in America' about the 'surrealism' in Ellison's work. He goes further to speculate that Ellison may have either 'provided an example or anticipated a trend' in subsequent black American writing.[11]

The idea is an intriguing one in so far as it is possible to argue, as Worringer did, that people who are not at home in the world will express that space-dread through various degrees of abstraction instead of in the more comfortable realist modes attributable to empathy. But it seems equally possible to read *Invisible Man* as a textualizing of Ellison's vision of an America too complex, diverse, heterogeneous, and polyphonic to be contained within what Bakhtin would describe as the monologic hegemony of social realism. Expressionism – and it is after all only one element in Ellison's polyphonic discourse – can be used to unsettle the unitary perspective of authority and to demonstrate the passionate, and political, struggle of the individual to say the self and, thereby, heal the soul. To the degree that *Invisible Man* succeeds in this, then it is indeed a subversive 'nay-saying' text.

In his discussion of the novel, 'Nightmare of a Native Son,' Jonathan Baumbach praises Ellison highly for his 'surrealism' but locates 'the novel's crucial flaw [in] its inconsistency of method, its often violent transformations from a kind of detailed surface realism ... to an allegorical world of almost endless imaginative possibilities.'[12] At the opposite extreme from the social realists, then, Baumbach finds Ellison's realistic passages 'tedious' and only his non-realist writing 'alive.' The fundamental complaint here involves the mixed style of the narrative ('its inconsistency of method') and is based on the assumption that a novel should be homogeneous. But Ellison clearly wanted a shifting style, or inconsistent method, *because* (as he said in the passage from 'The Art of Fiction') it allowed him to 'express both [the hero's] state of consciousness and the state of society.' Like Joyce, Eliot, or his admired jazzmen, he needed a variety of styles, rhythms, and tones.

Before turning to the text itself, I would like to make a number of preliminary observations about Ellison's remarks from 'The Art of Fiction.' First, the prologue, which was written last, is meant to establish the 'non-naturalistic effects' of the following narrative; at the same time, of course, it completes the crucial frame that controls and unifies the reader's relation to the text. The 'inconsistency of method' that bothered Baumbach is firmly located in the mind – and words – of the novel's paradoxical hero / author. Second, the text is neither realist nor surrealist: according to Ellison, 'a more naturalistic treatment was adequate' for the hero's southern experiences because, bizarre and brutal though they are, the young man's perception of himself and his world is still largely unquestioned. It is not until he reaches New York that he is really thrown off balance; 'his sense of certainty is lost and the style becomes expressionistic.' The surrealism for which *Invisible Man* is praised is, if we can trust Ellison's description, a 'somewhat surrealistic' style reserved for the latter stage in his hero's association with the Brotherhood. Third, these shifting styles – naturalistic, expressionistic, and 'somewhat surrealistic' – employed by the narrator *are* Ellison's method, and, theoretically at least, they mirror or express the narrator's consciousness. In so far as Ellison's method succeeds, it conveys a plurality, diversity, even a disorientation, shaped post-experientially by a single, highly articulate, and unified self-consciousness. It also gives artistic form to the tension between representation and iconic abstraction essential to an expressionist poetics.

Because the text is so firmly situated within the voice and consciousness of its nameless first-person narrator, any discussion of poetics must begin with him. What makes him exceptionally interesting *as an expressionist hero* is the temporal framework of his narrative. If we take the prologue and epilogue together, it is clear that he has succeeded in his quest where most heroes before him have failed; he has passed through *Aufbruch* to a secular and artistic *Erlösung* that enables him to speak for both himself and us. The magnitude of this achievement should not be lost sight of –

remember Kaiser's Cashier, O'Neill's Yank or Jim, and Barnes's Dr O'Connor; even Lowry's erudite, articulate Consul dies leaving his story to be told by another voice. Having survived his ordeals and learned from them, Ellison's narrator no longer suffers from the 'soul-sickness' of an expressionist hero. He has gained temporal, psychological, and philosophical distance from that suffering, and as a result the artistic perspective he provides is at a crucial remove from the timeless immediacy of anguished experience that engulfs the more typical expressionist hero. He has come back from Hell to tell us about the fire, something Geoffrey Firmin himself could not do. Technically, then, he is an expressionist hero in retrospect, *after* his ordeal is over. Moreover, he is sufficiently sophisticated and aware of his artistic, analytic, and communicative tools to modulate the narration of his ordeal, reserving only the most disoriented moments of his past for a full expressionist treatment. Rather than being caught up in and overwhelmed by the combined forces of his own 'soul-sickness' and a vicious society or being irrevocably trapped by the 'expressive fallacy,' he writes about these dangers from a position of relative certainty and health. *Invisible Man* is not, then, an attempt at the unmediated expressionist *Schrei*.

As soon as we move into the retrospective narrative proper, however, we encounter a familiar expressionist hero, even though his narrative is not always in the expressionist mode. What complicates and enriches his portrayal is the sympathetic, yet often ironic distance between the naïve, confused, suffering being he was and the articulate individual he has become. As readers we are invited to deplore his circumstances, sympathize with him in his repeated exploitation, identify with him against his white and black antagonists, share his violent disorientation, even smile at him for his earnestness, but we are never allowed to forget that he has come through. As an object of both his own later contemplation and ours, this young man is the expressionist dreamer (even before he arrives in his dream city) or somnambulist who will experience an escalating series of perceptual shocks before he is fully awake. He seems to float through life – whether driving Norton in the college limousine or walking the streets of Harlem – with external forces pulling his strings, and in a sense he does not fully wake up until he meets the grotesque distortion of himself in Tod Clifton's obscene Sambo dolls. It is this confrontation with Tod (Death) in chapter 22 that signals his last and most crucial *Aufbruch*.

Even though the novel as a whole cannot be described as an expressionist *Schrei*, we are none the less prepared for extremes of inner anguish by the prologue. In the italicized passages that mark his drug-induced descent, 'like Dante,' into the depths (12–15), the invisible man is assailed by all the voices and hallucinated images of his racial, cultural, and personal past. As he will in chapters 1 to 25 he stumbles about in the dark, haunted by footsteps, 'dazed, the music beating hysterically' in his ears, with trumpets blaring and (shades of O'Neill's *Emperor Jones*) 'a tom-tom beating like heart-thuds' (14–15). This nightmarish experience instructs the reader how to read the subsequent narrative by warning us that before we can surface to the cool control of the narrative present, we must experience the depths of the speaker's inner world or, in the closing metaphor of chapter 25, fall into the coal-hole and darkness of his soul. The climax/nadir of that descent (in itself a superb instance of the inversion topos already familiar in expressionist art) comes with the vision of the last chapter, the vision that in many respects echoes and continues the hallucinations of the prologue. This time, however, caught in 'a state neither of dreaming nor of waking,' what he sees is an expressionist vision of apocalypse with its full panoply of negative associations. By castrating him, his black and white tormentors precipitate the destruction of the world – as we may if we fail to heed the hero's warning in the text/memoir addressed to us. Perhaps in this sense more than any other, the narrator, whether during or after his ordeal, is an expressionist hero. He offers his vision to us as a warning; he lifts the veil on that possibility of ending, offering us the chance to see before it is too late.

The episodic structure of *Invisible Man* shares certain qualities with the *Stationen* structure of expressionist drama, in part because of the central focus on a bewildered, suffering hero and in part because his experiences of the world are radically fragmented. Reality as he knows it does not make epistemological or moral sense; the apparent motives of others seldom fit their actions. The disorientation and alienation that result from this confusion spring from his lack of a stable inner reference point and his failure to read the external signs in his social milieu. To complicate his dilemma further, that milieu itself changes. Thus, the world he inhabits is itself in flux, and this instability intensifies the 'sickness' within him. The extreme distortion of certain parts of the narrative is therefore both a mirroring of the narrator's inner turmoil and a critical imaging of the economic, political, social circumstances surrounding him.

Even before the narrator leaves the south, with its version of order provided by the college, signs of approaching vertigo appear. He remembers his past in vivid flashes – the Battle Royal, Trueblood's 'confession,' the Golden Day – without any attempt to explain them as part of a continuous and meaningful context. Each episode, though related in a language remarkable mostly for its syntactic simplicity, semantic coherence, or, in the case of Trueblood's story, with a sensitivity to real speech rhythms and idiom, stays in the mind (the reader's too) with a violent, visual power. By the time he reaches New York, the shock of his expulsion, which he cannot understand, has already begun to take effect, but with the increasing tempo of events both inner and outer reality become more and more confused. Chapter 7, when he first arrives in the city, begins in an objective tone with controlled phrasing. By chapter 9 the style has not changed, but the young man's perception of reality receives a jolt when young Emerson reveals the actual contents of Bledsoe's letter.

Then, without initially breaking the realist contiguities of the narrative, our hero describes the Liberty Paints Factory and its denizens in increasingly dramatic terms until, in the last moments of that chapter, he confronts a maniacal Lucius Brockway: 'He started toward me as in a dream, trembling like the needle of one of the gauges as he pointed toward the stairs, his voice shrieking. I stared; something seemed to have gone wrong, my reflexes were jammed' (196). The ambiguity of the opening sentence – 'He started toward me *as [if] in a dream*' – establishes the possibility that it is the narrator who is already dreaming the living nightmare of the approaching disaster. Whose dream is this, the narrator's or Brockway's? Or have inner and outer reality become so closely identified that the distinction is pointless? Is Brockway really trembling and shrieking, or is this distorted image the result of the narrator's emotional response to his own situation and the other man's anger? From this point until the end of chapter 11, the narrator is caught up in an extraordinary sequence of increasingly expressionist scenes.

Surrounded by disembodied voices and bright lights, shot through with pain and barraged by a wild variety of sounds – the crashing chords of Beethoven's Fifth Symphony, Sunday music, a trumpet, an organ, droning voices, and folk rhymes – he appears to himself to be lying in a glass and metal machine-cum-coffin at the mercy of vaguely medical personnel. Snatches of logical-sounding dialogue give way to passages of intense description of his raw feelings and confused perceptions. These, in turn, are followed by a lengthy verbal assault on his very identity: 'WHO … ARE … YOU?' (209–11) But even within this expressionist *tour de force*, the judgment of a wiser narrator can be heard. In retrospect he knows that he is no Samson and that the machine, with its cruel operators, is an apt symbol for a hostile, destructive American society: 'I had no desire to destroy myself even if it destroyed the machine; I wanted freedom, not destruction … When I discover who I am, I'll be free' (212).

Despite hints like this that the hero is *not* undergoing some major medical procedure, most readers interpret this episode as the description of a frontal lobotomy or electric-shock treatments. But Ellison has been deliberately vague about the physical realities of the ordeal because it is the hero's inner response to his felt situation of confusion, dread, and loss that is of paramount importance. Instead of straining for realistic explanations of the voices and events suggested here, it is possible and, I think, more fruitful to read them as the violent projections of his 'soul-sickness.' Here for the first time the hero experiences the full horror of his existence, and the truth of his insight into himself and his world is intensified by their distortion. This is the reality of emotion, the truth of terrifying vision, not the limited logic and facts of a material world. The sooner he recognizes that he carries 'part of [his] sickness within [him],' the sooner he will be free.

At the end of chapter 11, just as he leaves the factory, with its 'paint-fuming air,' the narrator provides a further important clue to the status of his narrative and to his state of mind: 'I had the feeling that I had been talking beyond myself, had used words and expressed attitudes not my own, that I was in the grip of some alien personality lodged deep within me ... It was as though I were acting out a scene from some crazy movie. Or perhaps I was catching up with myself and had put into words feelings which I had hitherto suppressed' (217). Although logically, coherently expressed, the narrator is suggesting here that the recent ordeal was the projection of an inner, not yet recognized self. Thus, the expressionist method – like the experience it gave rise to – reveals an inner truth he could not otherwise have faced. Both the factory scene with Brockway and his bizarre ordeal in the 'machine' (the latter reminiscent of the mad Dr Rotwang transforming the gentle Maria into a demonic robot by means of electric shocks) seem to make oblique references to Fritz Lang's apocalyptic allegory *Metropolis*, with its expressionist vision of the workers' city and their final salvation.

After Tod Clifton's death, the narrator draws more and more upon a surrealistic depiction of Harlem reality. With one or two exceptions (such as the expressionist monologue in chapter 22, to which I shall return, and the expressionist vision of chapter 25, discussed above), approximately the last third of the narrative could be described as being 'somewhat surrealistic.'[13] The key point to remember in distinguishing the surrealistic from the expressionistic mode is that the former maintains a primarily cerebral approach (Breton, like most surrealists, spoke only of the *mind*) towards objects in the external world, even though their significance is interpreted through dream, imagination, and symbolic association, whereas the latter concentrates upon the intense expression of subjective emotion as a means of tapping visionary truths, both personal and cosmic. While not as surrealistic as the Harlem riot that follows, the scene of Clifton's death provides a good example of the distinctions and of Ellison's clear sense of what he wanted to do.

At about the mid-point of chapter 20, the narrator, who has finally realized his isolation within the Brotherhood and stormed from the general meeting, stumbles by accident upon Clifton, who is selling Sambo dolls illegally on the sidewalk. The narrator is horrified yet mesmerized by his friend's degrading spiel and moves slowly away, pondering Clifton's fate. Moments later he turns a corner to witness Clifton's arrest and murder. He describes the sequence of events exactly as he sees them, vividly, precisely, but in fragments of action interrupted by traffic and scattering pigeons, then comments:

> He fell forward on his knees, like a man saying his prayers just as a heavy-set man in a hat with a turned-down brim stepped from around the news-stand and yelled a protest. I couldn't move. The sun seemed to scream an inch above my head. Someone shouted. A few men were starting into the street. The cop was standing now and looking down at Clifton as though surprised, the gun in his hand. I took a few steps forward, walking blindly now, unthinking, yet my mind registering it all vividly. (377)

The scene, which he registers coolly and meticulously in his mind, is frozen in time, disjunct in space, and free of emotional response. He makes no attempt to project his own feelings of dread or anger, nor does he try to capture the moment empathetically from the dying man's point of view. Yet there is certainly horror in this violent scene, not merely because of its content but because of the way it is described; it bears a dream-like quality in which things happen without connection, motiva-tion, or purpose, and the vivid elements of the scene – praying posture, newsman's hat, screaming sun, and gun – seem disjunct in space, occurring together in that instant as if by accident and hinting at some hidden, ominous meaning by their strange association.

From this point on, Ellison's hero sees the world around him as if through a surrealist painter's eyes. Brother Jack's glass eye sits like 'buttermilk' in a glass, 'distorted by the light rays' (*not* by his emotion) and 'staring fixedly at [him]' (409). It reminds this reader, at least, of a René Magritte canvas (*The False Mirror*, 1928, or *Portrait*, 1935). When he dons his Rinehart glasses and white hat, he not only disguises his own identity but becomes instantly capable of new angles of perception on Harlem itself. Thus, the crowd around the bar at Ballantine's Jolly Dollar resembles 'nightmare figures in the smoke-green haze,' and the jukebox lights up 'like a bad dream of the Fiery Furnace' (420). And later, when he is mistaken for Reverend Rinehart, he has a brief glimpse of the church interior, which quivers 'vague and mysterious in the green light' (430) before the door swings shut. The insights provided by these surrealistic images, however, are a function of his increased understanding, not the embellishments of a vivid imagination or the consequences of his emotional projections. By the end of chapter 23, the invisible man has learned to *read* the images well enough to see that he has been exploited by real, external forces (in the scene with the glass eye it is the light rays that distort and Brother Jack who manipulates). As a human being, he is still invisible to others and he formulates this truth in another surrealistic image: 'And now I looked around a corner of my mind and saw Jack and Norton and Emerson merge into one single white figure. They were very much the same, each attempting to force his picture of reality upon me' (439).

Rather than an impassioned outburst of emotion (which will come later), passages like this locate the hero's insights firmly in the mind, and in the mind's eye, through an evocation of disturbing yet precise images of external reality. There is no iconic abstraction here, no expressive distortion. Instead, the *logic* of Ellison's image is strongly reminiscent of the empty passages, arches, and repetitive, static white figures of Giorgio de Chirico and Paul Delvaux, and the sense of threat from reduplicated, hovering figures recalls Magritte's *L'Assassin menacé* (1926). But if there is any single surrealist canvas that speaks directly to the quality of Ellison's prose at this point in *Invisible Man* and whose iconography parallels the symbols his hero is deciphering here, it might well be Max Ernst's 1923 oil *Pietà, ou la révolution de la nuit*. Against a flattened, monochromatic, rudimentary yet precise urban background of brick wall, pavement, stairs, and railing kneels a large brown, slightly stylized man in bowler hat, suit, and tie, carrying in his arms the classic image of sightless, indifferent white Western culture – a Greek statue clothed in bright red pants and startlingly white chemise. The painting is as rich in cultural, social, and sexual tensions as is *Invisible Man*, but the central meaning of the painting, as of these scenes in the novel, is the terrible burden of sightlessness and invisibility conveyed in the static, lucid language of surrealism.

With the onset of the Harlem riot, real events happen so quickly and with so little direction that the entire night seems a surrealist fantasy: a tenement burns, gunshots ring out, milk runs in the streets, and people appear and disappear in the dark. Quiet, empty, and shadowed under a new moon at one moment, the streets are suddenly filled with Ras the

Exhorter become Ras the Destroyer on a black horse at another, but not before the narrator stumbles upon a scene lifted straight from the violent, pornographic world of Hans Bellmer:[14] 'Ahead of me the body hung, white, naked, and horribly feminine from a lamppost. I felt myself spin around with horror and it was as though I had turned some nightmarish somersault ... there was another and another, seven – all hanging before a gutted storefront ... They were mannequins – "Dummies!"' (481)

The final chapters of *Invisible Man* are by no means uniformly surrealistic. The text remains throughout in the dominantly realistic-confessional mode of the narrator, controlled by his logic and illocutionary intentions. One major aspect of the novel's expressionism remains to be examined, however, and this is the hero's own rhetoric, the dramatic speeches through which he expresses himself at moments of intense emotional involvement and, ironically, becomes useful to the Brotherhood. As spontaneous verbal constructs they constitute fine examples of the expressionist hero creating himself through language; as deliberately placed intertexts within the larger metanarrative of memoir they contribute both thematically and formally to Ellison's dramatic strategy, thereby uniting art and protest. Although there are several speeches that illustrate Ellison's use of an expressionist monologue to advantage, such as his protest against the Harlem evictions in chapter 13, his decidedly unscientific speeches for the Brotherhood, or his impassioned oration at Clifton's funeral, one comparatively short but effective passage from chapter 22 provides an especially apt example of the mode, because here there is no externalizing occasion, no represented audience (however irrelevant or abstract and symbolic that audience might be).

Brother Jack has been berating the hero at length for the refusal of party discipline demonstrated by his actions at Tod Clifton's funeral. In his rage the glass eye has popped from Brother Jack's head, and he shouts, struts, and slams the table in his desire to threaten and intimidate. But the narrator responds with the heightened emotional disorientation, or *Schrei*, that none the less enables him to express himself:

> I shook like a leaf. So that is the meaning of discipline, I thought, sacrifice ... yes, and blindness; he doesn't see me. He doesn't even see me. Am I about to strangle him? I do not know. He cannot possibly. I still do not know. See! Discipline is sacrifice. Yes, and blindness. Yes. And me sitting here while he tries to intimidate me. That's it, with his goddam blind glass eye ... Should you show him you get it? Shouldn't you? Shouldn't he know it? Hurry! Shouldn't you? Look at it there, a good job, an almost perfect imitation that seemed alive ... Should you, shouldn't you? Maybe

he got it where he learned that language he lapsed into. Shouldn't you?
Make him speak the unknown tongue, the language of the future. What's
mattering with you? Discipline. Is learning, didn't he say? Is it? I stand?
You're sitting here, ain't I? You're holding on, ain't I? He said you'd learn
so you're learning, so he saw it all the time. He's a riddler, shouldn't we
show him? So sit still is the way, and learn, never mind the eye, it's dead ...
All right now, look at him, see him turning now, left, right, coming short-
legged toward you. See him, hep! hep! the one-eyed beacon. All right, all
right ... Hep! hep! The short-legged deacon. All right! Nail him! The short-
changing dialectical deacon. There, so now you're learning ... Get it under
control ... Patience ... Yes ...   (410–11)

Shattered syntax, explosive punctuation, breathless ellipsis, and obsessive repetition express the hero's emotional chaos, reaching a climax in
the inner confusion that renders him outwardly passive: 'Should you,
shouldn't you?' The vertiginous climax of this monologue occurs with the
staccato questions, and the pronominal instability – '*You*'re sitting here,
ain't *I*? *You*'re holding on, ain't *I*?' – signifies the acute objective/
subjective disorientation of the self. At about this point in the monologue
the hero begins to regain a degree of control over language and feeling,
until he is able to contain Jack's threatening, distorted image in words. To
do this he draws, instinctively, upon idiomatic expressions ('What's
mattering with you?'), rejection of formal grammar ('ain't ... ain't'),
riddles, and the black oral tradition of the dozens. From here on repetition
facilitates rhythm – 'hep! hep!' 'all right, all right' – and rhythm signifies
control, a black, semiotic control that is the opposite of Brother Jack's
white discipline.

It is impossible, I think, to underestimate the centrality of speech in
Invisible Man, and most critics at least recognize it in passing. From an
expressionist perspective, however, it becomes the unifying factor of the
book. Not only has Ellison exploited the various speech registers and
patterns of black American culture and the rich oral traditions of folktale
within the mandarin English of an educated middle-class American,
together with a full (almost Joycean) range of modernist allusions and
styles; he has also cast his entire text in the form of a first-person direct
address to an implied, potential interlocutor: the reader. This invisible
man, after all, is cast as 'a disembodied voice' (503) who 'speaks' for and
to us. Speech-making, as the hero knows (331), started him off in life; and
he has continued to act under the influence of Trueblood's, Bledsoe's,
Norton's, Emerson's, and Jack's words. What he has misunderstood is
that the 'magic in spoken words' (330) will not work properly if the words

are merely borrowed. Until he wakes up to the reality of his situation in this expressionist monologue, he does not see the extent to which he has been a victim of words, a speech-making machine mouthing other people's ideas. Both the invisible man's victory and Ellison's protest exist within the same medium: drawing upon, manipulating, flaunting, and glorying in a polyphonic discourse, Ellison's speaker says himself into visibility.

In a long and detailed analysis of *Invisible Man*, Malcolm Lowry criticized the general lack of artistry in the last eight chapters that deal with the Brotherhood. The first two-thirds, indeed the novel in general, he described as 'electrifying' proof of how important and truthful modern fiction could be. Ellison, 'like Kafka,' so Lowry said, managed to 'strike at the soul of man himself.'[15] To an exceptionally skilled and artistically sympathetic reader like Lowry, *Invisible Man*'s success arose chiefly from its fusion of art and protest. Ellison's refusal to bow to the social-realist program did not mean that he had failed to address the plight of his people or the danger of racism in American society as a whole. Rather, like Ernst Toller, writing from exile in England before the war, Ellison believed in the inherent 'power of the word and the moral nature of art' (see chapter 1, note 3). Seeing Ellison's novel in the context of expressionist art helps one to appreciate the type of moral vision, as well as the type of art he espoused: his faith resembles Toller's; his vision of the city recalls Meidner or Kirchner; his black Everyman reminds one, time and again, of Döblin's abused hero Franz Biberkopf, and his portrait of the artist as protestor and iconoclast echoes Pechstein's *An alle Künstler!* (see Plate 8) far more than it suggests a parallel with Joyce's *Portrait*. In his ambivalent response to the conflicting attractions of regression and apocalypse, he seems to encapsulate many of the tensions that inform the expressionist / modernist mode.

Without the prologue and epilogue *Invisible Man* comes very close to inscribing a topos of inversion; not only does Ellison's hero fall down a coal-hole in a mad, sinister caricature of Alice; he resigns himself to being in this safe, warm hideout that, dark as night (or filled with his new-found light), protects him from the world outside. Worse still, he dreams of the ultimate male victimization – castration – after which he will be incapable of action. Thus, his choice apparently comes down to castration, or reabsorption by the mother. Such a case for regression, however, becomes difficult (though not impossible, as some critics have shown) to sustain when the prologue and epilogue are given due weight. To complicate an already ambiguous ending further, Ellison's vision of apocalypse is itself double. On the one hand he has conjured up images of sheer destruction in the riot and in the hero's dream, not only through the hero's graphic castration but also with the ominous symbol of the bridge that metamorphoses into an iron robot striding 'doomfully' (493). On the other, he has provided the type of hope familiar from the romantic, secular version of apocalypse, first by suggesting that this is *only* a dream – albeit a prophetic one – and second by stressing the importance of speech: in the last analysis, the narrator has succeeded in shaping an artistic communication out of his agony, and we have the chance to share that existential hope. *His* apocalypse is the unveiling, through language, of the already coded, previously constituted self.[16] In the last analysis Ellison's *Invisible Man* provides no easy answer to the regression/apocalypse question because 'all dreamers and sleepwalkers must pay the price, and even the invisible victim is responsible for the fate of all' (17). And they must pay because there is no pure origin to be tapped and no transcendent Logos to be appealed to.

But if Ellison rejects the 'expressive fallacy' and thereby refuses easy answers to the large ethical and socio-political questions he raises, he is not as hard to pin down stylistically. Clearly he saw the need for a mixed style within a type of narrative both expansive and flexible enough to accommodate his vision of America. Thus, his naturalism permits him to recount the facts of black history and social conditioning; his expressionism enables him to reveal and explore the forces *within* that contribute to his protagonist's 'soul-sickness'; and his surrealism facilitates a vivid, shocking anatomizing of an external world that refuses to see what exists. Together, and unified by the consciousness of the narrator, this heterogeneity establishes his freedom from illusions, asserts his empowerment, and celebrates the rich diversity of his discourse. Ellison may well have had Dostoevsky's Underground Man in mind while working on his novel, but, as Bakhtin has demonstrated in his analysis of Dostoevsky's dialogistic discourse, there are other lessons to be absorbed by a sensitive response to the Russian's fictional system. Although it was not recognized in the fifties, perhaps the most subversive aspect of Ellison's prose is its mixture of styles, its multiple voices, and its so-called inconsistent method, because that very heterogeneity and undecidability resists a centralizing, authoritarian reduction of the text. Looked at in Bakhtinian terms, Brother Jack's 'discipline' and 'sacrifice' are nothing less than the totalitarianizing of the word to which *Invisible Man* says 'nay.'

PART FOUR

The Expressionist Legacy

10 From Modernism to Postmodernism: Conclusions, Speculations, and Questions

By the end of the 1920s the ferment and fervour of early modernism were over: Dada was dead, having slipped beneath Breton's tamer, intellectualized Surrealism; *The Waste Land* (1922) was behind Eliot and he was moving towards a more classical form and an Anglican vision; Stravinsky's *Rite of Spring* (1913) and the compositions of George Antheil no longer scandalized audiences;[1] *Ulysses* was well on its way to canonization by those critics who would help to define it as quintessentially modernist; Vorticism was a distant memory, and Pound, who was writing the *Cantos*, was sliding further towards the political right, together with Lawrence, Dali, Heidegger, Lewis, the futurists, and Benn; Picasso had painted what some consider to be his last great cubist canvas – *Three Dancers* (1925)[2] – but the excitement and outrage of Cubism had already settled into the calm plasticity of Mondriaan and the De Stijl movement, and the non-iconic abstraction of Constructivism. The German expressionists were scattered and diffused, some stubbornly continuing to work within that aesthetic but many more turning further inward or abandoning an expressionist vision for the new objectivity, with others, like Kandinsky, moving towards non-iconic abstraction. What would happen to modern art in the Third Reich has already been told in chapter 1.

My point, and it is scarcely a new one, is that the early modernism of the first two decades of this century was enormously varied and vital. But this point needs stressing because, in looking back on those years prior to the Second World War, we have too often tended to see modernism as homogeneous, defined on the one hand by a select group of male artists and on the other by the visual abstraction and architectural impersonality characteristic of late, or high, modernism. Cubism, Surrealism, De Stijl, the Bauhaus, and in the English language, Eliot, Joyce, and Pound: these have been promoted as the parameters and arbiters of modernist art.[3] There is, however, much truth to the claim articulated by Serge Guilbaut in *How New York Stole the Idea of Modern Art* that, in the late forties, a group of American theorists and promoters of abstraction set out to establish American 'cultural hegemony [and] to shift the center of artistic creation from Paris to New York,' from Surrealism (with its communist and Trotskyist leanings) to a pure, non-political Abstract Expressionism that would better serve American imperialist ends.[4] And to a large degree, though perhaps not with the same political agenda, American and Canadian critics of Joyce, Pound, and Eliot performed a similar role in canonizing an ostensibly apolitical, universalist high modernism during the fifties and sixties.

To accept Ihab Hassan's 1982 schematic summary of modernist qualities – hierarchy, finished work, totalization, synthesis, centring, presence, readerly texts, 'master code' (which he contrasts with postmodernist 'idiolect' to stress the elitist level of modernist language), metaphysical, determinant, and transcendent – is to imagine a static, monolithic, and authoritarian art-form and to neglect utterly the distortion, rebellion, and intense subjective expressivity of early modernism.[5] Late modernism, American-style, has been taken for the whole. Writing twenty years earlier than Hassan, however, Stephen Spender and Irving Howe had a more discriminating perspective, though to be fair to Hassan, he is not so much interested in charting modernism as in exploring the parameters of *post*modernism. None the less, Spender and Howe were more sensitive to the explosive vitality of modernism, as well as to the differences between its early and later phases. For them, violent distortion, extreme subjectivity, and a 'jagged and fragmented expressiveness' were synonymous with modernism.[6]

A close consideration of Expressionism, such as the one offered in preceding chapters, despite its exclusions and limitations, modifies our generally received notions of modernism by stressing, and placing in perspective, the contribution made by Expressionism to the modernist enterprise. Indeed, Expressionism represented a somewhat different modernism from the dominant image of the period promulgated between 1945 and the mid-sixties.

And yet it is unwise to say *a* different modernism, because the singular implies a unity of program and style that was as foreign to Expressionism as it was to Dada and Surrealism. With a terrible historical irony, however, the virulent epithets hurled against modern painting, sculpture, and literature (in London, in New York at the Armory Show, at the first exhibits of the Group of Seven, and across Europe), then picked up and transformed into official doctrine by Hitler, became the terms by which Expressionism and its artists both inside *and* outside Germany were generally known: modernism was 'degenerate,' or in a slightly more tolerant vein perhaps, neurotic, emotional, irrational, meaningless, 'painterly,' nostalgic, and regressive. With such pejorative labels the art of Expressionism has often been categorized and dismissed. As recently as 1986 a North American couple visiting a splendid Munch exhibition was overheard loudly complaining: 'Let's get out of here, this is just crap!' What Ortega diagnosed in 'The Dehumanization of Art' (1925) as the unpopularity of modern art with the masses remains constant.

But Expressionism was neither 'degenerate' nor meaningless. Fundamentally informed by a rejection of realism, expressionist art none the less contains within it extremes of representation and iconic abstraction, of violent physicality and lyric spirituality. As a result it is defined not by distortion, frenzy, and irrationalism per se but by the functional tension between a number of conflicting tendencies and artistic possibilities; its aesthetics belongs on that axis, derives from that interface between extremes, leaning more towards 'empathy' here or abstraction there, towards representation in this work or semantic and syntactic abstraction in that.

An expressionist poetics must allow for and inscribe that tension, whether the writer wishes to express a personal subjectivity in the most strident tones or the anguish of a fictional character's soul, either of which may be conceived as participating in some mystic or cosmic force. Consequently, an expressionist poetics abstracts from and distorts a reader's perception of external reality by breaking the accepted conventions of narrative or dramatic form, of speech and character portrayal, and of language itself. The closer the text stays to the mimetic conventions of realism and to the socio-political concerns of the author, the more likely it will be that the resources of an expressionist poetics will serve a central, suffering, recognizable hero, as, for example, in the work of Toller, Kafka, O'Neill, Lowry, and Ellison. By contrast, the more symbolic and mythic the writer's intention, the more abstract the discourse will become, as can be seen in Kaiser, Döblin, Voaden, Barnes, and Watson. In the last analysis, however, difference among expressionist works is a question of tendency and degree.

This internal dynamic of an expressionist poetics creates a genuine potential for decentring and destabilizing a text. Thus, there is often a marked tendency towards what I have called, borrowing from Bakhtin, the 'carnivalesque' in expressionist discourse. Structurally, linguistically, and thematically an expressionist play or novel images displacement, disorientation, and breakdown by turning the familiar world of literary form and spoken or represented discourse upside-down, and this is true, to a degree, even in the works where the 'expressive fallacy' seems not to be recognized, let alone analysed (in Sorge's *The Beggar* or O'Neill's *Emperor Jones*, for example). In so far as a given work is carnivalesque, it is also potentially political or, at least, projects itself in the gesture of political resistance and critique. Moreover, that critique, however abstract and oblique (as it most certainly is in Watson's novel), or private and self-centred (as it is in O'Neill), originates in an apocalyptic eschatology; it is a story about last things, a warning of ends – and new beginnings.

This century has been preoccupied with death: the death of God, the death of class and capitalism, the death of the author and of the individual, the death of art. But if, as Derrida speculates in 'Of an apocalyptic tone recently adopted in philosophy,' *all* writing is apocalyptic, then it is important to stress that expressionist texts constitute one twentieth-century mode that is overtly, urgently so. Expressionist art addresses itself directly and painfully to the apocalyptic task: to speak / break out; to announce, to warn: 'LE GUSTA ESTE JARDÍN QUE ES SUYO? EVITE QUE SUS HIJOS LO DESTRUYAN!'[7] Romantic and Nietzschean, the expressionists more than other modernists strive desperately to close the gap between the end, any end ('Come back to me, if only for a day,' Lowry's Consul cries), and the hoped-for new beginning; hence the frequently strident pitch of the expressionist *Schrei*. When the attempted closure fails – or falls on nothingness – or when the speaker admits the impossibility of originary, unmediated expression, he or she erupts in violence and is destroyed or withdraws into a union with the natural world that offers release from action and consciousness. Seen in this way, as an aspect of a wider eschatology, such atavism combines a desire for primitive simplicity and spirituality with a longing for death that need not preclude rebirth. Regression, then, can be more than a final negation of life.

But expressionist literature struggles with and against that failure and negation. The author, character, or narrator pits him or herself against surrounding silence or a hostile bourgeois society or the 'soul-sickness' within in a struggle to articulate a vision of better things that centres upon the birth of the New Self or Man. Even when the effort fails within the text (as imaged in the characters or hero), the text itself exists, and it is Derrida's hope (as it was also Nietzsche's and Kant's) that the apocalyptic discourse itself can dismantle established contracts, undermine the hegemony of the 'general collucation' to reveal, unveil, and thereby subvert its false or authoritarian position: 'By its very tone, the mixing of voices, genres, and codes, and the breakdown (*le détraquement*) of destinations, apocalyptic discourse can also dismantle the dominant contract or concordat. It is a challenge to the established admissability of messages and to the enforcement or the maintenance of order.'[8] Such a 'mixing of voices,' of course, recalls Bakhtinian dialogism, both in its verbal heterogeneity and in its liberating activity. Furthermore, by announcing its array of endings – to bourgeois paternalism, urban mechanization, political repression, to the banality of surfaces, artistic illusion and spiritual torpor – an expressionist apocalypse invites the artist ('An alle Künstler!') to destroy the old forms of life and art and create the new.

In stressing the *différance* of Expressionism, however, I do not want to ignore its place as an aesthetic, a poetics, and a corpus of work within the wider context of the modern.[9] On the contrary, it seems to me that Expressionism belongs near the centre, not at the periphery of the modern movement in the arts. Certainly Ortega recognized this centrality of both the movement and the aesthetic, first in 'The Dehumanization of Art' and again in his 1949 *Partisan Review* article 'On Point of View in the Arts.' Expressionist literature shares with modernism its faith in language to convey meaning, its conception of the artist as creator and iconoclast, and its desire to create unified art-works. Thanks in large part to the expressionists the modern stage was freed from a slavish realism, so that, without a direct influence from the German stage, contemporary dramatists as varied as Arthur Laurents, Tennessee Williams, Adrienne Kennedy, and the authors of Vietnam plays in the United States and George Ryga, Robert Gurik, and Michael Cook in Canada, to name only a few, could write plays that require expressionistic handling on stage, exploit expressionist strategies for character presentation and thematic development, and assume an audience's understanding of the form.

Expressionism has also helped to free the modern novel from the strait-jacket of realist conventions by enabling the writer to reach for visionary, prophetic, and mythic power and to achieve a broad symbolic scope. The expressionist character and the various forms of represented speech needed to express him or her have contributed enormously to the available territory of narratorial investigation. For English-language writers, of course, the 'Circe' episode in *Ulysses* provided an early example of these possibilities. Post–Second World War American fiction owes a great deal indirectly to the expressionist vision that is integral not only to the novels discussed in Part Three but also to a wide range of writing that displays few obvious signs of the mode (such as the expressive style of Faulkner, the nightmare vision of West, the horrifying world of Hawkes's *The Cannibal*, which but for space might well have been considered with *Nightwood* or *Invisible Man*.[10] Speaking in the mid-sixties of what he described as the American 'novel of nightmares,' Jonathan Baumbach recognized in these works the combination of technical sophistication with the desire to investigate a 'Dostoevskian ... confrontation of man with the objectification of his primordial self and his exemplary spiritual passage from innocence to guilt to redemption.'[11] This confrontation is one that characterizes much contemporary American writing and that R.W.B. Lewis extends in 'Days of Wrath and Laughter' to include Barth, Burroughs, and Pynchon.[12]

By contrast with the American tradition, at least as it is outlined by Baumbach and Lewis, Canadian novelists have resisted the lessons of Expressionism. Until recently, and partly in response to Watson's *The Double Hook*, realism has remained the dominant mode in fiction and on the stage. Rarely has an apocalyptic tone entered the literature of a culture more receptive to the discourse of historical and natural continuities than to violent disruptions. Rather than supposing some 'excluded middle' (Derrida, 79) out there, Canadians feel as if they occupy that middle ground, with the result that they have preferred to create predominantly (though by no means exclusively) representational fictions that frequently conclude with images of social accommodation or union with the earth. There are exceptions, of course, beyond the decisively expressionistic novels examined in Part Three, such as some scenes in F.P. Grove's *The Master of the Mill* (1944), aspects of Margaret Atwood's *Surfacing* (1972) and of Timothy Findley's *The Wars* (1977), the intensely expressionist vision of Michael Ondaatje's *Coming Through Slaughter* (1971) or of Leonard Cohen's *Beautiful Losers* (1966), and a spectacular expressionist/surrealist mixture of styles in Denys Chabot's *Eldorado on Ice* (1981).[13] The generalization (for what it is worth) is tempting: Canadian expressionist literature tends more towards regression (as I define that term), with a marked preference for representation and empathy, while the American variety is more apocalyptic in its themes and more tolerant of abstraction. No sooner is that said, however, than one recalls the expressive abstraction of *The Double Hook* and the atavism of O'Neill's *The Great God Brown*, and with them the limited value of generalizations.

There are two aspects to the current revival of interest in Expressionism, and while there are some intriguing connections between them, there are also some important differences. On the one hand, the decade 1977–87 has enjoyed a feast of retrospectives and revivals, not only in Germany but across North America; on the other, the same period has seen the birth of so-called Neo-expressionism. It would be easy to say with the cynics that this apparent historical coincidence is a promotion trick, an artificially created taste capitalized upon by a few who made quick fortunes in a wildly escalating international art market and have already left the stage. It would be equally easy to agree with cultural pessimists who argue that this return to representation, with its recuperation of the past, parallels the neo-conservatism of late capitalism and the rise of an extreme political right in North America and much of western Europe, and that it signifies nothing more than a generalized nostalgia catered to by pastiche instead of genuine art. What these responses share is the attempt to understand what, if anything, our time has in common with the early decades of this century. The question they both address is why: why is Expressionism important to the arts in the eighties?

To undertake a thorough examination of these claims and questions, and of the new art that has provoked them, requires a separate study. But I would like to gather up a few threads of the argument here, if only to sketch some of the ways in which – as Ernst Bloch predicted in 1938 – the 'heritage of Expressionism has not ceased to exist because we have not yet even started to consider it.' First the revivals and retrospectives.

In my introduction and in chapter 2, I mentioned a number of European revivals of expressionist classics such as the Paris opera's *Woyzeck* (Plate 16), the splendid Essen production of *The Green Table* (Plate 15), and Peter Stein's 1987 production of *The Hairy Ape* (Plate 26). It is by no means unusual to find popular runs of plays by Wedekind and Kaiser in German theatres, and every local museum exhibits its expressionist holdings (however scanty) with great pride. Indeed, major and important retrospectives have been held in Berlin, Hamburg, Düsseldorf, Munich, Vienna, and Venice (to mention only a few) of expressionist painting, sculpture, and graphics, with accompanying displays of poetry, fiction, manifestos, and correspondence. The Austrian Egon Schiele, whose oil on canvas *Liebespaar 1* (1914) sold for over five million dollars in 1984, has received individual attention in several retrospectives, as have Max Beckmann and Oskar Kokoschka.

Nor has this flurry of attention to the masterworks of Expressionism been restricted to the continent. In 1977 the Metropolitan Opera in New York performed Alban Berg's *Lulu* (it received its American première in Santa Fé in 1963) to considerable acclaim. A few years later, the Toronto Opera Company mounted a highly expressionistic production of *Lulu*, which, though superbly sung, acted, and staged, was less successful with audiences than with the critics. Berg's *Woyzeck*, however, received its

Canadian première in Toronto in 1977 when it was reviewed as a 'brilliant' performance of 'the century's operatic masterpiece.'[14]

Georg Büchner's play fragment *Woyzeck*, on which the opera is based, has enjoyed consistent popularity with alternate theatres in Canada and the United States since the early sixties. But perhaps even more than the music and literature of Expressionism, it is the visual arts that have received the greatest attention. For example, in 1977 the University of Houston hosted an interdisciplinary conference on the movement featuring exhibits, film screenings, and a performance of Schönberg's *Pierrot Lunaire* (1911); in 1979–80 the Guggenheim in New York and the San Francisco Museum of Modern Art held the major exhibit 'Expressionism: A German Intuition, 1905–1920'; early in 1985 the massive centenary Beckmann exhibit that began in Munich in 1984 travelled to St Louis and Los Angeles (but not to Canada);[15] in 1985 and again in 1987 McMaster University in Hamilton exhibited its impressive holdings of expressionist graphics – both times to enthusiastic reviews; the Guggenheim held a superb retrospective of Kokoschka's work in 1986, the same year that the Vancouver Art Gallery celebrated the province's centenary with a major exhibition of Munch that demonstrated the dramatic parallels between his expressionist vision and that of Emily Carr.

An interesting feature of much of this activity is that North Americans who collected German art are now finding a more receptive audience for their collections. The McMaster exhibitions are a case in point. Another is the Expressionist Collection from the St Louis Art Museum, which travelled to Seattle during the winter of 1986–87, where it formed the centrepiece to a series of lectures on Expressionism in the arts. Special attention was granted to Beckmann, who was described as 'the spiritual ancestor of contemporary neoexpressionist painters.'[16] This direct link between Expressionism and the new art that began to emerge in Germany in the seventies is more carefully documented and substantiated in the exhibition that, to date, marks the climax of renewed attention to the movement: the 1985–86 Tate Gallery's 'German Art in the Twentieth Century.' Several articles in the catalogue, as well as the paintings themselves, stress the crucial mediary role of Ernst Wilhelm Nay (1902–68), himself branded 'degenerate,' between the work of Kirchner and Nolde and the contemporary canvases of Georg Baselitz, Berndt Koberling, and Karl Horst Hödicke. Not to be outdone, the Museum of Modern Art opened its retrospective on contemporary German art on 4 June 1987. 'BERLINART, 1961–1987' confirmed and consolidated the centrality of Neo-expressionism to the art scene of the latter half of this century and clearly demonstrated the capillary links between this art of our time and its early modern, expressionist heritage.[17] In the summer of 1988 the Vancouver Art Gallery showed 'The Expressionist Landscape: North American Modernist Painting, 1920–1947.' This exhibition, which began in Birmingham, Alabama, in 1987, marked the first serious attempt to chart the influences on and results of Expressionism for landscape painting on this continent. Between the autumn of 1988 and the winter of 1990 a small but fascinating exhibition curated by Joyce Zemans has been travelling across Canada; 'New Perspectives on Modernism in Canada: Kathleen Munn/ Edna Taçon' (1988) clearly demonstrates the impact of Expressionism (notably the abstract type of Marc and Kandinsky) on these Canadian painters.

Neo-expressionism, the term coined in the early eighties by New York galleries to describe the work of the Berlin 'neuen Wilden,' should not be confused with either historical Expressionism or with what, for lack of a better term, I would describe as the serious or straight use of an expressionist style or of expressionist techniques by contemporary artists and writers.

Among the writers, Tennessee Williams in *Camino Real* and George Ryga in *The Ecstasy of Rita Joe* provide interesting examples of this serious use of style and technique.[18] Briefly, Williams has exploited all the strategies of expressionist dramaturgy to create a profoundly disturbing vision of an America that is collapsing under the weight of its own corruption, materialism, and consumer mentality. Life on the *Camino Real* lacks utterly in faith, imagination, or joy; everyone is a huckster out to cheat each passer-by. For the hero, Kilroy, life is a stage dominated by screaming voices, flashing lights and signs, threatening figures symbolizing death, obscene charades, and violence. The events of this life follow each other without logical connection or recognizable motivation; certainly, Kilroy seems helpless to control his fate, even when he is apparently (and unconvincingly) reborn in the final moments of the play. Interestingly, the impetus for this symbolic renewal (presided over by the image of the phoenix that remains spotlighted throughout) is *not* Kilroy's moral regeneration or improved understanding but an idealistic belief in the power of the artistic imagination represented by the figure of Don Quixote. Like *Camino Real*, *The Ecstasy of Rita Joe* uses an expressionist form to expose social violence and injustice, except that in this case there is no straining after allegory and rebirth. A major part of the play occurs within the disturbed mind and memory of its central character and victim, the Indian woman Rita Joe. Assailed on all sides by the demands and accusations of a paternalistic, insensitive white society, Rita Joe suffers the hectoring voices of Magistrate, Social Worker, Teacher, and Priest

and is haunted by the memories of her own absent family until she collapses from an exhaustion both physical and spiritual. When she is released
from prison – it could be the third or the tenth time – she is raped and
murdered by a group of white thugs in a highly stylized yet intensely
emotional scene. Rebirth, even in the ambiguous sense of a return to the
countryside and the Indian reserve, is not an option.

What distinguishes these plays from the literature of Neo-expressionism
is their profoundly serious social commentary and their emphatic belief
(overt, even embarassing in Williams, quietly assumed in Ryga) that the
theatre can still be used to express and communicate the tragedy and
suffering of the human condition. Despite its sophisticated production
techniques, this is expressionist art in the tradition of early modernism:
we are asked to believe that the human *Schrei* and the artist's vision
matter. Irony is not directed against these human issues, and art is not
channelled into parodic forms (although a case for parodic effect could be
mounted for *Camino Real*). American playwright Sam Shepard continues
to keep this essentially expressionist vision alive in his series of 'family'
plays; the almost unbearably anguished monologues of Beth in *A Lie of
the Mind* (1985) are examples of his powerful evocation of the tormented
human soul.

The same continuity is apparent among the painters. Just as Kokoschka
continued to paint expressionistically throughout his long career, regardless of high modernist abstraction's complete rejection of the figure and
painterly brushwork, so too did certain younger expressionists in the
United States and Canada – Sigmund Menkes, Karl Knaths, Abraham
Rattner, Sam Borenstein, Maxwell Bates, and Bruno Bobak, for example.[19] Neo-expressionism, whether it is the art of the 'neuen Wilden' in
Berlin and Cologne or the later offshoots in New York, California, and in
several Canadian cities, places the emphasis on the *new*.[20] Neo-expressionism, I contend, relates to the postmodern as its predecessor did to the
modern; it is a part and yet critically apart.

German neo-expressionist painting encompasses a wide variety of
styles and artists, from Georg Baselitz (born 1938), in many ways the
originator of the movement, with Anselm Kiefer, Markus Lüpertz, and
Jörg Immendorff, to a younger generation of artists in Berlin like Rainer
Fetting, Helmut Middendorf, Elvira Bach, and the Cologne Mulheimer-
Freiheit group: Walter Dahn, Georg Jiri Dokoupil, and Peter Bömmels.
Donald Kuspit, the American apologist for these artists, describes their
art as 'acts of aggression' revealing the 'most vital' examples of contemporary art.[21] Like Wolfgang Max Faust, author of *Hunger nach Bildern*
(1982) and German champion of the new expressionists, Kuspit has had to
explain their art and defend them against leftist attacks. History, it seems,

repeats itself. Taking up the battle where Lukács, Brecht, and Kurella (not to mention Ellison's similarly motivated detractors) left it, Benjamin Buchloh and Douglas Crimp champion a continuation of high modernist hard-edge abstraction while dismissing Neo-expressionism as reactionary, decadent, and bourgeois. In 'Flak from the "Radicals": The American Case against German Painting,' Kuspit goes so far as to call Buchloh's onslaught a 'Marxist blitzkrieg.'[22]

Behind the political slurs and critical posturing of those critics who favour a modernism of non-iconic abstraction lies the same problem that occupied Worringer, Kandinsky, and most of the early modernists eighty years ago: how to renew jaded sensibilities, free limited perceptions and repressed emotions while addressing the complex pressures of twentieth-century life in the tired, empty language of realist conventions? Prior to the First World War the avant-garde answer began with the rejection of 'natural' illusion and an increasing play with or abstraction from the represented object: empathy versus abstraction. Realism was then, and is again now, the *bête noire* for these critics, although as Fredric Jameson warns us in his important concluding essay to *Aesthetics and Politics*, the historical context has changed significantly.[23] Today it has become popular among philosophers and cultural historians (Jameson mentions Foucault, Derrida, and Deleuze among others) to assimilate realism to mimesis and thereby to devalue it by association with neo-conservatism. However, to do so, he argues, is to forget, first, that the representation of nature and things was once a 'subversive concept' and, second, that modernism, which 'was once an oppositional and anti-social phenomenon in the early years of this century, has today [Jameson is writing in 1977] become the dominant style of commodity production and an indispensable component in the latter's ever more rapid and demanding reproduction of itself' ('Reflections,' 209). Late modernism, according to Jameson (and Guilbaut's analysis substantiates this critique), goes hand in hand with post-industrial, multinational corporate capitalism, and within this system modern art is easily transformed into 'cultural commodities.'

But what does the avant-garde do now, after forty years of conceptual art, minimalism, and so on? Claiming, like Jameson, that abstract art has itself become sterile, a mere stereotype open to mechanical abuse and appropriation, Kuspit makes a very convincing case for the new figural art. Neo-expressionism, he argues, accomplishes a 'critique of abstraction ... especially appropriate for our times':

> The Germans create an illusion of intense but bizarre naturalness,
> involving the invention of 'disfigured' forms that are recognizable as still
> existing within the horizon of the natural. These forms, transformed by the

experience of abstraction, so they become allegorical, are energetically – aggressively – asserted. They have at once the conceptual power of authoritative abstractions and the 'natural' power of things to which we are concretely – passionately – committed. They are double focussed.   ('Flak,' 45)

Because abstraction has lost its critical power to shock, arouse, and signify in the world of the eighties, it is 'painterly figuration' that fulfils that signifying function. Whether or not Kuspit is right (and it does not necessarily follow that, because non-iconic abstraction has reached a dead end, *only* a return to figuration can revive a faltering avant-garde), the battle-lines seem clearly drawn. Neo-expressionism rejects the basic tenets of high modernism (in painting, non-iconic abstraction) and by doing so joins forces with postmodernism.

A brief foray into the work of three postmodernists who demonstrate neo-expressionist tendencies may throw some light on a few of the nagging questions raised by both terms. I suspect that what is happening on a Baselitz canvas has a lot in common with postmodern fiction by Hubert Aquin and Thomas Pynchon, among many others. In his early work from the sixties Baselitz was disturbing enough, his anamorphic distortions of the human body blurring and unsettling the viewer's recognition of familiar form. But he really seemed to catch the art world off-guard with his large, inverted images of men's heads, female sunbathers, and the German eagle. In sweeping, rough brushwork and intense colour he flagrantly quoted Munch, Kirchner, and Nolde, daring the viewer to ignore the echo or dismiss as meaningless effect the at once comic and terrifying quality of the crudely painted, upside-down image. Thus, in *Last Self-Portrait (Munch)* (1982), its inverted, grotesquely distorted, fiery-red figure slashed with white, he gives us a parody of Munch's striking *Self-Portrait in Hell* (1903). Or again, in *Brücke Choir* (1984), the four Dresden artists (Mueller, Kirchner, Heckel, and Schmidt-Rottluff) who belonged to *Die Brücke* and who are familiar from Kirchner's *Four Painters from the 'Brücke' Group* (1925) reappear suspended between heavily painted areas of bright yellow, orange, or black as cadaverous ghosts with 'scream-like' heads. What recalls the Kirchner canvas, apart from the sly title, is the composition of the image.

But the painting I want to consider more closely is *Die Auferstehung* (1984) – *The Resurrection* (see Plate 30). Here the inverted Munch-like figure recapitulates the intentions of Baselitz's other canvases while pointing more overtly to the signifying process of his visual system. Rather than freeing us from tradition or destroying signification altogether, Baselitz's Christ (if Christ he is) addresses a profound contemporary ambivalence about the possibility of meaning and the human inability to escape it.[24] While apparently mocking an entire genre of painting, savagely deconstructing its iconography, and supposedly subverting its value as eschatological symbol, Baselitz nevertheless evokes and uses all the associations that the image commands. The result for the viewer is acute dis/ease. Is this an ugly joke or an appalling reminder of the impossibility of rebirth in today's world (and the hesitation here is as much a function of the black ground as it is of the inverted homunculus)? Is this crude figure a primitivist whim or an expression of the artist's rage? Is it a celebration or parody of the 'expressive fallacy'? Only one thing is certain; with Baselitz's canvases, nothing can be taken for granted. The irony, violence, comedy, and horror of his vision interrogate art history through a kind of visual intertextuality at the same time as they represent and defamiliarize a recognizable real world ignored by high modernism. The inversion topos so central to Expressionism resurfaces here as a deliberate, irreverent play with both the expressionists and with the classical figure of the *mundus inversus*. And because it is *played with*, it can no longer be clearly attributed to an atavistic regression; paradoxically, Baselitz's explosive paintings of inverted images challenge the apocalyptics of Expressionism as well.

Aquin and Pynchon, both masters of postmodern parody, have created nightmare visions of violence, personal and social disintegration, and self-consciously ironic reflexivity. They are metafictionists, to be sure, but they are that and much more. In *Neige noire* (1974; translated as *Hamlet's Twin* in 1979) and *Gravity's Rainbow* (1973), both writers draw overtly on expressionist film classics in order to provide historical texture, to establish thematic parallels, to develop a structural paradigm, and, most important of all, to create a definite aura of acute emotional disorientation, even vertigo in their readers. At the same time as both texts anatomize contemporary *Angst* (on the immediate level of the individual artist in *Hamlet's Twin* and on the more abstract and generalized level of society in *Gravity's Rainbow*), they also play with notions of realist character and reader participation versus empathy in profoundly unsettling ways, ways that seem increasingly central to postmodernist literature and to what Jean-François Lyotard describes as 'the postmodern condition.'[25]

I have discussed both novels in detail elsewhere.[26] Here, therefore, I simply wish to outline some of the ways in which these two texts participate in a common neo-expressionist postmodern discourse with Baselitz's art. What strikes me as immediately interesting is the way that all three *use* expressionist art. In the painting and the novels, the quotation is signalled clearly through multiple strategies: Baselitz echoes titles, places proper names in parentheses – *Last Self-Portrait (Munch)* – parodies subject matter and iconography, and imitates (or appears to) both the palette and the brushwork of several expressionist painters. Like him, Aquin and Pynchon quote, imitate, and in cryptic but unmistakable ways allude to great expressionist films: *Hamlet's Twin*, which is cast in the form of a screenplay with commentary, uses *The Cabinet of Dr Caligari*; but *Gravity's Rainbow*, which plays with the governing metaphor of narrative as film diegesis and text as movie screen, incorporates a wider range of references, with the films of Fritz Lang predominant among them (most notably *Dr Mabuse* and *Metropolis*).

The disorientation experienced by the viewer of Baselitz's inverted images is more than matched by the confusion a reader must face in working with Aquin and Pynchon. Aquin insists that he is making love to the reader, who must co-create the screenplay/commentary/text (it feels more like an assault), while Pynchon pretends to disregard the reader/movie-goer utterly, except at isolated moments when we are given snatches of ominous advice. Aquin's strategy is to seduce us into such intimacy and empathy with his artist/madman/murderer that we feel as if we are seeing ourselves when he stares obsessively at his face in mirror after mirror. As a result we quickly become implicated in and identified with his distorted perspective and violent actions. By contrast, Pynchon subjects us to such a wildly shifting cast of shape-shifting figures scattered across an intolerably vivid, yet grotesquely exaggerated, war 'zone' that it is impossible to follow the action, organize information, or make sense of either the temporally discontinuous plot or his characters' motivations. Though the method differs, the end result for the reader is similar. We seem to be reduced to helplessness within a world where everything is inverted and before some all-consuming obsession or scheme – sickeningly private with Aquin, horribly public with Pynchon – without being allowed reliable insight into the source of our victimization or its purpose. What Leo Braudy has said of expressionist film generally, that the mode is stylized, coercive, functionally manipulative, and 'closed,' is true of these novels.[27] While reading them we seem locked within a disorienting presentness; time stands still, so Aquin's narrator tells us, while Pynchon's overwhelms us with the detritus of history.

From extensive, deliberate quotation of expressionist works, Baselitz, Aquin, and Pynchon go on to exploit these intertexts as part of an artistic method whose intention seems to be to parody tradition, to disorient the reader/viewer, most forcibly by collapsing history into a perpetual presentness, and to project some more or less recognizable image of a contemporary world gone mad. In each case the topos of inversion sustains the vertigo – in Baselitz's inverted images, in the ecstatic sexual inversion that concludes *Hamlet's Twin*, and in the rocket's flight that will bring the world down on our heads at the end of *Gravity's Rainbow*. At the same time, however, they play with the concept of apocalypse in such radically ironic ways that it becomes impossible to decide whether the ecstatic vision that closes *Hamlet's Twin* or the impending catastrophe that *may* be approaching in *Gravity's Rainbow* are real options or elaborate hoaxes. Each of these postmodern examples of neo-expressionist art mixes codes and thus destabilizes the tendencies towards topoi of inversion *or* explosion that characterize Expressionism.

I say that these works *seem* to parody tradition because the status of this art is very much open to debate. Among art historians and critics of postmodern culture, its detractors see in it what Jameson calls a 'pastiche' that demonstrates and perpetuates the fundamental 'schizophrenia' (Jameson's term for temporal discontinuity) of late capitalism; its defenders, however, praise these postmodern works as avant-garde in the true sense of the word, that is, as critically resistant to the neo-conservatism of contemporary society and as forcing its audience to re-examine assumptions about history, tradition, the alienation of the individual and the fetishization of all cultural products.[28] At its best, this art, which Kuspit has called the 'new subjectivism,' has given 'fresh meaning to the language of immediacy ... by giving it an archeological depth – a new power to mediate the past'; it is, says Kuspit, an art that reveals 'the extremely vulnerable condition of the subject in the contemporary world.'[29]

Since 1982 the debate over the value and status of postmodernism has warmed up, but a final verdict must wait for at least two reasons. It is always next to impossible to pronounce on a contemporary movement, and both Neo-expressionism and postmodernism are unstable, actively ambiguous phenomena that evade our best typologizing and evaluative efforts. Neo-expressionism flaunts recent history in a kind of whirling strip-tease of events, dates, and possible facts; postmodernism, even if we limit it to so-called metafictional fiction, is a complex and varied textual strategy and sensibility. Even Jameson, who, more than most other critics of contemporary culture, has traced the historical unfolding of modernism through the debate over Expressionism, has not decided. On the one hand he nervously assesses the 'pastiche' of contemporary literature, music, and figurative art, while on the other he allows that this trend towards representation is less about nature (it is not a return to nineteenth-century realism) than it is about art itself ('Reflections,' 211). At best, Jameson suggests, postmodern art *may* be able to resist reification in contemporary consumer society.

Can anything, then, be claimed about the resurgence of Expressionism in our time? Let me dare a few conclusions, proffer some speculations, pose some ongoing questions. A clearer sense of the nature of neo-expressionist contributions to the culture and style of postmodernism must await further analysis, if only because postmodernism itself is profoundly heterogeneous. But this much does seem clear: Neo-expressionism is not Expressionism; its recapitulation, quotation, and intertextuality constitute a rebellion against late modernism by means of serious parody – not mockery alone (and not Jamesonian 'pastiche') but an ironic reminding about and alteration of its early modernist sources.[30] A key subject for neo-expressionist parody, of course, is the expressive act itself, which, contrary to Hal Foster's pessimistic prognosis in *Re-codings*,[31] is *capable* of deconstructing, dismantling, and de-mystifying concepts of origin, subjectivity, and the natural, unmediated, or uncoded self. This type of demystifying parody of the expressive act seems central to Enzo Cucchi's monumental oil-on-canvas *The Mad Painter* (1981–82), to Robert Zend's 1983 'neovel' *Oāb*, and *possibly* to David Lynch's neo-expressionist film *Blue Velvet* (1986).

The results of this parody, however, are seldom easy to assess. Although Baselitz, Aquin, and Pynchon shock and disturb, the ambiguity of their images is confusing and the outrageousness of their methods verges on a voyeurism and titillation that is at once emotionally arousing and depleting. Carnivalization in these works is ambiguous because the intensely claustrophobic, 'closed' (in Braudy's sense) systems of much neo-expressionist painting and film, and of postmodern fiction, tend inevitably to foreclose upon response, leaving their audiences captured or stranded, repelled and often confused. Lynch's highly ambiguous *Blue Velvet* is a case in point.[32]

And yet the very vitality, confidence, and urgency of much postmodernist art, especially when it exploits neo-expressionist strategies that include a carnivalization of form, cannot be ignored. After the thirty-year hegemony (roughly 1945–75) of high modernist abstraction in North American painting and the structuralist announcement of the death of the author, it is exciting to rediscover the human element in art, whether in a figurative painting, in a dialogistic discourse that captures the rich multiplicity of human speech, or in the overt mixing of genres presided over by an intrusive author. At the least these canvases and texts provoke debate, command attention, and force viewers and readers alike to ask new questions and question old assumptions. More importantly still, they seem to focus debate on broadly moral and socio-political issues by offering us atavistic images of total regression (what has been labelled the return of the repressed) and violent, nihilistic prefigurings of an apocalyptic destruction that hints at no new dispensation, earthly or divine, often in the same work. Their difference from Expressionism on this score cannot be underestimated. Where the expressionists (as modernists) clearly believed in the individual human imagination and the power of art – word, pigment, or plastic form – to transform the human condition, it is by no means clear that contemporary art shares that belief. Indeed, it seems to image what Derrida has described as 'an apocalypse without apocalypse, an apocalypse without vision, without truth, without revelation ... without sender or decidable addressee, without last judgement, without any other eschatology than the tone of Come itself.'[33]

By going back to the forgotten legacy of Expressionism, with all its artistic, moral, and political concerns, its tensions and central fallacy, neo-expressionist painting, film, and literature force the issue: does art, after all, not reflect life in some way, and what does it tell us about our lives if (or when) it does? Put slightly differently, the question is: does Neo-expressionism, like its predecessor, not interrogate and expose the conditions of life *and* of art by recuperating distortion, returning to iconic abstraction, and by the parody and self-reflexivity of its methods?

I think it does. Although the evidence is by no means all in, the ascendancy of the political right in our time, paralleling so closely (as both Habermas and Lyotard, despite their differences, recognize) the abstraction and totalitarianization of contemporary signifying systems, fuels the desire for presence inscribed in a neo-expressionist art that traces a simultaneous rupture with late modernism *and* an assertion of filiation and continuity with the past of early modernism. If there is nostalgia here, in either the renewed interest in Expressionism itself or in its ironic postmodern sister, it may well be a constructive longing for a recontextualizing of the human being in history and place.

Writing in the May-August issue of *Socialist Review* for 1986, Fred Pfeil lamented the 'collusive schizophrenia – or is it autism? – of recent theoretical work on postmodernism.'[34] Where, he wonders, are the 'questions of cultural-aesthetic strategy and aesthetico-political value like those engaged in by Bloch and Brecht against Lukács a half-century ago, as the first two sought to defend the practices of Expressionism and modernism, respectively, against Lukacs' denunciations' (128). The questions are there, however, though during the early eighties the angriest voices were raised about neo-expressionist painting rather than other aspects of postmodernism. The debate is escalating. It will not be long before it informs appreciation of literature as well, and when that occurs the literary expressionism examined in this study will take its place in the continuous development of a vital tradition and alternate vision for late twentieth-century art.

INTRODUCTION

1 From 'Diskussionen über Expressionismus,' *Erbschaft dieser Zeit* (Frankfurt: Suhrkamp Verlag, 1962), trans. Rodney Livingstone as 'Discussing Expressionism,' in *Aesthetics and Politics*, ed. Ronald Taylor, afterword Frederic Jameson (London: NLB 1977), 26–7. See also Mark Ritter, 'The Unfinished Legacy of Early Expressionist Poetry: Benn, Heym, Van Hoddis and Lichtenstein,' in *Passion and Rebellion: The Expressionist Heritage*, ed. Stephen Eric Bronner and Douglas Kellner (London: Croom Helm 1983), 151–65.

2 In *Modernism in the 1920s: Interpretations of Modern Art from Expressionism to Constructivism* (Ann Arbor, Mich.: UMI Research Press 1985), Susan Noyes Platt provides a thorough and convincing analysis of both the contribution made to modernism in New York by Expressionism and the prejudice of many Americans against the new German art. Indeed, American expressionists associated with Alfred Stieglitz at 291 (Marsden Hartley, John Marin, Arthur Dove, and Georgia O'Keefe) were praised while exhibits by the Germans were attacked. See Platt, 47–65.

3 A noteworthy absence in this study is that of Ernest Hemingway. In his monograph *Hemingway: Expressionist Artist* (Ames: Iowa State University Press 1979), Raymond S. Nelson argues that Hemingway's admiration for Cézanne led him to develop an essentially expressionist style and subject-matter. Nelson's argument is an interesting one, but his sense of what constitutes Expressionism is shaky, and as a consequence his discussion of Hemingway's style is often vague. I am not convinced that Hemingway was an expressionist or that the influence of Cézanne, who is more usefully thought of as proto-cubist (with the exception of some early portraits from the 1860s), could illuminate expressionistic elements in his work.

4 See Mark Clifton Williams, 'Remittance Bards: The Places, Tribes and Dialects of Patrick White and Malcolm Lowry,' PhD, University of British Columbia 1983, 299–306; Jack F. Stewart, 'Expressionism in *The Rainbow*,' *Novel* 13, no. 3 (Spring 1980): 296–315; Henry Schvey, 'Lawrence and Expressionism,' in *D.H. Lawrence: New Studies*, ed. Christopher Heywood (London: Macmillan 1987), 124–36; Ira B. Nadel, 'Joyce and Expressionism,' *Journal of Modern Literature* 16, no. 1 (1989): in press; Johannes Fabricius, *The Unconscious and Mr Eliot* (Copenhagen: Nyt Nordisk Forlag 1967). Expressionism in the work of Wyndham Lewis is discussed briefly in chap. 3. In 'Expressionism in English Drama and Prose Literature,' *Expressionism as an International Literary Phenomenon*, ed. Ulrich Weisstein (Paris: Didier 1973), 181–92, Breon Mitchell argues that although the plays of Kaiser and Toller were an important part of the London theatre scene during the twenties, they did not influence British dramatists. He also rejects the influence of German Expressionism on Joyce, Lawrence, Auden, and Isherwood. He makes no mention of Wyndham Lewis, a Canadian by birth who worked in England, or Malcolm Lowry, an Englishman by birth who adopted Canada as his home. Expressionism has also been influential on other writers (e.g., Pirandello and Borges) and literatures. See Naomi Lindstrom, *Literary Expressionism in Argentina* (Tempe, Ariz.: Center for Latin American Studies 1977).

5 This study has already begun with Robert K. Martin's 'Painting and Primitivism: Hart Crane and the Development of an American Expressionist Aesthetic,' *Mosaic* 14, no. 3 (1981): 49–62. There is less evidence of Expressionism in any modernist Canadian poet, although expressionistic tendencies are apparent in some poems by Bertram Brooker, Lawren Harris, F.R. Scott, and Dorothy Livesay. Among contemporary poets the American Peter Klappert in *The Idiot Princess of the Last Dynasty* (New York: Alfred A. Knopf 1984) and the Canadian Michael Ondaatje in *The Collected Works of Billy the Kid* (Toronto: Anansi 1970) provide especially noteworthy examples of expressionistic monologue and imagery.

CHAPTER ONE: Expressionism: History, Definition, and Theory

1 In this speech Goebbels proclaimed that 'Das Zeitalter eines überspitzen jüdischen Intellektualismus ist nun zu Ende, und der Durchbruch der deutschen Revolution hat auch dem deutschen Wesen wieder die Gasse freigegeben ... hier sinkt die geistige Grundlage der Novemberrepublik zu Boden.' ('The era of an exaggerated Jewish intellectualism is now at an end, and the breakthrough of the German revolution has again cleared the way for the essential German character ... here the basic spirit of the November Republic sinks into the ground.') Quoted in Hildegard Brenner, *Die Kunstpolitik des Nationalsozialismus* (Reinbek: Rowohlt Taschenbuch Verlag GmbH 1963), 47–8.

2 See Renate Benson, *German Expressionist Drama: Ernst Toller and Georg Kaiser* (London: Macmillan 1984), 18–19, 101–4. Toller was one of thirty-three Germans stripped of citizenship at this time.

3 *Seven Plays* (London: John Lane The Bodley Head 1935), ix–x. In 'The Last Testament of Ernst Toller' he wrote that 'The threatened culture can be saved only if the subjugated nations keep alert the desire for freedom, justice, and human dignity and if this desire becomes so elementary that the desire turns into will and will into action.' Quoted in Benson, *German Expressionist Drama*, 21.

4 In addition to the works cited in nn 1 and 2 above, John Willett's excellent study *Expressionism* (New York & Toronto: McGraw-Hill 1970) has been an invaluable source of information.

5 Benson, *German Expressionist Drama*, 9. The rediscovery and recuperation of German expressionist art is a moving story in its own right; see Paul Raabe, 'On the Rediscovery of Expressionism as a European Movement,' *Michigan Germanic Studies* 2, no. 2 (1976): 196–210.

6 See the illustrations in Brenner, *Kunstpolitik*.

7 Adolf Behne, *Entartete Kunst* (Berlin: Carl Habel Verlag 1947), 10: 'Muskelschwellend, schweissdampfend und alles ganz genau erkennbar, serviert zu knatternden Fahnen, paukenden, fanfarenden Festmusiken, Aufzügen schöner, nur andeutungsweise bekleideter Mädchen, des war die Kunst des Dritten Reiches: laut und bunt, banal und knechtisch – und für viele wunderschön.' For a discussion of this art see Joseph Wulf, *Die bildende Kunst im Dritten Reich: Eine Dokumentation* (Gütersloh: Sigbert Mohn Verlag 1963), and Henry Grosshans, *Hitler and the Artists* (New York and London: Holmes and Meier 1983).

8 Franz Roh, *'Entartete' Kunst: Kunstbarbarei im Dritten Reich* (Hannover: Fackelträger-Verlag Schmidt-Kuster GmbH 1962), 51

9 Roh, *'Entartete' Kunst*, 123–229. See also Willett, *Expressionism*, 208.

10 For a discussion of expressionist sculpture, including details on the destruction of various works, see *German Expressionist Sculpture*, a Los Angeles County Museum of Art Catalogue, ed. Barbara Einzig, Lynne Dean, Andrea P.A. Belloli (Los Angeles 1984).

11 Behne, *Entartete Kunst*, 48. Adolph Behne was a supporter of the November 1918 revolution and a president of the Berlin *Arbeitsrat für Kunst* (Working Council for Art), paralleling the soldiers' and workers' councils that were being set up across Germany and were modelled on the Soviet revolutionary councils. Many expressionist artists, writers, and architects were actively involved in the revolution. Behne, an art and architecture critic, had followed the development of Expressionism and the careers of many expressionist artists from well before the First World War.

12 For information on the historical, social, and political background to Expressionism, see Roy F. Allen, *German Expressionist Poetry* (Boston: Twayne 1979), 34–40; Frederick S. Levine, *The Apocalyptic Vision: The Art of Franz Marc as German Expressionism* (New York: Harper & Row 1979), 7–14; and two essays in Bronner and Kellner, eds., *Passion and Rebellion*: Douglas Kellner's 'Expressionism and Rebellion' and Henry Pachter's 'Expressionism and Café Culture.' According to Pachter, cafés became popular centres of

rebellion in Berlin bohemian society in part because they were the sole places of escape from tyrannical households and constant domestic surveillance.

13 For the story of Munch's first inauspicious exhibit in Berlin see Arne Eggum, *Edvard Munch: Paintings, Sketches and Studies*, trans. Ragnar Christophersen (London: Thames and Hudson 1984), 91–3. Eggum considers Munch the first expressionist and a seminal influence on German Expressionism. Munch's work became very popular among the younger generation in Germany and was frequently exhibited in Berlin, Cologne, Düsseldorf, and elsewhere between 1892 and 1912, when he was given a place of honour in the famous Sonderbund exhibit at Cologne. He was made a member of the German Academy in 1923 and an honorary member of the Bavarian Akademie der Bildenden Künste in 1925. A large retrospective of his work was held in Berlin in 1927, and eighty-two of his works were confiscated as 'degenerate' by the Nazis in 1937.

14 See Lionel Richard, *The Concise Encyclopedia of Expressionism*, trans. Stephen Tint (Secaucus, NJ: Chartwell Books 1978), 8. Tracing the roots and usage of the term 'expressionism' has become an obsession with some scholars. For sensible discussions of these questions see Allen, *German Expressionist Poetry* and *Literary Life*, Willett, *Expressionism*, who dates the major creative activity (as opposed to the popularization) of Expressionism from 1910 to the early twenties, and Peter Selz, *German Expressionist Painting* (Berkeley: University of California Press 1957). Marit Werenskiold argues that Expressionism as a pan-modernist movement originated with Matisse and that German proselytizers later adopted the term for an exclusively Germanic style. See *The Concept of Expressionism: Origin and Metamorphosis* (Oslo, Bergen, Stavanger, Tromsø: Universitetsforlaget 1984), trans. Ronald Walford.

15 For an excellent discussion of Expressionism's debt to Jugendstil, see Selz, *German Expressionist Painting*, 53–64. The international roots of Expressionism are discussed in detail by Willett, Weisstein, Selz, and many others. Nolde's remark in *Jahre der Kämpfe* (1902–14) that 'he had come to the works of Munch and Van Gogh in worshipful admiration and love' is typical of the way expressionists turned to foreign models and sources of inspiration. Quoted in *Expressionism: The Buchheim Collection*, trans. Norbert Messler, William Walker (Munich: Buchheim Verlag Feldafing 1983), 188.

16 Walter Sokel, *The Writer in Extremis: Expressionism in Twentieth-Century German Literature* (Stanford, Calif.: Stanford University Press 1959), 8–9.

17 See Marian Kester's discussion of Hegel in 'Kandinsky: The Owl of Minerva,' in Bronner and Kellner, eds. *Passion and Rebellion*, 252, Victor Lange's important discussion of Husserl in 'Expressionism: A Topological Essay,' *Review of National Literatures* 9 (1978): 25–46, and Michael Patterson's remarks on Schopenhauer and the negative impact of scientific and technological developments in *The Revolution in German Theatre, 1900–1933* (Boston & London: Routledge & Kegan Paul 1981), 17–18.

18 Douglas Kellner, 'Expressionism and Rebellion,' in Bronner and Kellner, eds., *Passion and Rebellion*, 10. Kellner argues convincingly that Nietzsche is the

prime source of expressionist philosophy because 'Nietzsche's ideas were "in the air" and helped create the intellectual atmosphere in which Expressionism emerged' (11). This view of Nietzsche's central importance to Expressionism is further corroborated by Donald E. Gordon in his fine study *Expressionism: Art and Idea* (New Haven and London: Yale University Press 1987). Gordon traces Nietzsche's influence in detail on pages 11–24. Theda Shapiro also stresses Nietzsche, pointing out that when Heckel met Kirchner, he quoted Nietzsche, who was read avidly by the *Brücke* artists, as was Whitman. See *Painters and Politics: The European Avant-Garde and Society, 1900–1920* (New York: Elsevier Scientific 1976), 28. See also Ivo Frenzel, 'Prophet, Pioneer, Seducer: Friedrich Nietzsche's Influence on Art, Literature, and Philosophy in Germany,' in *German Art in the 20th Century*, ed. Christos M. Joachimides, Norman Rosenthal, Wieland Schmidt, et al. (Munich and London: Prestel-Verlag 1985), 73–81.

19 Quoted in Allen, *German Expressionist Poetry*, 19

20 See Henry Pachter's 'Expressionism and Café Culture,' in Bronner and Kellner, eds., *Passion and Rebellion*, 43–54, for a discussion of life at Berlin cafés like the *Café des Westens*, where the charismatic editor and proselytizer Herwarth Walden (Georg Levin) held forth.

21 Perhaps the chief importance of *Passion and Rebellion* is to redress the imbalance in expressionist studies that has led to the view that Expressionism is an exclusively stylistic, narrowly artistic, or thematic phenomenon instead of a broadly cultural and politically sensitive movement. See Kellner's introductory essay and Barbara Drygulski Wright's 'Sublime Ambition: Art, Politics and Ethical Idealism in the Cultural Journals of German Expressionism,' 82–112. See also Ida Katherine Rigby's *An alle Künstler! War-Revolution-Weimar* (San Diego, California: San Diego State University 1983), which demonstrates eloquently and convincingly that expressionist artists were very involved politically between 1918 and 1922, both through their art (in posters and illustrations) and in radical artists' groups like the Novembergruppe and the Arbeitsrat für Kunst.

22 For reproductions of the ten drawings and an excellent discussion of this superb work, see *Max Beckmann, Die Hölle, 1919*, an exhibit catalogue by Alexander Duchers (Berlin: Kupferstichkabinett 1983).

23 'Betrachten wir daher den Expressionismus ruhig so, wie er sich selber verstand: als "Revolution", als Aufbruch, als Wandlung oder Erhebung – alles Worte, in denen der Wille zu einer grundsätzlichen Veränderung der bestehenden Verhältnisse zum Ausdruck kommt. Denn was auch immer die einzelnen Expressionisten unterscheidet: der Hang zum Extremen, Aufrührerischen, Intensiven, Radikalen, ja Weltumstürzlerischen ist allen gemeinsam. An dieser These lässt sich schwerlich rütteln. Was man bezweifeln könnte, ist lediglich die politische Konkretheit der expressionistischen Revolution.' ('We may very well look upon Expressionism as it understood itself – as revolution, awakening, transfiguration, or insurrection – all terms that express the desire for

fundamental changes in existing conditions. Whatever else sets the individual Expressionists apart from one another, they all share the predilection for the extreme, rebellious, intensive, radical, even cataclysmic gesture. This thesis cannot be easily refuted. What can be questioned is the concrete political outcome of the expressionist revolution.') *Michigan Germanic Studies* 2, no. 2 (Fall 1976): 109. Although I cannot fully accept Hermand's notion of the truly revolutionary nature of Expressionism lying in its abstraction, depersonalization, and denaturization (*'Entnaturtes,'* 116) – all qualities that in much cubist, futurist, abstract expressionist, and constructivist art seem to reify nature and the body by subjecting organic forms to the control of the intellect – he does make many important points about the two tendencies of Expressionism and about the need for broader, interdisciplinary approaches to the subject.

24 From 'Expressionism is Dying,' which originally appeared in the Belgrade review *Zenit* 1, no. 8 (1921): 9

25 'So wird der ganze Raum des expressionistischen Künstlers Vision. Er sieht nicht, er schaut. Er schildert nicht, er erlebt. Er gibt nicht wieder, er gestaltet. Er nimmt nicht, er sucht. Nun gibt es nicht mehr die Kette der Tatsachen: Fabriken, Häuser, Krankheit, Huren, Geschrei und Hunger. Nun gibt es ihre Vision.' 'Über den dichterischen Expressionismus,' in *Über den Expressionismus in der Literatur und die neue Dichtung* (Berlin: Erich Reiss Verlag 1919), 54.

26 Beckmann and Marc as quoted in and translated by Selz, *German Expressionist Painting*, 240, 239

27 Hermann Bahr, *Expressionismus* (1916), quoted and translated by R.S. Furness, *Expressionism* (London: Methuen 1973), 48. Oskar Kokoschka, *My Life*, trans. David Britt (New York: Macmillan 1974), 23. Kokoschka, the Austrian *enfant terrible* of Expressionism, was famed for his uncanny ability to paint his subject's soul or inner life. He saw Expressionism as a 'revolutionary movement' that 'held a chance of spiritual revival which remains unrecognized today' (66).

28 Kokoschka, *My Life*, 216–17; Kaiser, 'Vision und Figur,' in *Georg Kaiser: Stücke, Erzählungen, Aufsätze, Gedichte*, ed. Walther Huder (Köln, Berlin: Verlag Kiepenheuer 1966), 666

29 *Concerning the Spiritual in Art and Painting in particular*, trans. Michael Sadleir, Francis Golffing, Michael Harrison, Ferdinand Ostertag (New York: George Wittenborn 1947), 24, 26, 29, 31. It is worth noting here that Kandinsky was deeply influenced by Matisse during his year in Paris, 1906–07, and that Matisse was an important precursor of Expressionism as a modernist movement.

30 The pamphlet *An Alle Künstler!* is an interesting document of the socio-political aesthetic wing of the new revolutionary government. It was a call to all artists to join in creating a new art and social order as part of the wider revolution, and it included poetry (by Hasenclever, among others), illustrations, and socialist articles by Pechstein and Ludwig Meidner. The passage from Sorge's *The Beggar* (*Der Bettler*), first published in 1912, is translated by Walter H. and Jacqueline Sokel in *Anthology of German Expressionist Drama*, ed. Walter H. Sokel (Ithaca and London: Cornell University Press 1963), 41.

31 *Continental Stagecraft* (New York: Benjamin Blom 1964), 3. All subsequent references are to this edition of the text.

32 Dukes's translation of Kaiser's play first appeared in *Poet Lore: A Magazine of Letters* 31 (Autumn 1920): 317–63, and two years later as a book (New York: Bretano's 1922), with photographs of the Theatre Guild Production at the Garrick Theatre, New York, on 21 May 1922. The Gate Theatre in London opened in 1925 with a production of Kaiser's play in Dukes's translation, and it was so popular that it moved to the Regent Theatre with Claude Rains as the Cashier. The play enjoyed several London revivals in subsequent years, but it is advertisements for Rains's performance that Lowry's protagonist remembers in *October Ferry to Gabriola* (New York: World Publishing 1970), 116, 133.

33 *The New Vision in the German Arts* (Port Washington, NY: Kennikat Press 1971), 1. All subsequent references are to this edition. For a detailed discussion of attempts by various American literary theorists and theatre and art historians (including Scheffauer) to explain Expressionism to Americans, see Susan Noyes Platt's *Modernism in the 1920s: Interpretations of Modern Art in New York from Expressionism to Constructivism* (Ann Arbor, Mich.: UMI Research Press 1985).

34 In 1837 a poorly organized group of farmers, retired soldiers and sympathizers, from that part of British North America soon to be known as Upper Canada, gathered together under MacKenzie King's leadership in an effort to establish independence from England and a better economic situation for the working classes. The rebellion was abortive and quickly crushed by British troops. Shortly afterwards, representative government was established for Upper (Ontario) and Lower (Quebec) Canada, but Confederation was not achieved until 1867. Rebellion and insurrection have always been swiftly crushed by government force in Canada.

35 'Producing Methods Defined,' *Toronto Globe and Mail*, 16 April 1932, 15. During the twenties, the Vancouver Little Theatre paid close attention to new, expressionistic developments in the theatre with productions of plays such as Susan Glaspell's *The Verge* (in 1921), Capek's R.U.R. (in 1924), and Andreev's *He Who Gets Slapped* (in 1926). And in a short but informed, sympathetic article called 'Expressionism in Modern Drama,' *Vancouver Little Theatre News* 3, no. 7 (1928), W.G. Stephen concluded that expressionist theatre 'has resulted from the struggle to free the stage from its obsession with representation and imitation' and that 'it will leave a deep effect on the dramatic method of the future.' I would like to thank Canadian cultural historian Maria Tippett for bringing this article to my attention. By 1930 the theatre group was producing O'Neill and Elmer Rice's *The Adding Machine*; see 'Two Views on Expressionism and "The Adding Machine,"' *Scene* (Sept. 1931): 6.

36 'The Painter and His Model,' in *Open House*, ed. William A. Deacon, Wilfred Reeves (Ottawa: Graphic Publications 1931), 213–14. I am grateful to my colleague William H. New for bringing this collection of essays to my attention. Reprinted in *Documents in Canadian Art*, ed. Douglas Fetherling (Peterborough: Broadview Press 1987), 76–9.

37 Quoted in William Wees, *Vorticism and the English Avant-Garde* (Toronto: University of Toronto Press 1972), 120. See also Hugh Kenner, *The Pound Era* (Berkeley: University of California Press 1971), 256–7.

38 Wendy Steiner, *Exact Resemblance to Exact Resemblance*. For a comparison of Picasso's portrait and Stein's 'portraiture,' see page 147 and, in general, Steiner's chapter on 'Literary Cubism.' For a discussion of Joyce and Cubism in *Ulysses*, see Jo Anna Isaak, *The Ruin of Representation in Modern Art and Texts* (Ann Arbor, Mich: UMI Research Press 1986), 36–40.

39 Selz, *German Expressionist Painting*, 192

40 See *Gaudier-Brzeska: A Memoir* (New York: New Directions 1970), 82.

41 See Arnold's article 'Foreign Influences on German Expressionist Prose,' in Weisstein, ed., *Expressionism as an International Literary Phenomenon*, 79–96, and *Prosa des Expressionismus* (Stuttgart: W. Kohlhammer Verlag 1966).

42 Quoted in Wees, *Vorticism*, 15

43 Quoted in ibid., 12

44 *Marinetti: Selected Writings*, ed. K.W. Flint, trans. Arthur A. Coppotelli (London: Secker & Warburg 1972), 100. The writers who seem more dadist than expressionist include Rudolf Blümner, Kurt Schwitters (whose Merzbau collages are also dadist), and George Grosz. Even August Stramm displays dadist tendencies in his play with language – see page 59. For a further discussion of Dada's links with Expressionism see Richard Brinkmann, 'Dadaism and Expressionism,' in Weisstein, ed., *Expressionism as an International Literary Phenomenon*, 97–110, and Serge Fauchereau, *Expressionisme, dada, surréalisme et autres ismes*, 2 vols. (Paris: Denoël 1976). It is also true that the Berlin dadists of 1920 were much more politically committed than either the Zurich or Paris groups; see John Willett, *Art and Politics in the Weimar Period: The New Sobriety, 1917–1933* (New York: Pantheon 1978), 53.

45 Breton made a system of this theory of 'l'écriture automatique,' by which a text was created in the collective writing down of the flow of phrases rising from the subconscious. See Fauchereau, *Expressionisme*, 119ff.

46 Quoted in Wees, *Vorticism*, 162, from an advertisement for *Blast* in the *Spectator* 485 (13 June 1914). In *Vorticism and Abstract Art in the First Machine Age*, 2 vols. (London: Gordon Fraser 1976), Richard Cork makes only passing reference to Hulme's discovery of Worringer and downplays the similarities between Vorticism and Expressionism. In *English Art and Modernism, 1900–1939* (London & Bloomington: Allen Lane and Indiana University Press 1981), Charles Harrison explores this relationship in detail and concludes that Vorticism was essentially expressionist; see my discussion in chap. 8.

47 Tzara and Breton split in 1922, thereby dividing the dadist-surrealist coalition and creating a distinct surrealist movement around Breton.

48 Breton was enthusiastic about seances, mediums, and 'sommeils prophétiques,' and this led to further splits among the surrealists. See Fauchereau, *Expressionisme*, 135.

49 Robert Descharnes, *The World of Salvador Dali,* trans. Albert Field (London: Macmillan 1972), 75
50 Quoted in Fauchereau, *Expressionisme,* 264. This is not to say that the surrealists were uninterested in politics or social reform. By 1926 Breton, Aragon, and Eluard had become Communists and René Crevel split with the others over political dedication before committing suicide in 1935 (Fauchereau, 137 and chap. 6). During the thirties Breton corresponded with and visited Trotsky in his Mexican exile. But see Willett's sceptical assessment of their politics in *Art and Politics in the Weimar Period,* 172. For a discussion of the Quebec surrealists' split with the French, see André-G. Bourassa, *Surréalisme et Littérature Québécoise: Histoire d'une révolution culturelle* (Montréal: Les Herbes Rouges 1986). Paul-Emile Borduas' 1948 manifesto *Refus global,* with its stress on emotion, 'soul,' and humanity, closely parallels German expressionist statements. *Refus global* is reprinted in Fetherling, ed., *Documents in Canadian Art.*
51 Quoted by Brian Kenworthy in 'Georg Kaiser: The Ambiguity of the Expressionist New Man,' in *Georg Kaiser Symposium,* ed. Holger Pausch, Ernest Reinhold (Berlin: Agora Verlag 1980), 106
52 *Abstraction and Empathy: A Contribution to the Psychology of Style,* trans. Michael Bullock (London: Routledge & Kegan Paul 1953), vii. All quotations are from this edition and are hereafter included in the text. Worringer does not speak of Expressionism in his next major study, *Formprobleme der Gotik* (1910), but in a 1919 article he exclaimed that the 'exciting element of expressionism' was that 'it made the first completely consistent attempt to carry through the experiment of a complete spiritualization of expression.' Quoted in Selz, *German Expressionist Painting,* 9. In his 1921 *Künstlerische Zeitfragen* he announced the end of Expressionism because society had failed to respond to spiritual art (ibid., 328).
53 The most emphatic example of this tendency is Jost Hermand's 'Interdisziplinäre Zielrichtungen der Expressionismus-Forschung,' *Michigan Germanic Studies* 2, no. 2 (Fall 1976): 107–20. Hermand is critical and dismissive of emphatic and subjective tendencies while praising abstraction as truly revolutionary. See also Walter Benjamin's assessment of 'empathy' and Expressionism in *The Origin of German Tragic Drama,* trans. John Osborne (London: NLB 1977), 54–6.
54 In the following discussion of Worringer I am by no means endorsing his ideas, but this is not the place to challenge his theory on its own terms. The most cogent counter-argument I know to Riegl's and Worringer's line of thinking is E.H. Gombrich's *Art and Illusion* (Princeton, NJ: Princeton University Press 1960), in which Gombrich refutes their notion of *Kunstwollen* and refuses to discount the element of skill in understanding art history. In *Contemporary Theory of Expressionism* (Bern and Frankfurt: Herbert Lang 1974), Geoffrey Perkins recognizes and describes Worringer's contribution to expressionist theory, but he does not analyse Worringer's position (see chap. 2).
55 Worringer's notion of 'empathy' (*Einfühlung*) seems problematic because it

purports to describe a work of art (as in its 'naturalism' or degree of representation) in terms of the psychological response of human to environment or viewer to painting. It does not necessarily follow that a desire for empathy (identity or union) with the natural world impels an artist to paint a meticulous representation of a field or stream. Patterson's categories, though more truly comparable on stylistic grounds, seem equally arbitrary. But as Patterson recognizes, the two styles cannot be rigidly separated; when they are, we no longer have Expressionism. See *The Revolution in German Theatre*, 51–95.

56 I have found Levine's study of Marc, *The Apocalyptic Vision*, and his analyses of the interrelated themes of regression and apocalypse very useful to my understanding of Expressionism in general. See also Levine's 'An Example of Apocalyptic Regression in 1913 Expressionism,' *Michigan Germanic Studies* 2, no. 2 (Fall 1976): 133–48.

57 *Abstraction and Artifice in Twentieth-Century Art* (Oxford: Clarendon Press 1979). See in particular chaps. 2 and 3. Further references are included in the text.

58 'The perception of such qualities [as moods, feelings, aesthetic properties] is direct (we do *not* infer that the willow is feeling sad) and the qualities are perceived as objective properties of the thing we perceive not as subjective responses in ourselves, as when we see an unknown looming figure as ominous, threatening, sinister ... These qualities of perceived things are called "physiognomic" and when we see things in this way psychologists speak of "physiognomic perception"' Osborne, *Abstraction and Artifice*, 16.

59 See Julia Kristeva's discussion of the semiotic power of 'poetic language' in 'From One Identity to An Other' and her analysis of 'musicating' in 'The Novel as Polylogue.' Both essays are in *Desire in Language: A Semiotic Approach to Literature and Art*, ed. Leon S. Roudiez, trans. Thomas Gora, Alice Jardine, and Leon S. Roudiez (New York: Columbia University Press 1980).

60 See Wendy Steiner, *The Colors of Rhetoric: Problems in the Relation between Modern Literature and Painting* (Chicago: University of Chicago Press 1982), 65. In this study and in her *Exact Resemblance to Exact Resemblance: The Literary Portraiture of Gertrude Stein* (New Haven and London: Yale University Press 1978), Steiner makes some useful, discriminating points concerning abstraction and interartistic comparisons. See also Rudolf Arnheim's *Visual Thinking* (Berkeley: University of California Press 1969), 232–53.

61 Levine, *The Apocalyptic Vision*, 3

62 For a taxonomy of apocalyptic topoi see Douglas Robinson, *American Apocalypses: The Image of the End of the World in American Literature* (Baltimore: Johns Hopkins University Press 1985), 26–7.

63 Quoted in *Expressionism: A German Intuition, 1905–1920* (New York: Guggenheim Foundation 1980), 193.

64 For Hal Foster's analysis of Expressionism, see his chapter 'The Expressive Fallacy' in *Recodings: Art, Spectacle, Cultural Politics* (Seattle, Wash.: Bay

Press 1985), 59–77. The problem of the 'expressive fallacy' is considered
passim and in chap. 10 in connection with Neo-expressionism.
65 For discussion of dialogism and carnival, the best source is M.M. Bakhtin,
Problems of Dostoevsky's Poetics, ed. and trans. Caryl E. Emerson, intro.
Wayne Booth (Minneapolis: University of Minnesota Press 1984), in particular
chaps. 4 and 5. This study is hereafter referred to in the text as *PDP*, followed by
the page number. See also 'Discourse in the Novel' from *The Dialogic
Imagination: Four Essays*, ed. Michael Holquist, trans. Caryl Emerson and
Michael Holquist (Austin: University of Texas Press 1981).
66 See Tzvetan Todorov, *Mikhail Bakhtin: The Dialogical Principle*, trans. Wlad
Godzich (Minneapolis: University of Minnesota Press 1984), 98–9.
67 'Word, Dialogue, and Novel,' in *Desire in Language*, 87

CHAPTER TWO: German Expressionism in the Arts

1 A brief summary of expressionist painting cannot hope to do justice to the
variety of styles and subject-matter nor to the many interesting artists of the
movement. In addition to these two groups, there is also a group of Berlin
artists, including Ludwig Meidner, George Grosz, Carl Sternheim, and a group
of Rhineland expressionists who include August Macke – only briefly associated with *Der blaue Reiter* – Heinrich Campendonk, Paul Seehaus, and
Heinrich Nauen, whose *Cello Player* (1919) is a striking example of expressionist colour and energy. Macke, however, is the most interesting of the group for
his cubist qualities and affinities with Marc. Another related group of note is
from Düsseldorf and includes Otto Dix, Gert Wollheim, and Otto Pankok.
Wollheim's *Die Zirkusreiterin* (1923), with its whirling distortion, is a fine
treatment of a popular expressionist subject. See Kirchner's handling of the
theme, Plate 2. Pankok painted some of the most moving anti-war pictures
done by any of the expressionists. In general, the Berlin and Düsseldorf artists
were more critical of social and political abuses than either *Die Brücke* or *Der
blaue Reiter*. Painters with the stature of a Nolde, Beckmann, Kokoschka, or
Barlach must be considered individually, though all shared an expressionist
vision.
2 Selz describes the Moritzburg Lake district as the 'Argenteuil of the Brücke'
(*German Expressionist Painting*, 99) and discusses the visits to Dangast,
Nidden, and Fehmarn of individual *Brücke* artists. Both the Pechstein and
Mueller paintings are reproduced in Selz, Plates 100 and 151.
3 The mindlessness and assertion of physical and emotional power seems to be
the main point of Kirchner's *Self-Portrait with Model* (1907). Of course, few
expressionist portraits or self-portraits show the kind of representational detail
of conventional portraiture, but the faces of Kirchner's and Nolde's figures are
typically blurred and highly distorted, with blank, staring slits for eyes.
4 *Der Blaue Reiter Alamanac*, ed. Vasily Kandinsky and Franz Marc, was
originally published by Piper Verlag in Munich, 1912. See the New Documen-

258 Notes to pages 47–9

tary edition (New York: Viking Press 1974), ed. Klaus Lankheit, trans. Henning Falkenstein.

5 Quoted in and translated by Selz, *German Expressionist Painting*, 202. The note appears in Franz Marc, *Briefe, Aufzeichnungen und Aphorismen* (Berlin 1920), vol. I, 123.

6 Levine, *Apocalyptic Vision*, 44

7 For an extensive reading of *Fate of the Animals* (Plate 5) as prophetic of massive destruction, see Levine, *Apocalyptic Vision*, 79–85. However, without emphasizing the painting's title, it is equally possible to see it, together with *Birds, Tirol*, and other works from 1913–14, as the successful embodiment of what Levine describes as Marc's consistent goal: 'to liberate the instinctual life ... the harmonious essence of nature ... as an alternative mode of being' (55). In his last paintings, for example *Fighting Forms* (1914), Marc captured an image of the spiritual forces lying behind the war in a nearly non-iconic abstract canvas that, like the late work of Lawren Harris, whose views and evolution parallel Marc's, retains a strong sense of organic, natural forms.

8 Manfred Kuxdorf, 'The New German Dance Movement,' in Bronner and Kellner, eds., *Passion and Rebellion*, 350–60, and Christopher Innes, *Holy Theatre* (Cambridge: Cambridge University Press 1981), 54. Kirchner did two woodcuts of Wigman; *Totentanz der Mary Wigman* (1926–28) is especially dramatic.

9 Christopher Innes, *Edward Gordon Craig* (Cambridge: Cambridge University Press 1983), 114

10 See 'Dance of the Theatre: Impressions of the Dance in Four Countries,' *Dancing Times*, no. 274 (July 1933): 333–5.

11 Henry A. Lea, 'Musical Expressionism in Vienna,' in Bonner and Kellner, eds., *Passion and Rebellion*, 315. Further references to Lea are included in the text. Two essays in *Arnold Schoenberg – Wassily Kandinsky: Letters, Pictures and Documents*, ed. Jelena Hahl-Koch, trans. John C. Crawford (London: Faber & Faber 1984), provide valuable discussions of expressionist music. In 'Schoenberg's Artistic Development to 1911,' 172–86, Crawford argues that Kundry in *Parsifal* prefigures the expressionist-type character and that Strauss anticipated Schönberg by carrying 'Wagner's nascent Expressionism to greater lengths.' In 'Kandinsky and Schoenberg,' 135–70, Hahl-Koch places *Der gelbe Klang* and *Die glückliche Hand* within the 'context of German expressionist drama.'

12 Quoted in Victor H. Meisel, *Voices of German Expressionism* (Englewood Cliffs, NJ: Prentice-Hall 1970), 10. In 'Expressionism and Music,' *Expressionism Reconsidered*, ed. Gertrud Bauer-Pickar and Karl Eugene Webb (Munich: Wilhelm Fink Verlag 1979), Jost Hermand sees Expressionism continuing in music until 1928 and stresses the contribution of Schönberg, whom he describes as 'anti-Aristotelian': 'The specific expressionist quality of this music [such as *Moses and Aaron*, 1932] is not its exoticism, eroticism, or cult of intensity, but rather its explicit renunciation of any relation to nature, of all

programmatic or illustrative elements. This music no longer wants to reproduce, but to be a product itself' (68).
13 *Das Kinobuch* (Zürich: Peter Schifferli Verlag 1963). *Das Kinobuch* was originally published in 1913 with 'Kinostücke' by Walter Hasenclever, Else Lasker-Schüler, Max Brod, Alfred Ehrenstein, Pinthus himself, and others. In his original introduction Pinthus explained that in the film one will 'nicht nur etwas Realistisches sehen, sondern dies Realistische soll in eine idealere, phantastischere Sphäre erhoben sein. Die Welt soll mit Abenteuern und Seltsamkeiten gespickt sein ... eine plausiblere Logik soll obwalten, die Schwere und Kausalität soll von den Dingen abfallen' ('not only see something realistic, but rather this reality will be intensified into an idealized, fantastic sphere. The world will be packed with adventures and curiosities ... a plausible logic will prevail; the heaviness and causality will fall away from objects') (22).
14 The following studies have been useful to me in this discussion of expressionist film: Lotte Eisner, *The Haunted Screen: Expressionism in the German Cinema and the Influence of Max Reinhardt* (London: Thames and Hudson 1965); Siegfried Kracauer, *From Caligari to Hitler: A Psychological History of the German Film* (Princeton: Princeton University Press 1947); Roger Manvell and Heinrich Fraenkel, *The German Cinema* (London: Dent 1971).
15 For a discussion of Lang's *Metropolis* and some excellent stills from the film, see Frederick W. Ott, *The Films of Fritz Lang* (Secaucus, NJ: Citadel Press 1979). In 1984 Giorgio Morodor released his new version of *Metropolis* with a rock score and the addition of sequences missing from earlier prints. The new material contributes a much clearer sense of development to what seemed a totally illogical resolution, but *Metropolis* is still a highly sentimental treatment of class struggle and social reform. Nevertheless, it is a splendid portrayal of the *Aufbruch* and *Erlösung* of the New Man, and in its sets it provides a fine example of what Patterson thinks of as 'abstractionism.'
16 J.L. Styan, *Modern Drama in Theory and Practice*, vol. 3, *Expressionism and Epic Theatre* (Cambridge: Cambridge University Press 1981), 2–3
17 'My Works,' trans. Marketa Goetz, *Tulane Drama Review* 3 (March 1959): 100
18 Styan, *Modern Drama*, 24. For discussion of the influences on expressionist theatre, see Innes, *Holy Theatre*, Styan, Willett, *Expressionism*, Walter H. Sokel's introduction to *Anthology of German Expressionist Drama*, and n 28 below. Georg Büchner (1813–37) is considered an important German forerunner of Expressionism because of the subjects and style of his plays and because they received their first productions at the beginning of the expressionist movement: *Dantons Tod* in 1902 and *Woyzeck* in 1913. *Dantons Tod* became popular for its political content, but *Woyzeck*, a brilliant though unfinished play, provides a splendid example of what would become a typical expressionist hero – a little man who is abused by the military system and betrayed by a woman and who commits murder, then dies accidentally or

possibly by suicide. It is a bitter play that shows man regressing into helpless absurdity and sexual violence. Alban Berg's opera, based on Büchner's play, is a fully expressionist *tour de force*.

19 Wedekind's Lulu plays are complex and ambiguous, and I think it is impossible to say with Styan that Lulu is 'Strindbergian woman ... cunning, lustful and desirable' (*Modern Drama*, 20). Lulu is manipulated and abused by the males around her, who insist on seeing her in their own way; she is, finally, a much more sympathetic figure than any man in Wedekind's menagerie. For an interesting analysis of Wedekind's plays, in particular his treatment of women, see Peter Jelavich, 'Wedekind's *Spring Awakening*: The Path to Expressionist Drama,' in Bronner and Kellner, eds. *Passion and Rebellion*, 129–50.

20 *The Beggar*, trans. Walter H. and Jacqueline Sokel, in Sokel, ed. *Anthology of German Expressionist Drama*, 129–50

21 Styan, *Modern Drama*, 40

22 Ernst Toller, *Seven Plays* (London: Bodley Head 1935). *Masses and Man* is translated by Vera Mendel. In his note to the famous 1921 Volksbühne production, Toller wrote: 'I want to tell you myself that you have carried out my meaning. These pictures of "reality" [scenes 1, 3, 5, and 7] are not realism, are not local colour; the protagonists (except for Sonia [the Woman]) are not individual characters. Such a play can only have a spiritual, never a concrete, reality ... "Masses and Man," considered as a whole, is the presentation of such visionary insight [into reality]. It literally broke out of me and was put on paper in two and a half days' (111).

23 *From Morn to Midnight*, in *Five Plays* (London: Calder & Boyars 1971), trans. B.J. Kenworthy, Rex Last, and J.M. Ritchie, 18–73. As the Cashier shoots himself, his arms outspread against the Salvation Army cross, the lights go out and a rather bored policeman announces perfunctorily that 'There must have been a short circuit.' In the stage instructions Kaiser writes: '[The Cashier's] dying cough sounds like an "Ecce" – his expiring breath like a whispered – "Homo"' (73), underlining in one stroke the Christ-like yet ironic quality of this parodic gesture. This is the scene depicted in Plate 18.

24 For a useful discussion of *Erlösung*, see Douglas Kellner, 'Expressionist Literature and the Dream of the "New Man,"' in Bronner and Kellner, eds., *Passion and Rebellion*, 169–70. Because the words *Aufbruch* and *Erlösung* are impossible to translate succinctly, I have retained the German throughout.

25 *Five Plays*, 72. In *Holy Theatre*, 45–6, Innes notes how close Expressionism is to monologue at all times, not just when a play uses the mode, and he points out that dialogue is unimportant in comparison with mime, exclamation, and monologue.

26 *Anthology of German Expressionist Drama*, 10. There was considerable renewed interest in the theatrical potential of the mask. Craig was one of the first to recommend its extended use.

27 Trans. Joseph Bernstein, in Sokel's *Anthology of German Expressionist Drama*, 8. For a discussion of expressionist acting, see Innes, *Holy Theatre*, 47ff, and Patterson, *Revolution in German Theatre*, 80–1.

28 In *The Theatre of Edward Gordon Craig* (London: Eyre Methuen 1981) Denis
   Bablet notes the 'close connection between Craig's principles and the expressionist style of stage production' (112). Innes provides a more exhaustive
   analysis of Craig's development and influence in *Edward Gordon Craig*
   (Cambridge: Cambridge University Press 1983) and links him with Adolphe
   Appia (famous for his work on Wagner and his innovations in stage lighting),
   Reinhardt, and others. Craig was an eccentric character whose anti-semitism
   and support of fascism in Italy, not to mention his extravagant rhetoric, makes
   him difficult to appreciate today, but his early books, like *On the Art of the
   Theatre* (1911) and *Towards a New Theatre* (1913), were influential in their
   day and of special importance to Herman Voaden and Bertram Brooker, who
   are discussed in chap. 3.
29 Quoted in Willett, *Expressionism*, 117, from a 'Speech addressed to young
   writers' (1918)
30 Albert Soergel, *Dichtung und Dichter der Zeit: Im Banne des Expressionismus*
   (1925), quoted in Armin Arnold, *Prosa des Expressionismus*, 12
31 For an analysis of expressionist poetry and its links with Dada, see Fauchereau,
   Expressionisme, vol. I, 33–44, 215–45. In *The Language of Night* (The Hague:
   Servire Press 1932), 22, Eugene Jolas described the expressionist writers and
   the Zurich dadists as the most linguistically experimental of modernists.
   Jolas's theories are discussed further in chap. 4.
32 In *Prosa des Expressionismus*, 167–87, Arnold lists the expressionist fiction
   (stories, novellas, and novels) published yearly from 1900 to 1925. Among
   those who appear most frequently are Döblin, Heinrich Mann, Robert Walser,
   and Jakob Wassermann, and those whom Arnold discusses in detail – Franz
   Jung, Kasimir Edschmid, and Curt Corrinth. Kafka, Max Brod, and Ivan Goll –
   also appear frequently.
33 Eliot's essay, *The Three Voices of Lyric Poetry* (Cambridge: Cambridge University Press 1953) draws attention to Benn's *Probleme der Lyrik* and agrees
   with Benn that in lyric poetry of the first voice (Rilke's *Duino Elegies* and
   Benn's own monologues are examples) the poet speaks only to himself. See
   Breon Mitchell, 'Expressionism in English Drama and Prose Literature,' in
   Weisstein, ed., *Expressionism as an International Literary Phenomenon*,
   181–92, and my comment in n 3 to the Introduction.
34 For a brief description of the Twenty-One Gallery exhibit, see Richard Cork,
   Vorticism and Abstract Art in the First Machine Age, vol. II, 365–6. An earlier
   exhibit in 1910 at London's Grafton Gallery met with violent denunciation as 'a
   swindle,' 'a pornographic show,' and as 'anarchy and degeneration.' There
   were no German expressionists among the Cézannes, Gauguins, and Van
   Goghs, but the response was prophetic of what lay ahead for Expressionism.
   See Wees, *Vorticism and the English Avant-Garde*, 21–7. The first wave of
   curiosity about expressionist theatre occurred early in the twenties and was
   followed by renewed, sympathetic interest in the mid-thirties. According to
   Willett (*Expressionism*, 215), Kirchner, Nolde, and Schmidt-Rottluff, were
   exhibited in New York for the first time between 1936 and 1939, and the New

Burlington Galleries in London held a large exhibition of modern German painting in 1938 as a public protest against Hitler's 'Degenerate Art' exhibit.

35 'Die Menschheit,' *Das Werk* (Wiesbaden: Limes Verlag 1963), 45

36 Although an important aspect of the expressionist movement, poetry is beyond this study. For translations and discussions of the poetry, see Allen, *German Expressionist Poetry*, Fauchereau, *Expressionisme*, and the following studies: Anne Paolucci, 'Benn, Pound and Eliot: The Monologue Art of German Expressionism and Anglo-American Modernism,' *Review of National Literatures* 9 (1978): 10–24; J.M. Ritchie, *Gottfried Benn: The Unreconstructed Expressionist* (London: Oswald Wolff 1972); Mark Ritter, 'The Unfinished Legacy of Early Expressionist Poetry: Benn, Heym, Van Hoddis and Lichtenstein,' in Bronner and Kellner, eds., *Passion and Rebellion*, 151–65. For an interesting discussion of Benn and his infamous involvement with National Socialism, see Ingo Seidler, 'Art and Power: An Expressionist Dilemma and Gottfried Benn's "Solution,"' *Michigan Germanic Studies* 2, no. 2 (1976): 169–82. Only three major expressionists joined or supported the Nazis – Nolde, Benn (until 1934), and Hanns Johst – and this did not save Nolde from being branded 'degenerate.'

37 A.P. Dierick, 'Irony and Expressionism: An Examination of some short Narrative Prose,' *New German Studies* 7 (1979): 71–90. Though not a major issue to the Expressionism of early modernist prose examined here, irony becomes crucial to the parodic use of Expressionism in both Aquin and Pynchon. In his 1987 book *German Expressionist Prose: Theory and Practice* (Toronto: University of Toronto Press) Dierick discusses the socio-political commitment and thematics of much hitherto-neglected short fiction.

38 Sokel's studies include 'Die Prosa des Expressionismus,' in *Expressionismus als Literatur*, ed. Wolfgang Rothe (Bern and Munich: Francke Verlag 1969), 153–70, and *The Writer in Extremis*.

39 *The Writer in Extremis*, 30

40 *Prosa des Expressionismus*, 29–50

41 I shall use these three authors in the following discussion because they provide different examples of expressionist prose, and at least two – Döblin and Kafka – were known by the writers under study. Lowry was particularly interested in Döblin. Their works are currently in print and most are in reliable English translations.

42 *The Writer in Extremis*, 40

43 Quoted in Breon Mitchell, 'Expressionism in English Drama and Prose Literature,' in Weisstein, ed., *Expressionism as an International Literary Phenomenon*, 190

44 In 'The Unfinished Legacy of Early Expressionist Poetry: Benn, Heym, Van Hoddis and Lichtenstein,' in Bronner and Kellner, eds., *Passion and Rebellion*, 155, Mark Ritter notes Benn's use of metonymy in his poetry, but I am referring here not to the metonymy of classical rhetoric but to metonymy as an organizing principle of narrative structure, as discussed by Roman Jakobson in 'The Metaphoric and Metonymic Poles,' in *Fundamentals of Language* (The Hague: Mouton 1956), 76–82, and developed further by David Lodge in *The*

Modes of Modern Writing: Metaphor, Metonymy, and the Typology of Modern Literature (Ithaca, NY: Cornell University Press 1977).

45 See Dorrit Cohn's discussion of *erlebte Rede* in 'Narrated Monologue: Definition of a Fictional Style,' *Comparative Literature* 18 (1969): 97–112, repr. in *Transparent Minds: Narrative Modes for Presenting Consciousness in Fiction* (Princeton, NJ: Princeton University Press 1978), chap. 3.

46 *The Writer in Extremis*, 121; see also 118–19.

47 *Prosa des Expressionismus*, 73

48 Ibid., 33

49 'Expressionist Literature and the Dream of the "New Man,"' in Bronner and Kellner, eds., *Passion and Rebellion*, 190. For a critical analysis of Kaiser's use of this figure, see B.J. Kenworthy, 'Georg Kaiser: The Ambiguity of the Expressionist New Man,' in *Georg Kaiser Symposium*, ed. Holger Pausch and Ernest Reinhold (Berlin: Agora Verlag), 95–111.

50 By Worringer, Sokel, Levine, Patterson, and Selz, for example

CHAPTER THREE: 'The New Art of the Theatre' in New York and Toronto

1 Quoted from Floyd Dell's *Homecoming: An Autobiography* (New York 1969) by C.W.E. Bigsby in *A Critical Introduction to Twentieth-Century American Drama* (Cambridge: Cambridge University Press 1982), 5. This excellent study of American drama is referred to hereafter in the text as Bigsby.

2 The 1925 program included Walter Hasenclever's 1920 expressionist play *Jenseits (Beyond)*.

3 See *Accelerated Grimace: Expressionism in the American Drama of the 1920's* (Carbondale & Edwardsville: Southern Illinois University Press 1972), 20–3, and chaps. 5, 6. Kreymborg's plays are especially interesting for their use of mime, music, rhythm, and stylization. Even his themes – domestic and sexual tensions between men and women – demonstrate his affinity with German Expressionism and Strindberg. See *Plays for Poem-Mimes* (1918; Great Neck, NY: Core Collection Books 1976).

4 *The Verge, A Play in Three Acts* (London: Ernest Benn 1925), 47. All quotations are from this edition and are included in the text. *The Verge* has been reprinted in *The Plays of Susan Glaspell*, ed. C.W.E. Bigsby (Cambridge: Cambridge University Press, 1987).

5 Jacques Derrida, 'Of an apocalyptic tone recently adopted in philosophy,' *Semeia* 23 (1982): 89: 'By its very tone, the mixing of voices, genres, and codes, and the breakdown [le détraquement] of destinations, apocalyptic discourse can also dismantle the dominant contract or concordat. It is a challenge to the established admissability of messages and to the enforcement or maintenance of order.' See my discussion of apocalyptic discourse in chaps. 4 and 5.

6 Both Valgemae (*Accelerated Grimace*) and Bigsby (*Critical Introduction*) consider Claire to be insane by the end of *The Verge*, and Bigsby states that 'Clearly Glaspell is critical of Claire' (32). Linda Ben-Zvi, in 'Susan Glaspell and Eugene O'Neill: The Imagery of Gender,' *Eugene O'Neill Newsletter* 10, no. 1 (Spring 1986): 26, also sees Claire as insane but allows that Glaspell may

none the less 'leave her victorious' because within the play's structure of meaning madness signifies freedom. I would argue, however, that Claire's madness is no more nor less than the madness of vision and that her uncompromising rejection of patriarchy makes her a successful expressionist heroine. Christine Dymkowski draws a similar conclusion in 'On the Edge: The Plays of Susan Glaspell,' *Modern Drama* 31, no. 1 (1988): 101.

7 *The Adding Machine*, in *Seven Plays by Elmer Rice* (New York: Viking Press 1950), 76

8 Quoted from Anton Wagner's introduction to *A Vision of Canada: Herman Voaden's Dramatic Works* (Toronto: Simon and Pierre, forthcoming)

9 *Creative Theatre* (New York: John Day 1929), 189, 229. Though closely associated with Toronto and the University of Toronto, where he was educated, Mitchell moved to New York in 1921, where he remained actively involved in theatre work. See Renate Usmiani, 'Roy Mitchell: Prophet in our Past,' *Theatre History in Canada* 8, no. 2 (1987): 147–68. In British Columbia, from 1920 to 1923, another Canadian director-producer established an experimental theatre. Carroll Aikens had a thorough knowledge of German and French theatre, of the theories of Appia and Craig, and of the newest American trends, but his experiment had no direct impact on Canadian theatre traditions. See James Hoffman, 'Carroll Aikens and the Home Theatre,' *Theatre History in Canada* 7, no. 1 (1986): 50–70.

10 Volkoff, born Boris Baskakoff in Scheptievo, Russia, in 1900, studied in Moscow under Alexander Gorsky, who was teaching a non-classical ballet of gesture, emotion, and grotesque movement influenced by Isadora Duncan. Volkoff spent two years touring the Far East and spent a year in Chicago before settling in Toronto. In his own dancing Volkoff chose expressive, abstract parts, and he continued to choreograph experimental works, despite the conservative tastes of the public. He often used Canadian folklore or native legends for his subjects, as was the case with *Mala* and *Mon-Ka-Ta* and the 1949 *Red Ear of Corn* with music by John Weinzweig. See Lillian L. Mitchell, 'Boris Volkoff: Dancer, Teacher, Choreographer,' PhD, Texas Women's University 1982. For a discussion of Volkoff's successful program in Berlin, see 'Toronto Dancers to Compete at Olympics,' *Saturday Night*, 11 July 1936, and 'Artistic Dances Competition' by James D. Pape in *Canada at the XI Olympiad, 1936, in Germany*, Official Report of the Canadian Olympic Committee 1933–36, ed. W.A. Fry (Dunnville, Ont. 1936), 103–5. I would like to thank Canadian cultural historian Dr Maria Tippett for bringing Boris Volkoff to my attention and for telling me about another European who introduced avant-garde ideas to Vancouver – the expressionist stage-designer from Vienna, Harry Täuber. Täuber arrived in Vancouver in 1931 to teach classes in Expressionism, direct plays (including Kaiser's *Gas*), and to found, with Frederick Varley and Jock Macdonald, the British Columbia College of Arts. He was a disciple of Rudolf Steiner, and his impact on the artistic community was considerable; see Jack Shadbolt, 'A Personal Recollection,' *Vancouver Art and Artists, 1931 to 1983* (Vancouver Art Gallery 1983), 34–41.

11 *Six Canadian Plays* (Toronto: Copp Clark 1930) includes *The Bone Spoon* by Betti Sandiford, *The Motherlode* by Archibald Key, *Manitou Portage* by T.M. Morrow, *Lake Doré* by Jesse Middleton, *God-Forsaken* by Charles Carruthers, and *Winds of Life* by Dora Smith Conover. The winning plays, *Lake Doré*, *God-Forsaken*, and *Winds of Life*, were produced by Voaden at the Central High School of Commerce in April 1930.

12 *Six Canadian Plays*, 50. *Manitou Portage* is printed in *Six Canadian Plays*, 49–70.

13 For discussions of Brooker's painting, see Dennis Reid, *Bertram Brooker* (Ottawa: National Gallery of Canada 1973); Victoria Evans, 'Bertram Brooker's Theory of Art as evinced in his "The Seven Arts" Columns and Early Abstractions,' *Journal of Canadian Art History* 9, no. 1 (1986): 28–44; and Joyce Zemans, 'The Art and Weltanschauung of Bertram Brooker,' *Artscanada* 30 (1973): 65–8.

14 Voaden discusses Brooker and his two Workshop plays in an unpublished typescript, 'Symphonic Expressionism: A Canadian adventure in the direction of a more musical and expressive theatre' (1975), 70–5. Although Voaden found *The Dragon: A Parable of Illusion and Disillusion* (1936) to be more impressive than *Within*, the actual text suggests that Brooker was using expressionist abstraction to create a rather heavy-handed allegory.

15 Both *The Dragon* and *Within* have been published in *Canadian Drama* 11, no. 1 (1985): 256–68, 269–79, together with illustrations and an introduction. Copies of Brooker's *Within* manuscript are located in the Herman Voaden Collection at York University and in the Bertram Brooker collection at the University of Manitoba.

16 For a detailed discussion of Brooker's 'ultimatist' beliefs, see Sherrill Grace, '"The Living Soul of Man": Bertram Brooker and Expressionist Theatre,' *Theatre History in Canada* 6, no. 1 (1985): 3–22. A reproduction of Brooker's sketch for the sets appears with the article. Brooker's dislike of O'Neill's psycho-sexual excesses, especially in *Strange Interlude* (cited by Victoria Evans, 'Brooker's Theory of Art,' 38), should not obscure his affinities with the expressive abstraction privileged by Worringer, Kandinsky, and Marc and demonstrated by writers like Voaden and Sheila Watson (see chap 8).

17 Lawrence Mason, 'The Play Workshop,' *Globe*, 30 March 1935

18 *The Collected Plays of Gwen Pharis Ringwood*, ed. Enid Delgatty Rutland (Ottawa: Borealis Press 1982), 27–43

19 Ibid., 355–78

CHAPTER FOUR: Eugene O'Neill

1 'Trying to Like O'Neill,' in *O'Neill and His Plays: Four Decades of Criticism*, ed. Oscar Cargill, N. Bryllion Fagin, William J. Fisher (New York: New York University Press 1961), 333. Many important essays and commentaries are collected in this volume, which is cited hereafter in the text as Cargill.

2 As Travis Bogard has aptly put it: 'No one writing on O'Neill and his plays can

do so in a state of original innocence.' This is certainly true in my case, and I am happy to acknowledge, here and throughout this chapter, the help I have received from the fine scholarly work that has been done on O'Neill, such as the following studies: Travis Bogard, *Contour in Time: The Plays of Eugene O'Neill* (New York: Oxford University Press 1972); Jean Chothia, *Forging a Language: A Study of the Plays of Eugene O'Neill* (Cambridge: Cambridge University Press 1979); John Henry Raleigh, *The Plays of Eugene O'Neill* (Carbondale & Edwardsville: Southern Illinois University Press 1965); Tino Tiusanen, *O'Neill's Scenic Images* (Princeton, NJ: Princeton University Press 1968), and Egil Tornqvist, *A Drama of Souls: Studies in O'Neill's Supernaturalistic Technique* (New Haven and London: Yale University Press 1969).

3 See, for example, O'Neill's 1924 comments in 'Strindberg and Our Theatre,' in Cargill, *O'Neill and His Plays*, 108–9, and the following articles: C.T. Busch and A.J. Orten, 'Immortality Enough: The Influence of Strindberg on the Expressionism of Eugene O'Neill,' *Southern Speech Journal* 33 (Winter 1967): 129–39; William Clark, 'The Rise of American Drama: O'Neill and Expressionistic Tragedy,' in *Chief Patterns of World Drama* (New York: Houghton Mifflin 1946), 1006–12; Thomas C. Dawber, 'Strindberg and O'Neill,' *Players Magazine* 45 (1970): 183–5; Frederic Fleisher, 'Strindberg and O'Neill,' *Symposium* 10 (Spring 1956): 84–93; David McDermott, 'Robert Edmond Jones and Eugene O'Neill: Two American Visionaries,' *Eugene O'Neill Newsletter* 8, no. 1 (Spring 1984): 3–10. Also of importance in this connection is the excellent volume *'The Theatre We Worked For': The Letters of Eugene O'Neill and Kenneth Macgowan*, ed. Jackson R. Bryer and Ruth M. Alvarez, intro. Travis Bogard (New Haven and London: Yale University Press 1982), and discussions by Tiusanen in *O'Neill's Scenic Images* and Tornqvist in *A Drama of Souls*.

4 'O'Neill and German Expressionism,' *Modern Drama* 10 (1967): 111. Valgemae's article is important as well because it notes many parallels between O'Neill's and Kaiser's plays and points to the likely influence of *The Cabinet of Dr Caligari* and *Metropolis*. The *Selected Letters of Eugene O'Neill*, ed. Travis Bogard and Jackson R. Bryer (New Haven: Yale University Press 1988), appeared after this book had gone to press, but Travis Bogard tells me that no references to Fritz Lang or *Metropolis* have as yet been discovered in the correspondence; therefore, it is not yet possible to claim absolutely that O'Neill saw this film, but we do know from the letters that he thought very highly of it. Valgemae concludes, correctly I think, that O'Neill has 'a much closer affinity with the German expressionists than with Strindberg, in whose dream plays the consciousness not of the protagonist but of the author holds sway over the surreal action' (122). Further references to this article are cited as Valgemae, followed by the page number, but see also his book, *Accelerated Grimace*. Among others who stress the German connection are Louis Broussard, *American Drama: Contemporary Allegory from Eugene O'Neill to Tennessee Williams* (Norman: University of Oklahoma Press 1962), 4–6, 12; Peter Egri, 'European Origins and American Originality: The Case of Drama,' *Zeitschrift für Anglistik und Americanistik* 29, no. 3 (1981): 197–205; Virginia Floyd, ed., who writes in *Eugene O'Neill: A World View* (New York: Frederick Ungar 1979)

that O'Neill 'was following the lead of the German expressionists [she mentions Barlach and Kornfeld] who dramatized the need for spiritual, as well as social, reform and faith in God' (28); Horst Frenz, 'Eugene O'Neill and Georg Kaiser,' in Floyd, ed., *Eugene O'Neill: A World View*, 172–85; and Kenneth Macgowan in his 1929 essay 'The O'Neill Soliloquy,' in Cargill, 449–53. Macgowan, who had become a passionate and knowledgeable supporter of Expressionism (see his 1922 *Continental Stagecraft*, illustrated by Jones), was better placed than most to know whereof he spoke.

5 Quoted in *Eugene O'Neill's Critics: Voices from Abroad*, ed. Horst Frenz and Susan Tuck (Carbondale and Edwardsville: Southern Illinois University Press 1984), 31

6 Notably, Clara Blackburn, 'Continental Influences on Eugene O'Neill's Expressionistic Dramas,' *American Literature* 13 (May 1941): 109–33; Catharine Mounier, 'L'Expressionisme dans l'oeuvre d'Eugene O'Neill,' in *Expressionisme dans le théâtre européen*, ed. Denis Bablet and Jean Jacquot (Paris: Centre national de la Recherche Scientifique 1971), 331–40, hereafter cited in the text as Mounier, followed by the page number; and James A. Robinson's fine PhD thesis, 'O'Neill's Expressionistic Grotesque: A Study of Nine Experimental Plays by Eugene O'Neill,' Duke University 1975. It is worth noting here that Alexander Tairov of Moscow's Kamerny Theatre mounted highly expressionistic productions of *The Hairy Ape* and *All God's Chillun Got Wings* and that O'Neill was extremely enthusiastic about Tairov's works. See Tairov's essay on *All God's Chillun* and the production photographs in Frenz and Tuck, *Voices from Abroad*. O'Neill's comments after seeing the 1930 Paris productions of *Desire Under the Elms* and *Chillun* can be found in Cargill, 123–4; he felt that the Kamerny under Tairov had realized his dream, even through a translation.

7 Two exceptions do come to mind: Tiusanen's *Scenic Images*, a proto-structuralist study that slips into thematics, and Chothia's *Forging a Language*, although I do not agree with her use of the term 'realist.'

8 Unless otherwise specified, the dates given for O'Neill's plays are the approximate dates of composition as these are listed in Cargill, 480–2. All page references are to *The Plays of Eugene O'Neill*, 3 vols. (New York: Random House 1951), and are included in the text. Of the nine other full-length plays written during this period, several display expressionist qualities, and *Marco Millions* (1923–25) and *Mourning Becomes Electra* (1929–31) might have been considered here except that both seem to me to be seriously flawed constructions.

9 Robinson, 'O'Neill's Expressionistic Grotesque,' 282

10 O'Neill's reading is discussed by each of his biographers: Doris Alexander, *The Tempering of Eugene O'Neill* (New York: Harcourt Brace & World 1962); Arthur and Barbara Gelb, *O'Neill* (New York: Harper & Row 1962); and Louis Sheaffer, *O'Neill*, 2 vols. (Boston: Little, Brown 1968, 1973); Chothia provides a useful 'literary biography' of O'Neill's reading; see *Forging a Language*, 198–206. I have relied on the biographies, especially Sheaffer's, throughout for a multitude of essential facts and details.

11 See Sheaffer, *O'Neill*, 1: 352. Marsden Hartley, who was also a friend of

Djuna Barnes, is discussed again in chap. 6. For a description of these fascinating years, see Robert Karoly Sarlos, *Jig Cook and the Provincetown Players* (Amherst: University of Massachussetts Press 1982). In *The Eugene O'Neill Newsletter* (Summer-Fall 1986), 49, Sheaffer notes that Hartley and Charles Demuth, another painter whom O'Neill met during these years, were 'the chief models for Charles Marsden in ... *Strange Interlude.*' For a discussion of painting during these years, see Dorothy Gees Seckler, *Provincetown Painters, 1890's to 1970's* (Syracuse, NY: Everson Museum of Art 1977), 27–48.

12 Valgemae, *Accelerated Grimace,* 20–3

13 In 'Eugene O'Neill and Georg Kaiser' (Floyd, ed., *Eugene O'Neill,* 178–9), Horst Frenz states that it was out in the Autumn of 1919 and in May as a book. However, the play definitely appeared in *Poet-Lore* 21 (Autumn 1920): 317–63. Renate Benson, in *German Expressionist Drama: Ernst Toller and Georg Kaiser* (London: Macmillan 1984), only cites the *Poet-Lore* translation for 1920, but in *Accelerated Grimace* (30) Valgemae notes that Dukes's translation was published in England in May 1920, several months before the *Poet-Lore* publication. See p 253, n 32.

14 Sheaffer, *O'Neill* 2:546. This quotation is from a letter, dated 26 Jan. 1922, in the Beinecke O'Neill Collection at Yale. See Valgemae, *Accelerated Grimace,* 33–4.

15 In *Modern Drama in Theory and Practice 3: Expressionism and Epic Theatre* (Cambridge: Cambridge University Press 1983), 32, J.L. Styan describes Strindberg's play as 'more rigorously expressionistic' than his other chamber plays. See Donald Gallup, ed., 'Eugene O'Neill's "The Ancient Mariner,"' in *Yale University Library Gazette* 35, no. 2 (Oct. 1960): 61–86. James Light designed the masks, which were meant to intensify the drama, not to represent life, and O'Neill used expressionistic devices such as having the masked wedding guests 'walk like marionettes.' In a review of the production Macgowan said it went further beyond realism than expressionism in an effort to approximate the formalism of Noh drama; see n 3 above for McDermott, 'Robert Edmond Jones and Eugene O'Neill,' 3.

16 Quoted in Bryer and Alvarez, eds., *'The Theatre We Worked For,'* 46.

17 For good discussions of these years, see Valgemae, *Accelerated Grimace,* 41–59, and Styan's *Modern Drama in Theory and Practice,* 97–111. The Players were also producing more realistic plays, such as O'Neill's *Desire Under the Elms* in 1924 and *Diff'rent* in 1925.

18 *'The Theatre We Worked For,'* 31

19 Quoted in Gelb, *O'Neill,* 499

20 See n 6 above. Although Blackburn makes some fine points, her comparison of Mildred in *The Hairy Ape* with Indra's daughter in *The Dream Play* is strained, and she glosses over some of the important differences between Strindberg and the Germans, which, as Valgemae and Floyd have demonstrated, place O'Neill rather closer to certain German expressionists than to the Swede.

21 In 'O'Neill and Georg Kaiser' (see n 4 above), Frenz points to several parallels between O'Neill's plays and Kaiser's *Gas* and *The Coral.*

22 In *German Expressionist Drama*, Renate Benson argues convincingly that, unlike Toller, Kaiser was a self-centred individual who came to see mankind as unregenerate and corrupt (145). With few exceptions (*The Burghers of Calais* is one) he treated the idea of rebirth ironically, and in *The Raft of the Medusa* (*Das Floss der Medusa*), which is discussed further below, the hero chooses to die rather than return to society. This Kaiser has much in common with O'Neill.

23 See also Robinson, 'O'Neill's Expressionistic Grotesque,' Sheaffer, *O'Neill*, and Tiusanen, *O'Neill's Scenic Images*.

24 Quoted in Sheaffer, *O'Neill*, 1:194

25 Quoted in Walter H. Sokel, ed., *Anthology of German Expressionist Plays: A Prelude to the Absurd* (Ithaca and London: Cornell University Press 1984), 10. Goll's appreciation of the mask is influenced by the expressionist painters' and sculptors' handling of the form; see, for example, the splendid illustrations of Kirchner's work in *German Expressionist Sculpture*, ed. Barbara Einzig, Lynn Dean, Andrea P.A. Belloli, exhibition catalogue (Los Angeles County Museum of Art 1983). Primitive art, notably masks and sculpture, had a profound impact upon modern painting, from the work of Picasso and many of the expressionists, such as Nolde and Kirchner, to the post–Second World War COBRA painters. Many contemporary painters are again drawing inspiration from these art-forms: for example, in Germany, Markus Lupertz, in the United States, Sandro Chia, and in Canada, Jack Shadbolt.

26 *The Hairy Ape* is usually considered to have a more satisfying and sophisticated structure than *The Emperor Jones* because the former avoids the sharp break between inner and outer reality created by the framing scenes; see, for example, Bogard's discussion of *The Emperor Jones*, *Contour in Time*, 143–4.

27 See Gelb, *O'Neill*, 440–1, 444. The *Kuppelhorizont*, or sky-dome, was already being used to great effect in Germany.

28 For a critique of Peter Stein's West Berlin Schaubühne Company's 1987 production of *The Hairy Ape* at London's National Theatre, see Ann Massa, 'Intention and Effect in *The Hairy Ape*,' *Modern Drama* 31, no. 1 (1988): 41–51. Lucio Fanti designed the 'arresting' and 'impressive' sets, but Massa finds fault with Stein's mixture of realism and expressionism.

29 See Benson's discussion of *Transfiguration* (*Die Wandlung*), *German Expressionist Drama*, 30–1, where the promise of redemption is contemplated by the hero, Friedrich:

Perhaps through crucifixion only
Liberation comes;
Perhaps the powers of light
Spring only from his blood.
Perhaps through crucifixion only
Can redemption come,
The way to light and freedom.

In his September 1919 première of the play, Karl Heinz Martin used lighting extensively to aid interpretation and he used solo violin between scenes; see Benson, 36.

30 Kenneth Macgowan, 'The O'Neill Soliloquy,' in Cargill, 449–53. O'Neill's oft-quoted phrase comes from his remarks on the playbill for the 3 January 1924 Provincetown production of Strindberg's *The Spook Sonata*. O'Neill wrote: 'The old "naturalism" – or "realism" if you prefer ... no longer applies. It represents our Fathers' daring aspirations towards self-recognition by holding the family kodak up to ill-nature. But to us their old audacity is blague; we have taken too many snap-shots of each other in every graceful position; we have endured too much from the banality of surfaces' (Cargill, 108–9).

31 See comments by Blackburn, Busch and Orten, Tiusanen, and Tornqvist, chap. 5 (see nn 2, 3, 6 above), and most recently by Hinden (see n 37 below).

32 See Bigsby, *Critical Introduction*, who makes many fine points passim about O'Neill's characters' living through language that constantly fails them. Bigsby remarks that for them silence is 'an admission of impotence' (95), and I carry this point further in suggesting that speech and its opposite, silence, are the prime polarities in O'Neill's ontological and epistemological struggle. Interestingly, Bigsby sees O'Neill as an absurdist (and implicitly an expressionist), but he does not link the two as does Walter Sokel in *The Writer in Extremis* and in his introduction to *Anthology of German Expressionist Drama*.

33 In 'Linguistic Features of the Stream-of-Consciousness Techniques of James Joyce, Virginia Woolf and Eugene O'Neill,' *Annales Universitatis Turkuensis* 116 (1970): 54–69, Liisa Dahl analyses passages from *Strange Interlude* and notes the high degree of nomination and repetition in the sentences. Although she describes O'Neill as expressionistic, as opposed to the impressionism of Woolf, and suggests Joyce's influence on O'Neill, she is comparing interior monologue with thought-asides, and these should never be confused with O'Neill's expressionist monologues. What Joyce in fact achieves is a greater realism, which is also true of the thought-asides in *Strange Interlude*. The only extended expressionism in Joyce is in the 'Circe' episode of *Ulysses*, and there Joyce is parodying the expressionist drama. I have discussed 'Circe' in '"Midsummer Madness" and the "Day of the Dead": Joyce, Lowry and Expressionism,' a paper presented at the 11th James Joyce International Congress in Venice, June 1988.

34 Chothia, *Forging a Language*, 83, 89, and chap. 4

35 Lotte Eisner, *The Haunted Screen*, 110. Doubles were a great favorite of E.T.A. Hoffman, whose work was often adapted by film-makers. See also Robert Rogers, *A Psychoanalytic Study of the Double in Literature* (Detroit: Wayne State University Press 1970). Rogers's discussion of the narcissistic motivations for doubling are particularly interesting with regard to O'Neill.

36 In her exhaustive and meticulous study, *Pan the Goat-God: His Myth in Modern Times* (Cambridge, Mass.: Harvard University Press 1969), Patricia Merivale traces the origins of Pan and the many variations in his mythological and literary significance from classical times to the present. For her discussion of the two incompatible Christian interpretations of Pan (one as demon, the other as conflation with Christ), see 11–14. Merivale credits Swinburne with the creation of a new trend in thinking about Pan as the terrifying life-force

in all things that finds its way into the sinister Pans of late nineteenth- and early twentieth-century fiction and culminates in D.H. Lawrence, for whom 'the Christ principle and the Pan principle' keep up a constant battle (217). Speaking of O'Neill, Merivale points out that in *The Great God Brown* Pan is at first positive, and that his repression by the Brown forces of bourgeois complacency turns Pan into Mephistopheles. The ambiguity of Dion Anthony causes many interesting problems in the play. Swinburne may be one source for O'Neill's Pan idea and the Dionysus concept is Nietzschean, but Nietzsche does not combine Pan and Dionysus, and for him Christ is a repellent and negative figure.

37 In 'When Playwrights Talk to God: Peter Shaffer and the Legacy of O'Neill,' *Comparative Drama* 16, no. 1 (Spring 1982): 49–63, Michael Hinden sees Brown's death as an 'apotheosis sought by Dion' (55), but the highly ambiguous ending of the play cannot be summarized so tidily. Hinden provides an excellent discussion of O'Neill's monologues, which I refer to below.

38 The question of O'Neill's misogyny has recently been gaining attention, as the Summer-Fall 1982 issue of the *Eugene O'Neill Newsletter* testifies. Of particular importance on this matter is Sheaffer's perceptive remark in 'Correcting Some Errors in the Annals of O'Neill' (pt 2), *Eugene O'Neill Newsletter* (Spring 1984): 16–21. Speaking of Hickey, and of O'Neill's identification with him, Sheaffer writes: 'Hence the legion of dead wives and mothers in his plays, a far larger number than is generally realized, as the playwright-son took symbolic revenge again and again on addicted Ella O'Neill' (20). His *Mourning Becomes Electra*, I would argue, is a profoundly misogynistic work in which both mother and daughter are seen as destructive monsters or as manifestations of the monster Woman. For an interesting reading of the gender question, see Linda Ben-Zvi, 'Freedom and Fixity in the Plays of Eugene O'Neill,' *Modern Drama* 31, no. 1 (1988): 16–27.

39 In 'Fusion-Point of Jung and Nietzsche,' in Cargill, 408–14, Oscar Cargill argues that *Lazarus Laughed* is the great example of O'Neill's vision of Dionysian oneness, with laughter signifying unity, but Cargill also points out that underlying this vision is a stark nihilism for which the only answer to the evils of living is not to be. Bertram Brooker struggles with a similar problem in *The Dragon* (discussed in chap. 3), and his ending also fails to convince. In her discussion of *Days Without End*, 'The Way Out: The Many Endings of *Days Without End*,' in Cargill, 415–23, Doris Falk describes the play as 'an unconvincing drama and a philosophical whistling in the dark' (416).

40 In 'O'Neill's *Hairy Ape* and the Reversal of Hegelian Dialectics,' *Modern Drama* 31, no. 1 (1988): 35–40, Hubert Zapf sees the play as a deliberate deconstruction of the ideology of progress; Yank's regression is, then, a sign of that deconstructive process.

41 In 'Virility and Domination in Early Twentieth-Century Vanguard Painting,' *Feminism and Art History: Questioning the Litany*, ed. Norma Broude and Mary D. Garrard (New York: Harper & Row 1982), 292–313, Carol Duncan examines the sexual politics of Kirchner, among others. This article is treated

in greater detail in chap. 6. For a very different reading of *Welded*, see Bogard, *Contour in Time*, 184–98. It is extremely difficult to see how Eleanor can be 'forced into a role' (188) by Michael, as Bogard admits, and yet not see her as a victim (184) without completely endorsing Michael's solipsism; this is certainly what O'Neill wants, but the reader (or viewer) can resist O'Neill's text.

42 See Sandra Gilbert and Susan Gubar, *The Madwoman in the Attic: The Woman Writer and the Nineteenth-Century Literary Imagination* (New Haven and London: Yale University Press 1979), 359–62. The chief difference in the portrayal of the madwoman between *Jane Eyre* and *All God's Chillun* could be attributed to the genders of their authors and the sympathetic focus of viewpoint in each work (Jane in the novel, Jim in the play). However, I do not think that this radically changes the terrifying nature of the Bertha/Ella figure, who is a projection of deep-seated sexual fears of both authors and of the Victorian morality they are both labouring under. The difference lies in the conclusion and the men: Jim is no Rochester, which is all the worse for him.

43 See dates in Cargill, 480–2. *Long Day's Journey into Night* and *A Touch of the Poet* were both published posthumously in 1956 and 1957 respectively. The manuscript of *More Stately Mansions*, dated 1938, was found in 1957.

44 See Frenz and Tuck, *Voices from Abroad*, 9–10.

45 Benson, *German Expressionist Drama*, 164. As Benson points out, this rejection is haunted, as O'Neill's most certainly was, by Christianity. The final scene of this grim play is highly reminiscent of O'Neill.

CHAPTER FIVE: Herman Voaden's 'Symphonic Expressionism'

1 For biographical information I am indebted, here and elsewhere, in this chapter to Anton Wagner, 'A Theatre of Beauty: Herman Voaden's Symphonic Expressionism,' an introduction to *A Vision of Canada: Herman Voaden's Dramatic Works* (Toronto: Simon and Pierre, forthcoming); Geraldine Anthony, ed., 'Herman Voaden,' in *Stage Voices: Twelve Canadian Playwrights Talk about Their Lives and Work* (Toronto: Doubleday 1978), 28–54; and to conversations and correspondence with Dr Wagner and Herman Voaden.

2 Lawrence Mason, 'Genuine Canadian Drama,' *Toronto Globe*, 6 Dec. 1930, 21

3 'Is There a Canadian Drama?' in *The Canadian Imagination*, ed. David Staines (Cambridge, Mass.: Harvard University Press 1977), 155

4 'Producing Methods Defined' appeared in Mason's *Globe* column for 16 Apr. 1932, 15, with a brief introduction by Mason.

5 'Toward a New Theatre,' *Toronto Globe*, 8 Dec. 1934, 19

6 Voaden praises Craig in his early *Globe* articles 'What Is Wrong with Canadian Theatre?' *Toronto Globe*, 22 June 1929, 22, 'Producing Methods Defined,' *Toronto Globe*, 16 Apr. 1932, 15, 'Drama Festival Thoughts,' *Toronto Globe*, 26 Nov. 1932, 7, and 'Creed for a New Theatre,' *Toronto Globe*, 17 Dec. 1932, 5, and in his chapter of *Stage Voices* he reiterates the importance of Craig, O'Neill, and the German expressionists. In private conversation Voaden has said that he read Craig's books with great enthusiasm.

7 See his discussion of these points in 'What Is Wrong With Canadian Theatre?' and in his introduction to *Six Canadian Plays* (see chap. 3, n 11, above). The extremes of Kokoschka did not appeal to Voaden and in 'What Is Wrong?' he admits that even Craig could go too far so that the 'aesthetic quality is often at variance with the natural human emotional note of drama.'

8 'Dance of the Theatre: Impressions of the Dance in Four Countries,' *Dancing Times* 274 (July 1933): 333–5.

9 Voaden owns a copy of *Continental Stagecraft*, first published in 1922. See the discussion in chap. 1.

10 Macgowan, *Continental Stagecraft*, 39

11 Voaden completed his MA thesis in 1926, and in the summer of 1927 he began bibliographical work for a PhD on O'Neill at the University of Chicago. He abandoned these academic plans after an exciting fall in which he helped found the Sarnia Drama League and wrote his first play.

12 A typescript of the O'Neill thesis is held in the Voaden Collection at York University. This remark appears at the end of the thesis, 40 of the typescript. Voaden reviewed a performance of *The Emperor Jones* at the Metropolitan Opera for the *Toronto Globe*, 3 Feb. 1933, and he was critical of the 'heavy and unimaginatively realistic' style of the production, which, he argued, destroyed 'the play's inner meaning and truth.'

13 *Leaves of Grass* (London: Appleton 1911), 446. Whitman had a profound influence on other Canadian modernists such as Bertram Brooker, Emily Carr, and many early twentieth-century poets. For discussion of his impact on Brooker, see my article 'Figures in a Ground: Brooker and the Craft of Fiction,' and others in *Bertram Brooker and Emergent Modernism*, a special issue of *Provincial Essays* 7 (1989).

14 *Modernist Studies* II (1977), 15. Djwa's excellent study of modernist poetry is the first to explore the relationship between Canadian painting and poetry.

15 *Stage Voices*, 35, and the preface to *Six Canadian Plays*

16 *A Canadian Art Movement: The Story of the Group of Seven* (Toronto: Macmillan 1974), 190

17 'Creative Art and Canada,' in *Yearbook of the Arts in Canada, 1928–1929*, ed. Bertram Brooker (Toronto: Macmillan 1929), 184. Harris goes on to explain that the painter 'moves toward purer creative expression, wherein he changes the outward aspect of Nature, alters colours and, by changing and re-shaping forms, intensifies the austerity and beauty of formal relationships' (185).

18 *Lawren Harris*, ed. Bess Harris and R.G.P. Colgrove, intro. Northrop Frye (Toronto: Macmillan 1969), 131. The text comprises selections from Harris's essays, poetry, and notebooks. Seven Harris works, including three canvases of Lake Superior, were included in a 1988 exhibition of expressionist landscape painting; see *The Expressionist Landscape: North American Modernist Painting*, exhibition catalogue by Ruth Stevens Appelhof, Barbara Haskell, and Jeffrey R. Hayes (Birmingham, Ala.: Birmingham Museum of Art 1988), 139–44.

19 'Introduction,' *Six Canadian Plays*, xix–xx

20 All three will be published in *A Vision of Canada: Herman Voaden's Dramatic Works*.

21 Quoted from Anton Wagner, '"A Country of the Soul": Herman Voaden, Low-rie Warrener, and the Writing of *Symphony*,' *Canadian Drama* 9, no. 2 (1983): 207

22 H. Voaden and L. Warrener, *Symphony* in *Canadian Drama* 8, no. 1 (1982): 74–83. All references are to this publication and are included parenthetically in the text. For a discussion of Warrener and reproductions of his work, see John Flood's 'Lowrie Warrener,' *Northward Journal: A Quarterly of Northern Arts* 25 (1982): 11–28. The illustrations include several oils that are distinctly expressionist in the manner of Schmidt-Rottluff and a very fine expressionistic bust of Voaden, at present in Voaden's private collection.

23 See *Concerning the Spiritual in Art*, 56–67, for Kandinsky's elaborate and detailed discussion of the symbolic and psychological properties of colour. Warrener, who had studied art in Europe (Antwerp and Paris) in the twenties, may well have been introduced to Kandinsky's theories in addition to the more conventional systems of Munsell and Ostwald. Certainly, Harris, who like Kandinsky was a theosophist, was influenced by these theories and developed a highly symbolic/spiritual colour system in his own work.

24 *Wilderness* in *Canada's Lost Plays* III, ed. Anton Wagner (Toronto: Canadian Theatre Review Publications 1980), 97. Also reprinted in *Boréal* 11/12 (1978), 10–20. Further references are to *Canada's Lost Plays*.

25 'Canadian Plays and Experimental Stagecraft,' *Toronto Globe*, 23 Apr. 1932, 18

26 See the comments quoted in *Stage Voices*, 37–9.

27 I am grateful to Heather McCallum, former head of Theatre Special Collections at the Metropolitan Toronto Library, for permission to read the typescripts of *Hill-Land* and *Ascend as the Sun*; typescripts of these plays are also held in the York Voaden Collection. In 'Pioneers: Two Contrasting Dramatic Treatments,' *Canadian Drama* 10, no. 1 (1984): 56–64, Richard Perkyns compares Voaden's *Hill-Land* with Robertson Davies's satirical play about Susanna Moodie called *At My Heart's Core*.

28 *Earth Song* (Toronto: Playwrights Co-op 1976), 27. Further references are to this publication and are included parenthetically in the text.

29 See *Hill-Land*, in *Major Plays of the Canadian Theatre, 1934–1984*, ed. Richard Perkyns (Toronto: Irwin Publishing 1984), 25–63. In his *Toronto Globe* review, 'A Beautiful Play,' 14 Dec. 1934, 5, Mason writes of the Workshop performance of *Hill-Land* at the Central High School of Commerce, 13 and 14 Dec. 1934: 'The seemingly tragic story is given higher values of faith and courage so that death is swallowed up in victory, and a mood of exultation is induced which is rare in the modern theatre. This highly unusual drama was written for "a theatre of many voices," and the skill with which the author-producer has used drum, piano, off-stage singer and chorus, dancers, symbolic commentators, realistic actors, an allegorical death-figure, varied stage settings, and a continually changing investiture of living light with striking colour and shadow patterns, is beyond praise. The balanced blending of all these different elements is a remarkable achievement.'

30 *Murder Pattern*, in *Canada's Lost Plays* III, 100–17. In response to a critic's dislike of his expressionist method in the 1936 production of the play, Voaden wonders how a 'traditional concept of a play' could express the spirit of a northern landscape; *Canada's Lost Plays* III, 102. Further references are included in the text.

31 In 'Herman Voaden and the Test of Time,' *Canadian Theatre Review* 25 (Winter 1980): 95, Allan Field remarks that the 1936 production of *Murder Pattern* in which he performed achieved a 'thrill and electrifying response' from the audience. *Murder Pattern* was given a revival in Toronto, March 1987, by the George Brown College Theatre School, under the direction of Heinar Pillar. The production demonstrated clearly that the play has not dated and that the design, sets, and production style required for it are still able to challenge actors and designers and to move audiences.

32 In his as yet unpublished introduction to Voaden's *Dramatic Works*, Anton Wagner quotes several favourable reviews of the Hart House production.

33 'Ascend as the Sun' ts, 74

34 For a discussion of Voaden's *Emily Carr*, see Eva-Marie Kröller, 'Literary Versions of Emily Carr,' *Canadian Literature* 109 (Summer 1986): 87–98. Wagner also comments upon this and other of Voaden's post-1942 works in his introduction to *Dramatic Works*.

35 In *Emily Carr: A Biography* (Toronto: Oxford University Press 1979), 269–71, Maria Tippett discusses Dr Max Stern's discovery of Carr in 1944 and notes that he immediately recognized her affinities with Munch and some of the expressionists. Stern, who had left his native Germany in 1935, arranged a major exhibit of Carr at his Montreal Dominion Gallery for the fall of 1944. Since her death in 1945, Carr has received increasing attention, but few have recognized the essentially expressionist nature of her late painting. In an interview with me on 20 August 1986 the late Dr Stern stressed his view that Carr is expressionist and that she may have been influenced by Hodler and Munch. A comparison of Munch's landscapes, such as *Trolltrees in Fairytale Forest* (1899) or *Forest* (1903), with Carr's, such as *A Rushing Sea of Undergrowth* (1935) and *Sombreness Sunlit* (1937–40), illustrates the striking similarities between their works; not only is the subject-matter the same, but Carr's approach also has much in common with Munch's, especially in the handling of line and rhythm. That the conventional view of Carr's late work may be changing is suggested by the 1987–88 exhibition of North American expressionist landscape, Appelhof, et al.

36 In 'On the Edge: Michael Cook's Newfoundland Trilogy,' *Canadian Literature* 85 (Summer 1980), 23, 40, Brian Parker describes Cook's failure to convey the experience of environment, which is the subject of the plays. Where Cook succeeds, Parker says it is 'at some cost to the realism,' but in *Jacob's Wake*, for example, realism is properly displaced by symbolism and expressionism, a tendency that Cook's description of 'a stark skeletonized set' partially acknowledges. See *Jacob's Wake* (Vancouver: Talonbooks 1975), 9. For a discussion of Expressionism in Canadian theatre, see Sherrill Grace, 'The Expressionist

Legacy in Canadian Theatre: George Ryga and Robert Gurik,' *Canadian Literature* 118 (Autumn 1988): 17–58.
37 See, for example, Robert Kroetsch's remarks on the north in 'The Canadian Writer and the American Literary Tradition,' *English Quarterly* 4 (Summer 1971): 46–9.
38 See the comments made by Alexander M. Leggatt in 'Playwrights in a Landscape: The Changing Image of Rural Ontario,' *Theatre History in Canada* 1, no. 2 (1980): 140. For a well-informed and more sympathetic discussion of Voaden's plays, see Anton Wagner, 'Herman Voaden's "New Religion,"' *Theatre History in Canada* 6, no. 2 (1985): 187–201.

CHAPTER SIX: Djuna Barnes's *Nightwood*

1 *Nightwood*, intro. by T.S. Eliot (London: Faber and Faber 1936, 1958). All references are to the paperback edition.
2 In his biography, *Djuna: The Life and Times of Djuna Barnes* (New York: G.P. Putnam's 1983. repr. as *Djuna: The Formidable Miss Barnes* (University of Texas Press 1985), Andrew Field goes to some lengths to describe Barnes's style as 'grotesque ... not naturalistic' (33), but at a later point he insists that her vision is 'consistently Naturalistic' (146). Louis F. Kannenstine in *The Art of Djuna Barnes: Duality and Damnation* (New York: New York University Press 1977) makes some very useful comments about *Nightwood* and notes the 'expressionistic' qualities of *The Book of Repulsive Women*; however, his adoption of the term 'subjective-feminine' (108) for *Nightwood* is confusing at best; James B. Scott in *Djuna Barnes* (Boston: G.K. Hall 1976) calls the novel an '*apprehended* tableau' (106), which is vague, although it does suggest the highly pictorial quality of the text, and he wisely points out that to see it as surrealistic, as does Ulrich Weisstein in 'Beast, Doll and Woman: Djuna Barnes' Human Bestiary,' *Renascence*, 15 (Fall 1062): 3–11, is to make the novel too safe – in short, to tame it.
3 Hartley is, I think, central to an appreciation of expressionism in Barnes; in 'Becoming Intimate with the Bohemians,' *New York Morning Telegraph*, 14 Nov. 1916, she mentions Hartley, as she does again in 'Giving Advice on Life and Pictures,' also for the *Morning·Telegraph*, 25 Feb. 1917, where she remembers showing Mabel Dodge her own pictures in 1914 and, through Dodge, meeting Alfred Stieglitz. Barnes also did a sketch of Hartley (Field, *Djuna*, 62). In *Marsden Hartley* (New York: Whitney Museum of American Art and New York University Press 1980) Barbara Haskell argues convincingly that the first (up to the First World War) and final periods of his life were his best and most expressionist. By 1909 he had discovered Albert Pinkham Ryder, a key influence upon his 'Dark Landscapes' and possibly the inspiration for the name of the title character in Barnes's 1928 novel *Ryder*. By 1913, when he first visited Berlin, he knew Herwarth Walden and Kandinsky, whose *Über das Geistige in der Kunst* he had read in 1912. After his return to America in 1915, Hartley felt obliged to hide his love of all things German, and he entered a

period of weariness and withdrawal. In the twenties he vacillated, often condemning personal emotion in art, but in the thirties he was painting expressionistically once more. See *The Expressionist Landscape*, the exhibition catalogue for the 1987–88 show of North American modernist painting, where Hartley's work plays an especially strong role. For Hartley's influence upon Hart Crane, see Robert K. Martin, 'Painting and Primitivism: Hart Crane and the Development of an American Expressionist Esthetic,' *Mosaic* 14, no. 3 (1981): 49–62. According to Nicholas Joost, *Years of Transition: The Dial, 1912–1920* (Barre, Mass.: Barre Publishers 1967), 254, Barnes visited Walden's gallery during her time in Berlin.

4 Barnes praises the German theatre and cinema in 'Home Notes from Abroad,' an interview she gave to the *Greenwich Villager*, 11 Mar. 1922. One of the playbills in her papers at McKeldin Library, University of Maryland, for the Berlin Grosse Schauspielhaus contains an article by Kurt Pinthus, the expressionist theorist, on 'Das revolutionäre deutsche Drama.' However, Barnes did not read German well, so she would have had to rely on others to translate or explain. Her own later articles for the *Theater Guild Magazine* illustrate her ease with and knowledge of avant-garde theatre. One fine example is her article on 'Mordecai Gorelik,' *Theater Guild Magazine* (Feb. 1931): 42–5, illustrated with Gorelik's expressionistic designs for Andreev's *King Hunger*, Lawson's *Processional*, and for *The Golem*.

5 The portraits of Alice Rohrer, *Portrait of Alice* (1934), and Emily Coleman, *Madame Majeska* (ca 1935), are in the Barnes collection. In naming this portrait Barnes may have been making a punning reference to the bright ochre woman with blue hair on a red ground by Kees van Dongen called *Modjeska, Soprano Singer* (1908), or she may have been likening Coleman to the diva.

6 Both Thelma Wood and Barnes owned copies of Mayer's book *Expressionistische Miniaturen des deutschen Mittelalters* (Munich: Delphin Verlag 1918), and both copies are now in the Barnes collection.

7 Barnes acted and wrote for the Provincetown Players, both in Cape Cod and in Greenwich Village, where they opened their 1919 season with her one-acter *Three from the Earth*. She knew O'Neill, who admired her work, quite well and frequently wrote essays on the theatre for the *Theater Guild Magazine*, as well as doing the 'Playgoers' Almanac' from 1930 to 1931, for *Charm*, the *New York Morning Telegraph*, and so on. Her 'Portrait of Eugene O'Neill' in his sea-mother's son pose verges on caricature. Her friend and Provincetown associate, Alfred Kreymborg, published translations of plays by Wedekind and Andreev in magazines like *Glebe*, which he edited. Kreymborg was writing expressionistic plays before O'Neill (see chap. 3). For further biographical information, see Andrew Field's *Djuna* and Shari Benstock's *Women of the Left Bank: Paris, 1900–1940* (Austin: University of Texas Press 1986), 236–67.

8 I cannot accept Siegfried Kracauer's equation of tryanny, madness, and violence in the German silent film with a general social malaise and the rise of Nazism, but he does make some astute observations about the films themselves. For example, he notes that the post-war films were a kind of '*monologue*

intérieur' of the mind or soul and frequently used the double (*Doppelgänger*), vampires (or vampire-like figures), somnambulists, and fairground and circus settings (with emphatic circle imagery) to portray human obsessions and powerful instincts. See *From Caligari to Hitler: A Psychological History of the German Film* (Princeton, NJ: Princeton University Press 1947), and E.W. and M.M. Robson, *The Film Answers Back* (1939; New York: Arno Press 1972), 196–7, who describe the fair settings in all 'subjectivist' films, not only the German, as representative of chaos and human powerlessness. In 'Carnival of the Animals,' *Women's Review of Books* 1, no. 8 (Apr. 1984): 6–7, Jane Marcus argues that *Nightwood* should be seen as carnivalesque, combining many of the features of festival, transvestism and ritual that Bakhtin finds in Rabelais. The links among circuses, fairs, and the carnivalesque explored by Bakhtin shed interesting light on much expressionist literature (see chap. 1). See also Elizabeth Pochoda's 'Style's Hoax: A Reading of Djuna Barnes's *Nightwood*,' *Twentieth Century Literature* 22, no. 2 (1976): 179–91, for some interesting remarks on circle imagery and circus symbolism.

9 Walter H. Sokel, *The Writer in Extremis*, 118–19
10 See, for example, Wallace Fowlie's chapter on *Nightwood* in *Love in Literature: Studies in Symbolic Expression* (Freeport, NY: Books for Libraries Press 1965), 139–46, and Alan Williamson, 'The Divided Image: The Quest for Identity in the Works of Djuna Barnes,' *Critique: Studies in Modern Fiction* 7, no. 1 (Spring 1964): 58–74. Marcus's 'Carnival of the Animals' opens up a whole new way of looking at this theme.
11 Daubler is quoted by Patterson in *The Revolution in the German Theatre*, 56. For a translation of Brust's play, in which the frustrated heroine wants to be 'raped to death by a wolf,' see J.M. Ritchie and H.F. Garten, *Seven Expressionist Plays* (London: John Calder 1980).
12 Carol Duncan, 'Virility and Domination in Early Twentieth-Century Painting,' in *Feminism and Art History: Questioning the Litany*, ed. Norma Broude and Mary D. Garrard (New York: Harper & Row 1982), 309. I am grateful to my colleague Dr K Edgington for bringing this important book to my attention, and I refer to Duncan's excellent study in greater detail below.
13 Frederick S. Levine, *The Apocalyptic Vision*; see chap. 2. It should be noted as well that animals and animal imagery are consistently positive in Barnes's fiction, either as indicators of human betrayal and weakness or as symbols of freedom, power, and innocence; for example, in the stories 'A Night among the Horses,' 'A Night in the Woods,' 'No Man's Mare,' and 'The Rabbit,' and in the play 'To the Dogs.'
14 This sense of alienation and exile was typical of the so-called lost generation and widely shared by many modern artists. For an interesting commentary on the shape this took in the United States after the war and in conjunction with the rise of abstract expressionism, see Serge Guilbaut, *How New York Stole the Idea of Modern Art: Abstract Expressionism, Freedom, and the Cold War* (Chicago: University of Chicago Press 1984), 155–60.
15 See Eliot's introduction to *Nightwood*, Kannenstine's *The Art of Djuna*

Barnes, and Jack Hirschman's 'The Orchestrated Novel: A Study of Poetic Devices in the Novels of Djuna Barnes and Hermann Broch, and the Influence of the Works of James Joyce upon them,' PhD, Indiana 1961, 111ff, where he attempts to divide *Nightwood* into five acts, roughly analogous to classical tragedy.

16 Joseph Frank's discussion of spatial form in *Nightwood* in *The Widening Gyre: Crisis and Mastery in Modern Literature* (Bloomington: Indiana University Press 1963), 31. Frank's studies of spatial form were first published in 1945; he was perhaps the first to stress the non-naturalistic aspect of *Nightwood* and to link it with painting, specifically with Braque, the Fauves, and the cubists (28).

17 R.S. Furness, *Expressionism* (London: Methuen 1973), 18

18 Alan Singer, 'The Horse Who Knew Too Much: Metaphor and the Narrative of Discontinuity in *Nightwood*,' *Contemporary Literature* 25, no. 1 (Spring 1984): 72. Although Singer makes some valuable points about figurative language in *Nightwood* and its effects upon our concepts of genre and character, I cannot agree that the meaning of *Nightwood* should be reduced to the self-reflexive, at times parodic, process of its own production, or that the theme of tragic love and loss is 'banal.' Instead, the contingency and self-examining quality of the authorial imagination, the 'solipsistic darkness' of the characters, and the 'narcissistic isolation' caused by desire (all Singer's terms) affirm an expressionist reading and point directly to the problematic of the 'expressive fallacy.' Furthermore, where Singer rightly points out that Barnes's 'catachrestic metaphors' and 'disjunctive metaphors' 'nullify discriminations' (82) between narrative levels by refusing to situate an authoritative perspective within the story or outside it in an omniscient narrator, I would argue that this very conflation of inner and outer perspectives enacted by the text is essential to expressionism. So-called objective, authoritative, or conventional reality is shattered by the subversive figurative language of the text. Although Singer begins his study by taking Frank to task, they are, in fact, closer than Singer allows. Both stress the abstraction of the text (Frank's analogies with painting lead him to praise the 'autonomous structure' of the work of art and Singer goes further to privilege the linguistic abstraction, or productivity, of the text), and both dismiss the role of the human subject, the elements of representation, and the 'themes' of the novel, all of which provide a crucial balance for the abstracting power of the discourse. This tendency to underplay the representational and expressive qualities of *Nightwood* is reminiscent of the reception often given to Oskar Kokoschka's work, and Kokoschka strenuously protested all attempts to ignore the human subject in art.

19 See Julia Kristeva, 'From One Identity to An Other,' in *Desire in Language*, 124–47.

20 In addition to his own work with *transition*, founded by Jolas in 1927, he published work by many figures of the English and American avant-garde, including Barnes and several of her close acquaintances, and two monographs of note, *Revolution of the Word* (1929) and *The Language of Night* (The Hague: Servire Press 1932). Jolas reprinted his expressionistic manifesto from

Revolution in *The Language of Night, 33–4*. For his discussion of the expressionist and dadist attack on language, see 22–6. All further quotations are from this edition of *The Language of Night*.

21 Kristeva, *Desire in Language*, 140
22 Dorrit Cohn, 'Narrated Monologue,' 97–112
23 Each of these authors uses lengthy monologues within either a first- or third-person narrative point of view, but while they are always highly expressive of the speaker's inner turmoil, I am not suggesting that writers like Beckett or Faulkner are expressionists. There are other examples from German fiction that are expressionist, such as Carl Einstein's *Bebuquin* (1912), Robert Walser's *Jakob von Hoddis* (1909), or passages from Elias Canetti's *Auto da Fé* (1946), but whether or not Barnes knew of the first two of these novels is difficult to say. Both the title and the monologue form of *Die Nachtwachen* (1804–05) suggest that Barnes may have known of this proto-expressionist text, perhaps in the new 1916 edition, which caused some controversy and drew contemporary attention to the work. The sixteen discontinuous monologues present the nightwatchman Kreuzgang's chaotic perceptions of a world gone mad, where humans are reduced to manipulated puppets without purpose or meaning. Kreuzgang's misanthropic monologues, which become increasingly agonized as he drops his sardonic tone to reveal personal suffering, all take place at night, in a troubling night-world of the mind where nihilistic truths about the human condition – as Kreuzgang sees them – are more clearly revealed than during the conventionally controlled, deceptive conscious, or daytime, world. Kreuzgang is obsessed with two ideas: that life is a play and that everything is dead or dying. In a passage foreshadowing *From Morn to Midnight* he exclaims: 'Alles ist kalt und starr und rauh, und von dem Naturtorso sind die Glieder abgefallen, und er streckt nur noch seine versteinerten Stümpfe ohne die Kränze von Blüten und Blättern gegen den Himmel.' (Everything is cold and stiff and raw, and the limbs have dropped from the torso of nature, and it still stretches only its petrified stumps toward the sky without their garlands of blossoms and leaves.) *Die Nacht-wachen des Bonaventura*, ed. and trans. Gerald Gillespie (Edinburgh: Edinburgh University Press 1972), 158, 159. Although Kreuzgang speaks of himself as a 'Nachtwandler' (sleepwalker), his volubility bears comparison with O'Connor, not Robin. See Kannenstine's note on *Die Nachtwachen* in *The Art of Djuna Barnes*, 178.
24 Charles Baxter, 'A Self-consuming Light: *Nightwood* and the Crisis of Modernism,' *Journal of Modern Literature* 3, no. 5 (July 1974): 1175–87
25 Duncan, 'Virility and Domination,' in Broude and Garrard, eds., *Feminism and Art History*, 303. While Duncan's focus is not only upon expressionist painters, she does discuss their essentially misogynist views, and this aspect of the literature has been touched upon by Kellner in Bronner and Kellner, eds., *Passion and Rebellion*, 191–2, and discussed at some length by Peter Jelavich in 'Wedekind's *Spring Awakening*: The Path to Expressionist Drama,' also in *Passion and Rebellion*, 129–50. For a discussion of the identification of

Expressionism with the values of its male painters, see Alessandra Comini's 'Gender or Genius? The Women Artists of German Expressionism,' in Broude and Garrard, eds., *Feminism and Art History*, 270–91.

26 For example, in the expressionistic poem 'Suicide,' from *The Book of Repulsive Women*. The entire question of Barnes's feminism deserves careful attention because all her work, from *Repulsive Women* and *Ladies Almanack* to *The Antiphon*, is centred on women and their problems. Barnes could also joke about contemporary female stereotypes; see, for example, her 'Vampire Baby' sketch for *Vanity Fair* (July 1915).

27 Critical responses to Barnes tend to divide on precisely this point. Until recently critics have tended to see her depictions of women as negative, but Jane Marcus in 'Carnival of the Animals,' Susan Gubar in 'Blessings in Disguise: Cross-Dressing as Re-Dressing for Female Modernists,' *Massachusetts Review* 22, no. 3 (Autumn 1981): 477–508, and Sandra M. Gilbert in 'Costumes of the Mind: Transvestism as Metaphor in Modern Literature,' in *Writing and Sexual Difference*, ed. Elizabeth Abel (Brighton: Harvester Press 1982), 193–219, suggest new ways of reading *Nightwood* that permit us to see Barnes as celebrating a specifically matriarchal deity.

28 Quoted in Field, *Djuna*, 31, from 'Playgoers' Almanac,' *Theater Guild Magazine* (Jan. 1931)

29 Describing the female nudes of Kirchner, Munch, and Van Dongen as 'obedient animals' and the anxiety over male sexuality and its conflation with human creativity as the 'cult of the penis,' Duncan argues that the so-called liberated vanguard of modern art was, in an important way, extremely reactionary ('Virility and Domination,' 308). For a different reading of the expressionist position on this question, see Donald E. Gordon, *Expressionism: Art and Idea* (New Haven: Yale University Press 1987). On pages 7–8 Gordon considers the virulent prejudice against women in several influential books of the early twentieth century, such as Paul Julius Mobius's *On the Feeble-mindedness of Women* (1900) and Otto Weininger's *Sex and Character* (1903), but concludes that the expressionists resisted these views in favour of 'male-female equality' (8). He discusses sexual liberation, as he sees it, in specific works on pages 26–36.

CHAPTER SEVEN: Malcolm Lowry's *Under the Volcano*

1 In his introduction to the 1965 Lippincott edition of *Volcano*, Spender wrote that 'the most direct influence on this extraordinary book is not ... from other novelists, but from films ... The old, silent caption-accompanied movies – are felt throughout the novel' (xiii). For a discussion of the various screenplays of the novel, see 'The Sixty-Seventh Reading: Malcolm Lowry's Novel *Under the Volcano* and Its Screenplays,' *Proceedings of the London Conference on Malcolm Lowry, 1984*, ed. Gordon Bowker and Paul Tiessen (London and Waterloo, Ont.: University of London and Wilfrid Laurier University 1985), 45–61, by Wieland Schulz-Kiel, who co-produced, with Moritz Borman, the

film, and personally read sixty-two of the sixty-six screenplays written before the one by Guy Gallo that was chosen for the film. The directors who wanted to do *Volcano* include Luis Buñuel, Joseph Losey, and Ken Russell, and Gabriel García Márquez (on whom Lowry has had a profound influence) wrote a screenplay for the Mexican producer Luis Barranco.

2 The 455-page script of *Tender Is the Night* prepared by Malcolm and Margerie is held, with the vast majority of Lowry manuscripts and letters, in the Malcolm Lowry Collection of the University of British Columbia Library, Special Collections. For further information on the script see *Notes on a Screenplay for F. Scott Fitzgerald's Tender Is the Night* (Bloomfield Hills, Mich. and Columbia, SC: Bruccoli Clark 1976).

3 To provide authenticity for his brothel scene from chap. 12 of the novel, Huston imported real prostitutes from Mexico City. Such realism, however, supplants and displaces Lowry's far more important symbolic and visionary intentions. The American director David Lynch (*Elephant Man, Eraserhead, Blue Velvet*) would be a much more likely interpreter of *Volcano*.

4 *The Selected Letters of Malcolm Lowry*, ed. Harvey Breit and Margerie Bonner Lowry (Philadelphia and New York: J.B. Lippincott 1965), 80. All further references are included in the text.

5 For biographical information on Lowry, see Douglas Day' *Malcolm Lowry: A Biography* (New York: Oxford University Press 1973), Gordon Bowker, *Malcolm Lowry Remembered* (London: Ariel Books, British Broadcasting Corporation 1985), and Sheryl Salloum, *Malcolm Lowry: Vancouver Days* (Vancouver: Harbour Publishing 1987).

6 I have discussed Lowry's plans for the *Voyage* at length in *The Voyage That Never Ends: Malcolm Lowry's Fiction* (Vancouver: University of British Columbia Press 1982).

7 *Dark as the Grave* has received little serious critical attention, but see George Woodcock's 'Art as the Writer's Mirror: Literary Solipsism in *Dark as the Grave*,' in *Malcolm Lowry: The Man and His Work*, ed. George Woodcock (Vancouver: University of British Columbia Press 1971), 66–70, and my chapter on the novel in *The Voyage That Never Ends*. I would like to thank my graduate student Cynthia Sugars for the excellent insights into the text that she provides in her 1985 unpublished essay 'The Road to Renewal: An Analysis of *Dark as the Grave Wherein My Friend Is Laid*,' a revised version of which will appear in a critical book in preparation called *Swinging the Maelstrom: New Perspectives on Malcolm Lowry*, ed. Sherrill Grace.

8 For the influence of Maeterlinck on expressionists see Armin Arnold, *Prosa des Expressionismus*, 46. In his essay 'Foreign Influences on German Expressionist Prose,' in Weisstein, ed., *Expressionism as an International Literary Phenomenon*, 84–5, Arnold points out that Bang's novels and Jack London's supermen were popular with expressionists.

9 *Expressionism as an International Literary Phenomenon*, 23

10 *Selected Letters*, 68, 330. In *October Ferry to Gabriola* (1970), 61, Ethan insists that 'a novelist presents less of life the more closely he approaches what he thinks of as his realism.'

11 For a more detailed discussion of Lowry's aesthetics, see my article 'The Creative Process: An Introduction to Time and Space in Malcolm Lowry's Fiction,' *Studies in Canadian Literature* (Winter 1977): 61–8. Lowry was influenced, through Conrad Aiken, by Bergson, who had considerable impact upon Expressionism and Vorticism. Although Lowry does not appear to have been influenced by the English movement or by Wyndham Lewis, with whom he had much in common, he did know of Herbert Read's theories in the essays collected in *The Philosophy of Modern Art* (London: Faber and Faber 1952).

12 'Expressionism in Poland,' in Weisstein, ed., *Expressionism as an International Literary Phenomenon*, 301. Lipski offers many valuable insights into the nature of Expressionism and distinguishes it from symbolism in terms of its dualism, dynamism, and reverence for time.

13 *Expressionism as an International Literary Phenomenon*, 42

14 *Under the Volcano* (Harmondsworth, Middlesex: Penguin Modern Classics 1963), 362. Subsequent references to this edition are included in the text.

15 Lipski, 'Expressionism in Poland,' in Weisstein, ed., *Expressionism as an International Literary Phenomenon*, 301

16 Quoted and translated in Willett, *Expressionism*, 150. Arnold offers further examples in *Prosa des Expressionismus*.

17 'June the 30th, 1934,' *Psalms and Songs*, ed. Margerie Lowry (New York: Meridian, New American Library 1975), 48

18 In 'The Form of Carnival in *Under the Volcano*,' PMLA 92, no. 3 (May 1977): 481–9, Jonathan Arac describes *Volcano* as a Menippean satire, in the terms used by Bakhtin to characterize that genre. He pays particular attention to stylistic heterogeneity, threshold states, and carnival, and concludes that the text's carnival form makes it 'for all its copious variety, go round in one smooth circle in a carnival path of loss and return.' It seems to me, however, that *Volcano*'s ending cannot be so categorically situated in 'loss and return' and that, at most, the return of the Consul, within *Volcano*, like the novel's 'trochal' form, is an ambiguous metaphor.

19 Manuscript information makes it clear that the opening chapters of *Dark as the Grave* are a dream experienced by Sigbjørn. The editors' preparation of the text obscures this important point. See Grace, *The Voyage That Never Ends*, pages 64–6.

20 Lowry makes this remark in one of the two Mexican notebooks for *Under the Volcano*, with the *Volcano* mss in the Lowry collection.

21 See R.S. Furness, *Expressionism*, 18.

22 Sokel, *The Writer in Extremis*, 121

23 See my discussion in *The Voyage That Never Ends*, and see *Under the Volcano*, 198.

24 I discuss the novella in detail in '"An assembly of apparently incongrous parts": Intertextuality in Lowry's "Through the Panama,"' *Proceedings of the London Conference on Malcolm Lowry, 1984*, 135–64. For other discussions of Lowry's use of signs, see Richard Hauer Costa's 'The Grisly Graphics of Malcolm Lowry,' *Proceedings*, 98–106, and Paul Tiessen, 'Malcolm Lowry and the Cinema,' in Woodcock, ed., *Malcolm Lowry: The Man and His Work*,

133–43. In '*Under the Volcano*'s Colour Fields,' *Malcolm Lowry Review* 19–20 (1986–87): 82–102, Duncan Hadfield stresses the importance of the black / white opposition in the novel. This chiaroscuro (a possible echo of the black and white of early film) and the use of other strong colours intensifies the expressionist semiotics of the text.

25 *Lunar Caustic* (London: Jonathan Cape 1968), 36. Further references to this edition are included in the text.

26 The line is from the refrain to Oscar Wilde's poem 'The Ballad of Reading Gaol.'

27 Lowry collection, box 3:1, p 11

28 *October Ferry to Gabriola* (New York: World Publishing 1970) was edited by Margerie Lowry from Lowry's manuscript drafts and published posthumously. An examination of the manuscripts suggests that the published version does not represents Lowry's intentions very well. Nevertheless, it is clear that Ethan Llewellyn, the main protagonist, is more successful in his life's quest than was Geoffrey Firmin and that Lowry was striving for a more affirmative vision. Victor Doyen's discussion of the novel will appear as 'From Innocent Story to Charon's Boat: Reading the *October Ferry* MSS,' in *Swinging the Maelstrom*, (see n 7 above).

29 Lowry should be distinguished from Joyce and T.S. Eliot on this basis; his vision, at least in its expressionist qualities, is closer to that of D.H. Lawrence or Elias Canetti.

CHAPTER EIGHT: Sheila Watson's *Double Hook*

1 'What I'm Going To Do,' in *Sheila Watson: A Collection, Open Letter*, 3rd ser., no. 1 (Winter 1974–75), 183

2 The following works have been consulted for historical and topographical facts and for the stories that haunt the area: G.P.V. and Helen B. Akrigg, *Backroads of British Columbia* (Vancouver: Sunflower Books 1975); *The British Columbia Source Book*, ed. W.K. Cross, C.F. Gaulson, A.E. Loft (Victoria, BC: K.M. MacDonald, Queen's Printer, 1975); *Beautiful British Columbia's Cariboo* (Victoria, BC: Ministry of Tourism 1980). The Indians of the area are the Chilcotin, of the Athapascan language group, and during the early nineteenth century they were influenced by Roman Catholic missionaries. See Diamond Jenness, *Indians of Canada*, 7th edn. (Toronto and Buffalo: University of Toronto Press 1977).

3 'What I'm Going To Do,' 183

4 *The Double Hook* (Toronto: McClelland and Stewart 1959). All references are to this edition and are included in the text.

5 'What I'm Going To Do,' 183

6 These remarks come from an important interview, 'It's What You Say,' from *In Their Words: Interviews with Fourteen Canadian Writers*, Bruce Meyer and Brian O'Riordan (Toronto: Anansi 1984), 157–67. This interview is referred to parenthetically in the text as 'It's What You Say,' followed by the page

number. Watson does not remember when she wrote 'Deep Hollow Creek,' but evidence suggests either the late thirties or mid-forties. The short story 'Rough Answer' treats a young schoolteacher's disillusioning encounter with a rural community; it was published in *Canadian Forum* 18, no. 212 (1938): 178–80 under her maiden name Doherty. Watson provides valuable insights on her work in two other interviews: George Melynk's 'A Talk with Sheila Watson,' *Quill & Quire* (Sept. 1975): 14, where she describes her effort to create 'that emotional environment' operating on her characters' lives, and Daphne Marlatt's 'Interview / Sheila Watson,' *Capilano Review* 8–9 (1976): 351–60.

7 D.G. Jones, 'The Mythology of Identity: A Canadian Case,' in *Driving Home: A Dialogue Between Writers and Readers,* ed. Barbara Belyea and Estelle Dansereau (Waterloo, Ont.: Wilfrid Laurier University Press 1984), 54.

8 'Canada and Wyndham Lewis the Artist,' *Open Letter,* 95. This article was originally published in *Canadian Literature* 35 (Winter 1968): 44–61, and reprinted in *Wyndham Lewis in Canada,* ed. George Woodcock (Vancouver: University of British Columbia Press 1971), 60–77.

9 *Open Letter,* 184

10 Biographical information comes from my interview with Sheila Watson at McGill University in 1975, a further conversation with her in Vancouver on 5 Aug. 1986, and the interview 'It's What You Say.' In our 5 Aug. 1986 conversation Watson recalled seeing photographs of expressionist painting in Vancouver as early as 1930. In her extensive library she has *Three Plays by Ernst Barlach* (1964), one of her favourite artists, and the remarkable little Penguin paperback *Modern German Art;* the latter contains thirty-two plates, an introduction by Herbert Read, and a thorough discussion of the expressionists. 'Thoene' wrote the book in defiance of Hitler's 1937 'Degenerate Art' exhibit in Munich – hence his need for anonymity. She and her husband, the poet and playwright Wilfrid Watson, have a painting collection including works by Jack Shadbolt, Wyndham Lewis, and Emily Carr. During this conversation Watson also explained that in the geography of the novel, the community is located at Hat Creek, so that James's ride into Ashcroft (where there really was a parrot in the local hotel) would be possible within the time-frame of the action.

11 'Wyndham Lewis and Expressionism,' PhD, University of Toronto 1965, 382; referred to parenthetically in the text as Thesis, followed by the page number

12 Not until Charles Harrison's *English Art and Modernism, 1900–1939* (London and Bloomington, Ind.: Allen Lane and Indiana University Press 1981) does a scholar stress Lewis's expressionism. According to Harrison, Lewis's early drawings (1910–12) closely resemble contemporary German art and 'are unlike anything else' (77), and as a writer and painter his 'satirical modes are combined with expressionistic means' (76). Harrison concludes that 'Vorticism was in fact essentially an Expressionist movement' (111). Ulrich Weisstein, in 'Vorticism: Expressionism English Style,' *Expressionism as an International Literary Phenomenon,* and William C. Wees, in *Vorticism and the English*

Avant-Garde (Toronto: University of Toronto Press 1972), also see elements of expressionism in Lewis's work. Richard Cork, in *Vorticism and Abstract Art in the First Machine Age*, 2 vols. (London: Gordon Fraser 1976), dismisses the idea of much influence or similarity between Expressionism and Vorticism. See also Walter Michel, *Wyndham Lewis: Paintings and Drawings* (London: Thames & Hudson 1971), Hugh Kenner, *Wyndham Lewis* (Norfolk, Conn.: New Directions 1954), Fredric Jameson, *Fables of Aggression: Wyndham Lewis, the Modernist as Fascist* (Berkeley: University of California Press 1979), Jeffrey Meyers, ed., *Wyndham Lewis: A Revaluation* (Montreal: McGill-Queen's University Press 1980), and Jane Farrington, *Wyndham Lewis* (London: Lund Humphries 1980). For a contemporary evaluation of Vorticism, see Ezra Pound's *Gaudier-Brzeska: A Memoir* (New York: New Directions 1970), in which Pound repeatedly links Vorticism with Cubism and Expressionism and speaks of Futurism as 'accelerated Impressionism.' He also sees strong parallels between his own goals and those of Kandinsky in *Über das Geistige in der Kunst*.

13 Ulrich Weisstein, 'Vorticism,' in *Expressionism as a Literary Phenomenon*, 168

14 *Blast 2* (1915): 5–6. See Watson's discussion of Lewis's distinction in her thesis 'Wyndham Lewis and Expressionism,' 109.

15 Quoted by Wees, *Vorticism*, 162, from an advertisement in the *Spectator* 4485 (13 June 1914)

16 Hulme's key Worringer-inspired essay is 'Modern Art and Its Philosophy,' from *Speculations: Essays on Humanism and the Philosophy of Art*, ed. Herbert Read, frontispiece and foreword Jacob Epstein (London: Routledge & Kegan Paul 1924), 75–109. This essay, published posthumously (Hulme was killed at the front near Nieuport in 1917), was given as a lecture to the Quest Society in London on 22 Jan. 1914.

17 'Wyndham Lewis and Expressionism,' 118–19, and *Blast 2* (1915): 78

18 Differentiating between Vorticism and Expressionism, Weisstein writes that 'while soul states are manifestly present in Expressionist art, they are merely implied in its Vorticist counterpart. E. shows life in the raw ... whereas Vorticism seeks to absorb the machine [an image of transition from organism to mechanism] into the aesthetic consciousness' ('Vorticism,' in *Expressionism* 174). The phrase 'a patterned energy made visible' is Hugh Kenner's, from his discussion of the vortex in *The Pound Era* (Berkeley and Los Angeles: University of California Press 1971), 146.

19 In this 1927 speech in Munich, Worringer proclaimed that art was hopeless in this age of exhaustion. See 'Art Questions of the Day,' *Monthly Criterion* 6, no. 2 (Aug. 1927): 101–17.

20 In addition to the thesis and her remarks in 'Canada and Wyndham Lewis the Artist,' see also 'Unaccommodated Man,' *Open Letter*, 98–101, where she discusses Kurt Schwitters, whose *Merzbau* (actually his home in Hanover) was a totally collaged environment, and her 1982 preface to *West Window: The Selected Poetry of George Bowering* (Toronto: General Publishing 1982).

Watson is one of the very few scholars in Canada to speak easily of Expressionism and abstract expressionist art and to consider the slide between literature and fine arts a natural one.

21 Peter Selz locates the first use of the term in *Der Sturm X* (1919) in an article by the abstract painter Oswald Herzog called 'Der abstrakte Expressionismus.' See *German Expressionist Painting* (Berkeley: University of California Press 1957), 342.

22 Watson stresses the importance of this anti-mimetic, non-realist principle in 'What I'm Going To Do' and in her interview 'It's What You Say.'

23 In 'Symbolic Grotesque,' from her book *The Haunted Wilderness: The Gothic and Grotesque in Canadian Fiction* (Toronto: University of Toronto Press 1976), 88–94, Margot Northey speaks loosely of *The Double Hook* as 'gothic.' I am using the term, however, in Worringer's sense.

24 See Michael J. Hoffman, *The Development of Abstractionism in the Writings of Gertrude Stein* (Philadelphia: University of Philadelphia Press 1965). In 'Between One Cliché and Another: Language in *The Double Hook'* (see n 29 below), Barbara Godard offers a sophisticated discussion of text and language in the novel to date; see in particular her commentary on Watson's use of the words 'things' and 'glory.' I do not, however, agree with Godard that Stein influenced Watson's use of repetition; at most Stein helped to focus Watson's attention (as did other writers) on the challenges of language. For a structuralist analysis of Watson's prose, see Jan Marta (n 29) and for an excellent discussion of Watson's rhetoric, see Glenn Deer (n 29).

25 Quoted in Kenner, *The Pound Era*, 146

26 Kenner, *The Pound Era*, 507. The anthropologist Leo Frobenius (1873–1938) describes *paideuma* in his seven volume *Erlebte Erdteile*, and Kenner suggests that the concept validates the *Cantos*. It is a notion diametrically opposed to that of *Zeitgeist*. In 'Gertrude Stein: The Style is the Machine,' *Open Letter*, 170, Watson explains that there was 'nothing particularly revolutionary' in Stein's theory of style because the nineteenth-century German theorist, Konrad Fiedler, had already expounded a comparable theory. Watson concludes that 'each art moreover utters itself in its own form-language.'

27 Implicit throughout *Abstraktion und Einfühlung* is Worringer's belief that only abstraction in art is spiritually transcendent. Hulme went slightly further in his linking of abstraction with redemption. For Hulme, the extreme abstraction of geometric, as opposed to realistic, art signalled a change in world-view that he welcomed enthusiastically. See T.E. Hulme's Jan. 1914 lecture 'Modern Art and its Philosophy,' in *Speculations: Essays on Humanism and the Philosophy of Art*, and Weisstein's discussion of Worringer and Hulme in 'Vorticism,' 171–3. Kandinsky explicitly links abstraction with spiritual transcendence in his seminal monograph *Über das Geistige in der Kunst*.

28 'Wyndham Lewis and Expressionism,' 458, n 571. In 1924 Yvan Goll described Expressionism as 'an impotent man's fist clenched against the firmament in a fury,' quoted in Lionel Richard, *The Concise Encyclopedia of Expressionism*, 11.

29 See the following articles: Margaret Morriss, 'The Elements Transcended,'
   Canadian Literature 42 (Autumn 1969): 56–71; Leslie Monkman, 'Coyote as
   Trickster in *The Double Hook*,' *Canadian Literature* 52 (Spring 1972): 70–6;
   Beverley Mitchell, 'Association and Allusion in *The Double Hook*,' *Journal of
   Canadian Fiction* 2, no. 1 (Winter 1973): 63–9; Nancy J. Corbett, 'Closed
   Circle,' *Canadian Literature* 61 (Spring 1974): 46–53; Diane Bessai and David
   Jackel, 'Sheila Watson: A Biography,' *Figures in a Ground: Canadian Essays
   on Modern Literature Collected in Honour of Sheila Watson* (Saskatoon,
   Sask.: Western Producer Prairie Books 1978); Barbara Godard, 'Between One
   Cliché and Another: Language in *The Double Hook*,' *Studies in Canadian
   Literature* 3, no. 2 (Summer 1978): 149–65; Dawn Rae Downton, 'Messages
   and Messengers in *The Double Hook*,' *Studies in Canadian Literature* 4, no. 2
   (Summer 1979): 137–46; Jan Marta, 'Poetic Structures in the Prose Fiction of
   Sheila Watson,' *Essays in Canadian Writing* 17 (Spring 1980), 44–64; Steven
   Putzel, 'Under Coyote's Eye: Indian Tales in Sheila Watson's *The Double
   Hook*,' *Canadian Literature* 102 (Autumn 1984): 7–16; Stephen Scobie, *Sheila
   Watson and Her Works* (Toronto: ECW Press 1984); Helen Tiffin, 'The Word
   and the House: Colonial Motifs in *The Double Hook* and *The Cat and
   Shakespeare*,' *Literary Criterion* 20, no. 1 (1985): 204–26; George Bowering,
   Sheila Watson and The Double Hook (Ottawa: Golden Dog Press 1985), and
   Glenn Deer, 'Miracle, Mystery and Authority: ReReading *The Double Hook*,'
   Open Letter, 6th ser., no. 8 (1987): 25–43. See also discussions by John Moss
   in *Patterns of Isolation in English Canadian Fiction* (Toronto: McClelland and
   Stewart 1974), 166–88, and Margot Northey, *The Haunted Wilderness*, 88–94.
30 For a discussion of this figure, see Paul Radin, *The Trickster: A Study in
   Amerindian Indian Mythology* (London: Routledge and Kegan Paul 1976) and
   analyses of the Trickster in *The Double Hook* by Monkman ('Coyote as
   Trickster') and Putzel ('Under Coyote's Eye').
31 In 'What I'm Going To Do,' 183, Watson remarks: 'I don't know now, if I
   rewrote it, whether I would use the Coyote figure. It's a question. However, it
   begins with a dramatis personae, I suppose, and that is in the mouth of this
   figure who keeps making utterances all through the course of the novel.' In
   'Sheila Watson, Trickster,' *The Mask in Place: Essays on Fiction in North
   America* (Winnipeg, Man.: Turnstone Press 1982), 97–111, George Bowering
   argues that *The Double Hook* has important postmodernist features, one of
   which is the voice of Coyote. But see Steven Putzel's 'Under Coyote's Eye' for a
   good discussion of Watson's Trickster figure.
32 Weisstein, 'Vorticism,' 177
33 See Robert Kroetsch, *Essays*, ed. Frank Davey, *Open Letter*, 5th ser., no. 4
   (Spring 1983); Leslie Armour, *The Idea of Canada and the Crisis of Community* (Ottawa: Steel Rail 1981); Sherrill Grace, 'Duality and Series: Forms of the
   Canadian Imagination,' *Canadian Review of Comparative Literature* (Fall
   1980): 438–51; Eli Mandel, *Another Time* (Erin, Ont.: Press Porcepic 1977);
   and George Woodcock, *Odysseus Ever Returning: Essays on Canadian*

Writers and Writing (Toronto: McClelland and Stewart 1970), 190, and Stephen Scobie's discussion of *The Double Hook* in *Sheila Watson and Her Works.*

34 The parallels of Greta and James with Electra and Orestes and of the fortunes of the Potter household with the house of Agamemnon are merely suggestive, but according to the types in classical tragedy James can be seen as an *alazon*, Felix as the *eiron*, and Kip as the scapegoat (*pharmakos*) in the working-out of the community's *moira*, and, as I have suggested, Greta's suicide is reminiscent of *Elektra*.

35 That the female figures are all associated with the elements and that each is closely linked with a particular element is clearly demonstrated within the text: the link between Greta and fire is as obvious as that of Mrs Potter or Ara with water. I link Angel and Lenchen with the earth because of their active fertility (Lenchen, of course, conceives while lying on the earth) and the Widow Wagner with air because she constantly, although pointlessly, calls on God and because, according to Bettina Knapp, 'psychologically, air implies spiritual growth'; see *Theatre and Alchemy* (Detroit: Wayne State University Press 1980), 11. These analogies, however, should not be pressed too closely. Angela Bowering's book *Figures Cut in Sacred Ground: Illuminati in 'The Double Hook'* (Edmonton: NeWest Press 1988) appeared after my manuscript had gone to press. Her discussion of parallels between Watson's novel and classical literature and of female characters are especially interesting. As do I, she sees Mrs Potter as the central force of the text; see her discussion in chaps. 8 and 13.

36 Radin, *The Trickster*, ix. In his contribution to the book, part five, 'On the Psychology of Trickster,' Jung notes that Coyote is like Yahweh in his 'orgies of destruction' and his gradual 'development into a saviour' (196); he is also a 'collective shadow figure' (209). See also 'Trickster' in *Man, Myth and Magic: The Illustrated Encyclopedia of Mythology, Religion and the Unknown*, ed. Yvonne Deutch (New York: Marshall Cavendish 1983): 2881–5.

37 It has been suggested by Margaret Turner in 'Closure in the Works of Sheila Watson and Alice Munro,' a paper delivered at the Learned Societies of Canada Conference in 1986, that Watson uses language as a bulwark against an apocalypse that is seen as the collapse of language and communication. However, I believe Watson invokes apocalypse (cyclic destruction leading to rebirth) as *the articulation of* or *term for* disjunction and *différance*. Rather than restoring meaning through what Turner calls a forced harmony, Watson confronts and rejects regression (understood as the loss of language, art, mediating ritual) through the topos of apocalypse.

CHAPTER NINE: Ralph Ellison's *Invisible Man*

1 *Invisible Man* (New York: Signet Books, 1952), 497–8. All quotations are from this New American Library edition, and subsequent references are in the text.

Ellison began working on the novel in 1945, and the 'Battle Royal' chapter appeared as 'Invisible Man' in *Horizon* 23 (Oct. 1947): 104–7. It won the American National Book Award in 1953.

2 For a bibliography of Ellison studies up to 1971, see Jacqueline Covo, *The Blinking Eye: Ralph Waldo Emerson and His American, French, German and Italian Critics, 1952–1971* (Metuchen, NJ: Scarecrow Press 1974). Additional material can be found in 'A Selected Check List of Materials by and about Ralph Ellison,' compiled by Frank E. Moorer and Lugene Baily, *Black World* 20 (Dec. 1976): 126–30. See also John O'Brien, *Interviews with Black Writers* (New York: Liveright 1973), 62–77; John Hersey, *Ralph Ellison: A Collection of Critical Essays* (Englewood Cliffs, NJ: Prentice-Hall 1974); Ardner Cheshire, Jr, 'Invisible Man and the Life of Dialogue,' *CLA Journal* 20, no. 1 (Sept. 1976): 19–34; E.M. Kirst, 'A Langian Analysis of Blackness in Ralph Ellison's *Invisible Man*,' *Studies in Black American Literature* 7 (Spring 1976): 19–34; Kimberly Benston, 'Ellison, Baraka, and the Faces of Tradition,' *Boundary 2* 6 (Winter 1978): 333–54; Susan Blake, 'Ritual and Rationalization: Black Folklore in the Works of Ralph Ellison,' *PMLA* 94 (Jan. 1979): 121–36; Robert O'Meally, *The Craft of Ralph Ellison* (Cambridge, Mass.: Harvard University Press 1980); Berndt Ostendorf, *Black Literature in White America* (Sussex: Harvester Press 1982).

3 *Shadow and Act* (New York: Random House 1964), 178–9

4 See Lloyd Brown, 'The Deep Pit,' and Anthony West, 'Black Man's Burden,' in *Twentieth Century Interpretations of Invisible Man: A Collection of Critical Essays*, ed. John M. Reilly (Englewood Cliffs, NJ: Prentice-Hall 1970), 98, 102.

5 See Floyd R. Horowitz, 'Ralph Ellison's Modern Version of Brer Bear and Brer Rabbit,' and Therman O'Daniel, 'The Image of Man as Portrayed by Ralph Ellison,' in Reilly, *Twentieth Century Interpretations of Invisible Man*, 33, 89.

6 In 'On Initiation Rites and Power,' from *Going to the Territory* (New York: Random House 1986), 39, Ellison remarks that he found the same sensibility in jazz and *The Waste Land*. Many of the essays in *Going to the Territory* are important for the light they throw on Ellison's interests and his exposure to the arts at an early age. For example, in 'Remembering Richard Wright' he explains that he was familiar with the avant-garde music of Sergei Prokofiev while at Tuskegee because one of his teachers possessed several of the Russian composer's scores (200).

7 Ellison's essay 'The Art of Romare Beardon' was first published as the introduction to the exhibition catalogue *Romare Beardon: Paintings and Projections* (Art Gallery of the State University of New York at Albany 1968). It has been included in *Going to the Territory*. Beardon's collages have much in common with fauvist and expressionist colour and at times echo Kirchner's interiors (as in *Mamie Cole's Living Room*), but more often his technique is closer to that of the surrealists. For a brief discussion of his work, see Elsa Honig Fine, *The Afro-American Artist: A Search for Identity* (New York: Holt, Rinehart and Winston 1973), 156–8. When Ellison went to New York in 1936,

he intended to study sculpture with Richmond Barthé, who was well known in New York during the thirties and forties, and believed to be 'the leading black sculptor of the era,' according to David Driscoll in *Two Centuries of Black American Art* (New York: Alfred A. Knopf 1976), 69. Apart from slight echoes of Lehmbruck, Barthé's work is basically realist, but other black sculptors, like Barbara Chase and Selma Burke, were doing more avant-garde and expressionist work at that time.

8 *Collected Poems, 1909–1917* (London: Faber and Faber 1963), 24

9 For useful discussions of this debate, see Larry Neal, 'Ellison's Zoot Suit,' and George E. Kent, 'Ralph Ellison and the Afro-American Folk and Cultural Tradition,' in Hersey's *Ralph Ellison*, 58–79 and 160–70 respectively.

10 See in particular 'On Initiation Rites and Power,' *Going to the Territory*, 62–63. Ellison explains: 'In the very act of trying to create something, there is implicit a protest against the way things are.' Another important essay from this collection is 'The Novel as a Function of American Democracy,' 308–20.

11 Reilly, *Twentieth Century Interpretations of Invisible Man*, 8–9. Though he does not mention her work, the highly expressionist plays of Adrienne Kennedy are an excellent example of the mode used by a black American writer for reasons similar to Ellison's. See Kennedy's *Funnyhouse of a Negro* (1964), *The Owl Answers* (1966), and *A Beast's Story* (1969). For a discussion of her plays see Kimberly W. Benston, 'Cities in Bezique: Adrienne Kennedy's Expressionistic Vision,' CLA *Journal* 20, no. 2 (Dec. 1976): 235–44.

12 *The Landscape of Nightmare: Studies in the Contemporary American Novel* (New York: New York University Press 1965), 77

13 Ellison's remarks in 'The Art of Fiction' suggest that the naturalism, expressionism, and surrealism belong to roughly equal thirds of the novel, but it is neither possible nor even useful to try to categorize parts of the text in this procrustean way. What he has described are tendencies, not absolute distinctions that characterize parts of the text.

14 Hans Bellmer, a German surrealist (1902–75), constructed an almost life-size female doll in the thirties, which he used in so-called 'erotic researches' and for violently misogynistic images.

15 *The Selected Letters of Malcolm Lowry*, 315. The discussion of *Invisible Man* extends over three pages of a seven-page letter that Lowry wrote in May 1952 to his editor at Random House, Albert Erskine.

16 See R.W.B. Lewis's brief discussion of *Invisible Man* as apocalypse literature in *Trials of the Word: Essays in American Literature and the Humanistic Tradition* (New Haven & London: Yale University Press 1965), 218–20. Lewis sees Rinehart as 'the unmistakeable sign of the traditional loosening of Satan,' against which Ellison, like Nathaniel West, 'offers the counterforce of art.' However, it seems more accurate to say that where art is a deliberately offered counterforce to destruction in Ellison's novel, it provides little more than a way of representing chaos (whether in Tod Hackett's painting *The Burning of Los Angeles* or in the narrative of the novella) in *The Day of the Locust*.

CHAPTER TEN: From Modernism to Postmodernism

1 At his 4 Oct. 1923 concert at the Théâtre Champs Elysées, Antheil caused a riot, with Marcel Duchamp and Erik Satie arguing and shouting and the surrealists being arrested. See *Bad Boy of Music* by George Antheil (New York: Da Capo Press 1981), 7–8.

2 In *Cubism, Futurism and Constructivism* (London: Thames and Hudson 1974), 27, J.M. Nash remarks that Picasso's *Three Dancers* was 'also one of the masterpieces of Surrealism.'

3 Recent discussions about the nature of postmodernism and its complex relationship to modernity have served to remind us of the complexity and variety within modernism itself. See, for example, Andreas Huyssen, 'Mapping the Postmodern,' *New German Critique* 33 (Fall 1984): 5–52, repr. in *After the Great Divide: Modernism, Mass Culture, Postmodernism* (Bloomington and Indianapolis: Indiana University Press 1986). For another illuminating analysis of the scope and variety of modernism beyond the narrow parameters defined by a few major figures, see Shari Benstock, *Women of the Left Bank, Paris 1900–1940* (Austin: University of Texas Press 1986).

4 Guilbaut provides a revealing analysis of cultural, economic, and political manoeuvring in New York during the early years of the Cold War. The masterminds of American high modernist abstraction included Clement Greenberg, Alfred Barr, Harold Rosenberg, Frank O'Hara, and Leo Castelli. Increasingly during the fifties, according to Guilbaut, modern American art became representative of 'liberal American values' and was 'used as a powerful political instrument.' *How New York Stole the Idea of Modern Art*, trans. Arthur Goldhammer (Chicago: University of Chicago Press 1984), 5, 190.

5 Ihab Hassan, 'Postface 1982: Toward Postmodernism,' in *The Dismemberment of Orpheus* (Madison: University of Wisconsin 1982), 268. It is interesting to compare Hassan's list with the one Ortega drew up for *modern* art in his 1925 essay 'The Dehumanization of Art,' in *The Dehumanization of Art and Other Essays on Art, Culture and Literature* (Princeton, NJ: Princeton University Press 1968), 14: 'It tends (1) to dehumanize art, (2) to avoid living forms, (3) to see to it that the work of art is nothing but a work of art, (4) to consider art as play and nothing else, (5) to be essentially ironical, (6) to beware of sham and hence to aspire to scrupulous realization, (7) to regard art as a thing of no transcending consequence.' All references to Ortega are to this edition of his essays.

6 Irving Howe, 'The Idea of the Modern,' in Howe, ed., *The Idea of the Modern in Literature and the Arts* (New York: Horizon Press 1967), 29. See also Stephen Spender's conclusion to 'The Modern as Vision of the Whole': 'The idea of tradition as an explosive force, an unknown quantity almost, an apocalyptic mystery ... something disturbing and shocking, belongs to the early phase of modernism in poetry and fiction' (ibid., 58).

7 In *Under the Volcano* the Consul sees these words on a sign at key moments –

for example, in chap. 5, 132 – but Lowry used this warning on a separate page at the end of his novel; it translates: 'Do you like this garden which is yours? See that your children do not destroy it.'

8 'Of an apocalyptic tone,' 89
9 The neologism *différance* is a term coined by Jacques Derrida from the verbs 'to differ' and 'to defer,' and it signifies the supplementary play of meaning in words that prevents conceptual closure by deferring definition and activating, rather than resolving, difference, thereby resisting semantic reduction. As such, *différance* is a key element in the deconstructive process and thus in Derrida's theory of 'writing.' It signifies the potential dialogism and heterogeneity of language, of writing, and of texts. See *L'Ecriture et la différance* (1967).
10 *The Cannibal* (New York: New Directions 1949), with its deranged first-person narrator, apocalyptic vision of rebellion leading to a bizarre hope for rebirth, somnambulistic characters, and distorted Beckmann-like images, has closer affinities with expressionism than with the 'surrealism' that Albert Guerard suggests, 'for want of a better word,' in his introduction (xii). But the novel is an interesting case of a text that, because of its ironic tone and collapsing of history, might well be seen as a Neo-expressionist novel *avant la lettre*.
11 *The Landscape of Nightmare: Studies in the Contemporary American Novel* (New York: New York University Press 1965), 6, 15
12 See *Trials of the Word* (New Haven: Yale University Press 1965), 184–235. Various American critics trace these tendencies to the literature of the nineteenth century and earlier; see also Richard Chase, *The American Novel and Its Tradition* (New York: Doubleday 1957), and Raymond Olderman, *Beyond the Wasteland: The American Novel in the 1960's* (New Haven: Yale University Press 1972).
13 In 'Possessing the Land,' from *The Canadian Imagination: Dimensions of a Literary Culture*, ed. David Staines (Cambridge, Mass.: Harvard University Press 1977), George Woodcock describes Grove's early novel, *The Master Mason's House* (1906), as 'a late naturalist novel with expressionist overtones' (86). But Grove's later novel *The Master of the Mill*, first published in 1944, has many expressionistic touches and several echoes of Toller and of Lang's movie *Metropolis*. Speaking of Emily Carr and the Group of Seven, Northrop Frye comments upon their 'use of expressionist and fauve techniques' but fails to develop, indeed, miscontrues, their expressionism. See 'Sharing the Continent,' from *Divisions on a Ground: Essays on Canadian Culture* (Toronto: Anansi Press 1982), 60. Ondaatje's earlier *The Collected Works of Billy the Kid* (1970) also has expressionist moments, but it sits uneasily on a line between modernist sincerity and postmodernist irony. *Eldorado on Ice* was first published as *L'Eldorado dans les glaces* (1978).
14 William C. Reeve, 'Büchner's *Woyzeck* on the English-Canadian Stage,' *Theatre History in Canada* 8, no. 2 (1987): 174. In his article 'Büchner in Canada: *Woyzeck* and the Development of English-Canadian Theatre,' *Theatre History in Canada* 8, no. 2 (1987): 181–92, Jerry Wasserman traces the influ-

ence of the play through important productions by George Luscombe, John Herbert, Richard Rose, and Gordon McCall in the sixties, seventies, and early eighties. He explains that the play's appeal 'was grounded in documentary truth and so held special appeal for Canadians, whose unofficial national genre is the documentary. At the same time it offered up its truth in an expressionistic way, challenging the more conventional models of realism and naturalism' (184).

15 In 'Psychological Realist in a Bad Age,' *Time*, 14 Jan. 1985, 72, Robert Hughes observes that 'since one of the main facts of contemporary art is the resurgence of figurative expressionism, it seems ridiculous that the East should not see what ... amounts to the definitive exhibition of the man ... who was the greatest German painter of the 20th century.'

16 *Seattle Art Museum, Program Guide* (Winter 1986–87), 2.

17 See BERLINART, *1961–1987*, ed. Kynaston McShine (New York and Munich: Museum of Modern Art and Prestel-Verlag 1987).

18 *Camino Real* (New York: New Directions 1970), first produced in 1953, and *The Ecstasy of Rita Joe* (Vancouver: Talonbooks 1970), first produced in 1967, are complex explorations of North American society. Williams's play is highly allegorical, and its visionary ending threatens to render the entire action ridiculous and sentimental. Ryga's play, by contrast, is far more tightly controlled and overtly political. See Sherrill Grace, 'The Expressionist Legacy in the Canadian Theatre,' *Canadian Literature* 118 (Autumn 1988): 47–58.

19 For examples of work by these artists, see the catalogues listed in the Bibliography.

20 Among the chief artists considered to be neo-expressionists are, in the United States, David Salle and Julian Schnabel, and in Canada, Vicky Marshall, Brian Burnett, and Regine L'hériter. The American Fritz Scholder's work appears to be moving closer and closer to a parodic Neo-expressionism, largely through the influence of Francis Bacon.

21 Donald Kuspit's two-part study 'Acts of Aggression: German Painting Today,' first appeared in *Art in America* (Sept. 1982): 141–51, (Jan. 1983): 90–101, 131–5. It has been reprinted in his recent collection of essays, *The New Subjectivism: Art in the 1980's* (Ann Arbor, Mich.: UMI Research Press 1988). To be fair to Kuspit, it should be pointed out that he was not as enthusiastic about American painting as he was about the German; in 1981 he called the 'new (?) Expressionism' in the United States 'damaged goods.' See *The New Subjectivism*, 29–37.

22 'Flak from the "Radicals": The American Case Against Current German Painting,' *Expressions: New Art from Germany*, ed. Jack Cowart (Munich: St Louis Art Museum and Prestel-Verlag 1983), 43. I would like to thank my colleague Joel Kaplan for bringing this article to my attention. Further references are included in the text as 'Flak,' followed by the page number. Kuspit is replying to the diatribe on contemporary art by Benjamin H.D. Buchloh, called 'Figures of Authority, Ciphers of Regression: Notes on the Return of Representation in European Painting,' *October* 16 (1981): 39–68.

Buchloh attacks contemporary figural painting as regressive, nostalgic and complicit with resurgent fascism. He likens this art to the European art of the twenties and thirties, when leading artists, from Picasso on, abandoned avant-garde ideas for classical styles and tradition, both of which he appears to view as repressive forces. Although he touches on important issues, he does not argue convincingly, nor does he examine his own apparent privileging of non-iconic art. About one thing he is right, however; since 1980 Neo-expressionism has spread to North America.

23 'Reflections in Conclusion,' *Aesthetics and Politics* (London: NLB Press 1977), 196–213; hereafter cited as 'Reflections,' followed by the page number

24 In a 1984 interview with Henry Geldzahler, 'George Baselitz,' *Interview* (Apr. 1983), 83, Baselitz insists that, if an image 'stands on its head, it is delivered of all ballast, it is delivered from tradition.' In the same interview he denies any connection between his art and that of Expressionism. For thoughtful assessments of Baselitz, see Joel H. Kaplan, 'Rewrapping Lazarus: The Canadian Debut of Georg Baselitz,' *Issue* 2, no. 5 (May 1985): 31–3, a review of the major 1984–85 Baselitz exhibition at the Vancouver Art Gallery, and Kuspit's 1983 'The Archaic Self of Georg Baselitz,' in *The New Subjectivism*, 117–23.

25 In 'Answering the Question: What Is Postmodernism?' trans. Regis Durand, in *The Postmodern Condition: Report on Knowledge* (Minneapolis: University of Minnesota Press 1984), 71–82, Lyotard suggests that postmodernist art and literature, unlike modernist, attempt to present the unpresentable, or the sublime, through the act of presentation itself, and that this activity is a terroristic attempt 'to seize reality.' It seems clear that Lyotard prefers the abstraction of a Mondriaan and the pleasure of late modernism to the demotic parody and irreverence of postmodernism.

26 See Sherrill Grace, 'The "Paracinematic Lives" of *Gravity's Rainbow*,' *Modern Fiction Studies* 29, no. 4 (Winter 1983): 655–70, and ' "Dans le cristallin de nos yeux": *Neige noire, Caligari* and the Postmodern Film Frame-Up,' *New Comparison* 5 (Summer 1988): 89–103.

27 See *The World in a Frame: What We See in Films* (New York: Anchor Press / Doubleday, 1977), 44–57.

28 In 'Postmodernism and Consumer Society,' *The Anti-Aesthetic: Essays on Postmodern Culture*, ed. Hal Foster (Port Townsend, Wash.: Bay Press 1983), Jameson sees the predominant characteristics of postmodernism as pastiche in writing ('all that is left is to imitate dead styles, to speak through the masks and with the voices of the styles in the imaginary museum,' 115) and as schizophrenia in other spheres. In the burgeoning critical literature on postmodernism, the best places to begin are *The Anti-Aesthetic*, Lyotard's *The Postmodern Condition*, the articles and books by Huyssen and Hassan cited above in nn 2 and 4, Richard Rorty's comparison of 'Habermas and Lyotard on Postmodernity,' in *Praxis International* 4, no. 1 (1984): 32–43, Gerald Graff, *Literature against Itself: Literary Ideas in Modern Society* (Chicago: University of Chicago Press 1979), Charles Newman, *The Post-Modern Aura: The Act of Fiction in an Age of Inflation* (Evanston: Northwestern University Press

1985), and Arthur Kroker and David Cook, *The Postmodern Scene: Excremental Culture and Hyper-Aesthetics* (Montreal: New World Perspectives 1986).

29 *The New Subjectivism*, xvii

30 See Linda Hutcheon's discussion of parody in *Narcissistic Narrative: The Metafictional Paradox* (Waterloo, Ont.: Wilfrid Laurier University Press 1980), chap. 3.

31 See *Re-codings*, 35–48. According to Foster, Neo-expressionism 'satisfies [the capitalist demand for the irrational] in a coded, i.e., rational, manner. Like its subjectivism and primitivism, its "irrationality" is less an antagonist than an agent of the dominant order, which is simply to say that all these terms and values no longer exist in the same form or place, and that the "resolution" afforded them in expressionism cannot be adequate today' (48).

32 I discuss *Blue Velvet* in '"Dans le cristallin de nos yeux": *Neige noire*, *Caligari* and the Postmodern Film Frame-Up.' See also Pauline Kael's 'The Current Cinema,' *New Yorker* 22 (Sept. 1986): 99–103, and David Chute's 'Out to Lynch,' *Film Comment* 22, no. 5 (1986): 32–5, where Chute quotes Lynch as saying that the artist for whom he feels the greatest affinity is Kafka.

33 'Of an apocalyptic tone,' 94. Derrida's elaborate play on the word 'come' (*viens*), carries an added dimension in English, where it refers, colloquially, to orgasm. Certainly the orgasmic parallels with apocalypse do not escape either Aquin or Pynchon, who exploit the possibilites of 'coming' dramatically in the final episodes of *Hamlet's Twin* and *Gravity's Rainbow*.

34 'Postmodernism and Our Discontent,' *Socialist Review* 16, nos. 87–88 (May-Aug. 1986): 128

Select Bibliography

Complete bibliographical references to works by and about individual authors are provided in the notes to each chapter. This bibliography, therefore, is limited to selected primary texts and materials on German Expressionism, to general critical studies of use in preparing this book, and to exhibition catalogues. Materials dealing with contemporary literature and art, sometimes called Neo-expressionism, appear under Other.

EXPRESSIONISM

Aesthetics and Politics [Essays on Expressionism by Ernst Bloch, George Lukács, Bertolt Brecht, Walter Benjamin, and Theodor Adorno, with a conclusion by Fredric Jameson]. Ed. and trans. Ronald Taylor. London: NLB 1977

Allen, Roy F. *Literary Life in German Expressionism and the Berlin Circles.* Göppingen: A. Kümmerle 1974

– *German Expressionist Poetry.* Boston: Twayne 1979

Arnold, Armin. *Die Literatur des Expressionismus: Sprachliche und thematische Quellen.* Stuttgart: W. Kohlhammer Verlag 1966

– *Prosa des Expressionismus: Herkunft, Analyse, Inventar.* Stuttgart: W. Kohlhammer Verlag 1972

Anz, Thomas, and Michael Stark, eds. *Expressionismus: Manifeste und Dokumente zur deutschen Literatur 1910–1920.* Stuttgart: J.B. Metzler 1982

Bablet, Denis, and Jean Jacquot, eds. *L'Expressionisme dans le théâtre européen.* Paris: Editions du Centre National de la Recherche Scientifique 1971

Bahr, Hermann. *Expressionismus.* Munich: Delphin-Verlag 1920

Bassan, Raphaël. 'L'Expressionnisme: Un révélateur sociale.' *Revue du cinéma-image et son écran* 348 (1980): 131–3

Behne, Adolf. *Entartete Kunst*. Berlin: Carl Habel Verlag 1947
Benn, Gottfried. *Primal Vision: Selected Writings of Gottfried Benn*. Ed. E.B.
   Ashton. Norfolk, Conn.: New Directions by James Laughlin, 1960
Benson, Renate. *German Expressionist Drama: Ernst Toller and Georg Kaiser*.
   London: Macmillan 1984
Birren, Faber. *History of Color in Painting, with New Principles of Color
   Expression*. New York: Reinhold 1965
Bloch, Ernst. 'Diskussionen über Expressionismus.' *Erbschaft dieser Zeit*. Frank-
   furt: Suhrkamp Verlag 1962
Boudaille, Georges. *Expressionists*. Trans. I. Mark Paris. New York: Alpine Fine
   Arts 1981
Bronner, Stephen Eric, and Douglas Kellner, eds. *Passion and Rebellion: The
   Expressionist Heritage*. London: Croom Helm 1983
Büchner, Georg. *Danton's Death*. Trans. James Maxwell. London: Methuen 1979
Canetti, Elias. *Auto da Fé*. Trans. C.V. Wedgwood. London: Pan Books 1978
Dierick, A.P. 'Irony and Expressionism: An Examination of Some Short Narrative
   Prose,' *New German Studies* 7 (1979): 71–90
– *German Expressionist Prose: Theory and Practice*. Toronto: University of
   Toronto Press 1987
Döblin, Alfred. *Berlin Alexanderplatz: The Story of Franz B. Biberkopf*. Trans.
   Eugene Jolas. New York: Frederick Ungar 1968
Dube, Wolf Dieter. *Expressionists and Expressionism*. Trans. James Emmons.
   Geneva: Skira 1983
Edschmid, Kasimir. 'Über den dichterischen Expressionismus.' *Über den Expres-
   sionismus in der Literatur und die neue Dichtung*. Berlin: Reiss Verlag 1919
– *Lebendiger Expressionismus*. Munich: Verlag Kurt Desch 1961
Fauchereau, Serge. *Expressionisme, dada, surréalisme et autre ismes*. 2 vols.
   Paris: Denoël 1976
Furness, R.S. *Expressionism*. London: Methuen 1973
Gordon, Donald E. *Expressionism: Art and Idea*. New Haven and London: Yale
   University Press 1987
Hahl-Koch, Jelena, ed. *Arnold Schoenberg-Wassily Kandinsky: Letters, Pictures,
   and Documents*. Trans. John C. Crawford. London: Faber and Faber 1984
Hermand, Jost. 'Interdisziplinäre Zielrichtungen der Expressionismus-Forschung.'
   Michigan Germanic Studies 2, no. 2 (Fall 1976): 107–20
Hoffmann, Edith. *Kokoschka: Life and Work*. London: Faber and Faber 1947
Huder, Walther, ed. *Georg Kaiser: Stücke, Erzählungen, Aufsätze, Gedichte*.
   Cologne and Berlin: Verlag Kiepenheuer 1966
Kaes, Anton. *Expressionismus in Amerika: Rezeption und Innovation*. Tübingen:
   Max Niemeyer Verlag 1975
Kaiser, Georg. *Five Plays*. Trans. B.J. Kenworthy, Rex Last, J.M. Ritchie.
   London: Calder & Boyars 1971
Kandinsky, Vasily. *Concerning the Spiritual in Art and Painting in Particular,
   1912*. A version of the Sadleir translation with considerable re-translation by
   Francis Golffing, Michael Harrison, and Ferdinand Ostertag. New York:
   George Wittenborn 1963

Kayser, Wolfgang. *The Grotesque in Art and Literature.* Trans. Ulrich Weisstein. Bloomington: Indiana University Press 1963

Kokoschka, Oskar. *My Life.* Trans. David Britt. New York: Macmillan 1974

Kornfeld, Paul. 'Der beseelte und der psychologische Mensch.' *Das Junge Deutschland* (Berlin 1918): 1–13

Kraus, Karl. *The Last Days of Mankind: A Tragedy in 5 Acts.* Trans. Alexander Gode and Sue Ellen Wright, abr. and ed. Frederick Ungar. New York: Ungar 1974

Krispyn, Egbert. *Style and Society in German Literary Expressionism.* Gainesville: University of Florida Press 1964

Lange, Victor. 'Expressionism: A Topological Essay.' *Review of National Literatures* 9 (1978): 25–46

Lankheit, Klaus, ed. *The Blaue Reiter Almanac.* Ed. Vasily Kandinsky and Franz Marc, trans. Henning Falkenstein. New York: Viking Press 1974

Levine, Frederick S. 'An Example of Apocalyptic Regression in 1913 Expressionism.' *Michigan Germanic Studies* 2, no. 2 (Fall 1976): 133–48

– *The Apocalyptic Vision: The Art of Franz Marc as German Expressionism.* New York: Harper & Row 1979

Mann, Heinrich. *Man of Straw.* London: Hutchinson International Authors 1946

– *The Blue Angel.* New York: Frederick Ungar 1979

Marx, Henry. 'Expressionism in the Theatre.' *Michigan Germanic Studies* 2, no. 2 (1976): 183–95

Miesel, Victor H. *Voices of German Expressionism.* Englewood Cliffs, NJ: Prentice-Hall 1970

Nietzsche, Friedrich. *Thus Spoke Zarathustra.* Trans. R.J. Hollingdale. Harmondsworth: Penguin 1961

Ortega y Gasset, José. *The Dehumanization of Art and Other Essays on Art, Culture and Literature.* Trans. Helene Weyl. Princeton, NJ: Princeton University Press 1968

Paolucci, Anne. 'Benn, Pound and Eliot: Monologue Art of German Expressionism and Anglo-American Modernism.' *Review of National Literatures* 9 (1978): 10–24

Paolucci, Henry. 'Expressionism and the "Discontinuous Tradition": A Bibliographical Spectrum.' *Review of National Literatures* 9 (1978): 101–50

Patterson, Michael. *The Revolution in German Theatre 1900–1933.* Boston, London: Routledge & Kegan Paul 1981

Pausch, Holger, and Ernest Reinhold, eds. *Georg Kaiser.* Berlin and Darmstadt: Agora Verlag 1980

Perkins, Geoffrey. *Contemporary Theory of Expressionism.* Bern and Frankfurt: Herbert Lang 1974

Pickar, Gertrud Bauer, and Karl Eugene Webb. *Expressionism Reconsidered: Relationships and Affinities.* Munich: William Fink Verlag 1979

Pinthus, Kurt. *Das Kinobuch.* Zurich: Verlag Die Arche 1963

Platt, Susan Noyes. *Modernism in the 1920's: Interpretations of Modern Art in New York from Expressionism to Constructivism.* Ann Arbor, Mich.: UMI Research Press 1985

Raabe, Paul, ed. *The Era of German Expressionism*. Trans. J.M. Ritchie.
Woodstock, NY: Overlook Press 1974
– 'On the Rediscovery of Expressionism as a European Movement.' *Michigan
Germanic Studies* 2, no. 2 (Fall 1976): 196–210
Richard, Lionel. *The Concise Encyclopedia of Expressionism*. Trans. Stephen
Tint. Secaucus, NJ: Chartwell Books 1978
Ritchie, J.M. *Gottfried Benn: The Unreconstructed Expressionist*. London:
Oswald Wolf 1972
– ed. *Seven Expressionist Plays: Kokoschka to Barlach*. Trans. J.M. Ritchie and
H.F. Garten. London: John Calder 1980
Ritchie, J.M., and R.W. Last. 'Expressionist Drama in English: A Bibliography.'
New German Studies 6 (1978): 59–70
Roeder, George Holzshu, Jr. *Forum of Uncertainty: Confrontations with Modern
Painting in Twentieth-Century American Thought*. Ann Arbor, Mich.: UMI
Research Press 1978
Roh, Franz. *'Entartete' Kunst: Kunstbarbarei im Dritten Reich*. Hannover:
Fackelträger-Verlag Schmidt-Küster GMBH 1962
Roters, Eberhard, et al. *Berlin 1910–1933*. Trans. Marguerite Mounier. New
York: Rizzoli 1982
Rothe, Wolfgang, ed. *Expressionismus als Literatur: Gesammelte Studien*. Bern
and Munich: A. Francke Verlag 1969
– *Tänzer und Täter: Gestalten des Expressionismus*. Frankfurt am Main: Vittorio
Klostermann 1979
Samuel, Richard, and R. Hinton Thomas. *Expressionism in German Life,
Literature and the Theatre 1910–1924*. 1939; Philadelphia: Albert Saifer 1971
Scheffauer, Herman George. *The New Vision in the German Arts*. 1924; London:
Kennikat Press 1971
Seidler, Ingo. 'Art & Power: An Expressionist Dilemma and Gottfried Benn's
"Solutions."' *Michigan Germanic Studies* 2, no. 2 (1976): 169–82
Selz, Peter. *German Expressionist Painting*. Rev. edn. Berkeley: University of
California Press 1973
Short, Robert. *Dada & Surrealism*. London: Octopus Books 1980
Sokel, Walter H. *The Writer in Extremis: Expressionism in 20th Century German
Literature*. Stanford, Calif.: Stanford University Press 1959
– ed. *Anthology of German Expressionist Drama: A Prelude to the Absurd*.
Ithaca and London: Cornell University Press 1984
Stephen, W.G. 'Expressionism in Modern Drama.' *Vancouver Little Mountain
News* 3, no. 7 (Apr. 1928)
Stramm, August. *Das Werk*. Ed. René Radrizani. Wiesbaden: Limes Verlag 1963
Styan, J.L. *Modern Drama in Theory and Practice*. Vol. 3, *Expressionism and
Epic Theatre*. Cambridge: Cambridge University Press 1981
Thoene, Peter [pseud.]. *Modern German Art*. Trans. Charles Fullman; intro.
Herbert Read. Harmondsworth: Penguin Books 1938
Toller, Ernst. *Seven Plays*. London: John Lane, Bodley Head 1935

– 'My Words.' Trans. Marketa Goetz. *The Tulane Drama Review* 3, no. 3 (Mar. 1959): 99–106

Valgemae, Mardi. *Accelerated Grimace: Expressionism in the American Drama of the 1920s*. Carbondale: Southern Illinois University Press 1972

Vergo, Peter. *The Blue Rider*. New York: E.P. Dutton 1977

Walser, Robert. *Jakob von Gunten*. Trans. Christopher Middleton. New York: Vintage Books 1983

Wedekind, Frank. *The Lulu Plays & Other Sex Tragedies*. Trans. Stephen Spender. London: John Calder 1977

– *Frühlings Erwachen: Eine Kindertragödie* und *Der Marquis von Keith: Schauspiel*. Munich: Wilhelm Goldmann Verlag 1982

Weisstein, Ulrich, ed. *Expressionism as an International Literary Phenomenon: 21 Essays and a Bibliography*. Paris and Budapest: Didier & Akademiai Kiado 1973

Wellwarth, George E., ed. *German Drama between the Wars: An Anthology of Plays*. New York: E.P. Dutton 1974

Werenskiold, Marit. *The Concept of Expressionism: Origin and Metamorphosis*. Oslo, Bergen, Stavanger, Tromsø: Universitetsforlaget 1984

Werfel, Franz. *Franz Werfel, 1890–1945*. Ed. Lore B. Foltin. Pittsburgh: University of Pittsburgh Press 1961.

Willett, John. *Expressionism*. New York: McGraw-Hill 1970

– *Art & Politics in the Weimar Period: The New Sobriety, 1917–1933*. New York: Pantheon 1978

– *The Weimar Years: A Culture Cut Short*. London: Thames & Hudson 1984

Worringer, Wilhelm. *Abstraction and Empathy: A Contribution to the Psychology of Style*. Trans. Michael Bullock. London: Routledge & Kegan Paul 1953

– *Form in Gothic*. Trans. Herbert Read. London: Alec Tiranti 1957

CRITICISM AND GENERAL STUDIES

Altieri, Charles. 'Abstraction as Act: Modernist Poetry in Relation to Painting.' *Dada/Surrealism* 10/11 (1982): 106–34

Arnheim, Rudolf. *Visual Thinking*. Berkeley: University of California Press 1969

Bablet, Denis. *The Theatre of Edward Gordon Craig*. Trans. Daphne Woodward. London: Eyre Methuen 1981

Bakhtin, Mikhail. *The Dialogic Imagination: Four Essays*. Trans. Caryl Emerson; ed. Michael Holquist. Austin, Texas: University of Texas Press 1981

– *Problems of Dostoevsky's Poetics*. Ed. and trans. Caryl Emerson; intro. Wayne Booth. Minneapolis: University of Minnesota Press 1984

Banta, Martha. *Failure and Success in America: A Literary Debate*. Princeton, NJ: Princeton University Press 1978

Baumgarten, Murray. 'From Realism to Expressionism: Toward a History of the Novel.' *New Literary History* 6 (1974–75): 415–27

Bigsby, C.W.W. *A Critical Introduction to Twentieth-Century American Drama I: 1900–1940*. Cambridge: Cambridge University Press 1982

Bletter, Rosemarie Haag. 'Paul Scheerbart and Expressionist Architecture.' *VIA* 8 (1986): 126–35

Bourassa, André-G. *Surréalisme et littérature québécoise: Histoire d'une révolution culturelle*. Montréal: Les Herbes Rouges 1986

Braudy, Leo. *The World in a Frame: What We See in Films*. New York: Anchor Press/Doubleday 1977

Brenner, Hildegard. *Die Kunstpolitik des Nationalsozialismus*. Reinbek: Rowohlt Taschenbuch Verlag GmbH 1963

Broude, Norma, and Mary D. Garrard. *Feminism and Art History: Questioning the Litany*. New York: Harper & Row 1982

Canetti, Elias. *The Tongue Set Free: Remembrance of a European Childhood*. Trans. Joachim Neugraschel. New York: Farrar, Strauss & Giroux 1979

– *The Torch in My Ear*. Trans. Joachim Neugraschel. New York: Farrar, Strauss & Giroux 1982

Cheney, Sheldon. *A Primer of Modern Art*. 1924; 13th edn, New York: Liveright 1958

– *Stage Decoration*. New York: Benjamin Blom 1928

Cohn, Dorrit. 'Narrated Monologue: Definition of a Fictional Style.' *Comparative Literature* 18 (1966): 97–112. Repr. in *Transparent Minds: Narrative Modes for Presenting Consciousness in Fiction*. Princeton, NJ: Princeton University Press 1978

Comfort, Charles F. 'The Painter and His Model.' In *Open House*, ed. William H. Deacon and Wilfrid Reeves. Ottawa: Graphic 1931. Repr. in *Documents in Canadian Art*, ed. Douglas Fetherling. Peterborough: Broadview Press 1987, 76–9

Cork, Richard. *Vorticism and Abstract Art in the First Machine Age*. 2 vols. London: Gordon Fraser 1976

Craig, Edward Gordon. *On the Art of the Theatre*. 1911; London: Heinemann 1914

– *Towards a New Theatre*. 1913; New York: Benjamin Blom 1969

Dahlström, Carl. *Strindberg's Dramatic Expressionism*. Ann Arbor: University of Michigan Press 1930

Derrida, Jacques. 'Of an Apocalyptic Tone Recently Adopted in Philosophy.' Trans. John P. Leavey. *Semeia* 23 (1982): 63–97

Eggum, Arne. *Edvard Munch: Paintings, Sketches and Studies*. Trans. Ragnar Christophersen. London: Thames & Hudson 1984

Eisner, Lotte H. *The Haunted Screen: Expressionism in the German Cinema and the Influence of Max Reinhardt*. Berkeley: University of California Press 1969

Eliot, T.S. *The Three Voices of Poetry*. Cambridge: Cambridge University Press 1953

Fabricius, Johannes. *The Unconscious and Mr. Eliot: A Study in Expressionism*. Copenhagen: Nyt Nordisk Forlag 1967

Flint, R.W., ed. *Marinetti: Selected Writings*. Trans. R.W. Flint and Arthur A. Coppotelli. London: Secker & Warburg 1972

Frenzel, Ivo. 'Prophet, Pioneer, Seducer: Friedrich Nietzsche's Influence on Art,
    Literature and Philosophy in Germany.' In *German Art in the 20th Century*.
    Munich and London: Prestel-Verlag 1985, 73–81
Fuller, Peter. *Art and Psychoanalysis*. London: Writers and Readers 1980
Gombrich, E.H. *Art and Illusion: A Study in the Psychology of Pictorial Represen-
    tations*. Princeton, NJ: Princeton University Press 1960
Grosshans, Henry. *Hitler and the Artists*. New York and London: Holmes &
    Meier 1983
Guilbaut, Serge. *How New York Stole the Idea of Modern Art: Abstract
    Expressionism, Freedom, and the Cold War*. Trans. Arthur Goldhammer.
    Chicago: University of Chicago Press 1983
Harrison, Charles. *English Art and Modernism, 1900–1939*. London and Bloom-
    ington: Allen Lane and Indiana University Press 1981
Haskell, Barbara. *Marsden Hartley*. New York: Whitney Museum of American
    Art and New York University Press 1980
Hoffman, Michael J. *The Development of Abstractionism in the Writings of
    Gertrude Stein*. Philadelphia: University of Philadelphia Press 1965
Hughes, Glenn. *The Story of the Theatre*. New York. Samuel French 1928
Hulme, T.E. 'Modern Art and Its Philosophy.' In *Speculations: Essays on
    Humanism and Its Philosophy of Art*, ed. Herbert Read; frontispiece and
    foreword Jacob Epstein. London: Routledge & Kegan Paul 1924
Hutcheon, Linda. *Narcissistic Narrative: The Metafictional Paradox*. Waterloo,
    Ont.: Wilfrid Laurier University Press 1980
Innes, Christopher. *Holy Theatre*. Cambridge: Cambridge University Press 1981
– *Edward Gordon Craig*. Cambridge: Cambridge University Press 1983
Isaak, Jo Anna. *The Ruin of Representation in Modernist Art and Texts*. Ann
    Arbor, Mich.: UMI Research Press 1986
Jakobson, Roman. 'The Metaphoric and Metonymic Poles.' In Jakobson and
    Morris Halle, *Fundamentals of Language*. The Hague: Mouton 1956, 76–82
Jameson, Fredric. *Fables of Aggression: Wyndham Lewis, the Modernist as
    Fascist*. Berkeley, Los Angeles, London: University of California Press 1979
Jean, Marcel, ed. *The Autobiography of Surrealism*. New York: Viking Press 1980
Jolas, Eugene. *The Language of Night*. Transition series 1. The Hague: Servire
    Press 1932
Jonas, Ilsedore. 'The Shattered Image: Rilke's Reaction to the Artists of Expres-
    sionism and to Some Works of Picasso.' *Michigan Germanic Studies* 2, no. 2
    (Fall 1976): 121–32
Kenner, Hugh. *The Pound Era*. Berkeley and Los Angeles: University of Califor-
    nia Press 1971
Kracauer, Siegfried. *From Caligari to Hitler: A Psychological History of the
    German Film*. Princeton, NJ: Princeton University Press 1947
Kristeva, Julia. *Desire in Language: A Semiotic Approach to Literature and Art*.
    Trans. Thomas Gora, Alice Jardine, Leon S. Roudiez; ed. Leon S. Roudiez.
    New York: Columbia University Press 1980
Lewicki, Zbigniew. *The Bang and The Whimper: Apocalypse and Entropy in
    American Literature*. London: Greenwood Press 1984

Lewis, Wyndham. *Wyndham Lewis: Collected Plays and Poems*. Ed. Alan Munton, intro. C.H. Sisson. Manchester: Carcanet New Press 1979

Lodge, David. *The Modes of Modern Writing: Metaphor, Metonymy, and the Typology of Modern Literature*. Ithaca, NY: Cornell University Press 1977

Macgowan, Kenneth. *Continental Stagecraft*. Illus. Robert Edmond Jones. New York: Benjamin Blom 1964

Manvell, Roger, and Heinrich Fraenkel. *The German Cinema*. London: Dent 1971

Martin, Robert K. 'Painting and Primitivism: Hart Crane and the Development of an American Expressionist Esthetic.' *Mosaic* 14, no. 3 (1981): 49–62

Mitchell, Breon. 'W.H. Auden and Christopher Isherwood: The "German Influence."' In *Oxford German Studies*, ed. T.J. Read. Oxford: Clarendon Press 1966, 163–72

Mosse, George L. 'Bookburning and the Betrayal of German Intellectuals.' *New German Critique* 31 (Winter 1984): 143–55

Mueller-Mehlis, Reinhard. *Die Kunst im Dritten Reich*. Munich: Wilhelm Heyne Verlag 1976

Nash, J.M. *Cubism, Futurism and Constructivism*. London: Thames and Hudson 1974

Nelson, Raymond S. *Hemingway: Expressionist Artist*. Ames: Iowa State University Press 1979

Osborne, Harold. *Abstraction and Artifice in Twentieth-Century Art*. Oxford: Clarendon 1979

Ott, Frederick W. *The Films of Fritz Lang*. Secaucus, NJ: Citadel Press 1979

Pool, Phoebe. *Impressionism*. London: Thames and Hudson 1967

Poor, Harold L. *Kurt Tucholsky and the Ordeal of Germany, 1914–1935*. New York: Charles Scribner's Sons 1968

Robinson, Douglas. *American Apocalypses: The Image of the End of the World in American Literature*. Baltimore: Johns Hopkins University Press 1985

Robson, E.W., and M.M. Robson. *The Film Answers Back*. New York: Arno Press 1972

Ryan, Judith. 'Kunst und Kriminalität: Siegfried Lenz' Retrospective on Expressionism.' In *Expressionism Reconsidered: Relationships and Affinities*, ed. Gertrud Bauer Pickar and Karl Eugene Webb. Munich: Wilhelm Fink Verlag 1979, 35–41

Schmied, Wieland. 'Points of Departure and Transformation in German Art, 1905–1985.' *German Art in the Twentieth Century: Painting and Sculpture, 1905–1985*. Munich and London: Prestel-Verlag 1985, 21–74

Scobie, Stephen. 'Gadje Beri Bimba: The Problem of Abstraction in Poetry.' *Canadian Literature* 97 (Summer 1983): 75–92

Shapiro, Theda. *Painters and Politics: The European Avant-garde and Society, 1900–1925*. New York: Elsevier Scientific 1976

Steiner, Wendy. *Exact Resemblance to Exact Resemblance: The Literary Portraiture of Gertrude Stein*. New Haven and London: Yale University Press 1978

- *The Colors of Rhetoric: Problems in the Relation between Modern Literature and Painting.* Chicago: University of Chicago Press 1982
Stewart, Jack F. 'Expressionism in *The Rainbow.*' *Novel* 13, no. 3 (1980): 296–315
- 'Expressionism in "The Prussian Officer."' *D.H. Lawrence Review* 16, nos. 2–3 (1985–86): 275–89
Strindberg, August. *Strindberg: Five Plays.* Trans. Harry G. Carlson. New York: New American Library 1981
Todorov, Tzvetan. *The Poetics of Prose.* Trans. Richard Howard. Ithaca, NY: Cornell University Press 1977
- *Mikhail Bakhtin: The Dialogical Principle.* Trans. Wlad Godzich. Minneapolis: University of Minnesota Press 1984
Wees, William C. *Vorticism and the English Avant-Garde.* Toronto: University of Toronto Press 1972
Wulf, Joseph, ed. *Die Bildenden Künste im Dritten Reich: eine Dokumentation.* Gütersloh: S. Mohn 1963

EXHIBITION CATALOGUES AND ILLUSTRATED MONOGRAPHS

A Distant Harmony: Comparisons in the Painting of Canada and the United States of America. Catalogue and text by Ann Davis. Winnipeg Art Gallery 1982
An alle Künstler! War – Revolution – Weimar. Exhibition and catalogue essays by Ida Katherine Rigby, with works from the Robert Gore Rifkind Foundation Collection. San Diego, Calif.: San Diego State University Press 1983
An International Survey of Recent Painting and Sculpture. Exhibition catalogue by Kenaston McShine for the Museum of Modern Art. New York: Museum of Modern Art 1984
BERLINART, *1961–1987.* Ed. Kenaston McShine. New York and Munich: Museum of Modern Art and Prestel-Verlag 1987
Brücke-Museum: Katalog der Gemälde, Glasfenster und Skulpturen. Berlin: Bruder Hartmann 1983
Bruno Bobak, Selected Works 1943–1980. Exhibition catalogue for Sir George Williams Art Galleries, with text by Donald F.P. Andrus. Montreal 1982
Busignani, Alberto. *Pollack.* London: Hamlyn 1974
Carey, Frances, and Antony Griffiths. *The Print in Germany, 1880–1933: The Age of Expressionism.* New York: Harper & Row 1984
'Den globale dialog: primitiv og moderne kunst.' *Louisiana Revy* 26, no. 3 (May 1986)
Deutscher Expressionismus: German Expressionism, towards a New Humanism. Catalogue and text by Peter W. Guenther. Sarah Campbell Blaffer Gallery, University of Houston 1977
Die Aktion: Sprachrohr der expressionistischen Kunst. Eine Ausstellung des Städtischen Kunstmuseums Bonn. Cologne: Verlagshaus Wienand 1984
Doris Caesar, Chaim Gross, Karl Knaths, Abraham Rattner: Four American

Expressionists. Exhibition catalogue from the Whitney Museum of American Art. New York: Frederick A. Praeger 1959

Edvard Munch. Exhibition catalogue with essays by Jo-Anne Birnie Danzker, Arne Eggum, and Gerd Woll. Oslo and Vancouver: Munch Museet and Vancouver Art Gallery 1986

Erich Heckel: Paintings, Watercolours, Drawings, Graphics. Ottawa: National Gallery of Canada 1971–72

Ernst Ludwig Kirchner: Zeichnungen und Pastelle. Ed. Roman Norman Ketterer, Wolfgang Henze, Claus Zoege von Manteuffel. Stuttgart: Belser 1979

Expressionism: A German Intuition 1905–1920. New York: Guggenheim Foundation 1980

Expressionism: The Buchheim Collection. Trans. Norbert Messler and William Walker. Munich: Buchheim Verlag Feldafing 1983

Expressionist Landscape, The: North American Modernist Painting, 1920–1947. Exhibition and catalogue organized by Ruth Stevens Appelhof et al. Birmingham, Ala.: Birmingham Museum of Art 1988

Expressions: New Art from Germany. Ed. Jack Cowart. Munich: Prestel-Verlag 1983

Farrington, Jane. Wyndham Lewis. London: Lund Humphries 1980

Fritz Scholder. Texts by Scholder, Joshua Taylor, William Peterson, R. Andrew Maass, and Rudy H. Turk. New York: Rizzoli 1982

Georg Baselitz. Exhibition catalogue prepared by Jo-Anne Birnie Danzker. Vancouver Art Gallery 1984

German Art in the 20th Century: Painting and Sculpture, 1905–1985. Catalogue and essays ed. Christos M. Joachimides, Norman Rosenthal, Wieland Schmid et al. Munich and London: Prestel-Verlag 1985

German Expressionism and Abstract Art. Ed. Charles Kuhn. Cambridge, Mass.: Harvard University Press 1957

German Expressionist Prints from the Collection of Ruth and Jacob Kainen. Washington: National Gallery of Art 1985

German Expressionist Sculpture. Ed. Barbara Einzig, Lynne Dean, Andrea P.A. Belloli. Los Angeles: County Museum of Art 1983

Helmut Middendorf. St Gallen: Galerie u. Edition Buchmann 1982

Julian Schnabel. London: Tate Gallery 1982

Kathleen Munn / Edna Taçon: New Perspectives on Modernism in Canada. Exhibition and catalogue prepared by Joyce Zemans, Elizabeth Burrell, and Elizabeth Hunter. Toronto: Editions du GREF 1988 for the Art Gallery of York University

Marsden Hartley / John Marin. Exhibition catalogue for La Jolla Museum of Art. California: La Jolla Museum of Art 1966

Martin Disler. Ed. Zdenek Felix. Essen and Paris: Museum Folkwang and le Musée d'Art Moderne de la Ville de Paris 1985

Max Beckmann, Die Hölle, 1919. Berlin: Kupferstichkabinett 1983

Maxwell Bates: A Retrospective. Text by Ian M. Thom. Art Gallery of Greater Victoria 1982

Mulheimer Freiheit Proudly Presents the Second Bombing. Institute of Contemporary Arts and Scottish Arts Council 1983

Oskar Kokoschka: Das Portrait Gemälde, Aquarelle, Zeichnungen, 1907–1966. Karlsruhe: Badischer Kunstverein 1966

Peter Bömmels: Bilder, die die Welt bedeuten. Dortmund: Museum am Ostwall 1983

Rainer Fetting. Berlin: Raab Galerie 1983

Reid, Dennis. *Bertram Brooker.* Ottawa: National Gallery of Canada 1973.

Rosenberg, Harold. *De Kooning.* New York: Abrams 1974

Sam Borenstein. Texts by William Kuhns and Leo Rosshandler. Toronto: McClelland and Stewart 1978

Vienne 1880–1938: L'Apocalypse Joyeuse. Exhibition and catalogue organized by Jean Clair with Nicole Ouvrard, Jeanne Bouniort et al. Paris: Editions du Centre Pompidou 1986

Walter Dahn. Text by Patrick Frey. Exhibition catalogue from the Galerie Paul Maenz. Cologne 1982

Walter Dahn, 1983. Exhibition catalogue from the Galerie Paul Maenz. Cologne 1984

Wyndham Lewis: Paintings & Drawings. Catalogue by Walter Michel, intro. Hugh Kenner. London: Thames & Hudson 1971

OTHER

A New Spirit in Painting: Six Painters of the 1980's. United States 1984, 58 min. Written and narrated by Donald Kuspit; directed by Michael Blackwood. Print source: Michael Blackwood Prod.

Buchloh, Benjamin H.D. 'Figures of Authority, Ciphers of Regression: Notes on the Return of Representation in European Painting.' *October* 16 (Spring 1981): 39–68

Faust, Wolfgang Max. 'Notes on New German Art in the 20th Century, written 6 August 1985.' *Artscribe* 54 (1985): 20–5

– and Gerd de Vries. *Hunger nach Bildern: Deutsche Malerei der Gegenwart.* Cologne: Dumont Buchverlag 1982

Ferrier, Ian. 'Ecclesiastical Expressionism in Larouche.' *Canadian Art* 2, no. 1 (Spring 1985): 16–17

Foster, Hal, ed. *The Anti-Aesthetic: Essays on Postmodern Culture.* Port Townsend, Wash.: Bay Press 1983

– *Re-codings: Art, Spectacle, Cultural Politics.* Seattle, Wash.: Bay Press 1985

Guidieri, Remo. 'Georg Baselitz's Pastorale.' *Arts Magazine* 60, no. 10 (June 1986): 35–7

Hassan, Ihab. *The Dismemberment of Orpheus.* Madison: University of Wisconsin 1982

Hermand, Jost. 'Modernism Restored: West German Painting in the 1950's.' *New German Critique* 32 (1984): 23–41

Hughes, Robert. 'Upending the New German Chic: Neoexpressionism enters the flophouse of late modernity.' *Time* 11 Jan. 1982, 70

Huyssen, Andreas. *After the Great Divide: Modernism, Mass Culture, Post-modernism*. Bloomington and Indianapolis: Indiana University Press 1986

Kaplan, Joel. 'Rewrapping Lazarus: The Canadian Debut of Georg Baselitz.' *Issue* 2, no. 5 (May 1985): 31–3

Klotz, Heinrich. *Die Neuen Wilden in Berlin*. Stuttgart: Klett-Cotta 1984

Kroker, Arthur and David Cook. *The Postmodern Scene: Excremental Culture and Hyper-Aesthetics*. Montreal: New World Perspectives 1986

Kuspit, Donald B. 'Acts of Aggression: German Painting Today.' *Art in America* (Sept. 1982): 141–51, (Jan. 1983): 90–135

– 'Flak from the "Radicals": The American Case against Current German Painting.' In *Expressions: New Art from Germany*, ed. Jack Cowart. Munich: St Louis Art Museum and Prestel-Verlag 1983, 43–55

– 'Pandemonium, the Root of Georg Baselitz's Imagery.' *Arts Magazine* 60, no. 10 (June 1986): 24–9

– *The New Subjectivism: Art in the 1980's*. Ann Arbor, Mich.: UMI Research Press 1988

Lyotard, Jean-François. *The Postmodern Condition: Report on Knowledge*. Trans. Regis Durand. Minneapolis: University of Minnesota Press 1984

Pincus-Witten, Robert. 'Georg Baselitz: From Nolde to Kandinsky to Matisse, A Speculative History of Recent German Painting.' *Arts Magazine* 60, no. 10 (June 1986): 30–4

Index